Theatre Brief

Twelfth Edition

Robert Cohen

Claire Trevor Professor of Drama
University of California, Irvine

Donovan Sherman

Seton Hall University

Mc
Graw
Hill
Education

THEATRE BRIEF, TWELFTH EDITION

Published by McGraw-Hill Education, 2 Penn Plaza, New York, NY 10121. Copyright © 2020 by McGraw-Hill Education. All rights reserved. Printed in the United States of America. Previous editions © 2017, 2014, and 2011. No part of this publication may be reproduced or distributed in any form or by any means, or stored in a database or retrieval system, without the prior written consent of McGraw-Hill Education, including, but not limited to, in any network or other electronic storage or transmission, or broadcast for distance learning.

Some ancillaries, including electronic and print components, may not be available to customers outside the United States.

This book is printed on acid-free paper.

2 3 4 5 6 7 8 9 LWI 21 20 19

ISBN 978-1-260-05738-6
MHID 1-260-05738-0

Senior Portfolio Manager: *Sarah Remington*
Product Development Manager: *Mary Ellen Curley*
Product Developer: *Victoria DeRosa*
Marketing Manager: *Nancy Baudean*
Content Project Managers: *Susan Trentacosti, Lisa Bruflodt, Emily Windelborn*
Senior Buyer: *Laura Fuller*
Design: *Egzon Shaqiri*
Senior Content Licensing Specialist: *Ann Marie Jannette*
Cover Image: *©Paul Kennedy*
Compositor: *Aptara®, Inc.*

All credits appearing on page are considered to be an extension of the copyright page.

Library of Congress Cataloging-in-Publication Data

Names: Cohen, Robert, 1938- author. | Sherman, Donovan, author.
Title: Theatre : brief / Robert Cohen, Donovan Sherman.
Description: Twelfth edition. | New York, NY : McGraw-Hill Education, [2020]
  | Includes bibliographical references and index.
Identifiers: LCCN 2018051294| ISBN 9781260057386 (student edition: alk.
  paper) | ISBN 1260057380 (student edition: alk. paper)
Subjects: LCSH: Theater.
Classification: LCC PN2101 .C632 2020 | DDC 792—dc23 LC record available at https://lccn.loc.gov/2018051294

The Internet addresses listed in the text were accurate at the time of publication. The inclusion of a website does not indicate an endorsement by the authors or McGraw-Hill Education, and McGraw-Hill Education does not guarantee the accuracy of the information presented at these sites.

Preface

Robert Cohen and Donovan Sherman's *Theatre Brief* emphasizes that theatre is a reflection of ourselves, because at the core of any great art is a commentary on the human experience. The authors stress that theatre is not merely entertainment, but a way for people to connect with one another and express important ideas about our culture and society.

Theatre also immerses its readers in the world of theatre, giving them in-depth descriptions of many job functions and various aspects of a play's production from beginning to end. Through the coverage of design, acting, and directing, students are given a behind-the-scenes look at professional theatre artists performing their craft. The Photo Essay features that appear in multiple chapters include interviews with well-known figures both onstage and offstage. Conducted personally by the authors, they provide readers with firsthand accounts of what it's like to work in the field.

Every culture has developed theatre of some kind, and this edition makes a greater effort to include plays from non-Western countries in its examples. There is also greater attention to individual diversity within the U.S. theatre community. The authors incorporate more examples of women and ethnic minorities in both onstage and backstage roles, including a new profile on Young Jean Lee, the first Asian American woman to have her work staged on Broadway.

The text has also been updated to reflect the latest plays on Broadway, London's West End, and other international locations, as well as the latest trends in theatre production.

In addition to these general additions, the 12th edition includes the following content changes:

Chapter 1: A new introduction; new coverage on performance as it relates to theatre; a new Spotlight feature "Why Study Theatre?"

Chapter 2: A new introduction; extensive updating to reflect more traditions and innovations in global theatre.

Chapter 3: Fully revised content that is more inclusive of global acting techniques.

Chapter 4: Additional examples from non-Western playwriting traditions; inclusion of additional female and ethnically diverse playwrights; new coverage on devised theatre; a new excerpt from Harold Pinter's *The Homecoming*; new sections on award-winning playwrights Annie Baker, Ayad Akhtar, Young Jean Lee, and Tarell Alvin McCraney; a new Photo Essay feature that includes an exclusive interview with Young Jean Lee.

Chapter 5: New coverage of selective realism and a focus on new technological advances, such as motion-capture technology.

Chapter 6: A new section on global directors; a new Spotlight feature "Diversity and Casting"; a new Photo Essay that follows the step-by-step process of putting on a production of *The Tempest,* featuring 28 new images.

Chapter 7: Updated coverage on the relationship of ritual to theatre.

Chapter 8: A new introduction to define "modern drama"; a new section "Global Modern Drama"; a new Spotlight feature that includes an interview with Oskar Eustis, artistic director of the Public Theater in New York City; new coverage of different types of stylized theatre: expressionism (using the example of *Machinal* by Sophie Treadwell), contemporary allegory (using the example of *Dutchman* by Amiri Baraka), and postmodern farce (using the example of *Cloud Nine* by Caryl Churchill).

Chapter 9: New coverage on the cultural phenomenon *Hamilton.*

Chapter 10: Updated coverage in the "Theatre and Race" and "Theatre, Gender, and Sexuality" sections; new examples that are more global and diverse; a new section "Theatrical Innovators Today," which highlights the work of global theatre luminaries Ivo van Hove, Jesusa Rodríguez, Rimini Protokoll, and Ong Keng Sen.

Chapter 11: This chapter title has changed from "The Critic" to "The Audience" to emphasize the critical perspective all audience members can bring to the theatre.

Mastering Concepts

SMARTBOOK® Connect combines the content of *Theatre Brief* with award-winning adaptive tools that help students prepare for their time in class with you. The tools in Connect help students understand and retain basic concepts: parts of the theatre, the creative artists and technicians who make it happen, and the tradition and historical background from which theatre springs. When students successfully master concepts using McGraw-Hill's Connect, you can spend more class time discussing theatre and theatrical performances, fostering a greater appreciation for the course and inspiring students to become lifelong audience members. Connect is reliable, easy to use, and can be implemented on its own or paired with your school's learning management system. Contact your McGraw-Hill Higher Education representative to learn more or to speak with instructors who already uses Connect for their theatre courses.

Connect for *Theatre Brief* now includes two ways to read: an eBook and SmartBook. The eBook provides a simple, elegant reading experience, available for offline reading on a tablet. SmartBook creates a personalized online reading experience by highlighting the most impactful concepts that a student needs to learn. Students periodically test their knowledge as they read, and SmartBook adapts accordingly, highlighting content based on what the student knows and doesn't know. Real-time reports quickly identify the concepts that require more attention from individual students—or the entire class.

Does Your Course Cover Theatre History?

Seven history chapters, formerly included in the comprehensive edition *(Theatre),* are available for instructors who want a greater historical focus in their course:

- The Ancients
- The Middle Ages
- The Renaissance
- The Theatre of Asia
- The Royal Era
- The Modern Theatre: Realism
- The Modern Theatre: Antirealism

These history chapters are available in two ways:

1. In **SmartBook** at no extra cost. Simply order the 12th edition of *Theatre Brief* in SmartBook to get all-digital access to all 18 chapters.

2. Through **McGraw-Hill Create.** Add the history chapters of your choice to the chapters that you will cover in *Theatre Brief* for a tailored print solution.

create® Also available through SmartBook and Create is a theatregoer's guide written by Robert and Lorna Cohen called "Enjoy the Play!" McGraw-Hill Create allows you to create a customized print book or eBook tailored to your course and syllabus. You can search through thousands of McGraw-Hill Education texts, rearrange chapters, combine material from other content sources, and include your own content or teaching notes. Create even allows you to personalize your book's appearance by selecting the cover and adding your name, school, and course information. To register and to get more information, go to http://create.mheducation.com.

Acknowledgments

Many scholars, artists, and critics gave invaluable advice as this edition came to fruition. We, the authors, would like to extend our gratitude to Jerry Patch, Oskar Eustis, Young Jean Lee, and Patrick Stewart for letting us speak with them; special mention is owed to the staff at the Public Theater for helping arrange a meeting with Mr. Eustis. A big thanks to the whole team behind the New Swan production of *The Tempest* at University of California, Irvine: the production team of Eli Simon, Keith Bangs, Karyn D. Lawrence, Kathryn Wilson, Dipu Gupta, Vincent Olivieri, Wesley Charles Chew, Miriam Mendoza, and Paul Kennedy, and the actors, Ryan Imhoff, DeShawn Mitchell, Adrian Alita, Anita Abdinezhad, Greg Ungar, and Thomas Varga.

When assessing the current state of theatre and theatre education, we received helpful feedback from a host of scholars and artists; many thanks are especially due to Katrina Bugaj, Kate Elswit, Lindsay Brandon Hunter, Julia Reinhard Lupton, Elise Morrison, William Murray, Vincent Olivieri, Sara O'Toole, Kate DiMarco Ruck, Jon Foley Sherman, and Jonah Spear for their considerable insights.

We would also like to thank the reviewers who informed this edition: Robin Armstrong, Collin County Community College; Jim Bartruff, Emporia State University; Arthur Grothe, University of West Alabama; Richard Harmon, Seminole State College; Rick Kemp, Indiana

University of Pennsylvania; Mark E. Lococo, Loyola University Chicago; and Lisa McNiel, El Paso Community College, Valle Verde Campus.

The team at McGraw-Hill Higher Education has guided the creation of this edition with care and thoughtfulness. Susan Trentacosti and Lisa Bruflodt ably provided assistance to the digital aspects of production, Sarah Remington oversaw the many moving parts of the process with grace and resourcefulness, and Emily Tietz demonstrated considerable alacrity and inventiveness in researching new photographs. Finally, the authors are deeply grateful to the indefatigable Victoria DeRosa, who provided keen and incisive feedback through every step of the process; her unerring eye has made the text so much stronger and more cohesive.

Finally, we wish to thank Lorna Cohen for her assistance throughout the process.

About the Authors

ROBERT COHEN was the founding chair of the drama program at the University of California, Irvine, in 1965 and was the sole creator of the original edition (and nine subsequent editions) of *Theatre* starting in 1981. A prolific theatre scholar, teacher, director, playwright, translator, critic, and acting theorist for over fifty years as professor of drama at UCI, he is the author of twenty-three books (translated into six languages), thirty-six scholarly articles, numerous published and produced plays and play translations, and over four hundred published reviews of plays produced in America and around the world. He has also directed fifteen plays at the Utah and Colorado Shakespeare Festivals and ninety more at both regional and academic theatres in the United States and abroad. In addition to teaching at UCI, Cohen has served multiple times as master teacher at the Actors Center in New York City and at TVI Studios in New York and Los Angeles; he also speaks at and conducts acting workshops regularly, with residencies in Japan, Korea, China, Hungary, Finland, Estonia, Sweden, Poland, Costa Rica, Hong Kong, Canada, Romania, Australia, and approximately half the states in the United States. His books include *Shakespeare on Theatre, Acting Power: The 21st Century Edition, Acting in Shakespeare, Acting One, Acting Professionally, Advanced Acting, Creative Play Direction, Working Together in Theatre, Falling into Theatre, Jean Giraudoux: Three Faces of Destiny,* and various plays, translations, and anthologies.

UCI awarded Cohen its highest honor, the UCI Medal, in 1993 and conferred on him a Claire Trevor Professorship and Bren Fellowship in 2001 and the UCI Distinguished Faculty Award for Research in 2015. He has also received the Career Achievement Award in Academic Theatre from ATHE (the Association for Theatre in Higher Education), the Honoris Causa Professor degree at Babes-Bolyai University in Romania, and—for bringing the great Polish director Jerzy Grotowski to UCI for three years—the Polish Medal of Honor.

DONOVAN SHERMAN is an associate professor of English at Seton Hall University. His research focuses on the drama and performance of Shakespeare and his contemporaries, as well as theatre history, philosophy, and critical theory. Scholarly works include the book *Second Death: Theatricalities of the Soul in Shakespeare's Drama,* published in 2016 by Edinburgh University Press, along with essays on Shakespeare, performance studies, film, and early modern religion and philosophy in *Shakespeare Quarterly, The Journal of Medieval and Early Modern Studies, Literature/Film Quarterly, English Literary Renaissance, Upstart,* and *Theatre Journal.* Currently, he is working on a book about portrayals of ancient philosophy in early modern drama. As a theatre artist, Sherman has performed with the Actors Theatre of Louisville, the SITI Company, Steppenwolf Theatre Company, and several other regional theatres in the United States. Donovan received his doctoral degree from the Joint Program of Theatre and Drama at the University of California, Irvine, and the University of California, San Diego.

Brief Contents

create
create.mheducation.com

Contents

create.mheducation.com

©Sara Krulwich/The New York Times/Redux

Introduction

IT IS EVENING IN MANHATTAN. On Broadway the marquees light up, and "Performance Tonight" signs appear in front of double doors. Beneath a few box-office windows placards announce, "This Performance Completely Sold Out." At Grand Central Station and Penn Station, trains release eager suburbanites from Greenwich, Larchmont, and Trenton; students from New Haven and Philadelphia; and day-trippers from Boston and Washington. Out of the Times Square subways pour mobs of locals, inhabitants of the bustling island and the neighboring boroughs. They head to the TKTS booth to line up and buy the discount tickets that go on sale a few hours before curtain time for shows with seats yet to be filled. Now, converging on these few midtown blocks of America's most populated city, come buses, cars, taxis, and limousines, whose drivers search for a curbside slot to deposit their riders among the milling throngs of pedestrians. Wall Street bankers, college students, teenagers gazing at their smartphones, sleek executives in expensive suits, Brooklyn hipsters, arm-in-arm widows, out-of-town tourists and conventioneers, celebrities, honeymooners, old and young, people of all different cultures, classes, and identities—all commingle in this bizarre mass that is the New York Broadway audience. Even during (and perhaps especially during) troubled times in this vibrant city, it is as bright, bold, and varied a crowd as is likely to assemble at any single place in America.

It is eight o'clock. In close to forty theatres within two dozen blocks of each other, houselights dim, curtains rise, and spotlights pick out performers who have fervently waited for this moment to arrive. Here a hot new musical, here a star-studded revival of an American classic, here a contemporary English comedy from London's West End, here a new play fresh from its electrifying Seattle or Chicago premiere, here a one-woman show, here an experimental play that has transferred to larger quarters, here a touring production from eastern Europe, and here the new play everyone expects will capture this year's coveted Tony Award. The hours pass.

It's 10:30. Pandemonium. All the double doors open simultaneously, as if on cue, and once again the thousands pour out into the night. At nearby restaurants, servers stand by to receive the after-theatre onslaught. In the private upstairs room at Sardi's restaurant, an opening-night cast party gets under way; downstairs, the patrons rehash the evening's entertainment and sneak covert glances at celebrities. Actors sip their drinks while impatiently awaiting the reviews that will determine whether they will be employed next week or back on the street looking for new jobs.

Now let's turn back the clock. It is dawn in Athens, the thirteenth day of the month of Elaphebolion in the year 458 B.C.E. From thousands of low mud-brick homes in the city, from the central agora, and from temples and agricultural outposts, streams of Athenians and visitors converge on the south slope of the Acropolis, Athens's great hill and home of its grandest temples. Bundled against the morning dampness, carrying breakfast figs and flagons of wine, they pay their tokens at the entrance to the great Theatre of Dionysus and take their places in the seating spaces allotted them. They have

Plays were often the sources of films in the early days of cinema, but now major films are increasingly turned into plays—mostly musicals—and very successful ones (for example, *The Lion King, The Producers, Once*). This scene is from the 2012 Broadway hit *Newsies,* adapted by Disney from its 1992 film of that name; the musical won Tony Awards for both its score and choreography. ©*Sara Krulwich/The New York Times/Redux*

gathered for the City Dionysia festival, which celebrates the rebirth of the land and the long sunny days that stretch ahead. It is a time for revelry and for rejoicing in fertility and all its fruits. And it is above all a time for the ultimate form of Dionysian worship: the theatre.

The open stone seats carved into the hillside fill up quickly. The crowd of seventeen thousand comprises not only the majority of Athenian citizens but also thousands of tradesmen, foreign visitors, slaves, and resident aliens. Even paupers are in attendance, thanks to the two obols apiece provided by a state fund to buy tickets for the poor; they take their place with the latecomers on the extremities of the theatron, as this first of theatre buildings is called. Now, as the eastern sky grows pale, a masked and costumed actor appears atop a squat building set in full view of every spectator. A hush falls over the crowd, and the

actor, his voice magnified by the wooden mask he wears, booms out this text:

> I ask the gods some respite from the weariness of this watchtime measured by years I lie awake . . .

The entranced spectators settle in, secure in the knowledge that today they are in good hands. Today they will hear and see a new version of a familiar story—the story of Agamemnon's homecoming and his murder; the revenge of that murder by his son, Orestes; and the final disposition of justice in the case of Orestes' act—as told in the three tragedies that constitute *The Oresteia*. This magnificent trilogy is by Aeschylus, Athens's leading dramatist for more than forty years. The spectators watch closely, admiring but critical. Tomorrow they or their representatives will decide by vote whether the festival's prize should go to this work, or

Singer, songwriter, guitarist, thumb pianist, and now playwright, Jonatha Brooke, wrote and performed her one-woman play, *My Mother Has 4 Noses*, to great success off-Broadway in 2014, basing her play on the last years of her own mother's life—and playing both her mother and herself. ©*Sandrine Lee*

whether the young Sophocles, whose plays were presented in this space the day before, had better sensed the true pulse of the time.

Let's zoom ahead in time. It is noon in London, and Queen Elizabeth I sits on the throne. Flags fly boldly atop three of the taller buildings in Bankside, across the Thames, announcing performance day at The Globe, The Rose, and The Swan theatres. Boatmen have already begun ferrying theatregoers across the river, where The Globe will present a new tragedy by Shakespeare (something called *Hamlet*), and The Rose promises a revival of Christopher Marlowe's popular *Dr. Faustus*. North of town, The Fortune and The Curtain are likewise opening their gates for new plays of their own.

Now at The Globe, two thousand spectators have arrived for the premiere. A trumpet sounds, then sounds again, and then builds into a full fanfare. Members of the

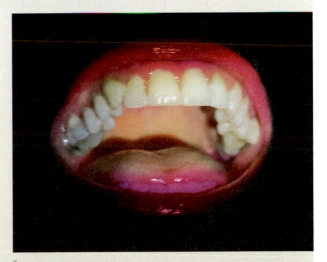

Theatre is not always grandiose. Samuel Beckett virtually revolutionized the theatre in 1958 with his *Waiting for Godot*, which basically shows two men under a tree waiting for a man who never comes. It was ridiculed at first, but by 2000 was cited as the greatest play of the century. From there his plays were steadily reduced in characters and actions until, in his 1972 *Not I*, there was but one performer—whose mouth, eight feet above the stage, is all the audience sees. This 2014 performance was performed by Lisa Dwan at the Brooklyn Academy of Music's Harvey Theatre. ©*Sara Krulwich/The New York Times/Redux*

Some plays never die. This Pulitzer Prize–winning 1936 production of Moss Hart and George S. Kaufman's farce *You Can't Take It With You* flooded the stage with fireworks in its 2014 Broadway revival, directed by Scott Ellis.
©Sara Krulwich/The New York Times/Redux

audience, standing on the ground before the stage or seated in bleachers overlooking it, exchange a few final winks with their friends old and new before turning their attention to the platform stage. Through a giant door a guard bursts forth, lantern in hand. "Who's there?," he cries, and across from him another guard hollers, "Nay! Answer me!" In two thousand imaginations, the bright afternoon has turned to midnight, London's Bankside has given way to the battlements of Denmark's Elsinore, and a terrified shiver from the onstage actor has set up an answering chill among the audience members. A great new tragedy has begun its course.

It is midnight in a basement in the East Village, or in a campus rehearsal room, or in a coffee shop in Pittsburgh, Seattle, Sioux Falls, or Berlin. Across one end of the room, a curtain has been drawn across a pole suspended by wires. It has been a long evening, but one play remains to be seen. The author is unknown, but rumor has it that this new work is brutal, shocking, poetic, and strange. The members of the audience, by turns skeptical and enthusiastic, look for the tenth time at their programs. The lights dim. Performers, backed by crudely painted packing crates, begin to act.

What is the common denominator in all of these scenes? They are all theatre. There is no culture that has not had a theatre in some form, for theatre is the art of people acting out—and giving witness to—their most pressing, illuminating, and inspiring concerns. Theatre is a medium through which a society displays its ideas, fashions, moralities, and entertainments, and debates its conflicts, dilemmas, yearnings, and struggles. Theatre has provided a stage for political revolution, social propaganda, civil debate, artistic expression, religious conversion, mass education, and even its own self-criticism. It has been a performance ground for priests, shamans, intellectuals, poets, painters, technologists, philosophers, reformers, evangelists, jugglers, peasants, children, and kings. It has taken place in caves, fields, and forests; in circus tents, inns, and castles; on street corners and in public buildings grand

and squalid all over the world. And it goes on incessantly in the minds of its authors, actors, producers, designers, and audiences.

Theatre is, above all, a *living* art form. It consists not only of plays but also of playing, and a play is not simply a series of acts but a collective ritual of acting. Just as *play* and *act* are both noun and verb, so theatre is both a thing and a happening, a result and a process: it is fluid in time and rich in feeling and human experience.

Above all, then, theatre is live and alive: an art that continually forms before our eyes and is present to an audience even as it is presented by its actors. In fact, this very quality of "presentness" (or, in the actor's terminology, "stage presence") defines every great theatrical performance.

Unlike the more static arts, theatre presents us with a number of classic paradoxes:

- It is spontaneous, yet it is rehearsed.
- It is real, yet it is simulated.
- It is unique to the moment, yet it is repeatable.
- The actors are themselves, yet they play characters.
- Audience members believe in the characters, yet they know they are actors.
- Audience members become emotionally involved, yet they know it is only a play.

These paradoxes comprise the glory of theatre. The actors may "live in the moment" during their performances, yet they have carefully studied, planned, and rehearsed the details of their roles beforehand. And audience members respond to their performance by rooting for their characters to achieve their goals, and then applauding the actors who play those roles during the curtain call. But this is also how we live our own lives, which we both experience and, at various points, present to others. The theatre shows us to ourselves in all of our human complexity.

And so this book about the theatre is also, ultimately, a book about ourselves.

Chapter

1

What Is Theatre?

©Evgenia Eliseeva

W HAT IS THEATRE? To start, let's look at the origin of the word. *Theatre* comes from the Greek *theatron*, or "seeing place." So on a basic level, a theatre is a place where something is seen. Already, with this simple definition, we gain an important clue about what theatre is. For something to be seen, after all, there must be people to do the seeing. So the theatre involves those who watch and those who are watched—the audience and the actors onstage.

Theatre depends on a separation of the viewer and the viewed. This separation need not be literal, however. In fact, some of the most powerful theatre happening today happens very intimately, with performers mere inches away from the audience. Rather, the separation of the theatre is something abstract, a feeling of distance between the viewer and what is seen. Theatre can simply be the result of a change in the attitude of the spectator: If I take on the attitude that I am watching life around me *as if* it were onstage, the everyday can suddenly take on a magical quality.

This kind of theatre—we might call this a theatre of perception—is demonstrated beautifully by a section of the High Line, a public park in New York City built on old railroad tracks elevated above the bustling city streets. In one section of the park, pedestrians can enter an "urban theatre"—a set of benches and aisles in front of a stage. But this "stage" is not typical: it's a big window that frames a busy intersection. Walkers on the High Line can sit on a bench and watch the spectacle of people rushing to work, hailing a cab, talking on their phones, laughing with their friends, and otherwise carrying on with their lives. When viewed as if they were on a stage, these actions take on a new sense of importance. Their circumstances are heightened. They might not realize it, but they are performing!

Another kind of theatrical separation can exist when audience members might not realize they are an audience. The "invisible theatre" of the Brazilian activist and director Augusto Boal often used this technique. Boal's actors would stage an altercation on the street, only to reveal to onlookers afterward that they were, in fact, just performing. Suddenly passersby became audience members, where before they were bystanders. And these audience members were forced to question their own "performances" in the play that took place: Did they help the person under attack? Or did they just watch or even inch away?

Most of the time, though, audiences and performers know that they are part of a theatrical event. They have a mutual understanding. The audience will watch and react to the play, and the performers will put on a show. Everyone knows that what happens will be different than everyday life. Even if the play attempts to emulate everyday life—and some of the theatre we will examine in this book does exactly that—it still does so in circumstances that make it, in some way, extraordinary.

To summarize our description thus far, *theatre* describes a set of heightened circumstances that depend

At the High Line park in New York City, spectators can sit at the "urban theatre" section to witness the ongoing play of the city itself. ©Francois Roux/Shutterstock

on a separation (whether acknowledged or not) of audience and performer. But we also use the word to refer to the physical space in which theatre often takes place. Theatre can occur in a theatre. It could also exist elsewhere, though. In this book, we will examine theatre that takes place in streets, in homes, in abandoned weapons factories, and in quarries—just to name a few examples. But even then, we refer to these spaces as a *theatre*. They transform, just as the performers do, from ordinary to exceptional.

Spotlight

Why Study Theatre?

Perhaps you are reading this book because you have a deep passion for theatre. However, chances are that some of you are also reading this book because you are just curious about theatre, or perhaps simply to get college credit. These are all perfectly fine reasons. One of the book's aims is to show you how knowledge of theatre can help you in many different settings, not just onstage. Regardless of your reasons for reading this book and of how frequently you engage with theatre afterward, knowing more about theatre can help you in both your professional and personal life.

This thought might give you pause. You might think, "Isn't theatre a lofty occupation?" It is, but it is also a highly pragmatic one. As we will discuss, it is first and foremost *work*. While studying theatre can be enormously rewarding for abstract reasons—for instance, it gives us an appreciation of culture and history—it also helps improve your occupational skills. And you do not even need to work in theatre to capitalize on your theatre studies. Theatre skills are crucial for work in law, education, and business. After all, if you study

and participate in theatre, you know how to work as a team, listen to other opinions, collaborate across different skill sets, and learn how to speak in front of a crowd.

People who have theatre degrees, or who have studied theatre in college, draw on their skills constantly. If you have to give a speech to your coworkers or superiors, if you have to devise a project with a group of people you don't know well but with whom you must collaborate, if you have an encroaching deadline and need to find a creative solution to a problem, or if you have to analyze a document and share your interpretation, then you are using theatre skills. You're not that different from an actor stepping onto the stage, a director meeting for the first time with an artistic team, or a performer picking up a script minutes before an audition.

Experiencing theatre gives us confidence, and it is not, contrary to some understandings of the word, a fake or negative kind of confidence. As we discuss in this book, theatre is about pursuing the truth, not artifice. It's an effort of a group of people trying to create something new—and can't the same be said for nearly every line of work? Studying theatre gives us what theatre scholar Nancy Kindelan calls "artistic literacy"—a fluency in thinking creatively in a variety of settings. Theatre skills help us constantly because theatre, in some form, is everywhere.

In addition to a theatre building, there's yet another way we can use the word *theatre*: the collection of artists who create the theatre. We call this collection the *company*. So the theatre can be a physical place, what happens in that place, and the people who create what happens in that place. To take one example, when we refer to the Guthrie Theater, we refer to (1) the actual building in Minneapolis called the Guthrie Theater: (2) what happens in that building—the performed actions and the audiences who watch them; and (3) the artists and administrators who create these occurrences.

Finally, we also use the word *theatre* to summon the professional occupation—and often the passion—of thousands of men and women all over the world. It is a vocation and sometimes a lifelong devotion. If someone says, "I work in theatre," they are telling you that they work in a theatre, they participate in the activity of theatre, they collaborate with other theatre artists, and—perhaps most importantly—that they are inspired by theatre. Theatre is an occupation and an art. To work in the theatre is not just to labor, but also to create.

We have already discussed one definition of theatre—the separation of actor and audience—so let's now examine the three other main definitions: theatre as a building, a company, and an occupation.

The Theatre Building

When you picture the space of the theatre, you probably imagine a big room with seats, a stage, and maybe a curtain. A theatre building is not always an enclosed structure, however. The most ancient Greek *theatron* was probably no

Shakespeare's Globe has been meticulously reconstructed near its sixteenth-century location on the South Bank of London's Thames River. The reconstruction was spearheaded by the late Sam Wanamaker, an American actor who labored many years to acquire the funding and necessary permits (the theatre has the first thatch roof laid in London since the Great Fire of 1666). This is scholarship's best guess as to the specific dimensions and features of The Globe in Shakespeare's time. Since its 1997 opening, this Globe has produced a summer repertoire of the plays of Shakespeare's age, seen on a stage much like the stages for which they were written. ©*Robert Cohen*

National theatre buildings in many European countries, generally supported by their governments, are often palatial. The National Theatre in Cluj, Romania, is regarded as the most beautiful building in this Transylvanian capital.
©Robert Cohen

more than a circle of bare earth where performers chanted and danced before a hillside of seated spectators. The requirements for building such a theatre were minimal: find a space to act and a space to watch and hear.

As theatre grew in popularity and importance, and spread out into different cultures and geographical locations, its structures grew larger and more elaborate. The theatre's producers had to seat larger and larger numbers of people, so the hillside soon became an ascending bank of seats, each level providing a good view of the acting area. And as the theatre grew, attention had to be paid to its *acoustics*, or sound quality (derived from the Greek *acoustos*, "heard"), so the sounds coming from the stage could be heard by the audience (from the Latin *audientia*, "those who hear").

Often, theatre spaces can be easily defined. The basic relationship set up in ancient Greece can still apply to theatres all over the world: the audiences are out in the seats, the actors are up on the stage. Occasionally, though, the spaces are merged together so that the actors mingle—and sometimes interact—with the audience.

Theatre buildings may also be complex. Greek theatres of the fourth century B.C.E.—the period immediately following the golden age of Greek playwrights—were gigantic stone structures, some capable of holding up to 17,000 spectators. Magnificent three-story Roman theatres, complete with gilded columns, canvas awnings, and intricate marble carvings, were often erected for dramatic festivals in the later years of the Republic. Grand, free-standing Elizabethan theatres dominate the London skyline in illustrated sixteenth-century pictorial maps of the town. Opulent theatres were built throughout Europe and in the major cities of the United States in the eighteenth

Theatre buildings need not be originally designed for theatre. Since 2007, audiences have flocked to the Park Avenue Armory in New York City to see theatre on a grand scale. In this 55,000-square-foot space, which was previously an ammunition storehouse, artists can realize spectacular visions, as with Heiner Goebbels's 2016 staging of Louis Andriessen's *De Materie*, pictured here. ©*Stephanie Berger*

and nineteenth centuries. Many remain in full operation today, competing with splendid new stages and serving as cultural centers for metropolitan areas around the world.

The Theatre Company

Theatre is a collaborative art that involves dozens, or even hundreds, of people working closely together on a single performance. Historically, theatre practitioners of various specialties have teamed up in long-standing companies. Since the fourth century B.C.E., such troupes of players have toured the countrysides and settled in cities to present a *repertory*, or collection of plays, as a means of earning a livelihood. Generally such players have included actors, playwrights, and technicians—and often combinations thereof—who make the company a self-contained production unit capable of writing, preparing, and presenting whole theatrical works. Some of these troupes—and the works they produced—have become legendary. The

Lord Chamberlain's Men, in London, counted William Shakespeare as a member. The Illustrious Theatre of Paris was founded and headed by the great actor-writer Molière. These companies remind us that the theatre depends on more than space; it also needs people. And these people represent the genius and creativity of theatre in ways that the buildings alone cannot.

The Occupation of Theatre

Theatre can be a full-time job for professionals or a hobby for amateurs. In either case, it is work. The fundamental act of theatre seems simple enough: actors impersonate characters in a live performance of a play. But an enormous amount of labor goes into this activity, including the design and creation of the set and props, the orientation of the lights, and the direction of the action to the actors—as well as countless other long hours spent honing specialized crafts and collaborating with other artists. We can organize this vast web of labor into four major categories: work, art, impersonation, and performance.

WORK

Theatre is difficult work. *Rehearsals,* when actors and directors meet to create and practice staging for the play, normally take a minimum of four to six weeks. These rehearsals are usually preceded by at least an equal amount of time—but often months or years—of writing, researching, planning, casting, designing, and creating a production team. After the rehearsal period, the entire artistic team—the company—gathers to combine all the different elements into one work of art. These final weeks before a play *opens* (when it is first shown to audiences) consist of an incredible amount of labor, frequently with twelve-hour workdays and seven-day workweeks.

The work of the theatre is generally divisible into a number of crafts:

Production includes securing all necessary personnel, space, and financing; supervising all production and promotional efforts; fielding all legal matters; and distributing all proceeds derived from receipts.

Directing consists of controlling and developing the artistic product to provide it with a unified vision, coordinating all of its components, and supervising its rehearsals.

Acting comprises the most famous and visible of theatrical work, in which performers take on roles in a play.

Designing entails the creation of visual and aural elements of a production, including the scenery, properties, costumes and wigs, makeup, lighting, sound, programs, advertising, and general ambience of the location.

Building includes the realization of the designers' vision through the work of carpenters, costumers, wig-makers, electricians, makeup artists, recording and sound engineers, painters, and a host of other specially designated craftspeople who construct the "hardware" of a play.

The *crew* consists of technicians who execute, in proper sequence and with carefully rehearsed timing, the light and sound cues and the shifting of scenery, as well as oversee the placement and return of properties and the assignment, laundering, repair, and changes of costumes.

Stage management consists of *running*, or coordinating in real time, a play production in all its complexity in performance after performance.

House management includes the responsibilities for admitting, seating, and providing for the general comfort of the audience.

There is one craft that does not take place during the enactment of a play but is absolutely critical to the whole production. This work is *playwriting*—and for musical theatre, *composing*—which is in a class by itself. Playwriting takes place elsewhere, sometimes even continents and centuries away from the productions they inspire.

Of course, the work of the theatre need not be divided exactly along these lines. In any production, some people perform more than one kind of work. For example, many of the builders also serve on the crew. And it is not uncommon for playwrights to direct what they write, for directors to act in their own productions, and for designers to build at least some of what they design. On some celebrated occasions, multitalented theatre artists have taken on multiple roles at the same time: Aeschylus, in ancient Greece, and Molière, in seventeenth-century Paris, each wrote, directed, and acted in their own plays, and probably designed them as well; William Shakespeare was a playwright, actor, and co-owner of the Lord Chamberlain's Men in Elizabethan times; Bertolt Brecht revolutionized both playwriting and acting when writing and directing his plays in Berlin after World War II; and recently, Lin-Manuel Miranda composed, wrote, and starred in his blockbuster musical *Hamilton.*

Theatre is also work in the sense that it is not play. Or, at least, not *only* play. "Play" is, after all, the word used to describe the main product of theatre work, so the word refers to both the activity of children who "play games" and adults who "play roles" or "put on a play" as a profession. This is not a coincidence. The French *jeu,* the German *spiel,* the Hungarian *játék,* the Mandarin Chinese *xi,* and the Latin *ludi* all share the double meaning of the English *play* by referring both to children's games and dramatic plays and playing. This association points to a relationship that is fundamental to our understanding of theatre: while it is a kind of work, theatre is also a kind of playing, and it is useful for us to see why this is so.

Theatre and games have a shared history. Both were born as Greek events: the Dionysian theatre festival and the Olympian athletic festival were the two great cultural events of ancient Greece. Each embodied a form of competition for excellence. The Romans then merged sports and theatre in public circuses, where the two were performed side by side, often in competition with each other. More than a millennium later, the Londoners of Shakespeare's time built "playhouses" that could accommodate dramatic productions on one day and bearbaiting spectacles (somewhat akin to bullfights) the next day. The association of dramatic and athletic entertainment continues today: flip through your TV channels and you'll see serialized dramas and comedies run alongside live recordings of basketball, football, and other sports. We love to watch "play" of all sorts.

This link between games and theatre is formed early in life. "Child's play" can be competitive and athletic, but also creative and imitative. Children love to dress up, mimic, or in any way pretend to be someone else—in short, they love to be theatrical. This kind of play is also educational because it helps children prepare for adult life. As we get older, more unstructured and spontaneous games become organized and instructional. Sometimes the lessons we learn from playing are quite serious. Hide-and-seek, an exhilarating and engrossing game, also offers an opportunity to act out one of childhood's greatest fears—the terror of separation from the parent. Hide-and-seek allows a child to confront this separation anxiety within a safe environment. In this context, fear loses much of its frightening power, and over time, through the act of playing, the child gradually learns to cope with life's challenges and uncertainties.

So while theatrical play is not real, it prepares us for reality.

Theatre and play have some important differences, as well. Unlike adult games, which are open-ended, every theatre performance has a preordained conclusion. The Patriots may not win the Super Bowl next year, but Hamlet definitely will die in the fifth act of *Hamlet*. The work of the theatre consists in keeping us invested in Hamlet while he is alive so that his death is moving and even surprising. We know he will die, but we are still emotionally affected when he does.

To return to an earlier point, theatre is not *only* play. We might say that theatre is the art of making play into work—specifically, into a work of art. It is exhilarating work, to be sure, and it usually inspires and invigorates the energies and imaginations of all who participate. But it is ultimately work. That is its challenge.

Sports, games, and theatre have always been related, and some plays combine these different "playing" motifs. Richard Greenberg's *Take Me Out* takes place in a baseball locker room in America, Eric Simonson's *Lombardi* in a football locker room, David Storey's *The Changing Room* in a rugby locker room, Andrew Lloyd Webber's *The Beautiful Game* on a soccer field in Ireland, and Thomas Meehan's musical adaption of the well-known film *Rocky* concludes in a boxing ring. Pictured here are Andy Karl and Dakin Matthews with World Middleweight Champ Gennady Golovkin making his Broadway debut in *Rocky* at the Winter Garden Theatre on July 23, 2014, in New York City. ©*Walter McBride/Getty Images*

ART

The word *art* brings to mind a host of abstract ideas: creativity, imagination, elegance, power, harmony, and beauty. We expect a work of art to capture something of the human spirit and to address some of the biggest questions in all of humanity, such as, Why are we here? and What does it mean to live a good life? Certainly great theatre, regardless of the play, can pose—if not answer—these questions. And theatre does so in playful, surprising ways. In theatre we can mix physical and emotional exuberance with philosophical reflections of our search for purpose.

Art is one of the great pursuits of humanity. It empowers both those who make it and those who appreciate it. Art also sharpens thought and focuses feeling by mixing reality with imagination. Think of a great work of art that you love: a song that makes you fight back tears or jump up and down in excitement, or a poem that expresses familiar emotions—like love or sadness—in new ways. We are drawn to works of art like these because they lend meaning to our lives. We might find similar values in religion as well, but art is accessible without subscribing to any particular set of beliefs. It is surely for this reason that so many religions have employed art and artworks (including dramatic art) in their liturgies and services from the earliest of times.

IMPERSONATION

A fundamental quality of theatre is that it involves actors who impersonate characters. Even when actors play "themselves," actors are viewed differently when in the theatre. They are viewed as artistic creations, rather than as people. Just as the New Yorkers walking by the High Line are seen as somehow more than everyday pedestrians when they are viewed as "onstage," people take on new significance when they are part of the theatre. They become characters.

When we see an actor impersonate a character, we know, on some level, that the character is not "real." However, oftentimes we act like it is. We react as if an actual person were going through real emotions. It can sometimes be difficult to separate the actor from the character. Even today, fans send tweets and post Instagram comments to movie stars to express their feelings about the people they play, not the people they are. (To take this a step further, we can think of our online selves as a kind of theatrical fiction; social media platforms like Twitter, Instagram, Facebook, and Snapchat are in the business of turning us from people into characters.) Movie fans clutter message boards with theories as to what a certain character "means" or what fate might befall them after the closing credits, as if they were real people.

Imagine how confusing this must have been in the early days of theatre! The very first plays and audiences didn't have centuries of conventions to remind them that an actor was not a character. How could they separate the performer from the fiction? The solution the ancient world found was the mask. Western theatre had its true beginning that day in ancient Greece when an actor first stepped out of the chorus and placed an unpainted mask over his face, thereby signaling that the lines he was about to speak were "in character." He was no longer Demetrius the olive-grower; he was Agamemnon, hero of the Trojan War. The mask provides both a physical and a symbolic separation between the impersonator (the actor) and the impersonated (the character), thus aiding onlookers in temporarily suspending their awareness of the "real" world and accepting in its place the world of the stage. In a play, it must be the characters who have apparent life; the actors themselves are expected to disappear into the shadows, along with their personal preoccupations, anxieties, and career ambitions.

Masks were used throughout the ancient Greek theatre period, and as we shall see in the pages that follow, they were also staples of many other theatres of the past, including the *mmanwu* masquerades of the Igbo people in Nigeria, the *noh* and *kyōgen* drama of Japan, and the *commedia dell'arte* of Italy. The theatrical mask endures, not only in these historic forms but also in many cutting-edge productions that continue to play with our understandings of theatrical impersonation. The most recognizable symbol of theatre, after all, is the side-by-side masks of comedy and tragedy.

PERFORMANCE

Theatre is a kind of performance, but what exactly does *performance* mean? Performance is an action or series of actions taken for the ultimate benefit (attention, entertainment, enlightenment, or involvement) of someone else. We call that "someone else" the audience.

All theatre is performance, but not all performance is theatre. What counts as performance is quite broad. One way of defining performance is through more of a perspective than an actual set of activities. In other words, we might view an activity such as a baseball game as a performance, rather than as something else (a cultural institution, an expression of local pride, etc.). The same goes for other activities not typically thought of as

Masks were fundamental to ancient theatre and often appear in contemporary productions, particularly in revivals of such classic works. Christina Uribe's masks, sculpted in the ancient Greek tradition, were employed in this Greek/ French production of Sophocles' *Antigone* directed by Philippe Brunet for his Demodocos company, which since 1995 has been devoted to the pursuit of what Brunet calls "Dionysian mystery theatre." The production, with costumes by Florence Kukucka, was featured at the 2008 Avignon Theatre Festival in France; shown here are two chorus members.
©*Laurencine Lot*

"performing": medical examinations, churchgoing, storytelling, and even aspects of our identity such as gender. When we view our cultural behavior as performance, it helps get us away from thinking of human activity as unchangeable. It reminds us that our identities depend on bodily enactment. The discipline of performance studies has taken this task to heart and offers many stirring analyses of human activity as a kind of endless performing.

But we need not be too academic about the issue. Performance is all around us. When two high school students arm-wrestle during lunch period, they may well be performing their physical prowess for the benefit of their peers. The student who asks a question in the lecture hall is often "performing" for the other students—and the

professor performs for the same audience when providing a response. Trial lawyers examining witnesses invariably perform—often drawing on a considerable repertoire of body language—for the benefit of the courtroom audience, the jury. Politicians kiss babies for the benefit of parents (and others) who are in search of a kindly candidate. Even stony silence can be a performance—for example, if it is in response to an overly eager admirer. In this sense, we are all performers.

The difference between theatre and performance is that theatre makes an *art* out of performance: it expands something we all do every day into a formal mode of artistic expression. When you sing along to a song in your car, you might be performing, but you are not creating theatre.

Presentational styles make little pretense of mimicking ordinary life. Here, director Susan Stroman creates a wonderful comedic moment in *The Producers* as the director Roger De Bris (played by Gary Beach) desperately tries to keep his wig on. Facial expressions around the room focus the action and intensify the hilarity. Matthew Broderick and Nathan Lane (*left*) are the producers from the musical's title. Scenic design is by Robin Wagner, costumes by William Ivey Long, and lighting by Peter Kaczorowski. *©Paul Kolnik*

The theatre makes use of two general modes of performance: *presentational* (or direct) and *representational* (or indirect). Presentational performance is the basic mode of stand-up comedy or concert singing. Presentational performers directly acknowledge the presence of audience members by singing to them, dancing for them, joking with them, and responding openly to their applause, laughter, requests, and heckling. Dramatic forms of all ages have employed these techniques and a variety of other presentational methods, including asides to the audience, soliloquies, direct address, and curtain calls.

Representational performance, however, is the more fundamental mode of drama. In representational performance, the audience watches behavior that seems to be staged as if no audience were present. As a result, the audience is encouraged to concentrate on the events that are being staged, not on the nature of their presentation; the audience believes in the play as if it were real. This belief—or, to borrow Samuel Taylor Coleridge's famous phrase, this "willing suspension of disbelief"—attracts audience

participation by encouraging a feeling of kinship with the characters. We can identify with their aspirations, sympathize with their plights, exult in their victories, and care deeply about what happens to them. When empathy is present, the audience experiences what is often called the "magic" of theatre. Well-written and well-staged dramas make people feel, not just think; they draw in the spectators' emotions, leaving them feeling transported and even somewhat changed.

Occasionally, presentational and representational styles are taken to extremes. In the late nineteenth century, the representational movement known as *realism* sought to have actors behave onstage exactly as people do in real life, in settings made as lifelike as possible. At times the representational ideal so dominated in certain theatres—for instance, the "Quiet Theatre" movement in Japan in the 1990s—that actors spoke with their backs to audiences, directors encouraged pauses and inaudible mumbling, and playwrights transcribed dialogue from fragments of randomly overheard conversations.

15

This production of Bertolt Brecht's sharply satirical *The Threepenny Opera*, directed by Robert Wilson at the Berliner Ensemble theatre (which Brecht founded in 1949), follows Brecht's representational concepts, with its bold colors, starkly white makeup, and deliberately artificial lighting. The production played in New York City in 2011. ©*Aris/Süddeutsche Zeitung Photo/Alamy Stock Photo*

Many theatre artists took the opposite approach, such as the twentieth-century German playwright-director Bertolt Brecht. Brecht advocated for a more presentational style that, by seeking to appeal directly to the audience on a variety of social and political issues, featured openly visible lighting instruments; signs, songs, slide projections, and speeches addressed directly to the audience; and a "distanced" style of acting intended to reduce emotional empathy or theatrical "magic."

No play can ever be completely representational or presentational, however. During naturalistic performances, we are always aware that we are watching actors perform for us, and the plays of Brecht and his followers, despite his theories, generate empathy when well performed. The fact is that theatrical performance is always both presentational and representational.

Two other aspects of theatre distinguish theatre from other forms of performance: theatre is live and, in most cases, is a scripted and rehearsed event.

Live Performance In contrast to movies, the theatre is a real-time event in which performers and audience members are fully aware of the others' immediate presence. The awareness of spectators can give performers an adrenaline charge and a magical feeling of responding and listening in the moment. Actors can feel the audience's energy, and audiences can feel the actors' focus. Everyone in the theatre is breathing the same air; all are involved at the same time and in the same space.

Live theatre also creates a relationship among the audience members. People attending a play arrive as individuals or in small groups, but they all quickly find themselves laughing at the same jokes, empathizing with the same characters, and experiencing the same revelations. Or perhaps they laugh at different moments, enjoy different characters, or arrive at different conclusions. Either way, they respond *together*; they become a community. While fans of TV shows and movies might exchange opinions online, theatre audiences experience the same social activity together, at the same time.

It is no wonder that political demonstrations often incorporate theatre. In creating a spectacle, theatre also creates an audience, and that audience becomes energized. In a celebrated example, the Depression-era *Waiting for Lefty* was staged as if the audience were a group of union members; by the play's end, the audience was yelling "Strike! Strike!" in response to the play's call to action. Theatre also has a long history of street performances that take advantage of this power. There's a reason why activists frequently stage plays in public, as opposed to screening films: nothing mobilizes a crowd like the theatre.

Finally, live performance has the quality of immediacy. The action of the play is taking place right now, as it is being watched, and anything can happen. Although in most professional productions the changes that occur in performance from one night to the next are so subtle only an expert would notice, the fact is that each night's presentation is unique and everyone present—in the audience, in the cast, and behind the scenes—knows it. When you are watching an actor onstage, you and that actor are in the same place at the same time. This awareness lends an excitement that cannot be experienced while watching films or video. One reason for the excitement of live theatre, of course, is that mistakes can happen in its performance. This possibility creates a certain tension, perhaps even an edge of fright, which can create a thrilling feeling in the audience—something could go wrong! But just as disaster can come without warning, so too can splendor. On any given night, actors are trying to better their previous performance, and no one knows when this collective effort will turn into something sublime.

Scripted and Rehearsed Performance

While theatre is always new and immediate, it is also scripted and carefully prepared. The art of theatre lives in the relationship between these two opposing principles: it is always spontaneous but also carefully and repeatedly rehearsed. In a popular phrase among theatre scholars, a play has "repetition with a difference." Theatre performances are largely prepared according to written and well-rehearsed texts, or play scripts. Sometimes theatre is instead devised rather than written. In these cases the play develops through workshops and collaborations, improvisation, and research. We will discuss this form of play creation in the chapter "The Playwright."

Mostly, though, plays depend on scripts. And in this way they are often distinguished from other forms of performance, such as improvisation and performance installations. Although improvisation and ad-libbing may play a role in the preparation process, and even in certain actual performances, most play productions are based on a script that was established before—and modified during—the play's rehearsal period, and most of the action is permanently set during these rehearsals as well. Professional theatrical productions, therefore, appear nearly the same night after night: for the most part, the Broadway production of *Wicked* that you see on Thursday will be almost identical to the show your friend saw on Wednesday or your mother saw last fall. And if you were to read the published text, you would see on the page the same words you heard spoken or sung on the stage.

But the text of a play is not, by any means, the play itself. The play fully exists only in its performance—in its "playing." The script is merely the record the play leaves behind after the audience has gone home. The script is to the play what a recipe is to a meal: it outlines the principal features of what you are preparing and gives you instructions for making it, but it can never capture the full sensations of the final product.

Published scripts are often an imperfect record. Often they carry over material left out of the actual production, or they include new material the author thought of after the production was over. The published texts of Shakespeare's plays include differing versions of many of his plays, including two versions of *King Lear* written several years apart. When American dramatist Tennessee Williams published his *Cat on a Hot Tin Roof* after the play's premiere, he included both the third act he originally wrote and the third act written at the request of the director, Elia Kazan. Williams invited readers to select their preferred version. Moreover, even a fixed script is often as notable for what it lacks as for what it contains. Plays published before the twentieth century rarely have more than rudimentary stage directions, and even now a published play tells us almost nothing about the play's nonverbal components. The simple direction "they fight" takes less than a second to read, but onstage it could be a breathtaking duel, a brawl, or a quick gunshot: it is up to the artists to bring the printed word to life.

We now have a good grasp on the many definitions of the theatre. It is a way of looking and a way of being seen. It can also be a building and a company; it can be work, art, impersonation, and performance; it consists of living performers and written, rehearsed scripts. It is a production: a collection of actions, sights, sounds, ideas, feelings, words, light, and, above all, people.

In reading our breakdown of these definitions, you may have noticed a pattern. As soon as we try to define an essential rule of the theatre, we admit that it can sometimes

Spotlight

Film Stars on Stage Acting

The vast majority of film stars got their start acting onstage in high school, college, or small theatres near their hometowns. Many of them—including the most successful—return to live stage performing. Film and TV stars such as Al Pacino, Viola Davis, Bryan Cranston, Michelle Williams, Daniel Radcliffe, Samuel L. Jackson, Scarlett Johannson, Andrew Garfield, Jude Law, Denzel Washington, Laura Linney, Daniel Craig, Mark Ruffalo, Uma Thurman, and Benedict Cumberbatch all found themselves acting on Broadway in recent seasons. Why would these actors, plus the likes of David Hyde Pierce, Neil Patrick Harris, Katie Holmes, Cate Blanchett, Ben Affleck, Matthew Broderick, Anne Hathaway, Patrick Stewart, Ian McKellen, Geoffrey Rush, John Lithgow, Dame Judi Dench, Anthony Hopkins, Ethan Hawke, and Meryl Streep, leave Hollywood for such vastly lower-paying stage work? Here are some of their replies:

There's that side of theatre that appeals to me, where you give something and the response to what you've created is a communion between you and the dark that contains however many people. It's thrilling not having a reflection other than through the people you're communicating with.

—BENEDICT CUMBERBATCH[1]

Theatre is about authenticity. It's in front of you; you feel it. It's so hard to feel stuff anymore from film. . . . It can get very remote.

—MERYL STREEP

I love acting for the camera. But in film your performance doesn't really belong to you. It belongs to the director and the editor and the producers. Onstage [in Arthur Miller's A View from the Bridge*], the audience saw everything I had, not some reshaped version of it. The same arc was there every night, of course, and yet it was a living, breathing thing.*

—SCARLETT JOHANNSON[2]

Cause, I love it, I love it! I love the theatre, it is how and where I started. . . . The way I was raised as an actor was in the theatre.

—DENZEL WASHINGTON[3]

I didn't want to make any films. I only wanted to be in the theatre. Shakespeare was my passion. And that's what I did, so it didn't matter.

—JUDI DENCH[4]

If my movie career was totally terminated, I would be saddened and disappointed . . . but if that were to happen with the live theatre, it would be devastating. [Theatre] is like a fountain that I have to return to.

—PATRICK STEWART[5]

One of the glorious things about the theatre is that it cannot be preserved. You can't look at it again; it's live. . . . Cinema's dead. You can laugh, you can cry, you can shout at the screen and the movie will carry on. But an audience in the theatre, whether it knows it or not, is affecting the performance. . . . That's the stream of life at its best, isn't it?

—IAN MCKELLEN[6]

In film, the challenge is to be able to shape a performance when the process is so piecemeal. And the absolute joy of being onstage is you get to surf that wave. It's a much more muscular experience.

—CATE BLANCHETT[7]

There is only so long you can go from film to film. Theatre is a more raw experience. For an actor a live audience is creative inspiration.

—JUDE LAW[8]

I love the stage, and I love being on stage, and the rush and the fear and all of that.

—DANIEL RADCLIFFE

Nothing was going to stand in my way of doing that play.

—ASHLEY JUDD, ON WHY SHE TURNED DOWN THE TITLE ROLE IN *CATWOMAN* TO BE ONSTAGE IN A NEW YORK REVIVAL OF *CAT ON A HOT TIN ROOF*

[1]Oldman, Gary. (2013, November 11). "Benedict Cumberbatch," www.interviewmagazine.com/film/benedict-cumberbatch.

[2]Isherwood, Charles. (2010, May 12). Scarlett Johannson quoted in "Definitely Didn't Get Lost in Translation," *The New York Times.*

[3]Gencarelli, Mike. (2010, June 13). "Interview with Denzel Washington & the Cast of Broadway's 'Fences,'" http://mediamikes.com/2010/06/interview-with-denzel-\washington-the-cast-of-broadways-fences/.

[4]Sturm, Rudiger. (2017, October 11). "Judi Dench: 'I Have an Irrational Fear of Boredom,'" http://the-talks.com/interview/judi-dench.

[5]Courtesy of Patrick Stewart.

[6]Crews, C. (2001, December 28). "At the Top of His Form by Chip Crews," *Washington Post.*

[7]Dobkin, M. (2006, February 27). "Hedda Steam," *New York Magazine.*

[8]Gibbons, F. (2001, January 12). "The Next Stage: Stars Pledge Millions for Theatre Ventures," *The Guardian.* Copyright Guardian News & Media Ltd. 2001. Used with permission.

Bryan Cranston has appeared in over 100 movies and TV shows, including his starring role in TV's *Breaking Bad*, and has won dozens of acting awards. It was not a surprise, then, that he scored the 2014 Tony Award for Best Performance in a Leading Role in a Play for his first Broadway role playing President Lyndon B. Johnson in Robert Schenkkan's *All The Way*, directed by Bill Rauch. More recently, Cranston recreated the Johnson role for television. He is shown here in his initial American Repertory Theatre production, with Betsy Aidem playing his stage wife, Lady Bird. *©Evgenia Eliseeva*

break this rule. The theatre is a building, but it *could* take place anywhere. Theatre depends on the separation of actor and audience, but it *could* still occur with the two sides mingling. Theatre uses scripts, but it *could* be improvised. Rather than become frustrated with theatre's ability to always find an exception to any stable definition, we encourage you to see this as one of its characteristics. In other words, one of the theatre's defining qualities is its resistance to definition! Time and again, as soon as one clear understanding of theatre has taken hold, artists and innovators have broken free of these constraints and introduced new ideas. You'll notice this throughout the textbook, right up until the present day. This is something to celebrate: the theatre, like all art forms, is alive. It simply needs to involve humans who want to create plays—and plays to put on.

But what exactly is a play? That question deserves a separate chapter.

Design Elements: *Spotlight Icon: ©McGraw-Hill Education; Theatrical Masks: ©Ingram Publishing/Alamy Stock Photo; Camera: ©Tatiana Popova/Shutterstock*

Chapter

2

What Is a Play?

©Robbie Jack/Corbis Historical/Getty Images

A PLAY IS, ESSENTIALLY, WHAT HAPPENS in theatre. A play is not a thing but an event, and not just any event. Rock concerts, stand-up comedy, poetry readings, storytelling, and cabaret performances all occur onstage in a highly theatrical manner, but they are not plays. Why not? What makes a play a play?

To answer that question, we can look at a related word, *drama,* whose origin is from the Greek *dran,* "something done." Simply put, a play supplies the theatre with drama. The word *theatron*, as we remember from the first chapter, means "seeing place," so we can put these terms together to learn that a play is both done (it supplies drama) and communally witnessed (it is theatrical). A play, then, is a form of perceived action, not just words in a book.

This definition of a play goes all the way back to the Greek thinker Aristotle (384–322 B.C.E.), who wrote one of the first works about the theatre, the *Poetics*. A play, Aristotle observed, is an "imitation of an action."

This kind of action, however, is not the kind we think of today—it is not merely movement. If a branch snaps and falls from a tree, it is not Aristotle's understanding of action. Rather, action must be willed, not accidental—it must result from thought. Action translates the inner landscape of our souls and minds into the external language of gesture, habit, and words. And since a play is an imitation of an action, rather than just the action itself, it is the poetic *interpretation* of human behavior. Plays take the raw material of our everyday lives and sculpt it into something that retains the truth, if not the exact reality, of our shared experience.

Around the same time Aristotle wrote the *Poetics,* another major text about drama emerged in ancient India. The *Natyasastra*, whose title roughly translates as "science of drama," is a vast compendium of instruction for how to create plays. While there are many differences between this work and Aristotle's, there are also some striking similarities. Both texts see plays as elevated and removed from the everyday: the *Natyasastra* organizes drama into different categories based on popular myths and stories of the gods. Both texts, too, are interested in how the audience responds. For Aristotle, a tragedy—and tragedies are for him the highest form of dramatic art—should create a *catharsis*, or purging, of pity and fear from the audience. The *Natyasastra,* for its part, defines drama as something that creates pleasure on the part of its spectators.

It is striking that, roughly 6,000 miles away from each other, two ancient cultures felt the need to codify playmaking into a set of practices for future generations to follow. Plays were important enough that their creation needed to be remembered. This need points to the *social* aspect of drama that both texts emphasize. Plays were fundamentally public, and performing plays had a beneficial effect on society. Based on our definition of *play* thus far, we can see what these beneficial effects are: plays give us structure that we lack in the more disorderly stream of sensations in life, but they also give us situations and ideas that reflect something truthful. We both recognize and are separated from what happens onstage in a play. They offer a heightened version of our reality so that we can reflect on our own circumstances. It is no wonder that Aristotle borrowed the word "catharsis" from medicine: he saw plays as a healing agent, an event of shared therapy.

Sometimes, though, when we talk about "plays," we are not speaking of an event but of a piece of literature. We see plays, but we can also read them. This is a relatively new understanding of the word. In the early seventeenth century—over two millennia after the *Poetics* and the *Natyasastra*—the celebrated Renaissance writer Ben Jonson collected all of his works—mostly drama, but also poems and epigrams—in one large bound edition, or "folio." Such a practice might seem common today for famous authors, but this action made Jonson a laughing-stock; it was perceived as a cocky and useless endeavor. Today, though, reading plays is the primary way we encounter them. Plays are often printed in literary anthologies, are intermixed with poems and short stories, or are given their own anthologies. One can now easily purchase the collected works of William Shakespeare, Arthur Miller, or Wole Soyinka.

But drama should not be thought of as merely a form of literature. It is foremost a live performance, of which some repeatable aspects may be captured in a written and published text. The plays that we read can be remarkably different from the plays we see. The texts exist between live performances. They can prompt new productions or serve as evidence of previous ones. When read, plays can be exhilarating, but it is far more vital to see and hear plays and, when possible, to do them yourself.

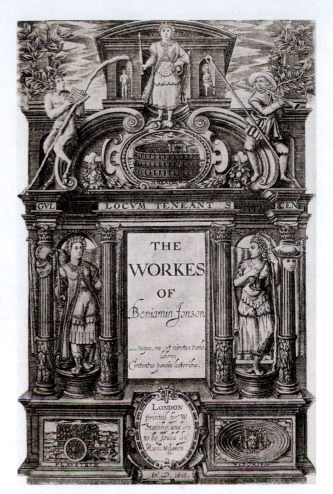

We commonly encounter plays by reading them, but this wasn't always the case. Pictured here is the 1616 "folio," or collected works, of the playwright Ben Jonson. At the time, the publication of plays (and the idea of reading them) was perceived as an anomaly. *©Universal History Archive/Universal Images Group/Getty Images*

Classifying Plays

Plays can present action that takes place in a single room or across continents, but even the most expansive plays have constraints. They are framed with a beginning and end, which—along with what happens in the middle—help determine what kind of play they are. These classifications are usually made according to the play's *duration* and *genre*.

DURATION

How long is a play? When celebrated American playwright Arthur Miller first thought of writing for the theatre, he admitted "How long should it be?" was his most pressing question. The answer is far from obvious, and the fact that

Tom Stoppard's three-part and nine-hour-long *The Coast of Utopia,* set in nineteenth-century Russia with more than seventy acting roles and covering some thirty-plus years, received ten Tony Award nominations in 2007, winning a record seven of them, including Best Play for its New York production—which certainly proves that long plays need not become tedious ventures. ©*Sara Krulwich/The New York Times/Redux*

even Arthur Miller had to puzzle over a play's duration makes it clear that a play's length is not just a technical consideration.

Historically, in drama that developed in Europe and the United States, a "full-length" play usually lasted between two and three hours. This is not an arbitrary period of time; it roughly represents the hours between lunch and dinner (for a matinee) or between dinner and bedtime. The seventeenth-century playwright John Webster wrote that the actor "entertains us in the best leisure of our life, that is between meals, the most unfit time either for study or bodily exercise." Webster was thinking of the afternoon performances in the outdoor theatres of his day. A few years earlier, speaking of indoor evening performances at court, Shakespeare's Theseus, in *A Midsummer Night's Dream*, asks for a play "to wear away this long age of three hours between our after-supper and bed-time." Elsewhere, Shakespeare refers to "the two-hours traffic of our stage," and this seems not to have changed much—plays on Broadway tend to run a little over two hours.

But plays can be much shorter or longer. One-act plays of an hour or less—sometimes even ten minutes—are occasionally combined to make a full theatre program. Short plays are often presented at dramatic festivals, school assemblies, social gatherings, street entertainments, cabaret performances, or other settings outside of a theatre building. One of the

shortest plays on record is Samuel Beckett's *Breath*, which can be performed in one minute. There are exceptionally long plays as well. *The Peony Pavilion,* a celebrated example of the traditional Chinese theatre known as *kunqu,* consists of 55 scenes and lasts three days. Also, the classical Indian drama known as *Kutiyattam,* a form of Sanskrit play inspired by the guidelines of the *Natyasastra,* consists of several acts that can last as long as forty-one days each.

In recent decades, more lengthy productions have also proven popular in the West. One of the hottest tickets in New York for the 2016 theatre season was Taylor Mac's *A 24-Decade History of Popular Music,* a daylong show that surveyed American musical forms from 1776 to the present day—each decade of music took up one hour—and saw audiences staying up, bleary-eyed, from noon on Saturday to noon on Sunday. In addition, audiences have flocked to the Royal Shakespeare Company's production of *Wolf Hall* (seven hours), Tom Stoppard's *Coast of Utopia* (nine hours), Peter Brook's *Mahabharata* (nine hours), Peter Stein's production of Aeschylus's *Oresteia* (seven hours), and Tony Kushner's *Angels in America* (six hours). (At the extreme end of this spectrum, Robert Wilson's *Ka Mountain* was once performed over 168 continuous hours.) Some plays are neither long nor short—they fall somewhere in between our usual categories. Take, for instance, David Mamet's *Glengarry*

Glen Ross. Mamet finished his script and worried that it was too short to be a full-length play and too long to be a one-act (the running time clocks in around 75 minutes). He sent a copy to his playwriting hero, Harold Pinter, and received the feedback that it was perfect as is. The play went on to win a Pulitzer Prize and has since been produced with regularity across the world.

Miller's question, it seems, does not have a precise answer: there are no concrete guidelines as to running time. Duration is critical but never set in stone.

GENRE

Genre provides a more subjective basis of classification than duration. No one argues how long a play lasts, but one could reasonably disagree over what genre it is. The word "genre" is directly derived from the French word for "kind" (it is also the root word for "gender"). So to classify a play by genre is to say what kind of play it is.

Just as there are different kinds of movies—comedies, westerns, action films, horror films, documentaries—there are different genres of plays. Historically, the first defined dramatic genres were tragedy and comedy. We are probably most familiar with comedy because of its popularity in films: we can easily recall moments and scenarios from movies that make us laugh just by thinking about them or describing them to friends. Tragedy, though, is not as common in films, or even in contemporary theatre. However, many of the great masterpieces of theatre are tragedies—from ancient Greece through the eras of Shakespeare and Jean Racine—and the genre deserves serious discussion.

Tragedy   A *tragedy* is a profoundly serious play that always ends in the death of one or more of its main characters and focuses on a resonant theme about human life and society. Tragedy was first described by Aristotle, who considered it the greatest kind of play. The greatest tragedy is, for Aristotle, Sophocles' *Oedipus Rex.* This play has in many ways become the fundamental and defining work of tragedy in the West. To understand why, we need to look closer at how Aristotle defines the genre.

In Aristotle's construction, the central character of a tragedy, the *protagonist*, is a person of high rank or stature. During the play, the protagonist undergoes a decline of fortune, which leads to suffering and usually to death. Integral to tragedy, according to Aristotle, is the protagonist's self-recognition (*anagnorisis* in Greek) of a fundamental mistake (*hamartia*). Self-recognition causes a reversal of fortunes (*peripeteia*) that in turn leads to demise. This dire outcome elicits pity and terror from the audience and

Shakespeare took Sophocles' blinding motif one step further in his tragedy of *King Lear,* some two thousand years later, in which Lear's friend, the Duke of Gloucester, is brutally blinded onstage by Lear's daughter and her husband. Here, Japanese actor Kazunori Akitaya plays the blinded Gloucester in a stylized Japanese production by the Globe Theatre of Tokyo. ©*Robbie Jack/Corbis Historical/Getty Images*

then a purging of those emotions (catharsis) aroused by the play's events.

In *Oedipus,* the title character, the King of Thebes, learns that his city is suffering from the plague because the killer of the previous king, Laius, is still on the loose. Oedipus vows to find and destroy this killer. Soon, however, Oedipus discovers that he himself had killed Laius some years ago at a crossroads (his mistake), without knowing his identity. He then finds out that Laius was also his father and that by marrying Laius's widow

Jocasta, he had married his own mother (his self-recognition). Jocasta kills herself at this discovery. Wracked with shame, Oedipus gouges out his eyes with brooches from his mother's gown, which causes the emotional release—the catharsis—of the audience.

Struggle, self-recognition, and catharsis are central to tragic drama, elevating the genre above mere sadness or sentimentality. The eighteenth-century philosopher David Hume proposed that tragedy must differentiate itself from the everyday violence of the world by producing a kind of beauty. This seems like a paradox: how can something so miserable also be beautiful? But this paradox is at the heart of what makes tragedy such an esteemed form of art. Tragedy cannot simply be sad or terrifying; it is neither pathetic nor maudlin. Instead, it focuses on greatness. By involving a bold, aggressive, heroic attack against huge, perhaps insurmountable, odds, tragedy is both recognizably human and larger than life. Tragic protagonists are always flawed in some way, but they are heroes, not victims. Their instigation of the play's action and their discoveries during its course bring the audience to deep emotional and intellectual involvement at the play's climax—and then great relief at its conclusion.

Tragedy is defined in part by its characters. The journey of the protagonist is complemented by the actions of the *antagonist* ("opposer of the action"). This duality gives tragedy its fundamental conflict. Tragic protagonists go forth against superhuman antagonists—gods, ghosts, fate—and their struggle, though doomed, takes on larger-than-life proportions. Through the heat of such conflict, they assume superhuman force and offer the audience a link outwardly to divine mysteries—or inwardly to the unconscious mind. The goal of tragedy is therefore to ennoble, not sadden, us. The tragic heroes we admire will fall, but not before they heroically challenge the universe. They carry us to the brink of disaster, but it is their disaster, not ours—at least, not yet. Experiencing a tragedy allows us to contemplate and rehearse in our own minds the great conflicts that may await us.

The basic structure of tragedy is not limited to the drama of the West; it is universal. The Kuwaiti playwright and director Sulayman Al-Bassam has noted the resonance of Aristotle's ideas with Islamic traditions, from the transcendental language of Sufism to the passionate conflicts of the traditional mourning play known as *ta'ziyeh,* a spectacular presentation that commemorates the bloody Battle of Karbala. Al-Bassam notes, "The themes of tragedy are with us: insanity in war, cruelty in the nature of the human condition, an individual's impulses to self-destruction." Tragedy prompts an unflinching look

Stagecraft

Genre-ly Speaking

Shakespeare often has brightly parodied the division of plays into genres, a practice that in his time was already becoming almost an affectation. In *Hamlet,* Polonius describes an acting company as "the best actors in the world, either for tragedy, comedy, history, pastoral, pastoral-comical, historical-pastoral, tragical-historical, tragical-comical-historical-pastoral; scene individable, or poem unlimited."

inward, a confrontation with our own deepest selves. This searching gaze is ultimately a human impulse.

Because tragedy is a universal form, its exact parameters are always evolving. There is no single recipe for tragedy: what constitutes a human conflict changes as humans change. In the 1950s, Arthur Miller's *Death of a Salesman* featured a central character, Willie Loman (that is, "low man"), who faces not gods but faceless bureaucrats, insensitive children, and an impersonal capitalistic system. Miller's vision was radical, yet the soul of this genre has remained more or less the same through the millennia. Frailty, freedom, self-sacrifice, and a yearning for the sublime will always be with us, and thus, so too will tragedy.

Comedy   Comedy is a very popular genre and has been a staple of the theatre since ancient times. Playwrights of all eras have written comedies—sometimes with serious themes, sometimes with particularly dark humor. At yet other times, playwrights have no purpose other than to create continuous hilarity through common devices such as full-stage chases, mistaken identities, lovers hiding in closets or under tables, sexual puns, switched potions, clever disguises (often involving cross-dressing), misheard instructions, and sheer physical buffoonery; such works are usually labeled *farce.* Comedies have been immensely popular in all ages, but because they are about ordinary life rather than larger-than-life heroes, they usually lose their popularity sooner. And because they rarely probe as deeply into human destiny as do tragedies, they offer less fertile ground for academic scholarship and are less frequently published in anthologies, examined in scholarly literature, or placed on college course syllabi. Nevertheless, some comedies (particularly those of Shakespeare and Molière) are considered true masterpieces of human observation. Comedy's

Arthur Miller's *Death of a Salesman* is often considered the American theatre's finest tragedy, since its protagonist, the likeable but morally flawed Willy Loman, experiences a decline of fortune that eventually leads to his suicide. Here, in a dream sequence from the much-heralded 1999 Goodman Theatre production, Brian Dennehy as Willy (*center*) leans on the shoulders of his two sons (played by Kevin Anderson and Ted Koch), not as they are now but as he remembers them from better days. ©AF archive/Alamy Stock Photo

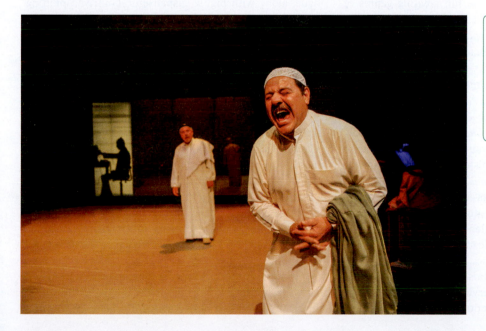

The genre of tragedy is truly universal. Pictured here is a scene from *Richard III: An Arab Tragedy,* adapted and directed by Sulayman Al-Bassam. This version of Shakespeare's tragedy changes its setting to an unnamed Persian Gulf country but retains the themes at its core. ©Richard Termine

The fact that drama is a category of literature does not mean that it is necessarily serious, much less profound. Shakespeare, for example, is best known for his tragedies, but his comedies are among the greatest theatrical achievements of all time. This hilarious 2014 production of *Comedy of Errors* was directed by Blanche McIntyre at the replica of Shakespeare's Globe Theatre in London, with Matthew Needham (*left*) as Antipholus of Ephesus and Jamie Wikes (*right*) as Dromio of Ephesus.
©Geraint Lewis/Alamy Stock Photo

place in the theatre world is every bit as secure as tragedy's, and comedy is as popular now as it was in the fifth century B.C.E., the era of the ancient Greek comic playwright Aristophanes.

Other Genres

Other genres are defined from time to time, and playwrights often have fun creating genres of their own. The *history play* first came to popularity in the sixteenth century when Shakespeare wrote plays that depicted events that occurred decades before he was born. We still occasionally see works that examine historical figures; examples include George Bernard Shaw's *Saint Joan*, Bertolt Brecht's *Galileo*, Alan Bennett's *The Madness of George III,* Lynn Nottage's *Las Meninas,* and, more recently, Mike Bartlett's *King Charles III,* which cheekily envisions the early reign of Britain's modern-day monarch in the verse of a Renaissance history play. More common today is the *documentary drama* (or *docudrama*), which makes use of actual documents—court records, for example, or transcribed interviews—to lend a sense of timeliness to the plot. The multitalented theatre artist Anna Deveare Smith is one of the leading lights of this genre. Smith's productions feature her embodying an array of roles, each a real-life person whose every spoken word is a direct transcription of an interview conducted by Smith herself. Recently, her production *Notes from the Field*

focused on race, education, and incarceration; her "characters" included a pastor, a protester, an imprisoned mother, and many more.

Many genres exist in between the major categories. *Melodrama*, whose heyday was the nineteenth century, is embellished with spectacular staging and flamboyant dialogue, along with highly suspenseful, contrived plotting. Melodramas lack the moral complexity, bleak endings, or catharsis of tragedy. When performed today, they are almost always staged as parodies of their originals and played for laughs. Other hybrid genres have resurged as of late, as with recent productions that blend docudrama with tragedy. In Beirut, at the Al-Madina Theatre, a 2014 production of Sophocles' classical Greek tragedy *Antigone*—a sequel of sorts to his *Oedipus*—featured a cast of actual Syrian refugees. The performers interspersed the ancient drama with monologues about their harrowing real-life stories. In this instance, the shocking relevance of a current issue melds with the universal themes of suffering in the ancient form.

Sometimes genres can bring in art forms outside of theatre altogether. The *Tanztheatre* (dance-theatre) of the late, celebrated director-choreographer Pina Bausch incorporates dramatic elements like impersonation and narrative, while also relying on the highly technical and physically daunting movements of dance. Is a Pina

I went up after her.

The Chilean theatre company Teatrocinema incorporates elements of film (animation, projection) with live performance, as demonstrated here in a scene from its critically acclaimed 2016 production *Historia de Amor.* ©*Krissi Lundgren/Photoshot/Newscom*

Bausch production a play or a dance? It's hard to say, which is the point. Her work provokes us by making us realize how thin the borders are between types of media. Many plays also incorporate film, as with the Chilean company Teatrocinema. (Like Bausch, this group combines two art forms in their name; "teatrocinema" means "theatre-cinema.") With live action and video, their work, such as the celebrated *Historia de Amor,* is hard to pin down as either theatre or cinema. Is it both? Or something new? Genres exist to be challenged and to challenge our expectations.

Furthermore, any system of classification should allow for the fact that each play is unique. The grouping of any two or more plays into a common genre is only a convenience for purposes of comparison and analysis. Maybe one person's tragedy is another's comedy. But applying genres can help us comprehend the broad spectrum of purposes to which plays may be put, and help us to perceive important similarities and differences between individual works. For the theatre artist, awareness of the possibilities inherent in each genre—together with knowledge of the achievements made in each—stimulates the imagination and aids in setting standards and ambitions.

Dramaturgy: The Construction of Drama and Dramatic Performance

A play is action, but it is *patterned* action. Unlike the action of, say, a street riot, dramatic action has clearly identifiable components and a specified beginning and ending. Even when improvised or radically experimental, a play's dramatic action tends to be crafted in patterns. We call these patterns a play's *dramaturgy.*

Action provides a play's thrills and excitement—Oedipus gouged out his eyes—while dramaturgy provides meaning by giving the action context—Oedipus gouged out his eyes *after finding out about his past* and *before he is exiled.* Dramaturgy leads an audience to see the play's action as consequential rather than as a random series of events. So while a street riot may be action, dramaturgy would lend structure and shape by determining how we *experience* the riot: Which characters do we follow? What events do we see unfold onstage? What information do we find out—and when? Action gives us the block of clay, but dramaturgy sculpts it. The most successful dramaturgy can create a profound engagement with the audience's thoughts and feelings.

The term "dramaturgy" also refers to the ingredients of the play: the elements that are needed to make it a play, such as plot, character, sound, and so on. These two different definitions of dramaturgy—the play's *components,* or what it is made of, and its *timeline,* or order of events—give us two different ways to analyze a play. As such, dramaturgy supplies us with a language to examine the theatre. Let's take a look at both aspects.

DRAMA'S COMPONENTS

The division of plays into components is an ancient practice begun by Aristotle. Although Aristotle spoke of tragedy in particular, his breakdown of dramatic elements has been influential to nearly all theatre since. He identified six components: plot, character, thought, diction, music, and spectacle—in that order of importance. With some modification, Aristotle's list still provides a helpful breakdown of the major elements of most dramas, although the importance of each component is a matter of debate. Let's take a look at each component, as well as the conventions of theatre.

Plot   Although we may think of *plot* as synonymous with story, the meanings of the two words are actually quite different. The story is simply the narrative of what happens in the play, as might be described by someone who has seen it. Plot refers to *why* things happen, not just *that* they do. Plot thus encompasses the means of storytelling. When we talk about plot, we refer to the order of characters' entrances and exits onstage as well as the order of what those characters do: the revelations, reversals, quarrels, discoveries, and actions that take place onstage. Plot is therefore the structure of actions, both external (a man shoots his brother) and internal (a man is overcome with guilt for committing murder). Perhaps Aristotle listed plot foremost among drama's six elements because it essentially makes drama dramatic. Without plot, we simply have a random series of events.

Character   The word *character* can mean different things today. We speak of someone "having character" in terms of having a particular quality or virtue, and we speak of the "characters," or letters, of an alphabet. This latter definition may seem to be an anomaly, but it is actually closer to the way Aristotle used the term: as something formed by text. An understanding of character both as something formed and as a container of particular qualities helps us understand what Aristotle meant. Characters are fictional (formed by writing) and yet they seem human (they possess qualities).

Sometimes characters are simple and contrived—sometimes on purpose!—and other times they are as deeply felt as people we know. Many theatre traditions, like Italian *commedia dell'arte* of the Renaissance or classical Chinese opera, intentionally use "types" of characters rather than fleshed-out individuals. These "stock" characters are then fleshed out in live performance, where actors improvise their lines and movement. Other characters are drawn in intense, lifelike detail on the page, right down to their posture, hair, clothes, and histories. Eugene O'Neill's play *Long Day's Journey Into Night* features characters taken from his own past, and the text is filled with precise descriptions recalled from his personal memories.

However the characters appear in the text, they ultimately become human only when they are performed. It is when we see actors take on a character that we react to them, and only then can the play be fully realized.

Thought   Aristotle used the word "thought" not in the sense of a mental picture or idea, but to refer to what a play is expressing: the arguments and concepts that emerge as a result of its performance. It is similar to the word "theme" as we use it today. A play's theme is an abstraction. It's not something you can point to, like an actor or a costume, and it's not immediately evident in the text, like plot. Some plays have obvious themes, such as Euripides' *The Trojan Women* (the horrors of war) or Molière's *The Bourgeois Gentleman* (the foolishness of social pretense). Other plays have less clearly defined themes, and the most provocative of these plays have given rise to much debate over what its theme is. In some cases, the lack of a clear theme is itself a theme: the plays lack conceptual unity just as the characters do, and the search for meaning becomes one of the play's central qualities. The recent play *An Octoroon* by Branden Jacobs-Jenkins begins with a surrogate of the playwright facing the audience and telling us that he isn't sure what he wanted to write about. The ensuing play—an adaptation of a nineteenth-century melodrama—becomes a vehicle for his own search for an understanding of his identity.

Sometimes a theme can change drastically over time. For example, Shakespeare's *The Merchant of Venice*, which features a complex portrayal of a Jewish character in an anti-Semitic environment, cannot help but seem different today than it did before the Holocaust. If you read reviews of current plays, you will no doubt see talk of "relevance." Usually what this means is that the play's themes take on a new meaning in light of the context of its production. *The Laramie Project,* a piece of theatre devised by a group of artists in response to the 1998 murder of Matthew Shepard, a gay college student, is a popular play in the United States,

but the play arguably took on even more relevance in a recent production in Uganda, a country that has outlawed homosexuality. Themes are ultimately *why* plays are produced—they are the beating heart of the theatre.

Diction   If the theme is *what* is expressed, then diction is *how.* We use the term to describe the quality of a play's language. At times, the language can be almost musical; consider, for example, this passage from Suzan-Lori Parks's *In the Blood*:

WELFARE: My dear husband.
    The hours he keeps.
    The money he brings home.
    Our wonderful children.
    The vacations we go on.
    My dear husband he needed
    a little spice.
    And I agreed. We both need spice.
    We both hold very demanding jobs.
    We put an ad in the paper: "Husband and Bi-Curious
      Wife seeking—"
    But the women we got:
    Hookers. Neurotics. Gold diggers!

The character is simply known as "Welfare," and here we see how the characteristics of her language reveal aspects of her personality. There is repetition in phrases ("My dear husband") as well as rhythm: the first five lines end quickly with a period. But the sixth line ends with a hanging phrase ("My dear husband he needed") and the seventh line picks up the end of the sentence ("a little spice"). This is a poetic technique called enjambment: after getting the audience used to a specific rhythm—the rat-a-tat of the first lines—we suddenly break the pattern. Why? Perhaps this is the moment when the character breaks, too—when she can no longer order her thoughts. We see here how diction affects the other elements. We learn about her character and the play's theme. (And the plot moves along, as well—the woman who answers the ad in the paper, Hester, is the protagonist of the play.)

Diction need not always be complicated or even beautiful. It can be simple. Some of the most devastating lines in drama are also the smallest: after a young woman in Anton Chekhov's *Uncle Vanya* asks her father if she can play piano with her distant stepmother, and thus begin a friendship with her, she returns and says, soberly: "He said no." The act ends, as do her hopes.

Music   Aristotle called music the "most pleasing" of the elements of drama. We should remember, however, that plays in Aristotle's time were sung or chanted, not simply spoken. That mode of presentation has all but disappeared, yet music, more broadly understood, remains directly or indirectly present in almost all plays performed today.

Such music can take many forms. Songs are common in the plays of Shakespeare; oftentimes in the Renaissance actors would break into a popular song (sometimes with little relevance to the play) to entertain the audience. More natural-seeming playwrights use music as well. Perhaps a recording is played onstage, or characters sing together, as in August Wilson's *Joe Turner's Come and Gone,* when a group of freed slaves erupts into a "Juba," or call-and-response song derived from African chants that had been sung on the plantation. This music is not simply adornment: it tells us something deep and profound about the characters' heritage and trauma.

Sometimes music underscores dramatic action but is not heard by the characters. This kind of music is a *score,* which is created and implemented by a sound designer. A score can do many things: it can punctuate the play's action, intensify its rising suspense and climaxes, or simply keep up the energy while one scene transitions into another. But no matter what, a score aims to move the audience to an ever-deepening engagement.

Of course, there are genres of theatre that depend entirely on music. The *musical* is the most obvious, and we will devote an entire chapter to that form later on. Similarly, some non-Western cultures have historically developed theatre and musical traditions together. The rough equivalent of Aristotle's *Poetics* in China is the *Yue Ji* ("On Music") written by Confucian disciples in the fifth to fourth century B.C.E. The Chinese performance scholar and artist William Sun calls Chinese theatre "a culture of music," and indeed, traditional Chinese theatre often blurs the line between musical and theatrical performance.

Spectacle   Aristotle's sixth component, spectacle, encompasses the visual aspects of production: scenery, costumes, lighting, makeup, properties, and the overall look of the theatre and stage. Spectacle need not be over-the-top; the word simply refers to its original definition, "something seen." Although this point may seem obvious, it is crucial. Theatre is as much a visual experience as it is an aural, emotional, and intellectual one.

Sometimes spectacle is the most memorable part of a play, as with the chandelier that crashes to the ground at the end of the first act of *Phantom of the Opera* or the helicopter that descends in *Miss Saigon.* But spectacle can be subtle, too. A simple arrangement of bodies and objects onstage—the term used by theatre artists is *mise-en-scène,* which means literally "seen in the scene"—can be just as startling as an awesome display of pyrotechnics. Some of the most powerful examples of spectacle are no more than a group of people in an everyday environment. The end of *Hamilton,* arguably the most famous piece of theatre in the world today, is strikingly straightforward: the actors walk to the edge of the stage and look out over the audience as they sing the final lines. There are no special effects, no splashy multimedia. The "spectacle" on display is nothing more than performers on a stage, yet it is profoundly affecting—we are reminded that these historical figures are, at their core, just people, as flawed and complex as any of us.

The crucial question to ask with spectacle is not "how big or small is it?" but "does it enhance the other elements of drama?" When spectacle works—when it is in sync with all the other elements—it serves the story, rather than existing for its own sake.

Convention   To those six Aristotelian components we can today add a seventh category: convention. Theatre conventions are, simply put, the agreements between audience and actor. Conventions are why audiences know that—for instance—when the stage lights fade out, the play (or act) is over. If a character walks onstage in the first seconds of a play and says, "This desert goes on for miles," we immediately understand that we are to accept the stage setting as a desert: we believe the character. Other common conventions of the Western stage over the centuries have included the following:

- When an actor turns directly away from the other actors and speaks to the audience, the other characters are presumed not to hear the actor. This is the convention of the *aside* (a line addressed directly to the audience, unheard by the other characters).

- When actors all leave the stage and then they or others reenter (particularly when the lights change), time has elapsed. And if one actor then says to another, "Welcome to Padua," we are now in Padua, even if in the previous scene was in Verona.

- When actors "freeze" and the lighting dims, time itself has stood still—the narrative has been paused. If one character continues to act while the others freeze, we are gaining access to the character's thoughts.

Conventions become most clearly defined when an audience witnesses theatre in another cultural setting. In the

According to one Chinese theatre convention, a man paddling with an oar signifies "boatman," "boat," and "water" alike. Here, multiple performers use this convention in *Dragon Boat Racing,* the Chinese dance-drama spectacular presented in 2016 at Lincoln Center in New York City. ©*Slaven Vlasic/Getty Images*

wayang kulit shadow puppet theatre of Bali, for example, the play is over when the "tree of life" puppet, previously seen only in motion, comes to a standstill at the center of the stage. In the ancient noh drama of Japan, the audience realizes that words sung by chorus members are to be considered speeches spoken by the actors who are dancing, and the audience interprets gestures with a fan to indicate wind, rain, or the rising moon. In the Chinese xiqu, or traditional opera, a character entering the bare stage while holding a boat paddle is understood to be rowing across a river, and one entering with a whip is understood to be riding a horse.

Playwrights and directors have long enjoyed subverting theatrical conventions or inventing new ones. The ancient Greek playwright Euripides ended his tragedy *Medea* with a mise-en-scène that was unthinkable at the time: a murderous sorceress atop the *skene* (the small houselike structure at the rear of the stage)—the place usually reserved for the gods. In one swift gesture, the play lets us know that divine order has been ruined. More recently, Peter Shaffer's 1965 *Black Comedy*, which is set in a room during a complete blackout, employs a simple but effective convention:

when the lights are off for the characters, the stage lights are actually on, and when the lights are on for the characters, the stage lights are off. In effect we, the audience, see them stumble around with perfect clarity and hear them speak calmly in the dark. Robert O'Hara's 2015 satire *Barbecue* employs two alternate casts, each with the same names and family relations, occupying the same public park. One cast is used for one scene, then the other for the next, then back to the first, and so on. The crucial difference is one cast is black and the other is white. The audience initially doesn't know what's going on: Are they the same characters? If they are different, why do they have the same names? We get our answer right before the intermission in a stunning revelation, but until then we are curious about what convention O'Hara is using. Indeed, there is no formal requirement for the establishment of theatrical conventions except that audiences must "agree" to suspend disbelief and accept them.

The seven components of every play—Aristotle's six plus the conventions that frame them—are the raw material of drama. Some plays emphasize one or more components; most great productions show artistry in all.

Balancing these aspects in theatrical presentations is one of the primary challenges facing the director, who may be called on to clarify and elaborate a theme, find the visual mode of presentation that best supports the action, develop and flesh out the characterizations to give strength and meaning to the plot, heighten a musical effect, or clarify the convention—the relationship between play and audience—that will maximize the play's artistic impact. As important as each of these components is to the theatrical experience, it is ultimately their combination and interaction, not their individual power, that are crucial to a production's success.

DRAMA'S TIMELINE

The *timeline* of dramaturgy focuses on the structure of experience: When are we held in suspense? When are we learning about the world of the play? When do we begin to breathe easy again? When do we know the play is over? We can divide the timeline into three major groupings: pre-play, play, and post-play. The play itself, of course, receives the most attention and includes additional elements of the timeline, including the exposition, conflict, climax, and denouement. However, the surrounding pre-play and post-play have been part of the overall theatrical experience from the theatre's earliest days and also deserve attention.

Pre-Play   Pre-play begins with the attraction of an audience. Theatre has had this responsibility in every era, for there can be no "seeing place" without those who see.

How do plays get an audience to show up? They advertise. The procession is one of the oldest known ways of publicizing the theatre. The circus parade, which still takes place in some of the smaller towns of Europe and the United States, is a remnant of a once-universal form of advertisement for the performing arts that probably began well in advance of recorded history. The Greeks of ancient Athens opened their great dramatic festivals with a *proagon* (literally, "pre-action") in which both playwrights and actors were introduced at a huge public meeting and given a chance to speak about the plays they were to present on subsequent days. The Elizabethans flew flags atop their playhouses on performance days, enticing hundreds away from their commercial and religious activities. The lighted marquees of Broadway theatres around Times Square and of West End theatres in London are modern-day equivalents of those flags, signaling their entertainments to passersby. Today, posters, email blasts, Facebook posts, multicolor subscription brochures, media events, elaborate press releases, tweets, and, in New York, flashy television commercials summon patrons out of the comfort of their homes and into the theatre.

Once gathered at the theatre's door, the audience remains a collection of individuals preoccupied with their daily concerns. Now the theatre must transform its spectators into a community devoted to the concerns of the play. Ushers may lead them into the audience area, showing them to their seats and providing them with written programs that will prepare them for what they are about to see. Pre-show music or sound effects may be used to set a mood or tone, while stage lights may "warm" a curtain or illuminate the revealed stage and scenery with a romantic or eerie glow, creating the anticipation of dramatic actions about to take place. The 2015 musical *Natasha, Pierre & the Great Comet of 1812* welcomed its audience members with a pierogi (a Russian dumpling); by sharing a meal, those in attendance felt more intimately involved with the play and with each other. Sometimes there is activity onstage when the audience enters. Perhaps a few actors are engaged in quiet pre-show activity as incoming audience members observe the scene. Some playwrights deliberately begin to build the world of the play in the pre-play before the play proper has begun: Sam Shepard's *Fool for Love* features one character, "The Old Man," rocking in a chair onstage as everyone enters. The play hasn't begun yet, but we are drawn into its world.

Finally, in the moments before the play begins, there is usually an announcement for audience members to turn off their cell phones. Then the houselights dim, and (if all goes well) the audience is transported into the world of the play. As the familiar theatrical saying goes, "It's magic time."

Play   In contrast to staged events such as performance art and stand-up comedy, a play normally contains a sequence of identifiable elements. Aristotle tells us that the plot of a drama has a beginning, a middle, and an end. This might sound obvious, but attention to how a play develops over time—how its sequence of events begins, builds, and concludes—is important to understanding how a play "works." Four fairly consistent features are routinely recognized in the orderly plot sequencing of a conventionally Aristotelian dramatic experience: exposition, conflict, climax, and denouement.

The Exposition.   No important play has ever begun with a character dashing onstage and shouting, "The house is on fire!" Such a beginning could only confuse members of the audience, who would have no way of knowing what house is on fire or why they should care about it. Most plays, whatever their style or genre, begin with dialogue or action calculated to ease us, not shock us, into the concerns of the characters with whom we are to spend the next two hours or so. Exposition is the background information the audience must have in order to understand what's going on in the action of a play. Sometimes the exposition is handled with little fanfare. In the "well-made plays" of the nineteenth century, a few characters—often servants (minor figures in the action to follow)—would discuss something that is about to happen and enlighten one another (and, of course, the audience) about certain details around which the plot will turn. Consider these lines from the opening scene of Henrik Ibsen's 1884 classic, *The Wild Duck*:

PETTERSEN, *in livery, and* JENSEN, *the hired waiter, in black, are putting the study in order. From the dining room, the hum of conversation and laughter is heard.*

PETTERSEN: Listen to them, Jensen; the old man's got to his feet—he's giving a toast to Mrs. Sorby.

JENSEN: (*pushing forward an armchair*) Do you think it's true, then, what they've been saying, that there's something going on between them?

PETTERSEN: God knows.

JENSEN: He used to be quite the ladies' man, I understand.

PETTERSEN: I suppose.

JENSEN: And he's giving this party in honor of his son, they say.

PETTERSEN: That's right. His son came home yesterday.

JENSEN: I never even knew old Werle had a son.

PETTERSEN: Oh, he has a son all right. But he's completely tied up at the Hoidal works. In all the years I've been here he's never come into town.

A WAITER: (*in the doorway of the other room*) Pettersen, there's an old fellow here . . .

PETTERSEN: (*mutters*) Damn. Who'd show up at this time of night?

After a few more lines, Pettersen, Jensen, and the waiter make their exits and are seen no more. Their function is purely expository—to pave the way for the principal characters. Their conversation is a contrivance intended simply to give us a framework for the action and impart information to the audience.

Sometimes plays can introduce themselves with startling simplicity. The noh theatre of Japan tends to begin with clear declarations by one character of his past and present circumstances. The play *Atsumori* begins with a priest who claims, "I am Kumagai no Naozane, a man of the country of Musashi [a famous samurai]. I have left my home and call myself the priest Rensei; this I have done because of my grief at the death of Atsumori, who fell in battle by my hand. Hence it comes that I am dressed in priestly guise." In a few lines, we are given a complex set of circumstances—the character addressing us killed someone and now is dressed as a priest. Similarly, the beginning of Thornton Wilder's play *Our Town*—a perennial favorite of community theatres and high school classrooms—starts with a character called "Stage Manager" walking onto a bare stage and telling us, "This play is called 'Our Town.' It was written by Thornton Wilder and produced by ____. In it you will see Mr. ____, Mr. ____, Mr. ____, Miss ____, Miss ____, Miss ____, and many others too numerous to mention. The name of our town is Grover's Corners, New Hampshire, just over the line from Massachusetts; latitude 42 degrees, 40 minutes, longitude 70 degrees, 37 minutes." The blank spaces are to be filled in by the names of the actual producer and actors in the production. Here, as with *Atsumori,* we learn not only information about the play's plot but also its conventions: actors in both plays can address us directly. For *Our Town,* we learn that the play is aware that it is a play: it is not pretending to represent accurately any specific place, and the actors are presented as actors, not just as characters. Exposition is educational: it teaches us not only *what* we are about to watch but *how* we are to watch it.

The Conflict.   *Now* is the time for the character to enter shouting, "The house is on fire!" Drama requires conflict; in fact, the word "drama," when used in daily life, implies a situation fraught with conflict. No one writes plays about characters who live every day in serenity; no one would ever choose to watch such a play. Conflict and confrontation are the mechanisms by which a situation becomes dramatic.

Why is this so? Why is conflict so theatrically interesting? Turning back to Aristotle, we can find reasons that have to do with plot, theme, and character. Plot can hold suspense only when it involves alternatives and choices: Macbeth, in Shakespeare's *Macbeth,* has strong reasons to murder the king and strong reasons not to. If he had only the former or only the latter, he would project no real conflict and we would not consider him such an interesting character. We are fascinated by such a character's actions largely in light of the actions he rejects and the stresses he has to endure in making his decisions. In other words, plot is about the "what if?" moments—the points in the action where another route could be taken, but isn't. In watching characters act, the audience must also watch the characters think, and a playwright gets the characters to think by putting them into conflict.

The playwright often introduces conflict early in a play, often by means of an "inciting incident" in which one character poses a conflict or confrontation either to

Drama requires conflict, and Shakespeare's tragedy *Othello* is filled with it: between father and daughter, soldiers and officers, and, fatally, husbands and wives. In the Royal Shakespeare Company's 2009 production directed by Kathryn Hunter, the tension simmers between Patrice Naiambana as Othello and Natalia Tena as Desdemona as he berates her in public while holding her like a child. ©Geraint Lewis/Alamy Stock Photo

another character or to himself. For example, read this passage from our earlier example of *Macbeth*:

FIRST WITCH: All hail, Macbeth, hail to thee, Thane of Glamis!

SECOND WITCH: All hail, Macbeth, hail to thee, Thane of Cawdor!

THIRD WITCH: All hail, Macbeth, that shalt be King hereafter!

BANQUO: Good sir, why do you start, and seem to fear Things that do sound so fair?

In this scene, the inciting incident involves a witch predicting that Macbeth will be king. Macbeth's friend Banquo reacts with surprise at Macbeth "starting," or making a sudden movement. It seems as if Macbeth flinches at this possibility. But why? Perhaps he has already had this thought himself. Here, we should be hooked—we have learned enough about these characters to care, but mysteries remain that keep us engaged.

The Climax.   Conflict cannot go on forever. In a play, as in life, when conflict becomes unbearable, something has to give. Every play culminates in some sort of dramatic release, like a kettle of water reaching a boiling point.

As we have seen, Aristotle describes that release, in tragedy, as the catharsis, a cleansing or purification. The catharsis, for Aristotle, releases the audience's pity and fear and thereby permits the fullest experience of tragic pleasure by washing away the terror that has been mounting steadily during the play's tragic course. The ultimate example of catharsis in ancient Greek tragedy follows Oedipus gouging out his own eyes and recognizing his true self.

For most dramatic forms, however, the climax need not be so gruesome, and our release need not be pity or fear. A climax is simply the conflict of a play taken to its most extreme—the moment of maximum tension. At the climax, a continuation of the conflict becomes unbearable and some sort of change is mandated. Climaxes in modern plays do not, as a rule, involve death or disfiguration. Instead, climaxes inevitably contain elements of recognition and reversal, and usually the major conflicts of a play are resolved by one or more of these elements. William Gibson's *The Miracle Worker*, for example, reaches its climax when Helen Keller, a blind, deaf, mute, and uncontrollable child, finally says a word ("wawa," which we understand to mean "water") for the first time, and the audience experiences a catharsis of long-delayed joy.

The Denouement. The climax is followed by a resolution, or *denouement* (the word in French means "un-knotting"), in which a final action or speech, or even a single word or gesture, indicates that the passions aroused by the play's action are now stilled and the conflicts are over. The tenor of the denouement tends to change with the times. In the American theatre of the 1950s and 1960s, a sentimental and message-laden denouement was the rule: for instance, in Dore Schary's *Sunrise at Campobello*, a young Franklin Roosevelt, recently paralyzed from the waist down, heroically makes his way to a convention platform. Today, we tend to look with suspicion on tidy virtues and happy endings, and more ironic and ambiguous denouements prevail. The denouements of contemporary theatre, as a result, find it harder to let the audience "off the hook," favoring instead a lingering sense of unease. Amiri Baraka's *Dutchman*, written in 1964—a time of deep racial tension and animosity in America—ends with a white woman on a train stabbing a black man (whom she has been seducing for the play thus far) and then instructing the other passengers to remove his body. She then sits next to another black man, as if beginning a new seduction and a new inevitable murder. This ending purposefully does not leave us feeling resolved, but it does give us a sense of a conclusion.

But while a denouement may be indeterminate, it must still provide at least some lucidity concerning the problems raised by the play, some vision or metaphor of a deeper and more permanent understanding. Perhaps the final lines of Samuel Beckett's absurdist masterpiece *Waiting for Godot* best represent the denouement of the current age:

ESTRAGON: Well, shall we go?

VLADIMIR: Yes, let's go.

They do not move.

Post-Play The last staged element of a theatrical presentation is the *curtain call*, during which the actors bow and the audience applauds. The curtain call is not simply a time for the actors to receive congratulations from the audience. Indeed, the actor's deeply bowed head was originally an offer for his patron—the nobleman who had paid for the performance—to lop off that head with his sword if the actor had not provided satisfaction! The curtain call remains a time in which the actors show their respect for the audience that has been watching them. It is a crucial convention that liberates the audience from the world of the play. In the best theatre, the invisible communication of the curtain call is a powerful experience—and it becomes even more powerful when the entire audience leaps to its collective feet in a standing ovation. Such a response becomes a sort of audience participation for theatregoers, who physically express their enthusiasm not only to the performers but also to fellow audience members standing and cheering around them.

What follows the curtain call? The audience leaves, of course, but the individual audience members do not disappear. Through them the production enjoys an extended afterlife—both in talk and in print—in late-night discussions and debates at a restaurant or bar and probing conversations on the morning after. In the days following the curtain call, there may be published and online reviews and actor appearances on talk shows; years later, there may be scholarly articles and books. The afterlives of all the plays discussed in this book are, in a way, part of their post-production.

Both the post-show chat and the formally published analysis are examples of what we may call dramatic criticism, which is the audience's contribution to the theatre. Criticism is as ancient as Aristotle and as contemporary as the essays and lectures that are presented daily in newspapers, journals, books, and academies all over the world. However, criticism is not solely an expert enterprise; criticism—which combines analysis and evaluation—is everybody's job. We look further at this key aspect of the theatre's art in the chapter titled "The Audience."

Chapter

3

The Actor

©Geraint Lewis/Alamy Stock Photo

S**HE STANDS ALONE IN THE** darkness and listens carefully. A few feet away, onstage, she sees her fellow actors awash under bright lights and speaking the lines she has heard so many times before. Soon—any moment now!—she will walk onstage. Her heart races as she tries to stay relaxed while feeling exhilarated by the sense of something about to engulf her.

The energy onstage is palpable: it is there in the eyes of the actors, the pace of the dialogue, the smell of the makeup, the sparkle of perspiration glittering in the lights, the bursts of audience laughter and applause.

She glances back. Backstage, there is energy, too. But this is a different energy. It is under the surface, restrained. Some of the other actors backstage bend their knees and roll their necks. Some gaze thoughtfully at the action of the play. Some stare at the walls, murmuring quietly to themselves. In one corner, a stage manager, his body hunched over a dimly lighted copy of the script, whispers commands into his headset.

Suddenly the onstage pace seems to quicken; the lines, all at once, take on a greater urgency and familiarity. It is almost her cue . . . she listens attentively . . . it is almost her cue . . . she takes a deep breath, a deeper breath . . . it is her cue! She bounds from the dimness into the dazzle and comes to life. She is onstage.

Acting is one of the world's most bewildering professions. On the one hand, it carries the potential for extraordinary rewards. The thrill of delivering a great performance, the roar of appreciation from an enraptured audience, the glory of getting "inside" a character—these are excitements and satisfactions that few careers can duplicate. An actor's rewards aren't purely artistic and intellectual, either: some become stars and make millions of dollars. The fame that can follow is legendary, even frightening: the private lives of the most universally admired actors become public property, the daily fare of television talk shows and Internet gossip.

On the other hand, the economic rewards are often paltry. The six- and seven-figure salaries of the stars bear little relation to the meager pay for which most actors work—if they're lucky enough to get paid at all. And although the stars billed "above the title" may be treated like celebrities or royalty and can be the most prominent aspect of a particular play, they are also, paradoxically, at the bottom of the pecking order. Actors take orders from directors, get bossed about by stage managers, and are hired and fired by producers; they are squeezed and fitted by costumers and wig dressers and poked and powdered by makeup artists. Being an actor offers the thrill of the spotlight, but it also offers the humility of knowing you are only a small part—albeit a very visible one—of the overall theatrical process. Because of its potential for sublimity, however, acting offers a tantalizing path for many people willing to risk its potentially less attractive qualities. As you are reading this, someone somewhere is deciding—with a mix of excitement and fear—to pursue acting as an occupation. Certainly no other profession entails such numbing uncertainties and sacrifices while offering such rich rewards.

Approaches to Acting

Acting is above all a craft. It is not simply a "gift" bestowed from the heavens—although historically it has been associated with divine connection. It takes work and practice. The craft of acting can be defined in two opposing ways. One way is that an actor creates a performance *externally,* first by imagining how his or her character should walk, talk, and behave, and then by imitating these imagined behaviors when performing the character. Another way is that acting is created *internally*, by concentrating not on imitating behavior but actually experiencing the life of the character—his or her emotions, memories, and

Actors are often celebrated for their virtuosity—their ability to embody a wide range of emotions, situations, and characters. Such skill was certainly on display in this celebrated 2017 production of Lillian Hellman's *The Little Foxes,* where Laura Linney (*left*) and Cynthia Nixon (*right*), pictured here with Michael McKean (*center*), alternated lead roles on different nights. ©Joan Marcus

The Irish English actor Kenneth Branagh is best known in the United States for his films (*Hamlet, Henry V, Much Ado About Nothing, Othello, Thor, Cinderella*) and for his 2013–2014 starring role in *Macbeth* in New York City. Globally, he is deeply admired on the stage for his dramatic passion, clearly apparent here in his 2008 performance in the title role of Chekhov's *Ivanov* in London. ©*Geraint Lewis/Alamy Stock Photo*

sensations—as if the actor really were the character, and not just performing.

For the sake of explanation, we will discuss an "external method" and an "internal method," even though there is no such thing as a *purely* internal or external approach to acting. However, there are techniques that emphasize one way over the other.

THE EXTERNAL METHOD

The external method, as the name suggests, starts from "outside" the character. When actors works externally, they will train their bodies intensively by seeking to master a wide variety of performance styles, such as singing, dancing, clowning, miming, and fencing. To take one example of an external technique, the director Anne Bogart has developed a method known as Viewpoints, adapted from a dance composition technique of the same name. Viewpoints consists of nine ways of thinking of time and

space onstage: tempo, duration, kinesthetic response, repetition, space, gesture, architecture, spatial relationship, and topography. Actors trained in Viewpoints are practiced and attentive to the exact position of their body and how it relates to the other bodies that share their space. They will learn to be both "in the moment"—responding to their scene partners and the shifting circumstances onstage—and capable of thinking of how they fit into the wider stage picture at all times.

The renowned Japanese director and teacher Tadashi Suzuki—who actually founded a theatre company with Bogart in 1992—has also developed an external method of performing. Suzuki's actors spend hours striking and holding physically excruciating poses, stomping on the ground, and learning what he calls a "grammar of the feet." His approach, which draws from many global influences, is less focused on creating a psychological "character" onstage than on creating a compelling presence.

Even if aspiring actors do not subscribe to Bogart's or Suzuki's methods, they will need to focus on external qualities in their approach. The two primary external qualities that all actors need, regardless of their philosophy, are their voice and body.

Throughout history, the actor's voice has received tremendous attention. Greek tragic actors were awarded prizes for their vocal abilities, and many contemporary actors, such as Patrick Stewart, James Earl Jones, Rachel Weisz, Audra McDonald, and Meryl Streep, are celebrated for their stunning tones. Voices can be dizzyingly diverse: resonant, mellow, sharp, musical, stinging, poetic, seductive, compelling, lulling, or dominating—and sometimes all of these qualities in the same performance. A trained theatrical voice can articulate complex ideas rapidly and explain subtleties clearly and convincingly. It can rivet attention while conveying nuances, can both thunder with rage and flow with compassion, and can, in major moments, hold audiences absolutely spellbound.

Actors' use of their body—the capacity for movement—is the other fundamental element of external acting. Most of the best actors are strong and flexible; all are capable of great physical self-mastery. The effects that can be achieved through precise and subtle stage movement are as numerous as those that can be achieved through voice: the gifted and well-trained actor's arched eyebrow, toss of the head, flick of the wrist, whirl of the hem, or even wiggle of a finger can command electric attention. Actors' command of their body has led to many memorably powerful moments in the theatre, such as Helene Weigel's powerful chest-pounding when, as Mother Courage, she loses her son; Laurence Olivier's breathtaking upside-down fall as Coriolanus; and Edward James Olmos's swift

Many theatre companies today combine acting techniques and ensemble members from a variety of world traditions. The Denmark-based company Out of Balanz stages physically dynamic and collaborative works such as 2013's *Next Door,* pictured here. In this typically kinetic stage picture, Troels Hagen Findsen is held aloft by Pekka Räikkönen. ©Tony Nandi

leap through a giant newspaper as El Pachuco. Entire traditions of acting depend fundamentally on learning specific bodily movement and conventions. Students of Chinese opera practice poses and facial expressions specific to the type of character they will eventually take on as their specialty. Japanese *kabuki* theatre similarly focuses on physical mastery in crafting characters; like Chinese opera, kabuki consists of a set of character types, each with its own specific regimen of positions and movements.

THE INTERNAL METHOD

In contrast to the external method, the internal method asks the actor to enter into the mind and emotional state of the character being played. Such an actor tries to "be" the character onstage, not just present the audience with a made-up imitation of an imagined individual. You have probably heard stories of actors becoming "lost" in roles to the extent that they insist on being called by their characters' names. These are exaggerated tales, but they carry a grain of truth: there are schools of acting philosophy that aim to replicate the character's inner circumstances exactly in the mind of the performer. In the United States, the internal method known simply as "the Method" was first developed by members of the Group Theatre in New York in 1931. The American tradition of realistic acting largely relies on the internal method that the Group Theatre—and later, from its ashes, the Actors Studio—created. This approach believes that theatrical performance must strive to replicate real life, and it must do so by delving into the biography and inner world of the character.

In developing their methods, the Group Theatre had been inspired by the work of the Russian acting theorist Konstantin Stanislavski (1863–1938). When Stanislavski and his Moscow Art Theatre visited the United States in 1924 and 1925, they astounded American audiences

No American actor in the past forty years has come close to equaling the achievement, both artistic and commercial, of Meryl Streep. Streep began in the theatre before crossing over into films. By 2015 she had received more Academy Award nominations (twenty) than any other performer, but Streep remains closely connected to the stage. She is shown here in 2006 taking a bow after playing in one of the most demanding roles in modern theatre, the title role of Bertolt Brecht's *Mother Courage and Her Children*. ©*Bruce Glikas/FilmMagic/Getty Images*

Edward James Olmos electrified audiences in the 1978 premiere of Luis Valdez's *Zoot Suit,* a seminal work of Latinx (a gender-inclusive way of referring to people of Latin American descent) drama. With his angular posture and unforgettable entrance—he slashes through a giant newspaper—Olmos demonstrated the power of physically embodying a role. Here, Olmos revises the role at a 50th anniversary celebration of the Center Theatre Group in Los Angeles, where *Zoot Suit* originally premiered. ©*Rich Polk/Center Theatre Group/Getty Images*

with an intensely realistic and convincing acting style. Stanislavski described his own system as the actor "living the life of his or her character on stage" and many American actors eagerly took up this charge. The wider American public first encountered Stanislavski's acting philosophy through his 1936 book *An Actor Prepares,* which declares that "our prime task is . . . to create the inner life of the character." By "inner life" Stanislavski meant all the messy, unruly aspects of our personalities that we typically hide—or try to hide—from our outward appearances, such as anger, love, fear, and confusion. But how can actors show these internal parts of themselves onstage? If they overdo it, the performance can

seem fake. If they hide their emotions, they can seem robotic and uninteresting. Stanislavski's ingenious solution was to suggest that actors base their performance on the pursuit of their character's task (in Russian, *zadacha,* which can also be translated as "problem" or "objective"). By concentrating on winning their character's task instead of simply being seen as great actors, Stanislavski discovered, actors can eliminate stage fright, be immersed in their character, and convincingly represent their character as a real and whole person rather than simply a fictional representation.

Stanislavski was not the first person to propose this strategy, but he was the first to turn it into an organized system. By focusing on motivations, he found a way to lend dignity and purpose to staged action. He declared: "Everything that happens onstage must occur for some reason or other. When you sit there, you must also sit for a reason, not merely to show yourself off to the audience."

Members of the Group Theatre adapted Stanislavski's system into the Method, which dominated the New York acting community until the end of the twentieth century. The Method in particular zeroed in on one aspect of Stanislavski's approach—its commitment to psychological realism—and deemphasized Stanislavski's more physical and analytical practices. The Method continues its popularity to this day through the teachings of the Actors Studio, which now has locations in New York and Hollywood and is currently under the leadership of Ellen Burstyn, Harvey Keitel, and Al Pacino. Variations of the Method became core beliefs of actors such as Paul Newman, Ann Bancroft, James Dean, and Marilyn Monroe. The Method, and through it Stanislavski's system, became world renowned through the success of these actors on the American stage and in American films.

Konstantin Stanislavski in the role of Vershinin in his 1901 production of Chekhov's *The Three Sisters* at the Moscow Art Theatre. ©*Sputnik/Alamy Stock Photo*

THE PARADOX OF ACTING

Great acting comes not from an external or internal approach but from both. In fact, the two methods are really inextricable. Even the most external-seeming techniques seek to develop inner psychology, and internal approaches still stress physical fitness. The two methods also have points of commonality. For instance, both Suzuki's physical approach and the more psychological American Method—as different as two techniques could be—share a similar interest in "animal energy." Lee Strasberg, one of the founders (with Stella Adler and Sanford Meisner) of the American Method, encouraged his students to study animals to discover more about their characters. Similarly, Suzuki believed that acting should unlock a primal, life-or-death force within us—an energy that other animals regularly experience. Even Strasberg's and Suzuki's techniques have overlap—neither is entirely internal or external.

But how can an actor work *both* from the inside and the outside? This situation creates a paradox: you have to act *as if* you were the character and yet also be aware of your technique—that is, your physical and vocal ability to project that character in a heightened manner. This paradox fascinated the ancients, just as it fascinates us today. In a famous dialogue by the Greek philosopher Plato (428–348 B.C.E.), the character Ion, a young man skilled in reading poetry, explains to Socrates that he often imagines himself *as* the character he is reading and that he is in the presence of the other fictional characters in the story. Yet Ion also admits that, even through his tears, he would regularly "look down on the audience from the stage, and behold their various emotions of pity, wonder, and solemnity stamped upon their countenances." He both "was" his character but still resolutely himself, a performer scanning the crowd for reactions.

A few centuries later, the Roman orator Quintilian (35–100 C.E.) envisioned his wife's and children's imaginary deaths with "extreme vividness" and became "so moved" during his speeches that he would be brought to tears, turn pale, and exhibit "all the symptoms of genuine grief." Yet Quintilian acknowledged that he created his performances with a "regularity and discipline promised by calculation." His advice could be highly precise to the point of absurdity, as when he warns that "it is never correct to employ the left hand alone in gesture" and that "the hand [must not] be raised above the level of the eyes." Quintilian felt the emotional pain of loss but was not overwhelmed with grief. He never lost sight of the precise movements of his body.

Daniel Radcliffe, famed for his film performances as Harry Potter, began his stage career as the leading actor in both the London and New York revivals of *Equus* and then the revival of the musical *How to Succeed in Business Without Really Trying*. Here he is shown as the title character in the 2014 Broadway production of Martin McDonagh's *The Cripple of Inishmaan*. ©Sara Krulwich/The New York Times/Redux

The actor must be spontaneous but disciplined, natural but highly trained. A great amount of effort must go into appearing effortless. The virtue of acting as purely a craft, rather than a process of becoming a character, became championed by the French essayist Denis Diderot, who proclaimed in his 1773 "Paradox of Acting" that "a great actor . . . must [only be] an unmoved and disinterested onlooker." Diderot argued fiercely that it is better for an actor to imitate anger than to actually be angry, and that actors should therefore play from the head, not from the heart. He declared, "Actors impress the public not when they are furious, but when they play fury well. . . . [A]ctors who play from the heart . . . are alternately strong and feeble, fiery and cold. . . . Tomorrow they will miss the point they have excelled in today. . . . But the actor who plays from thought . . . will be always at his best; for he has considered, combined, learned and arranged the whole thing in his head." Paradoxically, the only way an actor could convince an audience of a sincerely felt emotion was to *not* feel the emotion.

Diderot believed that audiences were moved by displays of precision. This remains true today: there are passages of Shakespeare that can still prompt tears even if—perhaps *especially* if—they were simply recited clearly, without an attempt to create a psychologically "real" character. The paradox of acting attests to the actors' power: they can affect an audience simply by dint of appearing on a stage. This power, in turn, helps explain the long-time association between acting and danger. In Renaissance Europe, the power of acting caused concern; many worried that actors could convince themselves and the audience that what occurred onstage was real—leading to illicit love affairs, confessions of crimes, and unregulated passions. This fear goes back as far as Plato. In his most famous work, the *Republic*, Plato sets out to design a perfect city-state. In doing so he firmly bans all theatre-making: the power of the actor's craft is too unpredictable for well-run political order.

This fear is not limited to Western traditions. In ancient China, the diplomat and philosopher Confucius (551–479 B.C.E.) demanded that actors be put to death. Like Plato, he worried about the power to beguile audiences. If an actor pretended to be the emperor, would an audience treat him like one? How is that different from pretending to be the emperor offstage? (This concern is a contemporary one, too: impersonating a police officer is a

The English-born, American-schooled Mark Rylance is one of the most versatile and accomplished actors in both of these countries today. He has been praised for his internal psychological realism as well as his external technical mastery. These qualities have led to a wide variety of roles, ranging from the unapologetic, alcoholic ex-Hippie "Rooster" (*bottom*) in Jez Butterworth's 2011 *Jerusalem,* and more recently his Olivia in the 2013–2014 *Twelfth Night* (*top*), which he alternated with the title role of Shakespeare's *Richard III.* Each performance netted him a Tony Award and near-universal praise.
Top: ©Geraint Lewis/Alamy Stock Photo; Bottom: ©Sara Krulwich/The New York Times/Redux

Stagecraft

Basic Acting Exercises

Acting is more easily understood by doing it than by reading about it. Even if you have never acted before, the following acting exercises can help you understand what acting is, both internally and externally.

REACH

Stand on your right foot; reach as high as you can with your left hand. Imagine there is something you greatly desire above your head, such as a beautiful jewel, a wad of thousand-dollar bills, or "the key to your true love's heart." Now reach again, and *really try to get it!* Repeat on the other foot, with the other hand.

This is the simplest acting exercise there is, and it illustrates the difference between presentational (external) and representational (internal) acting methods. When you're only asked to reach as high as you can, you will respond by acting from the outside since you will reach only because you were told to. This is not even acting—it's simply calisthenics. But when you *really* try to get something—even though it is imaginary—you will be acting from the inside because you are trying to achieve the character's goals. And the goals will come from your imagination: What kind of a jewel was it? How many thousand-dollar bills?

If you can fully commit to this, you will probably have stretched your arms out farther, breathed harder, found your pulse beating faster, and felt exhausted (and exhilarated) when you were done. You have done all you can to try to obtain something just out of your reach—just as your character will try hard to achieve performance goals that may seem impossible to achieve.

DANCE

Balancing on the balls of your feet, step forward on one foot while extending the same-side arm, wrist forward, in the same direction, letting your fingers follow after the wrist has reached its maximum extension. The movement is identical to throwing a Frisbee. At the moment when the fingers follow (or the imaginary Frisbee is released), cry "Dance!" Repeat with the other leg and arm, and keep repeating, in alternation, crying "Dance!" with each move.

Continue, switching to "Ballet!" As you step on your right foot, go up on the toes of your left foot, and vice versa. Say "Ballet!" in a way that encourages others to appreciate the beauty of ballet (whether or not you find it beautiful). Continue, switching to "L'amour!" (French for

"love," pronounced "lah-MOOR!") and imagining that you are casting beautiful flower petals. Really commit to the absurdity of the gesture.

Did those last two exercises make you feel a bit foolish? Good—that means you are learning what it means to perform behaviors beyond what you do in your everyday life. Actors do things all the time that would appear ridiculous if they did them in daily life—such as behave like an ass in *A Midsummer Night's Dream* or cry like a witch in *Macbeth*—yet these actors must believe in what they're doing, and believe they want to do those things.

CONTENTLESS SCENE: WHAT DID YOU DO LAST NIGHT?

Here is a short dialogue exchange written for two actors. It has no fixed content: it takes on meaning only when it becomes part of a context, which, in this exercise, can be any of the seven situations listed after the dialogue. To perform this exercise, one person memorizes the lines of role A and the other of role B. Then the players choose any of the seven situations and "perform" the scene accordingly.

This exercise is best experienced in a classroom where half of the participants learn one role and half learn the other and each participant tries the scene several times, changing both situations and partners on each occasion.

THE DIALOGUE

A: Hi!

B: Hello.

A: How's everything?

B: Fine. I guess.

A: Do you know what time it is?

B: No. Not exactly.

A: Don't you have a watch?

B: Not on me.

A: Well?

B: Well what?

A: What did you do last night?

B: What do you mean?

A: What did you do last night?

B: Nothing.

A: Nothing?

B: I said, nothing!

A: I'm sorry I asked.

B: That's all right.

felony in many countries.) Also, as we will discuss further in the chapter titled "Theatre Traditions," Islamic cultures have long debated the potentially blasphemous effects of acting. One of the Islamic *hadiths,* the teachings of the Prophet Mohammed, stipulates that one can become good by imitating someone good. If that's the case, then what if one were to imitate someone bad? As a result, in many traditional Islamic performances, such as the *ta'ziyeh* mourning plays, actors hold scripts and interact with non-actors to signal to the audience that they are *not* imitating a character but simply reading a character's speeches.

Throughout the world, then, there has been a concern over whether an actor "becomes" a character. Whether the performers take on an internal or external approach—whether they are focusing on their feet or on their characters' imagined biography—they still create something indelibly powerful, even dangerous, when they step onto a stage.

Becoming an Actor

It is not enough to have an approach to acting. You have to *train* yourself in that approach, or approaches, day in and day out. When you attend a play, you are seeing only a small sliver of the actors' work. For many hours, the actors will have been training both for their part and, more broadly, for their life as actors. If you were to sit in on a rehearsal, you would not simply see the actors stride into the space and begin bowling over everyone with their brilliance. You would see them warm up, try different line readings and movements, attempt wildly different interpretations of a scene, and in general take risks—and thus fail, many times, until getting it right. Just like any other craft, acting requires daily work.

The training of actors is a major endeavor in hundreds of colleges, universities, conservatories, and private high schools across the world. Of the number of acting students, the percentage who actually ascend to successful careers in the profession is relatively small. Acting is a tough trade to enter, and an even tougher one to sustain.

Much like the differing approaches to acting, there are internal and external components of training. First, there is the creation of a character—a mostly internal process. Second, there is the development of vocal and physical instruments, which naturally relate to external elements of performance. There is a third component, as well, that is neither purely external nor internal but is perhaps the most crucial: discipline. Let's look at each of these aspects of training.

CREATING A CHARACTER

One of the most globally popular elements of Stanislavski's system is his insistence on having a goal. Stanislavski-based training naturally focuses on the discovery of this goal. To do that, the actor has to read the script over and over and over again. The award-winning actor Anthony

Hopkins is renowned for reading and re-reading scripts—reportedly 250 times! Stanislavski actors collect evidence to find their character's goal, an overarching desire that helps clarify the actors' actions.

Most contemporary teachers also insist that these goals be achievable primarily through other characters in the play so that acting becomes, in almost all cases, *interacting* with other people. Juliet, in *Romeo and Juliet,* does not simply want to marry but to marry Romeo; Hamlet, in *Hamlet,* wants not just to seek revenge but to seek revenge for his father's death by killing Claudius. The more specific, the better the goal is. As a result, the acting becomes enlivened; it occurs in real time on-stage, with moment-to-moment live interplay between all the actors involved. And when there is no one else on the stage, the actor—for example Hamlet in his "O what a rogue and peasant slave am I" soliloquy—is interacting directly with the audience. He wants something out of *us*.

The second phase of the actor's approach, after finding a goal, is the identification of the *tactics* necessary to achieve that goal, or at least to avoid defeat. Juliet woos Romeo through wordplay, lyrical proclamations of love, and clever scheming; Hamlet secures Horatio's aid by speaking warmly to him, turns his mother against her husband by chastising her, disorients Polonius through clever wordplay and feigned insanity, and tries to steer his girlfriend Ophelia out of harm's way by frightening her. By means of these tactics, Romeo and Hamlet try to make their goals come to fruition. Actors who play tactics boldly and with enthusiasm, and who allow themselves to believe that if they try hard enough they will attain their goals (even if the play dictates that they won't), convey a deep sense of hope—and truth.

The third and most complicated element of the actor's approach requires research into the style of the play and the mode of performance that will govern the production, in which each role is just a single ingredient. This part of the process is, effectively, adaptation: actors merge their decisions with those of the other performers and the artistic staff to create a seamless whole. Every play is different. Some require more direct confrontation with the live audience. Others assume an environment in which the entire cast of characters employ elegantly refined speech. Still others assume an environment in which such speech is ridiculed as pretentious. Some plays contain several "worlds" of characters. For instance, Tony Kushner's *Angels in America* contains upper-class lawyers, buttoned-up Mormon missionaries, freewheeling *bon vivants,* and actual angels; the play spans conti-

nents and even celestial spheres. The actor's approach must lead to a deep and clear understanding of the nature of each layer.

THE ACTOR'S INSTRUMENT

Internal, Stanislavski-based approaches are not always appropriate for a performance. A purely physical approach may work for, say, a play (or production) that depends more on conventions of bodily movement than on the appearance of psychological realism. The *commedia dell'arte* plays of Renaissance Italy use improvisation based on character archetypes, and the actor interested in this mode of performance would have no real script to research. Instead, the actor would practice interacting with other performers, as well as practice a physically demanding repertoire of pratfalls, tumbles, and other stylized movements. One more extreme example of an external, bodily approach is the *bunraku* puppet theatre of Japan. To manipulate the large and complex puppets, *bunraku* actors spend a decade learning how to control the puppet's legs, another decade to control the left arm, and yet another decade to control the head and right arm. No research into the puppet's inner life and biography is needed, even though the final product creates, much like Stanislavski's system, a sense of truth.

Regardless of the convention, style, approach, or source material, performers need to train their bodies. The actor, like any artist, has an instrument. However, unlike a musician or a painter, the actor's instrument isn't outside of the body. In fact, the instrument *is* the body. The actor's voice is the perfectly tuned violin to be played or the sculpting clay to be molded. An actor is a portrait artist working from within to create characters with unique actions, utterances, and a physical presence. It is obvious that a great artist requires first-rate equipment. This does not mean that all actors need to look like fitness models. The theatre, in fact, thrives on a diversity of shapes and sizes. But regardless of body type, the actor's body must be capable of responding fluidly and precisely to the circumstances of the play.

Voice and speech, quite naturally, are the first elements of the actor's physiological instrument to be considered: "Voice, voice, and more voice" was the answer Tommaso Salvini, the famed nineteenth-century Italian actor, gave to the question "What are the three most important attributes of acting?" To train the voice, actors in voice- and speech-training programs learn a variety of means to achieve and enhance their breathing, articulation, pronunciation, resonance, and skills at mastering regional and foreign dialects. Great voices do not exist without training. Every day, great actors exercise their mouths and tongues, conduct breathing exercises, and pronounce (quickly and slowly) words and phrases that expand and clarify their voice's potential.

Physical movement is the second element of the actor's physiological instrument. Movement training typically involves exercises and instruction designed to create physical relaxation, muscular control, economy of action, and expressive gestures. Dance, mime, fencing, acrobatics, and circus techniques are traditional training for actors; regular trips to the gym are generally expected of them—and required by many acting schools. Most actors exercise regularly. Longtime British stage and film star Laurence Olivier, for example, contended that only sheer physical strength could provide the actor with the stamina needed to "hold stage" without strain or fatigue. In America, leading actor Jane Fonda became such a

fitness buff that she created a popular series of exercise training videos.

Control of the body permits an actor to stand, sit, and move on the stage with alertness, energy, and seeming ease. Standing tall, walking boldly, turning on a dime at precisely the right moment, extending the limbs joyously, sobbing violently, springing about uproariously, and occupying a major share of stage space (metaphorically becoming "larger than life") are among the capacities of the actor who has mastered body control through training and confidence. It is no wonder that some of the top actor-training programs in the world utilize intense vocal and physical workouts— students are up early to stretch, speak, sing, and train. The basic instructional technique for all of these exercises is nearly identical to those of athletic exercises: demonstration, memorization, repetition, and constant drilling. This is where the actor learns that to be part of

Acting traditions across the globe rely on training. Here, at the renowned school Kerala Kalamandalam in India, students practice poses, gestures, and facial expressions at a renowned school for *kathakali*, an ancient dance-drama. ©*Frédéric Soltan/Corbis/Getty Images*

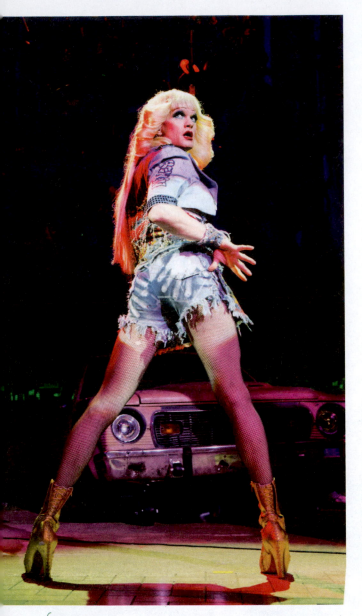

Neil Patrick Harris played the title character—a gender-queer East German rock singer—in the Broadway production of *Hedwig and the Angry Inch*, which won the 2014 Tony Award for Best Revival of a Musical. ©*Joan Marcus*

a play requires a tremendous amount of what can only be called work.

The actor's instrument also includes the psychological gift of imagination, and a willingness and ability to use it in the service of art. The liberation of imagination is a continuous process in actor training. Exercises and theatre games designed for that purpose are part of most beginning classes in acting, and many directors use the same exercises and games at the beginning of play rehearsal periods. Inspiration for acting can arrive from anywhere, and so an actor must always be curious, aware that anything could spark the imagination. Because the human imagination tends to become subdued as we get older, veteran professional actors have trained themselves to look at their roles, and the world, with the fresh eyes of a child.

Increasingly, actor training has also become international. The imagination required of an actor includes an open-mindedness to learning performance techniques from around the world. For instance, actors have long engaged in *mask work,* which consists of performing with neutral or expressive masks that liberate the body and imagination to explore new possibilities. Of course, as we have learned, masks have long been part of the theatrical and ritualistic traditions of nearly every culture, and at times this leads to fascinating exchanges between actor-training traditions. For instance, masks play a vital role in *topeng,* a Balinese dance-drama. In the past few decades, aspiring actors in the United States have taken classes that use topeng masks to work on honing their physical expressivity. International acting institutes have been modeled on these kinds of experiences, in which the actors are both turning inward to train their own selves and outward to expand their cultural horizons.

THE ACTOR'S DISCIPLINE

The third aspect of the actor's training is simply learning how to keep a job after you've got it—in other words, the actor's discipline. Artistic discipline keeps an actor within the established bounds and at the same time ensures artistic agility. The actor is not an independent artist, like a playwright, composer, or sculptor. The actor works in an ensemble and is just one employee in a large enterprise that can succeed only through collaboration. Although actors are sometimes considered by the public to be egotistical or temperamental, the truth is almost always the opposite: professional actors are among the most disciplined of artists, and the more professional they are, the more meticulous they are.

The actor, after all, leads a vigorous and demanding life. Makeup calls at 5:30 A.M. for film actors and both nightly and back-to-back weekend performances for stage performers make for exceedingly challenging schedules. In addition, the physical and emotional demands of the acting process—that is, the need for extreme concentration in both rehearsal and performance; for physical health and psychological composure; and for deep, attentive interaction with fellow performers—do not permit unprofessional behavior among the members of a professional cast or company.

The Actor's Routine

In essence, the actor's professional routine consists of three stages: *audition, rehearsal,* and *performance.* In the first, the actor gets a role; in the second, the actor learns the role; and in the third, the actor embodies the role every night in the theatre.

AUDITION

Auditioning is the primary process by which acting roles are awarded to all but the most established professionals, who may be offered roles without auditioning. In an audition, actors have an opportunity to demonstrate to the director (and possibly the producer or casting director) how well they can fulfill an available role. To show this, the actors are usually asked to present either a memorized monologue or more commonly a reading from the play being produced, often with other actors reading the other roles. All actors who are seriously planning for a career in the theatre will prepare several monologues to have ready when such opportunities arise. For the most part, these will be one- or two-minute speeches from plays. Each monologue must be carefully edited for timing and content (altering the text to make a continuous speech out of two or three shorter speeches is generally permissible), after which the piece is memorized and practiced. Any "staging" of the monologue should be flexible enough to adjust to the size of the audition space (which might be a stage but could just as well be an agent's office) and should not rely on costuming or the use of large props or furniture. More general auditions—for a repertory theatre or a Shakespeare Festival company, for example—will usually request two contrasting monologues (perhaps one in verse and one in prose, or one classical and one modern).

Reading from a selection of the script, or a *side,* presents actors with the opportunity to become familiar with the play they are auditioning for, as they will be speaking aloud from the actual play that is going into production. Most often, actors will be able to study the script in advance. In "cold reading" situations, however, they may be given the side just prior to the audition. Actors must train in giving excellent readings in both of these circumstances if they are to make progress toward a professional career.

The qualities a director looks for at an audition vary, but generally they include the actor's ease at handling the role; naturalness of delivery; physical, vocal, and emotional suitability for the part; spontaneity; power; and charm. Most directors also look for an actor who is well-trained, disciplined, and capable of mastering the technical demands of the part. They also tend to look for someone who will complement the company ensemble and who can convey that intangible presence that makes for "theatre magic." In short, the audition is the opportunity for actors to show the director that they not only know their craft but also can lend the production a special excitement.

REHEARSAL

The second phase of professional routine is rehearsal. Plays are ordinarily rehearsed in a matter of weeks: a normal period of rehearsal ranges from ten weeks for complex productions to just one week for many summer theatre operations. Much longer rehearsal periods, however, are not unheard of; the productions that Stanislavski directed himself were often rehearsed for a year or more. Three to five weeks is the customary rehearsal period for American professional productions—but these are forty-hour weeks and are usually followed by several days (or weeks) of *previews,* or runs of the production in regional theatres, with additional rehearsals between performances.

During the rehearsal period, actors continue to learn the role and investigate, among other things, the character's biography; the *subtext* (the unspoken communications) of the play; the character's thoughts, fears, fantasies, and goals; and the world envisioned by the playwright. The director will lead discussions, offer opinions, and issue directives with respect to some or all of these matters; the director may also provide reading materials, pictures, and music to aid in the actors' research.

The actors must memorize lines, execute movements (known as *blocking*), and follow directed stage actions (known as *business*—scripted or seemingly unconscious physical behaviors of the character, such as tugging an ear or playing with keys) during the rehearsal period. The actors must also be prepared to relearn these if they are changed, as they often are. In the rehearsal of new plays it is not unusual for entire acts to be rewritten between rehearsals and for large segments to be changed, added, or removed overnight.

The rehearsal period is a time for experimentation and discovery. It is a time for the actors to get close to the character's beliefs and intentions and to plumb the depths of the internal aspects of characterization that will lead to a fully engaged physical, intellectual, and emotional performance. It is a time to dig into the play's text and the director's mind for clues as to how the character behaves and what results the character aims for in the play. It is also a time to experiment with different acting techniques, both alone and with other actors. Acting in the rehearsal phase requires great risk-taking. Actors must be able to try something new and must be willing to fail in order to further explore their characters and the play.

Conversely, rehearsal is also a time for actors to become secure in their lines and movements through constant repetition—indeed, the French word for "rehearsal" is *répétition*. Rehearsals offer the actors an opportunity to explore all the possibilities of the role *and* to crystallize those possibilities into definite decisions. At its best, a rehearsal is both spontaneous and disciplined. It is a combination of repetition and change. It makes patterns and breaks them—and then makes them anew. It is an exciting time, though it invariably includes many moments of distress, frustration, and despair. It is a time, above all, when the actors learns a great deal about acting.

PERFORMANCE

Performance, finally, is what the theatre is about. It is before an audience in a live performance that the actors' mettle is put to the ultimate test.

Sometimes the results are quite startling. Actors who have been brilliant in rehearsal can crumble before an audience and completely lose the "edge" of their performance in the face of stage fright and apprehension. Or—and this is more likely—actors who seemed fairly unexciting in rehearsal can suddenly take fire in performance and dazzle the audience with unexpected energy, subtlety, and depth; a celebrated example of this latter process was Lee J. Cobb in the original production of Arthur Miller's *Death of a Salesman,* in which Cobb played the title role. Actors never really know how their performances will appear until they are performed before a live audience. While the changes that occur in front of a live audience might seem electric to the actors, the structure of the performance has largely been established. Sudden and dramatic change is not the norm as the performance phase replaces rehearsal, and most actors cross over from final dress rehearsal to opening night with only the slightest shifts in their behavior. While an audience's unexpected laughter or silence might make it tempting to question choices made in rehearsal, actors largely stand by their choices and commit to their interpretation wholeheartedly.

Even when the audience is silent and unseen—brightness of stage lights often renders the audience invisible to the actors—the performers will feel its presence. There is nothing supernatural about this. The absence of sound is itself a signal; when several hundred people sit without shuffling, coughing, or muttering, their silence indicates a level of attention for which the actors customarily strive. Laughter, gasps, sighs, and applause similarly feed back into the actors' consciousness—and unconsciousness—and spur their efforts. Veteran actors can determine quickly how to ride the crest of audience laughter, and how to hold the next line just long enough that it will pierce the lingering chuckles but not be overridden by them. They also know how to vary their pace when they sense restlessness or boredom on the other side of the curtain line. The art of "reading" an audience is more instinctual than learned. It is similar to the technique achieved by the effective classroom lecturer or stand-up comedian. The timing it requires is of such complexity that no actor could master it rationally; it can be developed only through experience.

In a way, performing is a continuation of an actor's training. There is, in fact, an ongoing debate in acting education about the relative merits of an *academic* model and an *apprentice* model. The former, which has been increasingly popular in American conservatory programs, gives students "room to fail" in a closed environment in which they are learning and experimenting in their smaller community. The apprentice model—for centuries the typical way actors all over the world have learned their craft—values the learning that happens in front of an audience. Apprentices would join a theatre company and study the work of their masters to become active parts of productions. Many training programs utilize both academic and apprentice models: pupils learn techniques and then get a chance to test what they've learned. For instance, at the Intercultural Theatre Institute of Singapore, students spend two years undergoing an intense intercultural training regimen for hours every day; in the third year, they collaborate with directors to create three new full-fledged productions.

Regardless of their training, stage actors face a special problem unknown to their film counterparts and seldom experienced by amateurs in the theatre: the problem of maintaining a high level of *spontaneity* through many, many performances. Some professional play productions run continuously for years, and actors may find them-

📷 Photo Essay: Actor Sir Patrick Stewart

1. In his dressing room, Stewart is creating a chart (in green) specifying where he is to make his entrances in the many different scenes of *Antony and Cleopatra*. During each performance he must leave the stage many times and go to his dressing room to change costume before reentering somewhere else each time. He feels safer with this "cheat sheet" on his dressing-room table to remind him of the location of each new entrance.
©*Robert Cohen*

Sir Patrick Stewart is known worldwide for his 176 episodes as Captain Jean-Luc Picard on television's *Star Trek: The Next Generation* and his long-time role as Professor Charles Xavier in the *X-Men* films, but he began his continuously ascending acting career with sixteen years of classical performances with England's Royal Shakespeare Company (RSC). During the course of a fifty-year career, he has performed in more than one hundred stage productions on Broadway, London's West End, and regional American theatres including Minneapolis's Guthrie, Washington's Shakespeare Theatre Company, the New York Shakespeare Festival, and Los Angeles's Ahmanson and Huntington Theatres. His post–*Star Trek* stage career is certainly his greatest, including stunning performances in the major Shakespearean roles of Othello, Macbeth, Prospero, Claudius, Malvolio, and Mark Antony (in *Antony and Cleopatra*)—and as Shakespeare himself in Edward Bond's *Bingo* at London's Young Vic. More recently, he played Robert in David Mamet's *A Life in the Theatre* on Broadway, and on both Broadway and London's West End, a double-bill (with Ian McKellen) in which he played Vladimir in Samuel Beckett's *Waiting for Godot* and Hirst in Harold Pinter's *No Man's Land* on alternate nights. With numerous cinema and television credits alongside his stage work, including a revival of his role as Professor X in the 2017 critical and box-office success *Logan,* Stewart is convinced that each medium can be a lead-in to all the others. "Sitting in all those thrones of England on the stage at Stratford-upon-Avon was nothing less than a preparation for sitting in the captain's chair of the *Enterprise,*" he said in an interview in 2007 with Robert Cohen, one of the authors of this text. "This is an exaggeration, of course, but there are parallels," he insisted, referring to his two long-standing artistic "homes"—England's RSC and America's *Star Trek.*

2. From his dressing room, Stewart checks with the wig room—ninety-two steps up—to see if his wig is ready. London's Novello Theatre, where the performance takes place, has dozens of individual dressing rooms scattered throughout the building's five backstage floors. The telephone is essential for communications with stage management before and during the show. *©Robert Cohen*

3. Onstage, the actors prepare with a physical and vocal warmup, led by voice coach Lyn Darnley (*standing*). Lying on the floor with the rest of the cast, Stewart is sounding his vowels as Darnley directs. *©Robert Cohen*

"*Star Trek* isn't written in naturalistic dialogue," Stewart continued. "It has a certain heightened quality, a tonality which is not like *CSI* or any of those contemporary shows. It has a five-act structure, which very much follows classical principles. And the bridge set is like an Elizabethan stage: it has a huge opening, the 'view screen' where the audience is, entrances down left and right and up left and right, and a raised area at the back with its own entrances. It is a very theatrical set, basically a stage format that hasn't changed much since the sixteenth century. And it is costume drama: no jeans or T-shirts, and, as with Elizabethan costumes, we have no pockets! No place to put our hands! And finally, the nature of the relationships of the principal cast very much conforms to what you might find in a Shakespearean history play. So there are many parallels!"

Stewart is also deeply involved in theatre education, currently as chancellor at the University of Huddersfield and previously as the Cameron Mackintosh Visiting Professor of Theatre at Oxford. He is also widely known to American theatre students through his many visits to

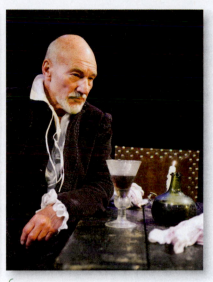

5. Wig on, Stewart applies the "pathetic little makeup" that he uses to play Mark Antony. He uses no base makeup, only a few very simple lines accented with an eyebrow pencil. Forty-five minutes before curtain, Stewart makes his final preparation, with light exercise and meditation, all intended to lead him to the ideal state of readiness for his first entrance. ©*Robert Cohen*

7. The actor plays a playwright: Stewart here performs the role of the aging William Shakespeare contemplating his future at a local pub after his retirement to Stratford-upon-Avon, in Edward Bond's *Bingo,* directed by Angus Jackson for London's Young Vic Theatre in 2012. ©*Geraint Lewis/Alamy Stock Photo*

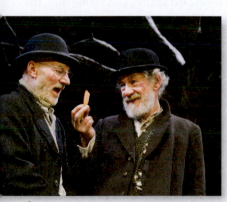

6. Sir Patrick Stewart as Vladimir and Sir Ian McKellen as Estragon study their last carrot in Sean Mathias's British production of *Waiting for Godot*, brought to Broadway in 2013–2014. ©*Geraint Lewis/Alamy Stock Photo*

campuses, first through the RSC's "theatre-go-round," which visited the University of California at Irvine in 1968, and then as the cofounder of the ACTER group of British performers (now called Actors from the London Stage), which has toured American colleges annually since 1976.

One of the remarkable aspects of Stewart's career is his easy crossover between English drama (by Shakespeare, Harold Pinter, and Tom Stoppard, among others) and American drama (by Arthur Miller, Edward Albee, and David Mamet). Born in the north of England, he had to lose his Yorkshire accent before acting in classic English plays, so finding the proper dialect was always part of his actor's preparation. Even today, forty-plus years into his professional acting career, Stewart joins the cast in pre-performance warmups that tone not only his voice but also the particular diction of the play he is in.

For his first American plays, Stewart admitted, "The biggest handicap was the accent. I was very aware of this in an early movie where I played an American and they wrote in a line about me saying, 'Oh, he was born in England.' Whenever you hear a line like that, you know it's about the accent!" Stewart attributed his now-polished American accent to vocal coach (and New York University faculty member) Deborah Hecht: "She completely transformed my experience and confidence in speaking American. That was for [Arthur Miller's] *Ride Down Mount Morgan* on Broadway. We were aiming at sort of a cultivated, cultured, New York Jewish accent, and she brought me to a point where I felt so good with it that I felt physically like a different person. The accent changed the way I moved, the way I behaved; certainly the rhythms of speech changed. And she was very, very precise with me, very exact. I worked with her again on [Edward Albee's] *Who's Afraid of Virginia Woolf?* and I went to her again for a film role. Once I had 'slipped sideways' into feeling like an American, everything became much easier. Indeed, a year ago, when we started to rehearse *Antony and Cleopatra* (in England), I was perpetually teased by stage management for my American vowels!"

Stewart obviously loves acting. As he told Cohen, "It's the liberty of total freedom, where I can be not myself—yet also purely myself. It is a kind of possession, where something takes over and I become everything I would like to be, and find a liberty to 'play' while knowing at the same time that there will be no consequences. Nobody's going to say, 'Oh, stop being a child! Stop being so selfish, so self-obsessed! Pull yourself together!'

"I thank God that I am an actor," Stewart concluded, "and that I spend my days in the company of people who behave with such dignity, honesty, and openness. That's what's truly meant by 'theatrical'—not something merely flashy, but doing what actors must do to help people understand what is really going on."

Courtesy of Patrick Stewart.

Keira Knightly, known primarily for her work in film, made her stage debut in London in 2009, in an updated version of Molière's seventeenth-century comedy *The Misanthrope,* pictured here.
©Geraint Lewis/Alamy Stock Photo

continuously for more than a year or two. However, the problem can become intense even after only a few weeks. How, as they say in the trade, do the actors "keep it fresh"? How can something seem new if it occurs over and over?

Actors have their own way of addressing this problem. Some rely on their total immersion in the role and contend that by "living the life of the character" they can keep themselves equally alert from first performance to last. Others turn to technical experiments—reworking their delivery and trying constantly to find better ways of saying their lines, expressing their characters, and achieving their objectives. Still others concentrate on the relationships within the play and try with every performance to find something new in each relationship as it unfolds onstage. A professional must find a way to walk onstage as if it were a totally new experience—to be "in the moment" and, ideally, to still find new aspects of the character, even after hundreds of performances.

The actors' performances do not end with the play. They live on in dressing-room conversations and in *postmortems* with the company, in which the actors reflect on what was done today and how it might be done better tomorrow. Sometimes the postmortem of a play is handled by the director, who may give notes to the cast. More typically in professional situations, actors simply rely on self-criticism, often measured against comments from the stage manager—whose job it is to maintain the director's vision—and from reviews in the press. Then the next day, they do it all again. An actor never truly perfects a role; it is always changing, always alive. It is perhaps this feeling of eternal work that draws the actor ever more deeply into the profession, for it is a feeling as well known to the amateur in a high school pageant as it is to the most experienced professional on Broadway: the need to try again, risk again, and keep exploring.

selves in the position of performing the same part eight times a week, fifty-two weeks a year, with no end in sight. Of course the routine can vary with vacations and cast substitutions, and in fact, very few actors ever play a role

Chapter

4

The Playwright

©Joel Moorman/Steppenwolf Theatre Company

Aт HOME, AS I GAZE at my computer screen, I am the master of my world. Scenes play out in my head; whole characters pop into my imagination; great speeches, scenes, and visions flow directly to my fingers as I type word after word. I mumble to myself, hearing each speaker shape each line, each monologue, each heated exchange. . . . These are *my* words, *my* ideas, *my* people, and *my* play—and they will soon be resounding in theatres around the world. Maybe, I idly wonder, my play will receive critical raves, and I'll start attending press interviews and speaking invitations as a result of my smashing success; I will mount the stage to accept countless "best play" awards, perhaps even sitting one day in Stockholm, next to my fellow Nobel Prize winners—that year's Einstein and Marie Curie who, like me, have forever changed the modern world.

But that's only at home, and only in my head. In reality, in the theatre, I am the loneliest of figures. I huddle inconspicuously in the back row, taking notes in the dark. I am unnoticed by the actors and, indeed, rarely allowed to speak directly to them. At the end of the rehearsal, when I politely offer to share my notes with the director, she glares at me. And when she finally listens, it's with a blank face before agreeing that, yes, she'll "think about all of this tomorrow."

This scenario is imaginary—and a bit extreme. But it addresses a strange truth: the playwright is both the most central *and* the most peripheral figure in the theatrical event. Obviously, playwrights are needed for nearly every production: the script, in most cases, is the starting point of the theatrical process. Yet that point of origin is also a point of departure. Once the script has been printed, duplicated, and distributed, the playwright's actual participation consists of mainly serving as the director's sounding-board and, if called for, script reviser. There are exceptions to this principle, of course. Some playwrights work from actors' improvisations, and others participate quite fully in rehearsals, even to the point of serving as director of their plays or even acting in them. But even when they are active and present in the rehearsal room, playwrights are still, in a way, isolated from the final product, which is largely a collaboration of other artists.

The tension between communal and individual desires informs the playwright's work. Playwrights must communicate their intimate selves *and* speak to the wider world. Plays may spring from a single mind, but they become part of something much bigger—as they should. We look to the theatre for a measure of guidance, for personal enlightenment derived from another's experience, for fresh perspectives, and for new vision. As such, a playwright cannot simply be a great textual writer but must have an understanding of the theatrical *event,* in all of its complexity. Simple mastery of certain conventional techniques will not suffice to enable a playwright to expand our daily lives.

Playwriting as Event Writing

If you take a look at the classes offered at your school's English department, you will probably see classes in drama: perhaps a Shakespeare course or a survey that incorporates some Greek or American plays. This makes sense because drama is a foundational form of literature. Many dramatic authors begin as poets or novelists, so it may seem that playwriting is primarily a literary activity. But it is not. Writing for the theatre is quite different from other literary forms. It helps to understand the word's origin: play*wright* is not play*write*. Although the words "write" and "wright" sound identical, "wright" is an old-fashioned way to say "maker"; a wheelwright, for instance, is a person who makes wheels. Therefore, a playwright is someone who makes plays.

Plays, as we discussed in the chapter "What Is a Play?," are live events, not texts. Thus a playwright is a creator of events: someone who sculpts narrative out of action. Most playwrights work with text as their medium—they write scripts on their computers or notepads—but even then, this text is charged with a potential for enactment. Picture this scenario: a playwright simply writes the words "they fight." In a novel or short story, the details of that fight would live in the mind of the reader, but for a playwright, what is created goes far beyond the words. There are infinite ways the characters onstage could fight. Fists? guns? knives? playful tickling? Hours of time will go into plotting these moves and incorporating them into the story of the play as a whole. The actors will find motivated actions, the director will enshrine the final movements as the official blocking, the designers will make sure that the

set and costumes can withstand the physical wear and tear, and a professional fight choreographer will train the performers to enact the scene safely and convincingly. All of that planning is because of two simple words! But this level of physical realization is true for all actions written in a play, such as "She crosses the room," "He drinks," and "They dance." And so too for the spoken words: there are always new ways to deliver lines of a script. The words are critical, but they are more of a blueprint than a final product. They are always linked to real, embodied performance. In fact, some of a play's most effective writing may look very clumsy as it appears in print. Take, for example, the following lines from Shakespeare:

Oh! Oh! Oh!	—*OTHELLO*
Howl, howl, howl, howl!	—*KING LEAR*
No, no, the drink, the drink. O my dear Hamlet, The drink, the drink! I am poisoned.	—*HAMLET*

These apparently unsophisticated lines of dialogue in fact provide great dramatic climaxes in an impassioned performance. The text as written is really a pretext for acting, which is ultimately far more crucial than literary eloquence to the art of playwriting.

Of course, some literary values are as important to the theatre as they are to other types of literature. The same formal devices that you may have learned in your English classes still apply: allusion, lyricism, imagery, figurative language, and a careful crafting of rhythm, diction, and syntax all contribute powerfully to dramatic effect. But they are effective only insofar as they are fully integrated within the whole of the theatrical medium—as they stimulate action and behavior through stage space and stage time in a way that commands audience attention and involvement. Mere literary brilliance is insufficient as theatre because theatre is, above all, the creation of an event, not a text.

Moisés Kaufman, the celebrated theatre director and playwright, describes his work as "writing performance." Kaufman's company, The Tectonic Theatre Project, takes this idea to the extreme by doing away with any original script. Instead, the company creates what it calls "moment work": company members write their plays through improvisation, interviews, and research. This kind of process is known as *devised* theatre, in which the entire play is created in rehearsal. Devised theatre practitioners may begin with an idea or question, but then create the text as a byproduct of their work together, rather than start with a script and explore how they can interpret it. The exact nature of the end product is, as a result, unknown at the start. Today, there are many celebrated companies that

The critically acclaimed Tectonic Theatre Project, based in New York City, uses "movement work" to create devised plays. Rather than start with a script, company members interview, research, and improvise to create their performance pieces. Pictured here is their 2017 production *Uncommon Sense,* based on work with people on the autism spectrum. ©Joan Marcus

create devised theatre, such as Elevator Repair Service and the Rude Mechanicals in the United States, and Complicite in the United Kingdom. One of the best-known plays that began as a devised piece is *Cloud 9* by Caryl Churchill. While Churchill is credited as the author, much of the text is a transcription of scenes created spontaneously by the Joint Stock Theatre Company, with whom she was working. Devised theatre is not merely a Western phenomenon: the *Kezairoku* ("Valuable Notes on Playwriting") is an influential 1801 Japanese text for authors of kabuki works that encourages playwrights to create their plays in collaboration with their performers. Because devised theatre blurs the line between playwriting and directing, we will discuss it further in the chapter on directing.

Whether playwrights work in isolation and create a polished script or devise work with a company—or engage in some process in between these extremes—all share human behavior as their primary medium. Ultimately,

their words and actions will be inhabited by actors. Fundamentally, then, the playwright works with two tools that both represent the externals of human behavior: *dialogue* and *physical action*. The inner story and theme of a play—the psychology of the characters, the viewpoint of the author, the impact of the social environment—must be inferred by the audience from the play's events as the audience sees them. It is this series of related events that constitutes the play's scenario or, more formally, its plot.

The events of drama are, by their nature, compelling. Some are bold and provocative, as in the Italian playwright and director Romeo Castellucci's *Four Seasons Restaurant,* in which women cut out their tongues while attempting to read poetry. Some are subdued, as when the military regiment in Chekhov's *The Three Sisters* leaves town at the play's end. And some are quite ordinary, as in the domestic sequences depicted in most modern realist plays—take, for instance, the work of Richard Nelson, whose 2016 trilogy *The Gabriels: Election Year in the Life of One Family* depicts a family gathering around a kitchen table at different points in the year. The Gabriels decorate cookies, eat dinner, and sort through old boxes of photographs. These actions are seemingly banal, but their careful construction adds up to a feeling of a richly realized, full life. Regardless of their content, events are always aimed at creating a memorable impression. To begin playwriting, one must first conceptualize events and envision them enacted in such a way as to hold the attention of an audience.

The events of a play can be connected to each other in a strictly chronological continuity. This has been a goal of the realistic theatre, in which dramatic events are arranged to convey a lifelike progression of experiences in time. Such plays are said to be continuous in structure and linear in chronology, and they can be analyzed like sociological events. The audience simply watches them unfold as it might watch a family quarrel in progress in an apartment across the way. One thing leads to another and to another; a clear cause-and-effect logic pervades.

Continuity, however, is by no means a requirement for play construction. Castellucci's *Four Seasons Restaurant,* for instance, precedes its aforementioned depiction of self-mutilation with the sound of a black hole, as recorded by NASA, filling the space in utter darkness. How does this sound relate to the women trying to read a poem? The audience must fill in the gaps. Yet while Castellucci is celebrated as an experimental artist, his discontinuous scenes are hardly a new innovation. The surviving plays of ancient Greece are highly disjointed: choral odes alternate with character-driven episodes in the tragedies, and choral interjections and direct speeches to the audience (*parabasis*) interrupt the action of Old Comedies. Most of Shakespeare's plays are structured in a highly complex arrangement of times, places, styles, songs, and subplots built around a theme or investigation of character.

To be clear, linear, point-to-point storytelling has not disappeared from the theatre. It remains the basic architecture of most popular and serious plays. Mastery of this form requires just as much craft as more experimental or complex structures. David Hare's play *Skylight* takes place in one evening in one room and consists, essentially, of a series of long conversations. But Hare imbues the proceedings with psychological, political, and erotic depth. While linear theatre is still popular, modern and postmodern audiences have proven increasingly receptive to less-conventional frameworks. Ella Hickson's 2016 play *Oil* spans 150 years, following a single, unchanging character in different times and places (northern England in the 1800s, turn-of-the-century Tehran, and 1970s Libya). Florian Zeller's *The Father,* also from 2016, forces its audience to experience the dementia of its main character by having actors play different roles and alternating the chronology of scenes. And the hit musical *If/Then* follows two parallel plots, each a different hypothetical life of the same character. Audiences flocked to these shows, proving that nonlinear structures can create powerful and sustained dramatic impact, provided they still fundamentally portray a dramatization of events that the audience can put together in some sort of meaningful and satisfying fashion.

The Qualities of a Play

As we have seen, plays can vary in their method of creation, length, and continuity. However, there are some qualities—abstract properties, as opposed to cut-and-dry characteristics—that most fine plays possess. Of course, as with any art form, the qualities that make up a good play only truly gain meaning in their combination and interaction—ways that cannot be dissected or measured. These qualities include credibility, intrigue, speakability, stageability, flow, richness, depth of characterization, gravity, pertinence, compression, economy, and celebration of life.

CREDIBILITY AND INTRIGUE

To be credible is to be believable, but it is not the same as being lifelike. It might be helpful to distinguish the "true" from the "real." Fantasy, ritual, and absurdity might not be "real," but they can all convey truth; and they have all proven to be enduringly popular theatrical modes.

Credibility is the audience-imposed demand that requires a play's actions to appear to flow logically from its characters, its situation, and the theatrical context the playwright provides. In a credible play, what happens in act 2 appears to be a reasonable outgrowth of what happened in act 1.

Credibility requires that the characters in a play appear to act out of their own individual intentions rather than serve as pawns for the development of theatrical plot or effect, or as empty disseminators of propaganda. Credibility requires that characters maintain consistency within themselves: their thoughts, feelings, hopes, fears, and plans must appear to flow from human needs rather than purely theatrical ones. Credibility, in essence, is a contract between author and audience, whereby the audience agrees to view the characters as "people" as long as the author agrees not to shatter that belief in order to accomplish other purposes. Even in the most absurd situations—perhaps especially in those situations—characters should reflect to us something familiar. Oftentimes, it is the tension between the familiarity of their qualities and the strangeness of the scenario that makes a play truly compelling.

Intrigue is the quality of a play that makes us curious (sometimes fervently so) to see "what happens next." Sheer plot intrigue—which is sometimes called "suspense" because it leaves us suspended (that is, "hanging")—is one of the most powerful dramatic effects. Whole plays can be based on little more than artfully contrived plotting designed to keep the audience in a continual state of anticipation and wonder. Shakespeare's *The Merchant of Venice* begins with the titular character proclaiming, "In sooth, I know not why I am so sad." So why is he sad? Even he doesn't know. We don't immediately find out—in fact, we never explicitly find out—but his statement keeps us wanting to know more.

Plot, however, is only one of the elements of a play that can support intrigue. Most plays that aspire to true insight develop intrigue in their characters and themes, not just in their plot. Most of the great plays demand that we ask not so much "What will happen?" as "What does this mean?" Most great plays, in other words, make us care about the characters and create a more grand sense of suspense than simply "What will happen?"—they create tension by inviting us to ponder the bigger mysteries of the human condition.

Look, for example, at the opening dialogue of Harold Pinter's 1964 play *The Homecoming*. In the living room of an old house in London, Lenny, a middle-aged man, sits on a couch while reading the paper; Max, an older man, enters from the kitchen and begins going through drawers in a sideboard, looking for something.

MAX: What have you done with the scissors? (*Pause.*) I said I'm looking for the scissors. What have you done with them? (*Pause.*) Did you hear me? I want to cut something out of the paper.

LENNY: I'm reading the paper.

MAX: Not that paper. I haven't even read that paper. I'm talking about last Sunday's paper. I was just having a look at it in the kitchen. (*Pause.*) Do you hear what I'm saying? I'm talking to you! Where's the scissors?

LENNY: (*looking up, quietly.*) Why don't you shut up, you daft prat?

Max lifts his stick and points it at him.

MAX: Don't you talk to me like that. I'm warning you.

He sits in a large armchair.

There's an advertisement in the paper about flannel vests. Cut price. Navy surplus. I could do with a few of them.

The scene creates tension in a typical, even banal, situation. What begins as a simple exchange between two men gains intrigue with its punctuation of aggression and a threat of violence—only to resolve, it seems, back to a discussion of the everyday. But why does it resolve? Was Max sincere in his threat to Lenny? Why is Lenny so unconcerned with Max? And how are they related to each other? Pinter, here, shows a mastery of creating intrigue subtly, rather than with forthright suspense.

Intrigue draws us into the world of a play; credibility keeps us there. In the best plays the two are sustained in a fine tension of opposites: intrigue demands surprise, credibility demands consistency. Combined, they generate a kind of "believable wonder," which is the fundamental state of drama. Credibility alone will not suffice to make a play interesting—just try transcribing a real-life dialogue directly as a script—and no level of intrigue can make a noncredible play palatable. The integration of the two must be created by the playwright in order to transcend our expectations but not our credulity.

SPEAKABILITY, STAGEABILITY, AND FLOW

The dialogue of drama is written on the page, but it must be spoken by actors and staged by directors. Thus the goal of the playwright is to fabricate speakable, actable, and stageable dialogue that flows in a progression leading to theatrical impact.

One of the most common mistakes of beginning playwrights is that their lines lack speakability. At times their speeches may sound brilliant when read silently, or as prose, but feel limp or difficult to follow when spoken aloud.

This is not to say that dramatic dialogue must resemble ordinary speech. No one imagines people in life speaking like characters from the plays of the ancient Greek dramatist Aeschylus, or of Shakespeare—when is the last time you heard someone speak spontaneously in poetic verse?—or of any number of other authors who write in a nonrealistic style. Brilliantly styled language is a feature of most of the great plays in theatre history, and lifelikeness, by itself, is not a dramatic virtue—nor is its absence a dramatic fault.

Speakability means that a line of dialogue should achieve its maximum impact when spoken. To accomplish this, the playwright must be closely attuned to the rhythm of sound that creates emphasis, meaning, focus, and power. Verbal lullabies and climaxes, fast punch lines, sonorous lamentations, sparkling epigrams, devastating expletives, pregnant pauses, and hushed whispers—these are

David Mamet is revered for his ability to create dialogue that is both believable and theatrically compelling. He won the Pulitzer Prize for his fiery *Glengarry Glen Ross,* portraying the cutthroat competition among employees in a Chicago real estate office. Alan Alda (*left*) and Liev Schreiber (*right*) face off in this 2005 Broadway revival of the play, directed by Joe Mantello. ©*Sara Krulwich/The New York Times/Redux*

some of the devices of dialogue that impart audial shape to great plays written by master dramatists. Look, for example, at the speech of the rakish and witty gentleman Millamant in the "proviso" scene of William Congreve's eighteenth-century comic masterpiece *The Way of the World.* When discussing the terms of his possible marriage, Millamant finally cries out in frustration:

> Oh, I hate a lover that can dare to think he draws a moment's air independent on the bounty of his mistress. There is not so impudent a thing in nature as the saucy look of an assured man, confident of success. The pedantic arrogance of a very husband has not so pragmatical an air. Ah! I'll never marry, unless I am first made sure of my will and pleasure.

When his conversation partner, Mirabell—who is in love with him—responds that Millamant could have "the first" (will) now and "the other" (pleasure) after agreeing to marry, Millamant responds with an *apostrophe,* or address to an abstract concept:

> My dear liberty, shall I leave thee? My faithful solitude, my darling contemplation, must I bid you then adieu? Ay-h-adieu—my morning thoughts, agreeable wakings, indolent slumbers, all ye *douceurs,* ye *sommeliers du matin,* adieu?—I can't do't, 'tis more than impossible.

No one would call this "everyday speech." Though it might be difficult to read at first—with its complex sentence structures, shifts to French, and exaggerated sounds ("Ay-h-adieu")—it is immensely speakable. Its cascading rhythm develops a rollicking momentum that leaves Mirabell enraptured and, with a great actor delivering it, the audience breathless.

Speakability also requires that the spoken line reflect the character's personality, not just the author's perspective. Actors use their lines to develop characterizations, and the script helps create an overall style for an acting ensemble. Thus the mastery of dramatic dialogue demands more than an impressive vocabulary—it requires a constant awareness of the purposes and tactics underlying human communication, as well as of the multiple psychological and aesthetic properties of language.

Stageability requires, as its name suggests, that dialogue be written so it can be spoken effectively onstage, but it also must be conceived as an integral element of a particular staged situation in which setting, physical acting, and spoken dialogue are combined. A stageable script is one in which staging and stage business—as well as design and the acting demands—are neither adornments for the dialogue nor sugarcoating for the writer's opinions, but are intrinsic to the very nature of the play. Like credibility, stageability is different from "realism." Suzan-Lori Parks (see the section "A Sampling of Current American Playwrights" later in this chapter) creates brilliantly stageable works, but the worlds of her plays are nothing

we would encounter in real life; for example, the opening stage directions of her *The America Play* are "A great hole. In the middle of nowhere." One hundred different directors could come up with one hundred different interpretations of that description, but the physical results would all reflect the more abstract truths that her play evokes—absence, history, amnesia, and trauma.

A speakable and stageable script flows rather than stumbles. *Flow* requires a continual stream of information, and a play that flows is one that is continually saying something, doing something, and meaning something to the audience. To serve this end, the playwright should address such technical problems as scene-shifting, entrances and exits, and act breaks as early as possible in the scriptwriting process. When drafting scenes, the writer should avoid exposition for its own sake. An old maxim of writing and acting still holds true today: "Show, don't tell." Rather than have a character say, "As your older brother, who once saved your life back when we lived in Oklahoma, I'm disappointed by your recent decision to divorce your wife," the author must try to have this information emerge organically in the natural behavior of the character.

Simon Russell Beale (*seated at left*) chats eloquently with Hayley Atwell as his daughter, Major Barbara, as both are surrounded by equally well-spoken friends and family in George Bernard Shaw's 1905 *Major Barbara,* directed by Nicholas Hytner at England's National Theatre in 2008. ©*Geraint Lewis/Alamy Stock Photo*

Leaden exposition and incomprehensible plot develop-ments can sink the sturdiest script in a sea of audience apathy.

RICHNESS

Depth, subtlety, fineness, quality, wholeness, and *inevita-bility*—these words are often helpful in describing plays we like. They are fundamentally subjective terms, eas-ier to apply than to define or defend, for the fact is that when a play pleases us—when it "works"—the feelings of pleasure and stimulation it affords are beyond concrete expression. Certainly richness is one of the qualities common to plays that leave us with this sense of satisfaction.

A play that is rich with detail is not necessarily one that is rife with detail; it is simply one whose every detail fortifies our insight into the world of the play. Going to a play is in part a matter of paying a visit to the playwright's world, and the more vividly created that world is, the greater the play's final impact will be. Detail lends speci-ficity: specific people are engaged in specific tasks in a specific place. In Margaret Edson's *Wit,* for example, Viv-ian, a terminally ill English professor, addresses the audi-ence from her hospital bed. Her tone is professorial and her vocabulary is filled with medical terminology, little of which the average audience member will understand, but in the context of an intellectual woman struggling against a fatal disease, Vivian's speech creates an immensely com-pelling and affectingly detailed portrait:

VIVIAN: I don't mean to complain, but I am becoming very sick. Very, very sick. Ultimately sick, as it were.

In everything I have done, I have been steadfast, resolute—some would say in the extreme. Now, as you can see, I am distinguishing myself in illness.

I have survived eight treatments of Hexamethophosphacil and Vinplatin at the full dose, ladies and gentlemen. I have broken the record. I have become something of a celebrity. Kelekian and Jason [her doctors] are simply delighted. I think they foresee celebrity status for themselves upon the appearance of the journal article they will no doubt write about me.

But I flatter myself. The article will not be about me, it will be about my ovaries. It will be about my peritoneal cavity, which, despite their best intentions, is now crawling with cancer. What we have come to think of as me is, in fact, just the specimen jar, just the dust jacket, just the white piece of paper that bears the little black marks.

Vivian's free use of seven-syllable words, her refining of words on the spot (from "very sick" to "very, very sick" to "ultimately sick"; from "steadfast" to "resolute"), her

public style of presentation ("ladies and gentlemen"), her parallel phrases ("I have . . . I have . . . I have . . . ," "just the . . . just the . . . just the . . ."), her use of alliteration ("just . . . jar . . . just . . . jacket, just") and her use of op-posing images ("white piece of paper . . . little black marks") tell us volumes about her character and how she is "distinguishing" herself in illness. Richness of linguistic detail lends a play authority and an aura of sureness.

Richness is not an easy quality to develop in writing. It demands of its author a gift for close observation, an unin-hibited imagination, a consummate vocabulary, and an astute sense of what to leave out as well as what to include. A person who can recollect personal experiences in great detail; who can conjure up convincing situations, peoples, locales, and conversations; and who is closely attuned to nuance can work these talents into the creation of plays.

DEPTH OF CHARACTERIZATION

Depth of characterization presents perhaps the greatest single stumbling block for novice playwrights, who tend either to write all characters "in the same voice" (nor-mally the author's own) or to divide them into two camps: good and bad. Capturing the depth, complexities, and uniqueness of real human beings, even seemingly ordi-nary human beings, is a difficult task.

Depth of characterization requires that every character possess an independence of intention, expression, and motivation. Moreover, these characteristics must appear sensible in the light of our general knowledge of psychol-ogy and human behavior. In plays as in life, all characters must act from motives that appear reasonable to them (if not to those watching them or to those affected by them). The playwright should bear in mind that all char-acters are, to themselves, important and worthwhile peo-ple, regardless of what others think. Thus even the great villains of drama must believe in themselves and in the fundamental "rightness" of their causes. Even if we never completely understand their deepest motivations (as we can't fully understand the motives of real villains such as Hitler, Caligula, or John Wilkes Booth), we should be able to sense at the bottom of any character's behavior a valid-ity of purpose, however twisted or perverse we may find it.

If masterfully drawn, with depth and richness, *any* character can engender our empathy. The British author debbie tucker green, who does not capitalize her name, caused a sensation with her 2008 play *Random,* about the effects of a gang-related killing on a black family in South London. The play is written for one actor, who takes on many different characters. *Random* ends with the sister of the victim leaving her deceased brother's bedroom:

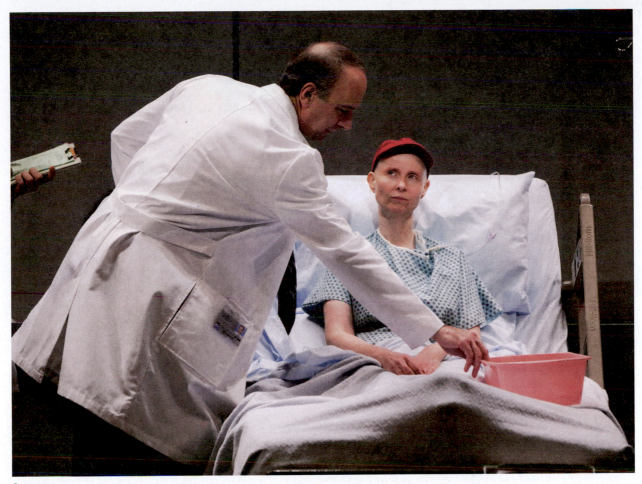

Margaret Edson's *Wit*—about an English professor dying of cancer—began as a blind submission to South Coast Repertory in California by the yet-unknown playwright; it was soon premiered by that company and awarded the 1999 Pulitzer Prize. This 2012 Broadway revival, directed by Lynn Meadow for the Manhattan Theatre Club, featured Cynthia Nixon as Dr. Vivian Bearing and Michael Countryman as one of her doctors. *©Sara Krulwich/The New York Times/Redux*

SISTER: Close back his
 drawer
 close back his
 door—
 keep his stink in.
 Step down the—too quiet stairs
 past the stank Dad still sittin in
 from the kitchen.
 Past the socked Support Officer
 struggling—
 in the best room
 with our . . .
 my
 destroyed Mum.

What is brilliant about this speech—and the play as a whole—is how it shows us, with startling brevity, a deep sense of interior life. Because this particular life is a black woman in a lower-class neighborhood, her depth of characterization is also a political act, one that gives a voice to someone often rendered invisible and rarely given a chance to speak out. Depth of characterization reminds us that everyone is capable of dramatic poetry. We can observe here, too, other elements of play construction we have discussed: the speakability (note the slant rhymes and small alliterative bursts, like "socked Support . . . struggling"), stageability (one need only speak these words on a bare stage to evoke the entire imagined space of the house), flow (the lines are arranged almost like music), and richness of detail—Dad is, in her patois, "stank"; her mother is "destroyed"; they sit in the "best room"; and the steps, like the brother, are now "too quiet."

Language is everything for Edward Albee, whose awards include three Pulitzer Prizes and three Tony Awards. One of his Pulitzer Prizes recognized his 1994 masterpiece *Three Tall Women*, shown here in its Tony Award–winning 2018 Broadway premiere starring Laurie Metcalf (*left*), Glenda Jackson (*center*), and Allison Pill (*right*) as the titular three women, simply named A, B, and C. The play's dialogue brilliantly builds suspense, with poetic ambiguity, as to the exact nature of their identities and relationship. ©*Sara Krulwich/The New York Times/Redux*

The small speech expertly balances these aspects of green's craft to create an overall impression of a living, breathing person.

GRAVITY AND PERTINENCE

Gravity and *pertinence* are terms used to describe the importance of a play's theme and its overall relevance to the concerns of the intended audience. To say a play has gravity is to say simply that its central theme is one of serious and lasting significance in humanity's spiritual, moral, or intellectual life. The greatest dramas—comedies as well as tragedies—are always concerned with universal problems—aging, discord, regret, insecurity, rejection, loss—for which we continually seek greater lucidity. Gravity does not mean somberness, however; it requires only a confrontation with the most elemental tasks of living. When an audience truly understands and identifies with a play's experiences, even the darkest tragedy radiates power and illumination.

Look, for example, at Bynum's speech in August Wilson's *Joe Turner's Come and Gone*. Bynum is what Wilson calls a "rootworker," or conjuror. A younger man, Jeremy, has just praised a woman as knowing "how to treat a fellow," and Bynum chastises him for his shallowness:

> You just can't look at it like that. You got to look at the whole thing. Now, you take a fellow go out there, grab hold to a woman and think he got something 'cause she sweet and soft to the touch. It's in the world like everything else. Touching's nice. It feels good. But you can lay your hand upside a horse or a cat, and that feels good too. What's the difference? When you grab hold to a woman, you got something there. You got a whole world there. You got a way of

life kicking up under your hand. That woman can take and make you feel like something. I ain't just talking about in the way of jumping off into bed together and rolling around with each other. Anybody can do that. When you grab hold to that woman and look at the whole thing and see what you got . . . why she can take and make something of you. Your mother was a woman. That's enough right there to show you what a woman is. Enough to show you what she can do. She made something out of you.

Using only a modest vocabulary (see, for a direct contrast, Vivian's speech in *Wit* earlier in this section), Wilson's Bynum probes at the heart of a profound subject: the vital possibility of deep, spiritual connection between people. The language grounds the speech in the specific circumstances of the play—we gain insight into the moral compasses of the speaker and the addressee, along with the social values of the era—but it marshals these particular details in service of a larger truth. Bynum's speech retains richness in its fine-grained examination of *these* people at *this* time while also prompting a revelation that can be understood by anyone. It is this connection of the specific to the universal that gives the passage gravity.

Pertinence refers to the play's touching on current audience concerns, both of-the-moment and timeless. Plays about current political situations or personalities are clearly pertinent; they may, however, quickly become outdated. In the wake of the tragic events of September 11, 2001, several plays emerged to grapple with the enormity of the disaster, such as Theresa Rebeck and Alexandra Gersten-Vassilaros's *Omnium-Gatherum,* which premiered a year afterward and received critical adulation—only to largely disappear from repertory productions after a few years. While powerful and timely, such pieces are not necessarily pertinent: they document events but may not transcend their historical specificity. Plays whose concerns are both timely *and* universal, however, will have a more enduring relevance. For example, Arthur Miller's *The Crucible* is about the Salem witch trials of 1692 but pertains as well to the McCarthy trials of the 1950s (when the play was written) and to corrupt investigations in all eras. The greatest plays are not merely pertinent to a given moment but also serve as archetypes for all time.

COMPRESSION AND ECONOMY

Compression and *economy* are also aspects of the finest plays. Compression refers to the playwright's skill in condensing a story (which may span many days, or even years, of chronological time) into a theatrical time frame. Economy relates to an author's skill in eliminating or

Roger Robinson plays the spellbinding healer Bynum Walker, a freed slave with mysterious insights, and Marsha Stephanie Blake is Mattie, a lost young woman seeking love but not knowing where to find it, in this 2009 Broadway revival of August Wilson's *Joe Turner's Come and Gone,* directed by Bartlett Sher. Costumes are by Catherine Zuber.
©*Sara Krulwich/The New York Times/Redux*

consolidating a play's characters, events, locales, and words in the service of streamlining its plot and ideas.

Many beginning playwrights attempt to convert a story to a play in the most obvious way: by writing a separate scene for every event described in the story (and sometimes including a different setting and supporting cast for each scene). Economy and compression, however, require that most stories be restructured in order to be dramatically viable. If the play is to be basically realistic, the playwright will rework the story to have all the events occur in one location, or perhaps in two locations with an act break between to allow for scenery changes. Events that are integral to the story but cannot be shown within the devised settings can simply be reported (as in Shaw's *Misalliance,* for example, in which an airplane crash occurs

No drama could have a more serious topic than *The Scottsboro Boys*, which depicts the true story of nine black teenage boys convicted of a crime that was never even committed during the period of racial segregation in the American South. However, David Thompson's script for the 2010 production, directed and choreographed by Susan Stroman, transforms the story into a black minstrel show being performed for white audiences. The play becomes both a scathing critique and a rousing spectacle—an example of how theatre's ability to celebrate does not undermine its capacity for political relevance. Colman Domingo and Forrest McClendon play the minstrel performers, with the jailed prisoners behind them. ©*Paul Kolnik*

offstage as the onstage characters gawk and exclaim). More common today—and, in fact, in many past eras, such as the Renaissance—is to integrate settings so that various places can be presented on the same set without intermission. Paula Vogel's *Baltimore Waltz*, for instance, hops among European locations so quickly that a theatrical ensemble must use a minimal, versatile set. At the other extreme, plays like Annie Baker's *The Flick* take place in one location, a run-down movie theatre, and occurs in "real time," which is to say that the characters and audiences experience time the same way. (See the section "A Sampling of Current American Playwrights" later in this chapter for more on Baker.) The minutes in *The Flick* tick by in tedium as the characters trade jibes and perform

mundane tasks. Yet there is still compression and economy: each word is carefully chosen and each pause carefully meted out.

The effects of economy and compression are both financial and aesthetic. Obviously, when scenery changes and the number of actors are kept at a minimum, the costs of production are minimized as well. But beyond that, compression and economy in playwriting serve to stimulate intrigue and focus audience expectation: a tightly written play gives us the feeling that we are on the trail of something important and that our destination is right around the next bend. Thus, economy and compression actually lead to intensity, which is one of the theatre's most powerful attributes.

CELEBRATION

Ultimately, a great play does not simply depict or analyze life—it celebrates it. After all, the first plays were presented at festivals that were essentially joyful celebrations. Even the darkest of the classical Greek tragedies sought to exalt the human spirit. And ancient Sanskrit dramas in India were joyous public occasions—in fact, as we learned in the chapter "What Is a Play?," the *Natyasastra,* which dictates how such plays should be written, requires that audience members feel pleasure.

The theatre can never successfully venture too far from this source. No one wants to buy tickets to be lectured for two hours; such a purely didactic theatre has never satisfied either critics or the public. Although the word "theatrical" usually suggests something like "glittery" or "showy," it better describes more fundamental aims: to extend our known experience, to illuminate life, and to raise existence to the level of art.

On the other hand, dramas intended to be merely uplifting by relying on happy endings and noble sentiments do not celebrate life but instead merely whitewash it. The truest and most exciting theatre has always been created out of a passionate, personal vision of reality and a deep devotion to expressing life's struggles and splendors. Writing, producing, and attending plays are acts of affirmation: they attest to the desire to share and communicate, as well as to celebrate human existence, participation, and communion. Purely bitter plays, no matter how justly based or how well grounded in history or experience, remain incomplete and unsatisfying as theatre, which simply is not an effective medium for nihilism. The most seemingly bleak of modern plays radiates a persistent hopefulness, even joyousness.

For a recent example of a play that proved to be celebratory without seeming simplistically uplifting and moving without seeming overly maudlin, see *Come from Away,* the 2016 musical by Irene Sankoff and David Heln. This drama—based on a true story—details the tragic events of September 11, 2001, in a curious setting: a small Canadian town where passengers aboard an American airplane were forced to land after the Twin Towers fell in New York City. Rather than look head-on at the horror of the historical event, the play instead finds joy and pathos in its depiction of a universally recognizable virtue: the capacity for a community to band together to help visitors feel welcome. The play proved to be a hit on Broadway. Audiences clearly want to feel celebration in times of darkness—and feelings of deep empathy amid joy.

The Playwright's Process

How does one go about writing a play? It is important to know the elements of a play (as discussed in the chapter "What Is a Play?") and the characteristics of the best plays—credibility, intrigue, speakability, stageability, flow, richness, depth of characterization, gravity, pertinence, compression, economy, and celebration—as discussed in the preceding sections. But these are abstract ideas. One must still confront the pragmatic, practical task of writing.

There is no consensus among writers as to where to start. Some prefer to begin with a storyline or a plot outline. Some, like the writers of *Come from Away,* begin with a real event and write the play to explain why that event occurred. Some begin with a real character or set of characters and develop a plot around them. Some begin with a setting and try to animate it with characters and actions. Some begin with a theatrical effect or an idea for a new form of theatrical expression. Some write entirely from personal experience. Some adapt a story, a legend, a biography of a famous person, a play by an earlier playwright, or even a remembered dream.

The process of writing a *documentary* play might begin with a transcript of a trial or a committee hearing. Other documentary plays might begin with interviews conducted by the theatre company. Others, as we have learned, are devised in collaboration with other artists. Some are compilations of material written over the course of many years or collected from many sources.

The fact is, writers tend to begin with whatever works for them and accords with their immediate aims. Oftentimes writing is simply the process of following your intuition without knowing where the process will lead or why you are pursuing it. On the one hand, because playwrights usually work alone, at least in the initial stages, they can create as they please whenever they want: there is no norm. On the other hand, certain steps can be followed as introductory exercises in playwriting, which may in fact lead to the creation of an entire play.

DIALOGUE

One common playwriting exercise is to transcribe dialogue from previous observation and experience, such as an overheard non sequitur on the subway or a brief heated exchange between a couple at a coffee shop. Because we remember conversations only selectively and subjectively, a certain amount of fictionalizing and shading inevitably creeps into these transcriptions. Often without even meaning to do so, authors transform people from their memories into characters in their scenes. For example, the comedians Nick Kroll and John Mulaney created their Broadway play *Oh, Hello* after they observed two older New Yorkers chatting away as they purchased copies of the same book at a bookstore. Kroll and Mulaney then spun out characters from these two men and created an entire absurd plot around their imagined friendship.

Writing scenes of imagined dialogue is the logical next step. Now the author extends the situation beyond memory and into the area of "what *might* have happened." The dialogue then constructed will be essentially original, yet in keeping with the personalized "characters" developed in the earlier transcription. The characters now react and respond as dramatic figures, interacting with each other freshly and under the control of the author. Many fine plays have resulted from the author working out, in plot and dialogue, hypothetical relations between real people. See, for instance, Tom Stoppard's *Travesties,* which depicts a production of Oscar Wilde's *The Importance of Being Earnest* in Zurich under the management of the author James Joyce. While such a production did actually occur, Stoppard fills in the gaps of Joyce's interactions with Henry Carr, an English actor in *Earnest;* Vladimir Lenin, the architect of the Russian Revolution; and Tristan Tzara, the founder of the Dada art movement. Clearly drawn to the historical curiosity that all of these figures were in the same place at the same time, Stoppard avoids simply depicting reality and instead propels the drama with his own imagination. The success of *Travesties's* revival in London in 2016, and its move to Broadway in 2018, proves that the drama clearly goes beyond a history lesson and possesses universal ideas and struggles.

CONFLICT

Scenes of conflict make the dialogue dramatic and help define a play. If a writer can create a convincing conflict that gets inside each of the characters involved and not merely one of them, then there is a good chance of making that scene the core of an exciting play—especially if it incorporates some subtlety and is not dependent entirely on shouting and denunciation. The best conflicts make the audience members feel ambivalent because they can understand each character's point of view. What is more, such a scene will be highly actable because the actors will have motivated psychological reasons to become engaged.

How does a playwright know if conflict is effective? Oftentimes writers will test out their work with actors. Having performers on hand to read a new draft of a scene gives playwrights the advantage of testing their work as it progresses. Playwrights can then quickly assess its impact. Sometimes a searing conflict on paper becomes limp

when acted out; other times, rising tension can only become palpable if real people embody the scripted action. Moreover, the performance of such a scene can generate enthusiasm for a theatrical collaboration that could create a fuller theatrical experience.

STRUCTURE

The development of a complete play demands more than stringing together a number of scenes. At some point in the writing process the playwright will confront the need for *structure*. Structure is not the same as plot. Plot, as we've learned, is the cause-and-effect chain of events: this event happened *because* of something else. Structure is the overall order of scenes. When we describe the plot of a play, we discuss how one occurrence (for example, Hamlet sees his father's ghost) leads to another (Hamlet pledges revenge on his father's murderer), and even more after that (Hamlet kills Laertes and Claudius and then dies). When we discuss structure, we refer to how all the scenes in the play are ordered. Does the murder happen before the play begins? Does the play end before a real resolution has been reached? Where in the play does a major revelation occur? We can discuss plot without taking into account all the scenes in the play. In our earlier example, "Hamlet takes revenge for his father's death" is an accurate description of the plot. However, discussion of structure would dwell instead on where in the play Hamlet does this, what scenes follow, and when (and if) he actually gets his revenge. We might also note that a play begins and ends in the same locale or with the same line (as David Henry Hwang's *M. Butterfly* does—with the single word "Butterfly"). When we speak of structure, we speak of symmetry, resonances, and connections among scenes.

Many playwrights develop outlines for the structure of their plays after writing a scene or two; some have an outline ready before any scenes are written or even thought of. Other playwrights never write down anything except dialogue and stage directions, yet they find an overall structure asserting itself almost unconsciously as their writing progresses. Authors like Sam Shepard and August Wilson likened their writing to music—they would start on a theme but improvise and follow their feelings as they wrote, often surprising themselves with where they were led. Indeed, many more writers with improvisational processes have mastered structure. Their intuitive and meandering first drafts were exactly that: *first.* It is a truism of theatre that playwriting is in fact *re*writing—editing an initial draft over and over to organize and reorganize the play's staged actions and events.

Some plays, particularly in the contemporary postmodern era, dispense altogether with conventional structure in favor of a collage of events, images, and poetic perceptions. Sarah Kane's last play, *4:48 Psychosis*, treats disorientation, death, and despair in an entirely nonlinear way. Shown here is a moment of extreme anguish from Poland's TR Warsawa company's production, performed at the Edinburgh International Theatre Festival in 2007. Magdalena Cielecka plays the unnamed central character. ©*Geraint Lewis/Alamy Stock Photo*

The Playwright's Rewards

There will always be a need for playwrights. There are always new stories to tell—and old stories that need retelling. As you read this, producers are eagerly reading their way through stacks of play submissions on their desks; aspiring playwrights are attending elite writing programs; and groups of new and experienced playwrights are meeting to support and constructively critique each other's work. Nearly every play receives a reading before it is fully produced. This reading may be simply a group of actors at a table speaking the lines aloud or a *staged reading* with scripts perched on music stands as the performers embody the roles more fully.

The rewards that await successful playwrights can be very fulfilling. Playwrights receive compensation according to their commercial success; they may acquire influence and prestige on the basis of their personal vision. As of late, it has become common for newer playwrights to combine their theatre work with television writing. The writers' rooms of recent critically acclaimed shows such as *The Americans, House of Cards, Orange Is the New Black, The New Girl, Daredevil*, and *Shameless*—to name but a few—are populated by active playwrights. There are, certainly, many financial gains from such a combination, but playwriting remains the true focus for many of these writers. Rather than undermine the quality and volume of innovative new theatrical work, writing for television has provided sustenance and publicity for young voices—and, for television, sophistication and praise.

However, the true rewards of playwriting go beyond calculation. The profound impact of playwrights such as Arthur Miller, Lillian Hellman, Tennessee Williams, Lorraine Hansberry, Tony Kushner, August Wilson, Lynn Nottage, David Mamet, and Suzan-Lori Parks on American social thought and cultural mores is undeniable. At its best, playwriting is more than a profession and more than just another component of the theatrical machine. It is a creative political and cultural act that enlarges human experience and enriches our awe, understanding, and appreciation of life.

A Sampling of Current American Playwrights

Literally hundreds of American playwrights are producing works on professional American stages today, and several have international reputations. In this section, we focus on five contemporary writers who have made a major impact on the national theatre scene and from whom we may eagerly expect to see new and important works in the decades ahead: Young Jean Lee, Annie Baker, Tarell Alvin McCraney, Suzan-Lori Parks, and Ayad Akhtar. Lee is also featured in this chapter's photo essay, in which she goes into depth on her writing and collaborating process. These dynamic writers have little in common except their ability to entrance and surprise; each, in fact, has a dramatically different work process and philosophy. In looking over their work, then, we hope to demonstrate not any conclusion about playwriting but instead revel in the diversity of forms it can take. In very different ways, each author is challenging our conception of what the theatre can do, and thus celebrating its potential. As you read these profiles, note too how their work combines—in many different ways—the assorted qualities surveyed in this chapter.

YOUNG JEAN LEE

In 2018, Young Jean Lee made history as the first female Asian American playwright to have her work presented on Broadway. This accolade, however, is precisely the kind of well-meaning honor that Lee herself skewers in her drama, which unflinchingly examines our culture's obsession with—and fear of—identity politics. Her Broadway debut, after all, was *Straight White Men*, a title that should rightfully give us pause. Straight white men have dominated the dramatic landscape for ages as performers and playwrights; it seems willfully perverse to celebrate a marginalized voice achieving fame with a play that appears to conform to the dominant culture.

The play itself, however, is deeply aware of this perversity. Lee's cheeky drama, which had been workshopped at Brown University, the Public Theater, and the Steppenwolf Theatre in Chicago, is both a deconstruction of and sincere homage to the kind of "living room naturalism" that she had long rebelled against. Even though *Straight White Men* is ultimately about, well, straight white men, the script contains a note that the "pre-show music, curtain speech, and transitions are an important part of this play. They should create a sense that the show is under the control of people who are not straight white men." Furthermore, the first voice is not from one of the main characters but instead a "Stagehand-in-Charge" who is to be "transgender or gender nonconforming" and "preferably a person of color" and who begins the show with this announcement: "Throughout this performance, the actors will stay in character and pretend not to see you, unless they hear your cell phone ring or see you taking photos or video, in which case they may come into the audience and attack you. We hope you enjoy the show." These funny and unsettling gestures—brilliant devices for creating intrigue—remind us that what we expect as "normal" conventions of a realistic play are, in their own way, quite odd: they refuse to acknowledge us (even though this is the premise of all naturalistic theatre) and their identities, while often thought to be dominant and powerful, are not in charge.

Lee has never written the same play twice—not close to it. Her work has spanned period-drama parody (*The Appeal*), solo rock-cabaret monologue (*We're Gonna Die*), cultural satire (*Songs of the Dragons Flying to Heaven*), and even pantomime (*Untitled Feminist Play*). What unites these works is a recurring interest in uncomfortable questions, such as What are the unsaid taboos that govern our social habits? How can a cultural identity be presented onstage without conforming to our expectations? and perhaps most prominently To what extent can a play cause discomfort on the part of the audience?

To that latter point, *Songs of the Dragons Flying to Heaven* begins with a character named "Korean-American" addressing the audience in a profane, discomforting, and utterly politically incorrect monologue about how "Asian-Americans" are "slightly brain-damaged" because of their Asian parents, who are like "retarded monkeys." This is surely offensive, but it truthfully reflects the character's rage—remember, as we discussed in an earlier section, that dialogue must be in the voice of the character, not the playwright. Yet if we are distanced from this character—even if we laugh despite ourselves—we may feel an odd kind of sympathy for her later when she and three other characters named Korean 1, Korean 2, and Korean 3 appear less and less frequently onstage, and two other characters—White Person 1 and White Person 2—start taking up more and more time lounging about and speaking at length on boring subjects. What Lee does here, as in much of her work, is meld the formal construction of her play—dialogue, structure, conflict—with its thematic concerns. Just as Asian Americans are shunted to the side in life, so too are they here, onstage; the characters gain depth as we become aware of their placement in the play as a whole.

This investment in dramatic diversity began early in Lee's career when, under the tutelage of her influential playwriting mentor Mac Wellman, she learned to confront her deepest discomforts and dislikes onstage. By focusing on what agitated or scared her, rather than attempting to emulate the work of artists she admired, she found a way to combine, with poetic and comedic flair, a sincere vulnerability with an adventurous and experimental sense of dramatic construction. Her early works attained critical raves in the heady downtown New York City theatre scene, and she has been awarded a Guggenheim Fellowship, two Obie (off-Broadway) Awards, and numerous other residencies and fellowships. Her recent arrival on Broadway, which was greeted with positive reviews, marks a cause for celebration for her blossoming career and for the expansion of theatre culture more broadly. (For more on Young Jean Lee, see the interview with her in this chapter's photo essay.)

ANNIE BAKER

Often, when Annie Baker's plays are produced, audience members walk out. Those remaining will often leap to their feet. Many cry, many laugh, and many scrunch their brows in confusion. Couples who see her work will fight with one another—one loved it, the other is mystified.

Just what is so powerful in Baker's plays that prompt such a wide array of responses? Are her plays bold, provocative, in-your-face displays of violence and spectacle?

The most devastating satires are often also the funniest; in Young Jean Lee's uproarious *Songs of the Dragons Flying to Heaven,* a group of intentionally stereotypical Asian American women (pictured here at a performance in Zurich, Switzerland, in 2007) give voice to utterly inappropriate, liberating opinions—yet underneath the ensuing laughter is the discomfort of confronting Lee's brilliant depiction of contemporary bigotry. ©*Walter Bieri/Keystone/AP Images*

In fact, while Baker's plays are certainly provocative, they are the opposite of flashy. Characters pause, stammer, and engage in the awkward and minor activities that constitute daily life: they clean up popcorn, take a cigarette break, gossip, and sip lukewarm tea. And they wait, and wait, and wait in long stretches of silence. Baker's work moves these marginal activities to the center of the action; we, as audience members, are aware of characters' rich inner lives but witness only their disconnected outer signs. Yet these moments add up to something bigger than simple minutiae—they constitute a sense of humanity and at times of surreality. Actual life, after all, is quite strange if taken at face value. We all fill our speeches with non sequiturs, elisions, mumbled asides, and half-forgotten thoughts.

However, as we learned in an earlier section, speakability is not the same as a real-life transcription. Baker's genius is, like that of her dramatic hero Anton Chekhov, to find the musicality in the everyday. (It is no wonder that she adapted Chekhov's *Uncle Vanya*, a masterpiece of misunderstandings and missed opportunities.)

Baker gained national recognition in 2009 with *Circle Mirror Transformation*, a play that details a series of acting exercises at a community theatre in a small town. (Raised in western Massachusetts, she sets many of her plays in isolated locales in the Northeast.) The play captures the odd intimacy that can emerge among strangers. She followed this up with *The Aliens*, about a trio of young and middle-aged men at a café in Vermont. Here, Baker's vision became distilled into a clear depiction of fumbling attempts to connect. At one point, the teenager who works at the café expresses frustration with his mother, whom he has just snapped at over the phone: "She like—she does this thing? She does this thing where she like asks what kind of—like if I want cauliflower or carrots with dinner and then if I like tell her carrots she's like well your father doesn't—and it's like just like whatever I say

The work of Annie Baker explores the seemingly banal spaces in our day-to-day lives. Her breakout play *Circle Mirror Transformation* (pictured here in its 2009 production, directed by frequent collaborator Sam Gold) finds profundity and insight in the relationships that develop at a small-town acting class. Baker's genius is to find beauty in the flawed and messy way her characters communicate. ©*Sara Krulwich/The New York Times/Redux*

she like contradicts me and I'm just like—Nevermind. It's stupid." His conversation partner nods appreciatively but then launches into an unrelated monologue about how he couldn't stop saying the word "ladder" when he was a child. He then proceeds to say "ladder" 127 times in a row. The dramatic action—the conflict—comes to a screeching halt, but midway through his recitation he begins to cry. Why? We will soon find out, but only obliquely; we may still not be satisfied.

Baker's 2017 work *The Antipodes* similarly features a mystery that never becomes solved. A group of executives sit around a bland conference table and start brainstorming ideas for . . . what, exactly? A TV show? movie? Some kind of narrative, surely, but that isn't important. What *is*

important is how they interact with each other, the casual and imperceptible ways they jostle for dominance and the way they listen—or more often *don't*. A paradox of her work is that we gain a depth of characterization despite— or perhaps because of—the characters' refusal to open up.

No other playwright on this list matches Baker's obsession with richness: she oversees and thinks through each play's design carefully, going so far as to choose the precise quality of film that will be projected in her 2013 Pulitzer Prize–winning play *The Flick*. The film isn't even visible to the audience, who will see only the shimmering beam of light from the projector, yet Baker's vision is so exacting that only one particular hue will do. It is this balance of intense care and seeming haphazardness that marks her plays as singular: what seems chaotic and structurally messy is, in fact, the result of a deep, obsessive mastery of the craft.

TARELL ALVIN MCCRANEY

When Tarell Alvin McCraney accepted his 2016 Best Adapted Screenplay Oscar for *Moonlight*—which went on to win Best Picture—much of the world learned who he was. But to many passionate theatregoers around the world, he was already quite famous. Heralded early on as a *wunderkind*, McCraney began attracting attention in 2007 when his play *The Brothers Size* premiered in New York while he was still in graduate school at the Yale School of Drama. *The Brothers Size* proved a deeply ambitious work that wove together Yoruban mythology with a richly textured look at small-town black life in Louisiana. It also proved to be only the beginning of his charmed career: the next year, at the age of twenty-eight, McCraney

received more raves for *Wig Out!,* his joyous celebration of drag queens. He also went on to create a sequel (*Marcus, Or the Secret of Sweet*) and a prequel (*In the Red and Brown Water*) to *The Brothers Size,* along with several other works for theatre companies in the United States and in England, where he served as the International Playwright in Residence for the Royal Shakespeare Company in 2008.

McCraney's work can be both epic and specific. His plays center on specific locales—often in the Deep South—yet his language is infused with poetry that makes the struggles of his characters seem almost cosmic. His play *Head of Passes,* an adaptation of the biblical Book of Job (in which God tests Job, a loyal and faithful man, with increasingly punishing trials and losses), perfectly demonstrates this balance in its richness of detail and deeply felt gravity. Set in a rambling house in the titular area, where the Mississippi River meets the Gulf of Mexico, the play's first half observes a familiar drama unfolding: estranged children return, old family traumas are revisited, and

In Tarell Alvin McCraney's 2017 *Head of Passes*, based loosely on the Book of Job, Shelah (Phylicia Rashad, *center*) celebrates her birthday with friends and family before her life—literally and figuratively—collapses around her.
©Caitlin Ochs/The New York Times/Redux

sibling rivalries resume. We feel as if we are watching a meticulously crafted midcentury American play, not an explosive new work.

However, the second half of the play literally destroys this impression: the house collapses in a torrential hurricane and nearly everyone dies, leaving only the matriarch of the family standing in a pool of water. Like Job, she cries out to God; unlike Job, she hears only silence in response. The effect is devastating: we feel as if we are witnessing mythology unfold, but we also—due to McCraney's gift for depth of characterization—feel as if we know *this specific* woman alongside the archetype she represents. It is highly credible even though it is fantastic, and the questions the play prompts are both profound (Can a biblical tragedy occur among the everyday? Can we continue living if we are not affirmed in the face of devastating loss?) and pertinent to our current moment (What does it mean for a black family to take on a dramatic model of suffering—tragedy—that was originally created for white audiences and by white authors?).

McCraney has long demonstrated a knack for tapping into our cultural present while simultaneously linking human lives to the transcendent. His ability to imbue characters with poetry is reminiscent of his mentor, August Wilson, whom McCraney assisted in a production of *Radio Golf,* Wilson's final play. Like Wilson, McCraney demonstrates an interest in the complex histories of black culture—histories both horrifying, as with slavery and incarceration, and uplifting, as with African myth and the creation of community. Currently McCraney's rise suggests he may reach the heights of recognition that Wilson attained; in 2017—the same year as his Oscar win—McCraney also became head of the playwriting program at his alma mater, the Yale School of Drama. He has received a MacArthur Fellowship, along with many other awards, and already has new work on the horizon.

SUZAN-LORI PARKS

The plays of Suzan-Lori Parks do not merely create new characters or situations within a recognizable world; they invent new worlds altogether. Her work abides its own internal logic, far from the recognizable structure and language of traditional—or much untraditional—drama. Many of her plays, such as *In the Blood* (mentioned briefly in the chapter "What Is a Play?"), include passages of wounded, broken, misspelled, and abbreviated language. At times the script marks the name of characters without giving them any lines, as if they wanted to speak but couldn't; rather than "pause," they "rest" as if playing a musical score. And *In the Blood* is one of her more accessible works! Other

plays feature long footnotes and murky stage directions and descriptions of place—the "great hole" that lies "in the middle of nowhere" in *The America Play*, as noted in the section on stageability, is a perfect example of this. Speeches are slurred and filled with inscrutable slang, as if characters were making up a language on the spot.

Yet these many seemingly "difficult" aspects combine onstage to electric effect. Her work is a perfect example of how speakability and flow can result from language that looks difficult on the page. Her speeches reveal themselves brilliantly and musically. Like Samuel Beckett, the modernist master, Parks gets at essential and theatrical truths through abstraction, not direct imitation of reality. Parks's first play, *The Sinners' Place*, earned her cum laude honors in English but was turned down for production by her college's theatre department on the grounds that it lacked stageability. Her next play, however, *Imperceptible Mutabilities in the Third Kingdom* (1989), won her a coveted Obie Award and led to subsequent positions as resident dramatist at both Yale Repertory Theatre and the New York Public Theater, each of which has subsequently produced several of her plays. Her later work, the critically acclaimed *Father Comes Home from the Wars (Parts 1, 2, and 3)*, signals new directions: while retaining her trademark abstract touches and lyrical, otherworldly language, this play follows a more traditional structure. Indeed, its narrative derives from one of the most traditional works in the literary canon, *The Odyssey*. Parks transplants Homer's story from ancient Greece to Civil War–ravaged America to turn a primal, mythological event into the tale of a slave who enlists to fight with the Confederate Army.

While universal in her themes, the specificity of Parks's work has long focused on the black experience in America, in all of its trauma—slavery, lynchings, poverty, discrimination, minstrelsy, and racism. In her hands, such horrors become both grotesque and beautiful, terrifying and sublime. With the speech of Mrs. Aretha Saxon from *Mutabilities*, for example, Parks vividly and indelibly describes the process of packing human cargo into the *Brookes*, an English slave ship:

> Six seven eight nine. Thupp. Ten eleven twelve thirteen fourteen fifteen sixteen. Thupp. Seventeen. Eighteen nineteen twenty twenty-one. And uh little bit. Thuuup. Thuup. Gotta know thuh size. Thup. Gotta know thuh size exact. Thup. Got people comin. Hole house full. They gonna be kin? Could be strangers. How many kin kin I hold. Whole hold full. How many strangers. Depends on thuh size.

The rhythm of her sentences, with their repetitions of sounds and noises, creates a startling, poetic effect.

A black slave named "Hero" (played by Sterling K. Brown) is attacked by the white Colonel (Ken Marks), who declares, "I am grateful every day that God made me white," in Suzan-Lori Parks's Civil War drama, *Father Comes Home from the Wars*. This thrilling 2014 production at the New York Public Theater includes Parts 1, 2, and 3 of what Parks plans to become a nine-part epic drama, modeled in part on Homer's *Odyssey*. The production was directed by Jo Bonney and coproduced by the American Repertory Theatre in Cambridge, Massachusetts. ©*Sara Krulwich/The New York Times/Redux*

Parks's other work has also discovered startling resonance in the ravages of history. *Venus* (1996) portrays the true story of a nineteenth-century African woman, Saartjie Baartman, who, because of her enormous buttocks, was displayed throughout America as a freak. Parks's Pulitzer Prize–winning *Topdog/Underdog*, staged by playwright-director George C. Wolfe at the Public Theater in 2001, while set in present-day America is also fixed on the past. It features a violently contentious pair of brothers named Lincoln and Booth. Lincoln, now a retired master of Three-Card Monte, a sidewalk con game, is impersonating President Lincoln in an arcade show, while Booth, a shoplifter, acts as a competitor in a complex game of sibling and status rivalry. Parks's continuing, vital presence on the American theatre scene continues to inspire and disturb: the Signature Theatre, in New York, devoted its entire 2016–2017 season to her work, and the packed houses and rapturous reviews show that she remains frighteningly relevant.

AYAD AKHTAR

The most-produced play of the 2014–2015 season of American theatre was Ayad Akhtar's *Disgraced*; and the most produced playwright of that season was . . . Ayad Akhtar. There is clearly something deeply pertinent about his work—it is finding deep resonance with our cultural moment.

Akhtar's plays are not simply ripped-from-the-headlines affairs. They do more than stage our culture's latest neuroses (although they do that too). They reach into something primal, even feral, that lurks under our polite decorum. Like other masters of the domestic chamber drama, such as Edward Albee and Yasmina Reza, Akhtar knows that the most seemingly joyful moments of conversation are often the most fraught and fragile. So it is with *Disgraced*, a realist work that charts the downward course of a dinner at a posh Upper East Side apartment in New York. Its characters are precisely drawn individuals but also seem to stand in for different voices and communities: there's

Amir, an American Muslim lawyer; Amir's white artist wife, Emily; Amir's nephew, Abe; Jory, a black female lawyer; and Jory's husband Isaac, a Jewish art dealer.

It would seem obvious how a gathering of these characters would proceed, and yet Akhtar masterfully subverts our expectations. It is Amir who seems to dismiss many facets of Islamic culture—to the consternation of his nephew—and Emily who embraces Islamic art (and who vocalizes her pain at the racism that Amir faces). Yet Amir also controversially defends an imprisoned imam (an Islamic leader). He is torn between his heritage and his journey of self-definition. While certainly speaking to our times, Akhtar also draws on an ancient recipe for inner conflict. Needless to say, an outer conflict also ensues, replete with screams, accusations, and even spousal abuse. These explosive events are all credible; they all build logically from previous events. Yet Akhtar is not afraid of ambiguity. Even though *Disgraced*'s titular word appears in a speech by Abe about the mistreatment of Muslims by the West—"They disgraced us. And then they pretend they don't understand the rage we've got?"—the play ends without settling *who* is truly disgraced: Amir for his repression? Emily for her casual adoption of Islam? Abe for feeling historical injustice? When *Disgraced* won the 2013 Pulitzer Prize for Drama, it conferred a sense of timelessness to a work that also questions (without settling) the passion of our most closely held beliefs.

Akhtar has been producing work at a fervent clip. He is the rare author to achieve success in prose and dramatic forms; his mostly autobiographical novel *American Dervish* told the story of a Muslim boy's upbringing in a small midwestern town. His interest also extends to film: a screenplay written while he was at Columbia University became the 2005 movie *The War Within*—which he also starred in. While this array of skills is impressive, it is his playwriting that has garnered the most praise and attention. In 2017, his play *Junk* was one of the most anticipated new works on Broadway, with feature after feature in major newspapers expressing their excitement.

Junk examines a different sense of religious faith—instead of Islam, it focuses its sights on the church of money. The play details the heady days of the 1980s, when Wall Street lured alpha males by the dozens into its fold. But like Shakespeare's history plays—an influence on Akhtar—this play has some chilling messages for our own current day. "You *are* what you *have*," advises one broker in *Junk*; and the terrifying materialism of this sentence (and the religious fervor with which it is expressed) reads today like an omen from the past. With characteristic precision, Akhtar has once again cut to the core of our current obsessions and taboos. Whatever topic he chooses to examine next, it surely will prove just as relevant and alarming in equal measure: a cracked mirror held up to the present day.

In Ayad Akhtar's Pultizer Prize–winning *Disgraced* (pictured here in its 2012 Lincoln Center production), the tensions and rifts between an interracial couple slowly boil over into shocking violence. Amir is played by Aasif Mandvi (*right*), and Emily is played by Heidi Ambruster (*left*). ©Sara Krulwich/The New York Times/Redux

Photo Essay: Playwright Young Jean Lee

1. Lee directs a 2017 production of *Straight White Men* at the Steppenwolf Theatre Company, in Chicago. ©*Joel Moorman/Steppenwolf Theatre Company*

Young Jean Lee is one of the most exciting playwrights working today. She became a sensation in New York's downtown theatre scene with provocative, critically acclaimed plays such as *The Shipment, Untitled Feminist Show,* and *Songs of the Dragons Flying to Heaven.* Donovan Sherman, one of your authors, spoke with Lee about her collaborative process, the need to be "egoless" in the theatre, and advice for young playwrights today. (For more about Lee's work, see the section "A Sampling of Current American Playwrights" in this chapter.)

DS: I'd love to hear how you define what you do. How do you think about what your role is?

YJL: I'm the leader of a collaboration. I like to work with lots of voices, lots of input from actors and assistant directors and associate directors and my dramaturg and strangers and audience members and people who are Facebook friends. I like lots and lots of input. And so I sort of see my job as being a little bit unconventional for a playwright, because the idea of a playwright is that they sit in their room by themselves at their desk, and then they just write this thing and then it becomes part of this collaborative process. And for me, from day one the whole process is collaborative and I'm working with other people and I'm just leading the charge.

DS: There are some specific moments in your plays in which you point out something in the dramatic action, or you reference the specific actors; it sounds like that's a sort of byproduct of this collaborative nature for work.

YJL: Definitely. For me it's difficult to just look at a script as a literary element, as opposed to at the same time being a documentation of what happened.

DS: It is a snapshot of the process, not a primary artifact from which other people must interpret it.

YJL: I would never say that the scripts are so detailed in the stage directions that any director had to follow that exactly. At the same time, there's a specificity that is essential to the work.

DS: How do you relate, today, to your time as a graduate student studying Renaissance theatre? Do you think about drama in a different way than you do now?

YJL: I think that all of the reading of Shakespeare that I did—so much Shakespeare and Ben Jonson and [Christopher] Marlowe, so much great drama in that period. People think of Shakespeare today as being this canonical, traditional, almost conservative playwright, but Shakespeare's *crazy.* He's a messy, crazy writer; he loves having strange characters and criminals and liars. So I think that reading so much Shakespeare

2. Lee reworks her script while chatting with Theo Germaine, who plays the Stagehand-in-Charge, during a rehearsal for *Straight White Men* at the Steppenwolf. ©*Joel Moorman/Steppenwolf Theatre Company*

3. *Straight White Men* received acclaim in its run at the Public Theater, in New York City, in 2014. That production, pictured here, featured (*from left to right*) Austin Pendleton, Gary Wilmes, Pete Simpson, and James Stanley. In 2018, it transferred to Broadway. ©*Ruby Washington/The New York Times/Redux*

was great training, actually, for being an experimental playwright. The part that I think was extremely destructive was the critical thinking that I was trained to do. It is helpful in the sense that because of my critical training my brain has all those pathways that are very useful when I'm in the editing process, in the later stages of a project. But in the early stages, when your brain just needs to be able to be creative and come up with stuff and not have that editing function on, it's very bad.

DS: That's interesting because in a way your work is like great criticism. It challenges my assumptions just like great criticism does. That seems to be one of the themes in your work: not taking anything for granted.

YJL: Absolutely. You know, I took one of those personality tests. I remember taking the test and I expected that I was going to be a creative artist, and actually the category that I got was "scientist." And I think that what you are describing is actually the result of an almost scientific approach to making a show, where there's constant testing on actual audience members. And that's why it's so collaborative also, because I'm constantly testing responses.

DS: The first thing that you mentioned is that you were a leader of a collaboration. But what does it mean to lead a process that is essentially collaborative?

YJL: What it means is that you have to be sort of egoless. And if you're the leader, and you get the final word on everything—and I've been very much in control of the process: I'm the producer and the director and the writer and nobody above me is calling the shots—as the person with the final word, I come into the room and I'm like: I've gathered you all here because you know more about a bunch of things that I need to know about in order to do a good job on this play. Even though I actually have all of the power in this room in a traditional sense, I actually am pretty low status when it comes to level of expertise because every show is a different genre that I'm not familiar with. And I am never the expert when I come into the room. So people in the room see that even though I'm in charge, it's really not about me. It's about the project. And this causes the collaborators to then become very egoless.

DS: That's a really compelling way to think of it: you are both without any ego and also the leader. How then do you choose your collaborators?

YJL: There's always a conversational aspect of the collaboration and you can tell pretty quickly if someone is going to be a fun person to talk to you or not. You know, it's almost like a date. You know: Do they seem narcissistic? Do they babble on and on? You just watch out for all these things and you just find those people who are capable of really listening and who are insightful and who are articulate. And that's probably the most important quality in a collaborator for me.

DS: So now you have a play headed to Broadway. And it's fascinating to think of *Straight White Men* on Broadway because it is in some ways an engagement with a tradition that has flourished on Broadway: a bunch of men in a room hashing out their problems. So the play both has the ability to deliver what I imagine a Broadway audience is expecting, a traditional kind of family drama. And yet it is also a critical engagement with that tradition. Is that something that you were conscious of in the conception of the play?

YJL: All that was done very consciously. The problem in the play is that the main character [Matt, a forty-something man who lives with his father] doesn't have a hero's journey that is acceptable to his family, and the play also doesn't have an acceptable hero's journey. Therefore the play's form reflects its content because you don't get the traditional hero overcoming obstacles to achieve it. The play is *structured* that way but, because what he wants is not considered something that somebody should want in his position, it doesn't work that way.

DS: How do you consider an audience's reaction? There seems to be a kind of almost clichéd answer, which is "Not at all, it's all about the work." And yet there's always a consideration of the audience in your work.

4. Much like her recent *Straight White Men,* Lee's 2009 play *The Shipment* challenged conceptions of race; the play's first half features black performers embodying stereotypically "black" roles, whereas the second half (pictured here) details a traditional drawing-room comedy, with the same performers taking on stereotypically "white" roles. Shown here is its 2009 premiere at the Kitchen, in New York City; from left to right are Amelia Workman, Douglas Scott Streater, Okieriete Onaodowan, Mikéah Ernest Jennings, and Prentice Onayemi.
©Sara Krulwich/The New York Times/Redux

YJL: Constantly. I told you that I have almost a scientific approach because I'm constantly thinking about testing it in front of audience members.

DS: You are from a small town. What kind of advice do you have for people without access to Broadway, or to touring companies, about how they can start making theatre in those circumstances?

YJL: I would say that the most valuable thing they can do is to read plays, as many plays as they can. Go to the library, and read through every play they have. And I would also advise them to read the *New York Times* and read the theatre reviews and Critics' Picks so they can know what types of plays are being written in New York right now. A lot of those plays end up being published, or are already published, and if the library doesn't have them, they can buy the plays, or they might ask their library to buy the play so they can see what's being done by contemporary playwrights. One of the obstacles that I encountered early on was that I had read so many classic plays and had no idea of what theatre people were doing today. And if you want to be produced, you need to know what's happening now and what's been happening in the last twenty years.

DS: What was the moment when you first encountered what was happening at the time and broke out of the more classical tradition that you were reading?

YJL: I had looked up all of the playwriting faculty at the Yale School of Drama—and now actually I'm teaching at Yale in that Master's program—and I read a play by each of the playwrights teaching. And there was one really weird play called *70 Scenes of Halloween* by this playwright named Jeffrey M. Jones. And so I reached out to him and asked him if he would meet with me. And he met with me and said, "If my play was your favorite play, then you like weird experimental theatre, and you're going to like all these other people." So he gave me this list of artists, and so I went to New York and started seeing all of these people's work. And that was my introduction.

Chapter

5

Designers and Technicians

©Geraint Lewis

WHEN AN ACTOR FIRST STEPPED onto the stage as Jocasta, the tormented Queen of Thebes in Sophocles' ancient Greek tragedy *Oedipus Rex*, he wore clothing similar, but not identical, to his everyday outfit. It was a robe, just as he would wear to the marketplace, but its shape and color were altered to indicate that he was playing a woman—and not just a woman, but a royal woman. This robe serves the basic purpose of design: to transform something so that it may be seen, by a willing viewer, as something else.

There would have been other differences, too. The robe's sleeves would have been narrower than the sleeves of an everyday gown so the actor's movements could be clearly seen from the back of the amphitheatre. Also, the actor would have worn a mask to enlarge his face, amplify his voice, and provide a fixed expression that even from a long distance could be quickly seen as both powerful and tragic.

When the costumed and masked "Jocasta" strode through the giant *skene* (stagehouse) door onto the sun-drenched stage, the audience saw not an actor walking onto a platform but a tragic queen leaving the royal palace to greet her equally gowned and masked husband, King Oedipus, who was grieving with his citizens on the palace steps.

Nothing in the text of *Oedipus* refers to the clothing, mask, or door just described, yet these elements, which create the look of the play, are absolutely crucial to the drama in its performance. They constitute its design: its costumes (gowns), scenery (door, wall), makeup (mask), lighting (sun), and sound (voice as amplified through the mask). And that design has artistic, as well as dramatic, characteristics: color, scale, line, balance, harmony, punctuation, and surprise. All these design elements came into play with the first drama, and all have even greater importance today.

The playwright creates the play's words, and the actors execute its actions and impersonate its characters, but the theatre designers determine what the stage and characters look like. Indeed, design comprises most of what we see when we go to the theatre—and much of what we hear. Designers, and the technicians who implement their ideas, create what the actors wear, sit on, and stand before. They determine how the actors are illuminated and how they—and their environment—sound. Sometimes they even create what we smell. Nearly every sense in the theatre has been carefully planned by the designers; they help create the experienced world of the play.

The Design Process

Put simply, design emerges from what occurs or is implied in the text. The action Sophocles outlined in *Oedipus Rex* implies a door, so most designers provide one. The moment also requires a chorus and characters that enter and leave the staging area, so suitable points of entry/exit are created as well. Sometimes—even in ancient times—characters physically fly through the air, so machines are designed and built to execute these superhuman actions.

Today, of course, scenery, lighting, and costumes can create realistic-looking environments, such as living rooms, Roman piazzas, barrooms, and butcher shops—and imagined locales such as the Land of Oz. They also can create uniquely conceived visualizations that layer interpretations and social, political, or aesthetic references on the scripts they accompany. Sound designs can create scores that enhance the play's actions with musical themes to emphasize romance, tension, or grief—or they can punctuate and disrupt the play's actions with the cacophonous noise of traffic, jungle cries, or warfare.

The first stage in creating a play's design is conceptual. At this time, often well before actors have even been cast, ideas emerge from reading the script, researching its context, and imagining its potential impact on the expected audience. These ideas are shared with the play's director (who may have initiated this process with ideas of their own), playwright (if a living playwright is part of the conceptual process), and other designers. Although the director normally oversees these conversations, artistic collaboration is absolutely fundamental to this conceptual period of a play production's creation.

For the visual designer, conceptual ideas may be almost instantly translated into mental images, both general and specific. Such images may be expressed first in words—such as "gloomy clouds," "Picasso angles," "delicate archways," "broken bottles," "black, black, black"—but they soon will lead to attempts at representation: quick sketches, photos torn from magazines, color samples, or swatches of fabric. The sound designer may likewise contemplate impressions of "medieval chanting," "random gunfire," "baroque harpsichords," or "wind in the reeds," and then compose or hunt down sounds that could give others on the design/directing team a sense of where they are heading at this stage.

Designers follow their own schedule. Scenery and costumes typically have longer timelines, so when rehearsals begin, most of these elements have been set in place. Meanwhile, sound, video, and lighting typically have more flexible processes. Designers are often responding to the work that comes out of the rehearsal process as the actors and directors generate new ideas about the staging, so communication among these elements is of the utmost importance. Though certain elements may already be determined, the play's vision may change, so designers who make decisions later in the process must ensure that they are still in harmony with aspects that were finalized earlier in the process.

Gradually, though, a comprehensive design emerges that is normally guided by the director and, of course, the budget. For the visual designer, a physical presentation of proposed designs normally involves colors (primary, earthy, gloomy, pastel), textures (rough, shiny, delicate, steely), shapes (angular, spiraling, blockish, globular), balance (symmetrical, natural, fractal), scale (towering, compressed, vast), style (realistic, romantic, period, abstract, expressionist), and levels of detail (gross, fine, delicate), as rendered in drawings, digitized representations, three-dimensional models, fabric samples, and other media. For the sound designer, designs may include music underscoring (retreating brass bands, lush violins, ominous chords), ambient noises (distant sirens, gunfire, ocean waves), and enhanced, reverberated, or digitally manipulated live sounds (voices, footsteps, door slams).

All these representations are shared among the artistic and technical staff, analyzed for cost and required labor in construction, and evaluated for their individual merit as well as their joint impact. How will the combination of all these designs feel? How will it propel the action of the play? What will it communicate to the expected audience? How will it tie the actors to the audience, the drama to the theatre in which it is staged, and the play's events to the real life that goes on outside the theatre's door?

Those are the questions the designer considers from the initial moment of conception to the opening performance.

Peter McKintosh's realistic set and costume design for this 2015 London production of Noel Coward's *Hay Fever* help anchor the comic performances with rich detail and naturalism. Here Simon Shepard (*left*) and Felicity Kendall (*right*) play a married couple who quarrel over drinks. *©Elliott Franks/eyevine/Redux*

What Design Does

Theatrical design in the twenty-first century presents a wide-open field for artistic creativity. While a play normally has thousands of lines for the actors to speak and hundreds of implicit or explicit stage directions for the director to stage, it rarely provides more than brief descriptions for its setting or costumes. At the beginning of *Waiting for Godot*, for example, Samuel Beckett simply writes, "A country road. A tree. Evening." He then launches directly into the opening dialogue, leaving us to wonder: What sort of road should this be? What sort of tree? Where is it in relation to the road? And how dark an

"evening" is it? Later in the play Beckett provides another stage description: "The light suddenly fails. In a moment it is night. The moon rises at back, mounts in the sky, stands still, shedding a pale light on the scene." But how is all this accomplished? How much darker does the stage get? What does the "moon" look like: full? crescent? How quickly does it rise? How suddenly does it stop? And what is it made of: projected light? a wooden cutout on a wire? And if a wire, is it meant to be seen or should it be invisible to the audience? Or is the moon simply a lantern carried by an actor—as in the *Pyramus and Thisbe* play embedded in Shakespeare's *A Midsummer Night's Dream*? And what else might be there besides the road, tree, and moon?

Some of the most fundamental elements—water and fire—can also be the most exciting. Here, in Lucas Hnath's *Red Speedo* (2016), the audience can see actors submerged in an actual swimming pool. The lighting mixes with the set design to startling effect, adding texture to the bright-blue water and drawing our focus to the actor's movement and, of course, to the titular piece of swimwear, worn here by Alex Breaux. Set by Riccardo Hernandez, lighting by Yi Zhao. ©*Joan Marcus*

And what do Godot's actors wear? We read in the dialogue of bowlers, boots, and coats, but what do these garments look like? What colors should they be? How should they be worn? Are they clean or dirty? Are they well-fitted, or too large, or too small?

More questions: How old should the characters appear to be? Should any have long hair? facial hair? fat bellies? missing teeth? And what sounds might surround them: birds? wind? passing cars or airplanes? sounds of war? nothing? Should the characters' voices sound natural? be amplified? reverberate?

Those sorts of initial questions are posed and addressed by the production's designers and the technicians who execute their designs. But they also lead to questions of a different order. What are the dominant feelings the audience members might be expected to experience when they first see the stage? What feelings should be evoked afterward? Should audience members find the environment mundane? shocking? hopeful? depressing? Is the environment human or otherworldly? ancient or futuristic? archetypal or unpredictable? What world should the audience enter when the curtain or lights come up and the play begins?

There are certainly as many designs for *Waiting for Godot* as there are designers to tackle this particular script.

The same is true of any play. No matter how detailed the playwright's directions may be, the design team and their collaborators ordinarily shape the production's visual and audio elements as they see fit.

Scenery

Scenery is usually what we first see—either when the curtain rises in a traditional proscenium production or as we enter the theatre if there is no curtain—and the scenic designer is usually listed first among designers in a theatre poster or program. Scenery, however, is a relatively new design area. Costume, makeup, and masks are far more ancient. Scenery played little part in early Greek or Roman drama, save to afford entry, exit, and sometimes expanded acting space or, later in the classical era, to provide a decorative backdrop. In much Asian theatre, scenery remains rare or even nonexistent; this is the case in public presentations of Indian kathakali, most Chinese xiqu, and—apart from the elaborate stage house itself—in Japanese noh drama as well. Nor was scenery of paramount importance in the outdoor medieval or outdoor public Elizabethan theatres, apart from a few painted set pieces made to resemble walls, trees, caves, thrones,

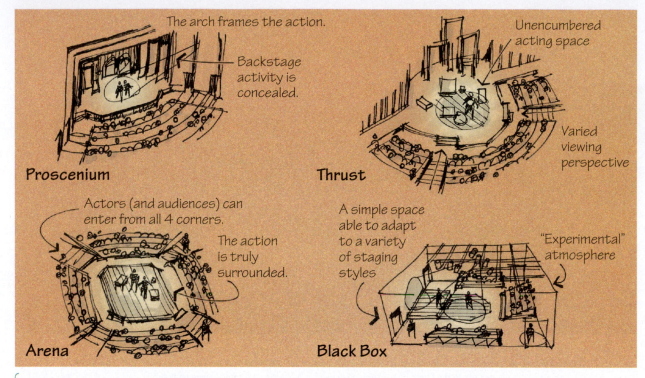

The arch frames the action.

Backstage activity is concealed.

Proscenium

Unencumbered acting space

Varied viewing perspective

Thrust

Actors (and audiences) can enter from all 4 corners.

The action is truly surrounded.

Arena

A simple space able to adapt to a variety of staging styles

"Experimental" atmosphere

Black Box

Illustrated here are the four basic staging formats: proscenium, thrust, arena, and black box. Deciding where to locate the stage in relation to the audience is the first consideration in theatre design. ©*John von Szeliski*

tombs, porches, and the occasional "Hellmouth." Prior to the seventeenth century, most of drama's scenic aspects were part of, or dictated by, the architecture of the theatre structure itself.

The development of European indoor stages, with their artificial lighting and flat scenery, fostered the first great phase of scenic design. Working indoors, protected from rain and wind, the scenic designers of the Renaissance for the first time were able to erect and position painted canvases and temporary wooden structures without fear of having the colors run and the supports blow away. Additionally, with the advent of controllable indoor lighting in the nineteenth century (first by gas, then by electricity), designers could illuminate settings and acting areas as they wished and leave other parts of the theatre building, such as the audience area, in the dark for the first time. Designers could now create both realistic illusions and extravagant visual spectacles—and have the audience focus on their work without worrying about the weather outside the theatre doors.

The result was that a new class of theatre artists rose to prominence. Early designers such as Sebastiano Serlio (1475–1554), Aristotile da Sangallo (1481–1551), and Giacomo Torelli (1608–1678) in Italy; Inigo Jones

(1573–1652) in England; and the Frenchman Jean Bérain (1637–1711) became as prominent as the playwrights whose plays they designed. Indoor stage scenery, painted in exquisite perspective, took on even greater sophistication under the artists of the Royal and Romantic eras in the eighteenth and nineteenth centuries. The proscenium format, which was created primarily to show off elegant settings, has largely dominated theatre architecture ever since.

The painted flat scenery that the proscenium gave rise to has been only one of many competing scenic formats in the modern era, usually divided into two general categories. *Realistic scenery* attempts to depict, often in great detail, a specific time and place in the real world where the play's events are presumed to take place. *Metaphoric scenery* favors, instead, visual images that seek to evoke (or to suggest, abstract, or make a visual statement about) the production's intended theme, mood, or social/political implications. Metaphoric scenery tends to remind us—at least when we first see it—that we are in a theatre, not in a bedroom or butcher shop, and seeks to draw us more deeply into the play's larger issues and concerns.

Realistic settings carry on the tradition of "illusionism" established in eighteenth-century painted scenery. At that

Shakespeare's plays can be staged in any number of ways, from the realistic to the metaphoric. The latter technique became world-famous when Sally Jacobs designed Peter Brook's 1970 production of Shakespeare's *A Midsummer Night's Dream* (shown here) for England's Royal Shakespeare Company. Employing a plain white set with rectangular walls and doors, clothing from all eras and of all styles, actors who were hoisted on cables when their characters fell asleep, and a circuslike atmosphere overall, the play proved an extraordinary success and toured throughout the world for nearly a decade, changing the way classical plays were seen almost everywhere. *Photo by Reg Wilson ©RSC 1970*

In Sean Graham's 2015 London production of *Othello* (shown here), produced by the Frantic Assembly, director Sean Graham and designer Laura Hopkins had Desdemona (Kirsty Oswald, *right*) and Emilia (Leila Crerar, *left*) discuss their views about men and their "peevish jealousies" while wearing modern clothes in a shabby and totally realistic bathroom of the present day. *©theatrepix/Alamy Stock Photo*

time, an ingeniously arranged assembly of *wings* (vertical, flat scenery pieces to the left and right of the stage), *borders* (horizontal, flat scenery pieces hung above the stage), and *drops* (short for "backdrops": large, flat scenery pieces at the rear of the stage), along with the use of forced perspective (a technique that creates the illusion of depth on a flat surface), created the lifelike appearance of offices, dining rooms, servants' quarters, and factory yards of many a dramatist's imagination. By the nineteenth century, this *wing-and-drop set*, as it became known, yielded to the *box set* (sometimes called a *black box set*): a three-dimensional construction of interconnected hard-covered "flats," representing the walls and occasionally the ceilings of a real room, which was then filled with furniture and objects taken from real-world environments. The box set is very much alive today and is indeed a major scenic format for contemporary domestic drama (particularly comedy) on New York's Broadway, in London's West End, and at many community and college theatres across America. Though no longer in fashion (it rarely wins design awards), the box set fulfills the staging requirements of a great many domestic comedies, thrillers, and linearly structured dramas, particularly those requiring interior settings. Moreover, by adding three-dimensional features, box sets allow for acting and playwriting opportunities unachievable in wing-and-drop scenery by providing solid, three-dimensional staircases to descend, doors to slam, windows to climb through,

With an eye to European modernism, Robert Edmond Jones revolutionized American design. He helped lead the "New Stagecraft" movement, which emphasized clear-eyed minimalism with selective attention to realistic elements. Here, his elegant design for a 1925 production of *Hamlet,* starring John Barrymore, emphasizes the title character's loneliness and isolation. ©*Mander and Mitchenson/University of Bristol/ArenaPal/The Image Works*

bookcases to stash revolvers in, and grandfather clocks in which to hide characters. Public fascination with realistic scenery reached its high-water mark in the theatre of the late nineteenth century, during which the box set helped foster a uniquely architectural theory of theatre: that it should represent life exactly as it is normally lived, but with one wall removed so the audience could look in upon it.

Metaphoric scenic design, in contrast, tends to be more conceptual than literal, more kinetic than stable, and more theatrical than photographic. The use of scenic metaphor is hardly new. In Chinese xiqu opera, sparse elements such as a desk or chair could denote a wide array of items—a ship, a throne room, a rock—according to its precise placement onstage and how the actors interact with it. In his prologue to *Henry V*, Shakespeare apologizes for the "unworthy scaffold" of his stage and begs his audience to use their "imaginary forces" to complete his scenic illusion—which during that play probably included a door opening

under the stage balcony where the audience could imagine the English army storming "unto the breach" of a castle wall in France. These are scenic "abstractions" in the most elemental sense: they present reality by a sign—or simply an invitation to imagine—rather than by trompe l'oeil ("eye-deceiving") realism. One of the most famous examples of metaphoric scenery is Peter Brook's celebrated 1970 production of *A Midsummer Night's Dream*, which featured an all-white box set with hidden doors and trapezes. The design looked nothing like the woods surrounding ancient Athens, but it evoked some of the core themes of the play, such as childhood, whimsy, and the excesses of love and passion.

Realism and *metaphor* are terms best described as end points on a scale, rather than purely exclusive categories. Today, in the United States, we are more likely to see a combination of these elements, in part because of an American tradition in scenery design known as *selective realism* that mingles the expressive with the lifelike. Selective realism began with pioneering designer Robert Edmond Jones, who in turn was influenced by the work of Caspar Neher, a collaborator of theatrical innovator Bertolt Brecht's. Neher's simple, direct sets did not let the audience escape into another world—the sets never let the audience members forget they were watching a play. Jones incorporated some of Neher's ideas but also retained the trappings of realism; in his groundbreaking design for the French melodrama *The Man Who Married a Dumb Wife,* in 1915, Jones used clean, simple lines to create a dynamic and expressive setting that complemented, rather than overwhelmed, the dramatic action. Jones served as a mentor for Jo Mielziner, who would go on to become the most famous and celebrated American scenery designer of all time, known for his landmark collaborations with the playwright Arthur Miller on plays such as *Death of a Salesman* and *All My Sons*. Like Jones, Mielziner created sets that carried metaphorical and poetic meaning without sacrificing the texture of real life.

Postmodern design elements made their appearance in the theatre of the 1980s and 1990s. Because the postmodern emphasizes disharmonies and associations, it travels a somewhat different path from the departures of modernist innovators such as Jones and Mielziner. Much as postmodernism, as a dramatic movement, suggests the "death of isms"—that is, a lack of any single, overarching idea or set of rules—postmodern design disrupts unifying stylistic themes and replaces them with seemingly random assemblages of different and unrelated styles. We can think of postmodern design as "quoting" historical periods or intellectual sources to disrupt the linear flow of consistent imagery or effect. Postmodern design also tends to

Most Americans can imagine what a shabby motel room in California's Mojave Desert might look like, but Bunny Christie's scenic and costume design for this 2006 London production of Sam Shepard's *Fool for Love*, with lighting by Mark Henderson, beautifully sets up the bleak but sensual atmosphere (notice the red dress and the blue and yellow light pouring through the closed blinds) for the action of this explosive drama of lust and longing. Juliette Lewis is the intensely passionate May, and Martin Henderson is her on-and-off boyfriend Eddie. Lindsay Posner directed at the Apollo Theater. ©*Geraint Lewis/Alamy Stock Photo*

reconfigure, or blatantly refer to, the theatre facility itself through, for example, painted scenery deliberately made to look "fake" (particularly in contrast to seemingly arbitrary found objects strewn about the set) and with theatrical devices meant to comment on—and to mock— their own "theatricality."

Successful postmodern design is not merely an intellectual exercise, however. Its ability to combine disparate historical elements and highlight theatrical artifice can, at its best, surprise and provoke the audience while resonating with the deeper themes of the play. Paul Steinberg's design for the 2017 revival of David Henry Hwang's *M. Butterfly* did not create a unified stage picture. Instead, with its towering screens and projected images of Communist propaganda or traditional Chinese art, it created a jarring sensation of eras and styles colliding—much

as the play itself centers on a clash of sensibilities and cultures. Jan Versweyveld's Tony-nominated design for 2016's revival of Arthur Miller's *A View from the Bridge* did not attempt to follow Miller's staging notes at all. Instead, it simply consisted of a white rectangle on the floor and a few benches that surrounded it. As a result, the focus of the play was entirely on the actors—their bodies, dynamics, and exertions—and the play was distilled to its essence: a story of attraction, repulsion, and aggression.

Whatever its guiding philosophy, the best scenic design today is so much more than mere "backing" for the action of a play. When fully realized, it is instead intrinsic to the play's action. It is the place where the play exists; it also determines exactly *how* the play exists and, along with other factors, helps reveal the play's deepest meanings.

◎ Spotlight

Henslowe's Diary

How can we research the theatre design of the past? We can, of course, study the ruins of the buildings or piece together evidence from references to the theatre in literature and in the plays themselves. But occasionally a truly enlightening resource survives from an older era that provides access to the physical reality of playmaking. For the Renaissance—arguably the theatre's greatest period of artistic innovation—we are lucky to have just such a source of information. The diary of Philip Henslowe, the owner of The Rose theatre and producer of many of the plays of Christopher Marlowe, allows us to peer into the day-to-day reality of theatre management.

In the diary, Henslowe listed daily profits for productions, tracked countless loans and expenses, recorded payments for the rights to new works, and portrayed the general ebb and flow of popularity and interest in the Elizabethan stage. One of the most illuminating sections is his inventory of props, which gives us precious insight into the design elements of the past. Some of the props are still unexplained, such as a "black lether gearken, & Nabesathe." Other entries, however, give us a crisper image of celebrated plays, as with "one caldron [cauldron] for the Jew" (for Marlowe's *The Jew of Malta*) and "the sittie of Rome" (a model of that city for Marlowe's *Doctor Faustus*). These fragments have helped us better understand the theatre design of this earlier era as a historical reality.

SCENIC MATERIALS

Scenic designers begin their work with the words of the text and the images in their minds, but at a certain point they begin to concentrate on the materials with which a design will be physically realized. The traditional materials they have been using over the past four centuries—wood, canvas, and paint—were in the twentieth century extended to include nearly every form of matter known to (or created by, or discovered by) humankind, including metals, plastics, masonry, fabrics, earth, stone, fire, water, fog, smoke, rain, light projections, and live animals.

Platforms, flats, and *draperies* are traditional building blocks of stage scenery and remain important. The platform is perhaps most fundamental: as the old saying goes, all theatre requires is "two boards and a passion." The "boards" here represent the platform stage that elevates the actor above the audience. In the chapter "What Is Theatre?" we noted that the only elements truly needed for theatre to exist are a performer and an audience; a platform is one of the simplest ways to separate these two fundamental components. Multiple platforms can create different height levels that provide actors with elevated spaces where they can be seen over the heads of other actors and stage furniture. A stage setting with several well-designed platform levels, normally with the highest at the rear of the proscenium (stage), permits the audience to see dozens of actors simultaneously. Flats—sturdy wooden frames covered in various hard surfaces (such as plywood) and then painted or otherwise treated (cut for doors and windows, adorned with paintings or moldings)—can realistically represent walls, ceilings, or pretty much any surface a designer might wish. Drapery is the great neutral stuff of stage scenery: black hanging drapes are conventional to *mask*, or hide, backstage areas and overhead lighting instruments, and a stage curtain may separate the stage from the audience to indicate, with its rise and fall, the beginning and end of an act or of the entire play.

In addition to these three primary components of stage settings, designers employ special objects, or *set pieces*, that often become important for the themes and action of the play. The tree in *Waiting for Godot*, for example, symbolizes both life and death. The moment when Vladimir and Estragon "do the tree"—a kind of exercise in which each man stands on one leg with the tree between them—is a profound moment in which set piece and actors combine into a single image that echoes the biblical scene of Jesus' crucifixion, where, as Vladimir recollects earlier in the play, two thieves died alongside Christ. Similarly, the massive supply wagon hauled by the title character of Bertolt Brecht's *Mother Courage* creates a powerful visual impression of struggle that may last long after the characters' words are forgotten. Recently, Sarah DeLappe's 2016 play *The Wolves,* about a girls' soccer team, uses elements of the sport as set pieces integral to the dialogue: characters pound the pitch and kick the ball in percussive bursts to emphasize their emotional ferocity. Such unique set pieces spring from the imagination of author, director, designer, and scene technician alike, and in some cases provide the dominant image of the production.

A host of modern materials and technological inventions add to the primary components from which scenery is created. Light as scenery (as opposed to stage lighting, discussed later) can create walls, images,

The "scenery" designed by Katrin Brack for Chekhov's *Ivanov*, as produced by Berlin's Volksbühne in a 2008 Los Angeles tour, consisted almost entirely of stage fog. Within a towering rectangular surround of white fabric, Brack created a "wall of mist" that billowed up from the floor, dividing the stage in half so that characters could make their entrances and exits by simply walking forward or backward through the fog. Because the play is largely about a Russian community beset by depression, despair, and anxiety, Brack's setting—with great support from Henning Streck's lighting—completely captured the confusion of the characters and the malaise of their pre-Revolutionary society. Bulgarian-born Dimiter Gottscheff directed. ©*Thomas Aurin*

and even—with laser holography—three-dimensional visualizations. Banks of sharply focused beams sent through dense atmospheres (enhanced by electronically generated haze that simulates smoke, dust, or fog) can create trenches of light that have the appearance of solidity yet can be made to disappear at the flick of a switch. Image projections (discussed later in the section "Puppets and Projections") can be realistic or abstract, fixed or fluid, precise or indefinite. *Scrim*, a loosely woven, gauzy fabric, long a staple of theatre "magic," is opaque when lit from the audience's side but almost transparent when lit from behind, and is thus employed to make actors and even whole sets seem to instantly appear or disappear.

Stage machinery—power-driven turntables, elevators, hoists, fully tilting stage floors (or "decks"), effortlessly gliding rooms (on "wagons"), and the like—can create a virtual dance of scenic elements to support and accompany the dramatic action. The ancient Greeks well understood the importance of such mechanical devices and used flying machines and rolling carts to deliver gods and corpses to the onstage action. More tricks and sleight-of-hand techniques were invented in the medieval theatre (where they were called "trucs" and "feynts") that imparted a certain sparkle of mystery that Shakespeare and his contemporaries picked up in the Renaissance. For example, *Macbeth* includes three mysterious "apparitions," a reappearing "ghost," and the stage direction "*witches vanish*." Today, the choreography of these appearances and disappearances may be as much a part of the performance as the scenery itself.

Stagecraft

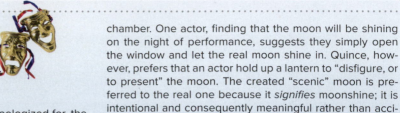

Quince's "Significant" Moon

Shakespeare understood, and at times apologized for, the pictorial limitations of the scenery of his time ("Piece out our imperfections with your thoughts," the chorus advises the audience in the prologue to *Henry V*). But he also appreciated its capacity to signify—rather than merely depict realistically—the world of his plays. In Shakespeare's *A Midsummer Night's Dream*, the character Peter Quince directs a production of "Pyramus and Thisbe" with a group of amateur actors and ponders the "hard things" this play requires, such as the effect of moonshine in a bedroom chamber. One actor, finding that the moon will be shining on the night of performance, suggests they simply open the window and let the real moon shine in. Quince, however, prefers that an actor hold up a lantern to "disfigure, or to present" the moon. The created "scenic" moon is preferred to the real one because it *signifies* moonshine; it is intentional and consequently meaningful rather than accidental and therefore meaningless. To indicate a "wall" in the same play—the other "hard thing"—Quince refrains from bringing in a real wall and instead has another actor put on "some plaster or some loam" so as "to signify wall."

Life may be a tale, as Shakespeare's Macbeth says, "full of sound and fury, signifying nothing," but the theatre tells tales that signify a great many things. Thus scenery's function is not merely to depict but also to signify—to "make a sign," to "be significant."

Sound is also considered by the scenic designer, who must plan for the actors' footfalls as well as for the visual elements around them. The floor of a Japanese noh stage, for example, is meant to be stamped on, and it must be designed and constructed to produce a precisely "tuned" vibration. The European scenographer Joseph Svoboda designed a stage floor for a 1997 production of *Faust* that could be either resonant or silent, depending on the arrangement of mechanisms concealed underneath. When Faust walked upstage, his steps reverberated; when he turned and walked downstage, his steps were suddenly silent—and we knew that the demon Mephistopheles had taken his body.

Properties, or props, and furniture are often handled by artists called *prop masters*, who work under the guidance of the scenic designer. They are crucial not only in establishing realism but also in enhancing mood and style. Although furniture often functions in the theatre as it does in real life—to be sat on, lain on, kicked over in a fit of anger—it also has a crucial stylistic importance. Often properties such as ashtrays, telephones, letters, and tableware are functional in realistic plays, but they can also have aesthetic and symbolic significance. How these props are designed helps shape the plot and the audience's perception of the characters. Some props are even raised to titular importance, such as the glass figurines in Tennessee Williams's *The Glass Menagerie* and the rare coin in David Mamet's *American Buffalo*. No prop is too small or too insignificant to escape the attention of the scenic designer and prop master.

Bill Clark's highly realistic setting for Virginia Stage Company's 2014 production of Patrick Meyer's adventure drama *K-2* portrays a ledge in the Himalayas. ©*Jay Westcott/The Virginian-Pilot/AP Images*

This verdant set, dominated by a giant beehive at its center, was designed by Tim Hatley and proved the virtual star of Charlotte Jones's *Humble Boy*, which played at the New York City Center in 2003. *©Sara Krulwich/The New York Times/ Redux*

Mark Wendland's highly theatrical 2007 setting for *Richard III*, directed for New York's Classic Stage Company by Brian Kulick and Michael Cumpsty—who also played Richard (seen here being crowned)—was largely made up of hanging chandeliers, which rose and fell to change the varying locales of the play. *©Richard Termine*

Neil LaBute's *The Mercy Seat*, about a couple who were presumed killed in the September 11, 2001, World Trade Center attack, but who were actually having a secret affair in an apartment across town, lends itself to both realistic and highly stylized stagings. Robert Jones's realistic staging (*top*) beautifully sets off the intimate complicity of Sinead Cusac, as Abby, and John Hannah, as Ben, in London's Almeida Theatre production of 2003, while Thomas Schulte-Michels's production (*bottom*) of the same play in the same year, at the Deutsches Theatre Berlin, focuses instead on space and isolation rather than on its characters. The result is more of an emphasis on the play's conceptual elements, rather than its emotions.

©Donald Cooper/Photostage

©picture-alliance/Newscom

THE SCENIC DESIGNER AT WORK

The scenic designer's work inevitably begins with several readings of the play, normally followed by research on the play and its original historical period (and the periods in which it may be set), a consideration of the type of theatre in which the play is to be produced, and extensive discussions with the director and other members of the design and production team. Scenic design usually is a collaborative process engaging the director, other designers, the principal technical staff, and whoever establishes and manages the budget.

The discussion phase normally proceeds simultaneously with the designer's preparation of a series of *visualizations*. These may begin with collected illustrations (for example, clippings from magazines, notations from historical sources, color ideas, and spatial concepts) and move on to sketches of individual settings, or storyboards, which illustrate how the sets will be rearranged or used in each scene. The designer will also use digital or hand-crafted color renderings of the set elements, and often three-dimensional models, which will help the director and design team fully understand how the set will work and be put together. Eventually, these early sketches lead to a set of working drawings and other materials that will guide the eventual scenic construction.

Throughout the process, of course, the designer must gain the approval of the director and producers and reckon with the constraints of the budget and the skills of the construction staff. Successful designers thus have to remain pragmatic and cooperative while freely exercising their creativity. Part architect, part engineer, part accountant, and part interpretive genius, the scenic designer today is one of the theatre's premier artists.

Rob Howell's scenic design for *Matilda the Musical*, which won him a 2012 Olivier Award (the English equivalent of a Tony), features a classroom at its center that disintegrates into blocks of letters at its margins, enveloping the audience and creating a psychological as well as physical space. ©*Nick Ansell/Press Association/AP Images*

📷Photo Essay: Scenic Designer Scott Pask

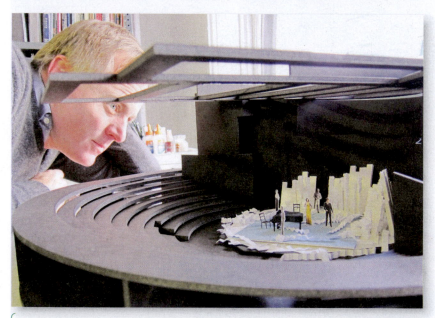

1.   Scott Pask at his design table in his studio overlooking
      New York's Union Square. ©*Robert Cohen*
2.   Pask studies his model for the 2012 production of Stephen
      Sondheim's *Merrily We Roll Along*, which he is designing
      for the Cincinnati Playhouse in the Park. ©*Robert Cohen*

Scott Pask is one of the leading scenic designers in America today. His outstanding design record in theatre—including over 50 productions on Broadway—has won him three Tony Awards (for *The Book of Mormon, The Pillowman*, and *The Coast of Utopia* trilogy). He has designed other stellar Broadway productions, including 2018's *Mean Girls,* 2017's critically acclaimed *The Band's Visit, Something Rotten, Finding Neverland, It's Only a Play, Airline Highway, Pippin, Pal Joey, Casa Valentina, Hair, Les Liaisons Dangereuses, Macbeth, Nine, La Cage aux Folles, Speed the Plow,* and *Promises, Promises*.

This is how Scott answered some of Robert Cohen's questions when they met up in 2013 at Pask's office in New York City near Madison Square Park:

RC: Why did you head into design?

SP: I first trained as an architect, but while pursuing that education, I started thinking about narrative structure and remembering how much I was intrigued with theatre. So I decided to take an elective course at the music theatre department at the university, and I loved it. Then I trained in Italy for a semester, studying the architecture and how the Baroque and Renaissance architects explored fluidity and space, and how they manipulated the space to make it more dramatic. That was a huge revelation. So when I finished my degree in architecture I knew what I wanted to do—come to New York and work in theatre design.

I began working with people who were creating performance art projects downtown and in experimental dance companies. Then I interned on a film and afterward did quite a bit of art direction. But as the films were getting bigger and the schedules were getting longer (and I was getting a little older, having been in New York for five years), I realized I had to move with that trajectory in

1c... "Two by Two"   THE BOOK OF MORMON

3.

3a... Ugandan Village   THE BOOK OF MORMON

4.

3. Pask's model for the first scene of *The Book of Mormon*, showing the false proscenium, which is seen throughout the play and shown here in the opening Salt Lake City scene. ©*Robert Cohen*

4. When the action moves to Uganda, the set model changes radically. ©*Robert Cohen*

mind if I was going to study theatre—and that's when I decided to go to Yale. A kind of "now or never" moment.

RC: And what is your basic process?

SP: Whether a musical or a dance or film or opera, I have to start with the script. I tend first to do small thumbnails—little sketches to put some thoughts and ideas on the page. And then I research and start looking at images, whether it's the period of the play or a place for the action. And then I'll storyboard, first very roughly, and then I'll go into a rough model to get spatial relationships and try to articulate some of my ideas in three dimensions. Then I start modeling, talking back and forth with the director and choreographer, showing them the development, hearing their responses, and honing our work to where we want it to head as the model becomes more developed and more detailed.

RC: How did you develop *The Book of Mormon*?

SP: I imagined it as a pageant, which is why the portal for the show is so important . . . we are always experiencing the material of the show through that viewfinder. I had been a part of a religious pageant or two while in elementary school, so putting it within the context of that frame seemed important from the beginning.

From there the design moved in stages. The first pageant in the opening moments of the show dissipates, and we're suddenly in a dark blue void singing "Hello!" and then at a training room with a vista of Utah behind it, all very bright and colorful and shiny. We used metallic automotive paint with an inherent glitter to make it sparkle, to make it all luminous. I collaborated with Brian [MacDevitt, the lighting designer] to give everything a halo—every piece of architecture, each planet, each tree—which would have light emanating from every possible angle. And then we go from these cool colors—the blues, the ice blues, the royal blues of Utah—to a very expressionistic and textured world of Africa (the opposite of the very presentational views of Utah), with warm and darker colors within burnt, distressed portals of tattered and torched fabric wings and borders.

5. Pask's design for Broadway's *Something Rotten* (2015), a musical farce about musicals and William Shakespeare as a young playwright, consisted mainly of 17 painted drops, mostly based on what Pask called a "Tudor ghetto"—a "downtrodden collage of Tudor buildings and a theatre at the center of it." Here, Christian Borle plays Shakespeare for a crowd of Elizabethan spectators while on a platform surrounded by medieval lanterns. ©*Joan Marcus*

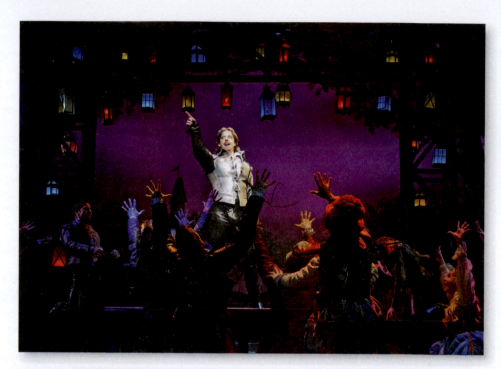

6. "The real star of the show is Scott Pask's astounding set . . . so solid and hyper-real you can almost smell the sun hitting the asphalt," said reviewer Hugh Iglarsh, *Newcity Stage*, of Pask's design for Pulitzer finalist Lisa D'Amour's *Airline Highway*, set in a rundown hotel in New Orleans. The play's 23 actors, directed by Joe Mantello, include hookers, addicts, beatniks, and exotic dancers. The play was initially produced by the Steppenwolf Theatre in Chicago; it reopened in New York City in 2015. ©*Michael Brosilow*

RC: And how about *Hair*, which you first did in Central Park and then moved to Broadway?

SP: We really did three productions of it. First, it was a summer concert in Central Park's Delacorte Theatre, for which we had simply painted the floor black and put in a bandstand since that was about all we had time and money for. But that taught us a lesson about scale; *Hair* has an energy that wants to come into the audience, and when we came back to the Delacorte for a full production the following year, we wanted to embrace the expanse of it, while making the production feel intimate. So I created a semicircular wall nearly midway on the expansive stage that reflected the architecture of the theatre. It became something the "Tribe" [the group of 1960s hippies that comprise the cast] climbed over to invade the space, make it theirs, and thus begin their evening. I wanted to have nature as close as

7. Pask's setting and costume design for Martin McDonough's grim 2010 *A Behanding in Spokane*, about a man (played here by Christopher Walken) who is still searching for his left hand that was severed 47 years ago, captures the pathos of the main character's life and environment, exemplified by the brightness of the light behind him—which might be seen as the promise of his long-lost youth. Zoe Kazan (*right*) plays a con artist who pretends to know where his hand is. ©*Sara Krulwich/The New York Times/Redux*

possible, so we did tons of planting right behind that constructed wall, to match the existing architecture of the theatre. People walked in and said, "They're using the Delacorte without a set?" Many had no idea that our wall was built and distressed to match the existing wooden texture, color, and age [of the theatre], and that there were trees brought in and grass—and that's what it should be: an authenticity of space and a complicity of gesture, an architectural intervention by which the Tribe came in, invaded the space, and put on their show. Because it had been such a success in the park, moving into a Broadway theatre that fall created a real challenge. The one thing I had on my side was that energy can be more easily contained onstage indoors, where the play's optimism and hope and excitement can come right at you. Indoors, people are looking up at the stage rather than down onto an amphitheatre, and so the wall motif—the architectural intervention—is very important. Indeed, it's the statement of the show. So the Tribe

came in and threw their rugs down and painted something on the wall and called it their space, claimed it as their own. And by the end, when sunlight and the mural's color has completely faded, and there's snow and they all put coats on, the optimistic commentary has gone away and is replaced by a plea for "let the sun shine in—Please!" I feel that true art can come from a place of upset, from people trying to find their way in the world, and from the "what's-next" of things, so the wall became a character of its own.

RC: So your design is more about narrative and ideas than about decor?

SP: For me *decorative* is a bad word. I'll even look at something of my own work mid-process and think—is that just decorative?—What is it trying to say? What is it doing? You can create the realistic elements that are there, but how do you make it theatrical? How do you address the space where we watch the action? In whatever era the play takes place, we all know we're watching it today; that's the main thing. That's something I

obsess about—keeping the theatre that I help to create as contemporary and progressive as I can.

RC: Do you have any advice to young potential designers?

SP: I began as an artist, and I think art classes are always going to be useful—any class that has you manipulating materials and paint. I also think it's important to develop your visual acuity, to go see exhibitions, to pick up on what art things are happening, to visit cities, travel, find spaces that are inspiring. Go to Washington, D.C., and see the Capitol and the museums. Go to any major city and seek out their museums and cultural institutions. There are amazing things at our fingertips useful toward understanding visual perception and space.

But basically, I think design is intuitive. It's about your gut. Intuit as much as you can. Be sensitive to the things around you—and to yourself, and especially to how it relates to the piece you are working on. Listen to what your mind or instincts are telling you.

Courtesy of Scott Pask.

David Zinn's ingenious set for Stephen Karam's *The Humans,* shown here in its 2016 Broadway production, balances intimacy with grandeur. The two levels of a middle-class New York residence allow the audience to see multiple family relationships play out at once, all while appreciating the precision of each individual character. Zinn won the Tony Award for Best Scenic Design for this play. ©*Joan Marcus*

Lighting

The very word *theatre*, derived from the ancient Greek word for "seeing place," implies the crucial function of light. Light is the basic precondition for theatrical appearance. Without light, nothing can be seen.

But stage lighting is not simply used for illumination. *How* we see is just as important as *what* we see—and what we don't. While the creative use of lighting dates back to the earliest surviving plays, lighting design became more psychological and symbolic as plays increasingly tackled more complex and interior elements of human life. Aeschylus's *Agamemnon* was staged so the watchman's spotting of the signal fire heralding Agamemnon's return to Argos coincided with the actual sunrise over the Athenian skene. It is also probable that the burning of Troy at the conclusion of Euripides' *Trojan Women* coincided with the sunset that reddened the Attic sky. Modern plays, on the other hand, commonly use light in symbolic ways, such as the blinking

neon light that intermittently reddens Blanche's quarters in Williams's *A Streetcar Named Desire*, and the searching follow-spot (a swivel-mounted lighting instrument that can be pointed in any direction by an operator) that Samuel Beckett calls for to train on the hapless, trapped characters in his play *Play*. In *Streetcar*, the light does more than realistically texture the setting—although it does that too. The flashes of red reflect Blanche's own psychological fragility and hint at the emotional explosions and revelations to come. In *Play*, the follow-spot enhances the characters' feelings of isolation onstage—and in the world.

In addition to coordinating the timing of their plays to the sunrise and sunset, the ancient Greeks paid a great deal of attention to the proper orientation of their theatres to best take advantage of the sun's rays. The medieval outdoor theatre, though as dependent on sunlight as the Greek theatre was, made use of several devices to redirect sunlight, including halos made of reflective metal to brighten the faces of Jesus and his disciples. In one production, a highly

Individual pools of light illuminate the parasols and costumes—and the isolation—of ladies waiting for the soldiers' return at the beginning of *Much Ado about Nothing*. This Indiana Repertory Theatre production was directed by Libby Appel, with lighting design by Robert Peterson. ©*Indiana Repertory Theatre*

polished metal bowl was held over Jesus' head to concentrate the sun's rays. Surviving instructions indicate that when cloudy skies obscured the sun, medieval stagehands would substitute blazing torches for the bowl.

It was on the indoor stage, however, that lighting technology attained its first significant sophistication. In a 1439 production of the *Annunciation* in Florence one thousand oil lamps were used for illumination, and a host of candles were lighted by a "ray of fire" that shot through the city's famous cathedral. One can only imagine the spectacle. Leonardo da Vinci designed a 1490 production of *Paradise* with twinkling stars and backlit zodiac signs on colored glass. By the sixteenth century the great festival lighting of indoor theatres, located in manor houses and public halls, served as a symbol of the intellectual and artistic achievements of the Renaissance itself, a mark of the luxury, technical wizardry, and exuberant humanism of the era. People went to theatres in those times partly to revel in light and escape the outside gloom—in much the same way today's moviegoers might go to the cinema to escape the heat of summer days.

How were these astonishing lighting effects created? The ingredients were actually quite simple: tallow, wax, and fireworks. With these limited components, lighting artists could orchestrate immense spectacles. Raphael "painted" the name of his patron, Pope Leo X, with thirteen lighted chandeliers in a dramatic production; Sebastiano Serlio inserted sparkling panes of colored glass (the predecessors of today's gels—colored plastic lenses) that, illuminated from behind, created glistening and seductive scenic effects. The "Sun King" of France, Louis XIV, ordered a 1664 presentation at Versailles that featured twenty thousand colored lanterns, hundreds of transparent veils, bowls of colored water, and a massive display of fireworks—all displaying his (literal) brilliance.

The inventions of gaslight in the nineteenth century and electric lighting thereafter—first in carbon arcs and "limelight" lighting, later in incandescence, and most recently with light-emitting diodes (LEDs)—have brought stage lighting into its contemporary phase, allowing lighting to shape dramatic action rather than simply being "showy." Ease and flexibility of control are the cardinal virtues of both gas and electric lighting. By adjusting a valve, a single operator at a "gas table" could raise or dim the intensity of any individual light or preselected "gang" of lights just as easily as we can raise or lower the flame on a gas range stove with the turn of a knob today. And with electricity—introduced in American theatres in 1879 and in European theatres the following year—the great fire hazard of a live flame (a danger that had plagued the theatre for centuries and claimed three buildings a year on average, including Shakespeare's Globe) was at last over. The round-the-clock staffs of fire crews in every major nineteenth-century theatre were dismissed, and the deterioration of scenery and costumes from the heat, smoke, and carbon pollution produced by a live flame similarly ended.

Electrical lighting also had the great advantage of being fully self-starting—it did not need to be relit or kept alive by pilot lights—and it could easily be switched off or dimmed up and down from a distance. With electricity, one could reconnect lighting units simply by fastening and unfastening flexible wires. Within a few years of its introduction, electricity became the primary medium of stage lighting in the Western world, and great dynamo generators were installed as essential equipment in the basements of theatres from Vienna to San Francisco.

Electricity provides an enormously flexible form of lighting. The incandescent filament is a reasonably small, reasonably cool point of light that can be focused, reflected, aimed, shaped, and colored by a great variety of devices invented and adapted for those purposes, and electric light can be trained in innumerable ways upon actors, scenery, audiences, or a combination of these to create realistic or atmospheric effects. Today, thanks to the added sophistication of computer technology and microelectronics, it is not uncommon to see theatres with nearly a thousand lighting instruments all under the complete control of a single technician seated in a comfortable booth above the audience.

CONTEMPORARY LIGHTING DESIGN

Since the mid-twentieth century, the lighting for most productions has been conceived and supervised by a professional lighting designer. The lighting designer has a complicated role, one that blends the more rigid design elements (architecture and scenery) with the evolving patterns of the movements of the actors. By skillfully manipulating the hanging positions, angles, colors, and shadows of the instruments, the lighting designer can illuminate a dramatic production in both subtle and more forthright ways.

Visibility and focus are the primary considerations of lighting design: visibility ensures that the audience sees what it's meant to see, and focus ensures that it sees this without undue distraction. The *spotlight*, a development of the twentieth century, has fostered something akin to a revolution in staging. Contemporary productions now routinely feature a darkened auditorium (a rarity prior to the 1880s) and a deliberate effort to illuminate certain characters (or props or set pieces) more than others—in other words, to direct the audience's attention toward those visual elements that are dramatically the most significant.

Verisimilitude, or lifelikeness, and atmosphere also are common goals of the lighting designer, and both can be achieved largely through the color and direction of lighting. Verisimilitude is crucial in realistic dramas, where the style generally demands that the lighting appear as if emanating from familiar sources: as from the sun, from *practical* (physically present) lamps on the stage, or from moonlight, firelight, streetlights, neon signs, or perhaps the headlights of moving automobiles. Atmospheric lighting, by contrast, need not suggest any particular source and can be used simply to evoke a mood appropriate to a scene or to a moment's action: gloomy, for example—or oppressive, nightmarish, funereal, or regal.

Sharp, bold lighting designs are often employed to create highly theatrical effects, from the glittery entertainments of the Broadway musical to the stark, simple lighting of a smaller production. A "theatricalist" use of lighting, which does not attempt to disguise the theatre's artifice, is now widespread, even in more traditional plays. Moodier plays may employ dense or unnatural colors, or patterns that break light beams into shadowy fragments, such as leaf patterns. There may be atmospheric fog effects that make light appear misty, gloomy, or mysterious. The big Broadway musical, by contrast, often makes splashy use of banks of colored footlights and border lights, high-intensity follow-spots that track actors around the stage, "chaser" lights that flash on and off in sequence, and an intense, almost unbearable brightness that makes a finale seem to burn up the stage. In fact, this traditional use—or overuse—of light has done as much to give Broadway the name "Great White Way" as the famous illuminated billboards and marquees that line the street have.

Stylized lighting effects are also often used to express radical changes of mood or event. The use of lighting alone to signal a complete change of scene, without any changes to the physical set, is an increasingly common technique. The smash hit musical *Hamilton* employs a simple, versatile set—a series of ropes and platforms—that can evoke a ship, a battlefield, or a government office. As such, the play depends on its lighting to signal shifts in

The lighting by Peter Mumford makes Tim Hatley's setting for Noel Coward's *Private Lives* an enchanting hotel facade, whose Mediterranean-facing balconies offer the promise of an elegant—but perhaps empty—life. Alan Rickman and Lindsay Duncan starred in this production on Broadway in 2002. ©*Sara Krulwich/ The New York Times/Redux*

environment. Lighting can also change the mood of a particular scene or character. Merely by switching from full front to full overhead lighting, for example, a designer can throw characters into silhouette and make their figures appear suddenly ominous, grotesque, or isolated. The illumination of actors with odd lighting colors, such as green, or from odd lighting positions, such as from below, can create mysterious, unsettling effects. And the use of follow-spots can quite literally put a character "on the spot" and convey a sense of terror. Highly expressive lighting and projections, when applied to a production utilizing only a *cyclorama* (a scenic backdrop at the rear of the stage that often represents the sky), neutrally clad actors, and a set piece, sculpture, or stage mechanism, can create an infinite variety of convincing theatrical environments. It is here, in the area of stylization and expressive theatricality, that the modern lighting designer has made the most significant mark.

THE LIGHTING DESIGNER AT WORK

The lighting designer ordinarily conceives of the design by researching the action and ideas of the play and discussing concepts and approaches with the director and other members of the design team. Other, more pragmatic realities affect the design: the physical characteristics of the theatre building (its lighting positions, control facilities, and wiring system), the scenery and costume designs, the movements of the actors, and the available lighting instruments. Because not all of these variables can be known

from the outset (for example, the stage movement may change from one day to the next, right up to the final dress rehearsal), the lighting designer must be skilled at making adjustments and must have the opportunity to exercise a certain amount of control, or at least to voice concerns about possible lighting problems.

Ordinarily, the two major preparations required of the lighting designer are the *light plot* and the *cue sheet*. A light plot is a plan that shows each instrument's characteristics: its placement, type, wattage, size, wiring, color, and sometimes its physical movement, since lighting instruments are increasingly electronically programmed to move via remote control. A cue sheet is a list of the precise moments in the script that the lights are to move and/ or change color or intensity. Both light plot and cue sheet are developed in consultation with the director and other members of the design team, who may take major or minor roles in the consultation depending on their interests and expertise. Some productions use hundreds of lighting instruments and require thousands of individual cues. In these cases, the complexity of the plot and cue sheet can be extraordinary, with weeks or months of preparation. In today's theatre, the cues that result from this lengthy process are almost always then programmed into a computer capable of executing them with the necessary speed and precision.

The lighting designer works with a number of different types of lighting instruments and must know the properties of each well enough to fully anticipate how it will perform when hung and focused on the stage. If you

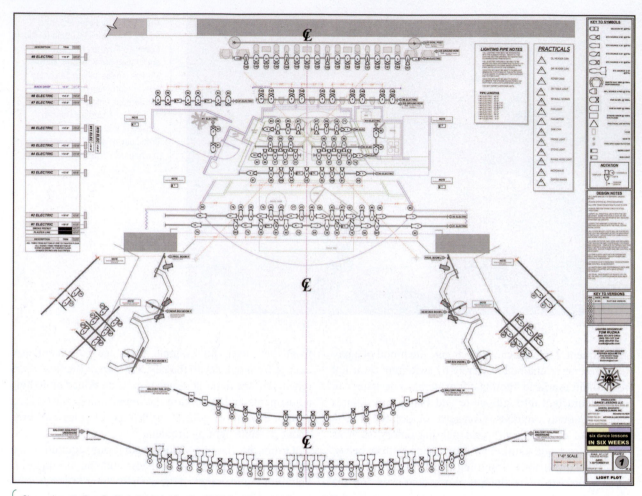

Shown here is Tom Ruzika's light plot for the 2003 Broadway production of *Six Dance Lessons in Six Weeks*. The photo is looking down from the theatre's ceiling; the stage is at the top of the drawing, and the audience area (the "house") is at the bottom. The gray rectangles on each side indicate the vertical sides of the proscenium, the "CL" symbol is the center line of the stage and house, and each bomb-shaped symbol is a specific lighting instrument. The light plot tells the electrical staff where instruments are to be hung, roughly where they are to be aimed, and how they are wired to the board. ©*Thomas Ruzika*

glance up at the grid above the stage or at the pipes above and to the sides of the audience, you will see the huge range of instruments from which the designer makes a selection.

Fixed-focus spotlights are the main instruments for lighting stage action; they come in two main forms. The ellipsoidal reflector spotlight, or ERS, has a sharply defined conical shape and is the instrument of choice for intense, hard-edged, and closely focused lighting. The circular ERS beam is easy to manipulate: four shutters can frame it from different sides, an iris can tighten its radius, and gobos—metal templates—placed into the instrument can project silhouettes of almost any variety. By contrast, the fresnel (pronounced "fren-ELL") spotlight, named for its French-designed lens, has a less-defined and less-shapable beam. It is most often used for general (wash) lighting, backlights, and downlights.

Other common lighting instruments are even less focused. Parabolic aluminized reflectors, or PARs ("cans"), can be used for color washes and general lighting. Striplights, banks of PARs or floodlights, are used to light drops, cycloramas, and other broad areas. Specialty instruments include follow-spots—whose high intensity and manual operation allow for following an actor (for example, during a solo dance number)—and automated lights, which can be computer-programmed to instantly change direction, color, and beam size at the mere touch of a button. Though more common in musical theatre, follow-spots

Lighting designer Rainer Casper's radically contrasting lighting colors—even in the same scene—create wholly different indoor and outdoor environments in Bert Neumann's set for Frank Castorf's critically acclaimed 2003 adaptation of Dostoevsky's *The Insulted and Injured*. ©*Thomas Aurin*

and automated lights are beginning to make an impact in nonmusical theatre as well. The most exciting recent development in lighting technology is the *LED*, which creates an electroluminescence that can deliver sufficient lighting intensity and color control to rival many incandescent sources. Though costing more at the outset, LEDs prove considerably less expensive in the long run because they are vastly more energy-efficient and environmentally friendly than incandescent bulbs. LEDs are now widely found in PAR cans, strip lights, moving color washes, and the "LED walls" used in large image and video projections (see the "Projections" section later in this chapter).

Because few theatres have the time or space to permit much on-site experimentation in lighting design, the development of the light plot and cue sheet takes place primarily in the imagination and, where possible, in workshops apart from the main theatre facility. This limitation places a premium on the designer's ability to predict instrument performance from various distances and angles and with various color elements installed. It also demands sharp awareness of how various lights will reflect off different surfaces.

Once the light plot is complete, the lighting instruments are mounted, or "hung," in appropriate positions, attached to the theatre's circuits, "patched" to proper control channels, called "dimmers," aimed and focused in the desired directions, and colored by the attachment of frames that contain colored plastic lenses, or "gels."

Once the lighting units are in place and functioning, the lighting designer begins setting the intensities of each instrument for each cue. This painstaking process involves the programming of thousands of precise numerical directions into the computer software from which an operator will execute the cues during performances. Finally, the lighting designer presides over the working and timing of the cues, making certain that in actual operation the lights shift as subtly or as boldly as desired to support and complement the play's action and achieve the design aesthetic.

Great lighting design contains thousands of details, most of them pulled together in one or two final weeks.

Photo Essay: Lighting Designer Don Holder

With his two Tony Awards (for the 1997 Broadway production of *The Lion King* and the 2008 Lincoln Center revival of *South Pacific*) and experience as a lighting designer in over one hundred Broadway and off-Broadway shows—including 2018's *My Fair Lady* and 2017's *Anastasia* on Broadway, along with *Oslo, Fiddler on the Roof, The King and I,* and *On the Twentieth Century*—Don Holder is clearly at the very top of the American lighting design field. In addition, he has had the opportunity to catch the new wave of technological sophistication that has propelled a truly revolutionary new era of stage design.

Like many designers, Holder became fascinated by lighting at a very young age. A self-admitted "music and drama addict" from the days his parents drove him from their Long Island home into Manhattan to see symphonies, ballets, and Broadway musicals, Holder began to light shows while still in junior high. "I did band concerts, high school plays, everything I could. I was also the guy at scouting camp who was always lighting the campfires and putting smudge pots on the trails," he recalls during an interview with Robert Cohen.

1.

Adoring the outdoors, Holder majored in forestry at the University of Maine's Orono campus, but he also played in jazz bands and the Bangor Symphony during the school year and worked summers as a technician and actor at Maine's Theater at Monmouth. Inspired by a designer there, he applied for graduate training at the Yale School of Drama, enrolling first as a stage technician and eventually as a lighting designer under the mentorship of fabled Broadway designer Jennifer Tipton. After Yale, Holder headed directly into a New York career, working first in small off-Broadway and off-off-Broadway companies and then making his Broadway debut with Richard Greenberg's *Eastern Standard* in 1989.

Holder describes his design aesthetic as supportive: "My basic goal is to bring out the play's text, the composer's music, and the director's vision. I strongly feel our job as designers is to adapt our own style and design aesthetic to the specific production: to help tell the story, of course, but also to augment the story's context and style." The path to excellence, however, is in the details. "I suppose I am characterized as

2.

1. In a workroom above the Mark Taper Forum stage in Los Angeles, where he is designing a production of the musical *Pippin*, lighting designer Donald Holder makes final marks on his light plot. Soon he will turn it over to the theatre's electricians to hang and focus the hundreds of lighting instruments that will be used in the show. *©Robert Cohen*

2. In the light booth, Holder looks up at stage left (the right side of the stage, as seen from the audience) to see how the lighting will work with the scene as described in his script. *©Robert Cohen*

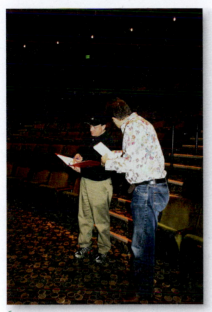

4. As technical rehearsals begin, Holder and his two assistants, in the light booth at the rear of the auditorium, enter the light cues into computers that will be used to operate the lighting during the show. *©Robert Cohen*

3. In the front rows of the audience, Holder discusses the scene with *Pippin* director Jeff Calhoun. *©Robert Cohen*

5. Color and individual punctuations are the key elements in Don Holder's consummate lighting design of this outdoor Iowan scene in the 2014 Broadway musical *Bridges of Madison County,* shown here with Kelli O'Hara and Steven Pasquale singing a duet. *©Sara Krulwich/The New York Times/Redux*

6. in Don Holder's lighting for 2013's *Big Fish* on Broadway, the illumination of the townspeople in a haunted forest (populated by dancing trees and a towering giant) makes them gleam in what would realistically be dark and gloomy surroundings. ©*Paul Kolnik*

meticulous," Holder freely admits. "My work tends to be quite detailed—specific rather than general, layered rather than spare. I'm certainly obsessive about craft—I start with a strong take on each scene and then detail each moment. This means that my lighting tends to be very densely cued and shaped." Holder cites as an example his 2009 production of the musical *Pippin* at the Mark Taper Forum in Los Angeles on which he was working at the time of this interview: "It's just two hours long but it has six hundred light cues. But every detail retains the sense of the big picture."

With a strong background in music, Holder finds himself often engaged in shows "that require a romantic, lyrical, and above all musical treatment"—but this is not limited to the music in musicals (like *Pippin*) alone. Indeed, he

accounts his love of music as a reason why he has often been tapped to design the premieres of August Wilson's nonmusical plays: "I think that August's work is so poetic and operatic, his storytelling is so rich, his sense of history, religion, and magic have such a depth, and there are so many undercurrents running through the body of his work that there's always much more underneath these plays than what you see on the page. I think my style of lighting is well suited to Wilson's work, since so many of his characters seem like they're stepping out of straight dramatic acting and singing arias. His work has a musicality, an operatic quality, a mythic proportion that I simply love. So there's a certain amount of freedom and liberty I can take by stepping out of reality, heightening things, making things larger than life, and responding

to the play emotionally rather than intellectually. And so my work becomes very personal."

Holder's career has taken flight during an extraordinary evolution of lighting technology, which has fit exceptionally well with his careful craftsmanship. He recalls, "When I broke into the theatre, the theatres I worked at were still employing manual dimming systems, so my work was wholly dependent on the skill of the person running it. Indeed, I was at the mercy of the light board operator. And as my work requires every light to be specifically cued and crafted, I would become despondent when mistakes were made. So I greeted the age of computerized control with open arms. For me it changed everything: my lighting could become more fluid and more creative, and I didn't have to lower my expectations because of

7. Holder's exquisite lighting in the 2014 Broadway revival of *You Can't Take It with You* at the Longacre Theater includes overhead "ceiling" lighting, table lamps, wall lamps, a dark blue sky overhead, and of course spotlights on Annaleigh Ashford, who is dancing on center stage, and Will Brill, who is peering over the staircase balcony to see her. ©*Sara Krulwich/The New York Times/Redux*

technical issues. And then came automated lighting [AL]—motorized moving lights that I first used when I designed *The Lion King*. That show was huge—with scenery constantly flying in and out, an animal parade through the audience to begin the show, and a band that played in the theatre's boxes above the audience. [Director] Julie [Taymor] had conceived the show within a constantly changing skyscape, a 'lightscape' actually, that included a whole spectrum of colors—not just three or four—that were to continuously cross-fade with each other. I needed to have six colors on every single surface of the setting!

And since I simply didn't have enough space in the theatre to hang all the lights I wanted, or to provide the level of detail and specificity the show required, or even to light the environment—the 'dance space on steroids' as we called it—I simply had to use AL. It was incredible—as, for example, in the opening sequence, when several luminous clouds were to rise in sequence while at the same time the sky was changing from twilight to dawn to noon and everything was in a constant state of motion. With AL, one instrument can replace fifty, and so that's how I did it. And when the director wanted to change something, I could do it right

from my seat—without ever taking out a ladder or refocusing a light or changing a gel [color agent]. This became a revelation to me!"

Holder thinks of his lighting as impressionistic. He explains, "The artists I'm most inspired by are the impressionists; they speak to me in a profound way." But his lighting is, at the same time, specific: "My mantra is craft, sweating the details, really controlling the composition, which must be impeccably crafted." When these two elements are brought together, the art of stage lighting rises to luminous achievements.

———————————

Courtesy of Don Holder.

Gradations of light, difficult to measure in isolation, can have vastly differing impacts in the moment-to-moment focus and feel of a play. Because light is a medium rather than an object, audience members are rarely, if ever, directly aware of it; they see only its illuminated target. But everyone who works professionally in the theatre knows what a crucial role lighting plays in the success of the theatre venture. The light that illuminates the theatre also glorifies it; it is a symbol of revelation—of knowledge and humanity—upon which the theatrical impulse finally rests.

Costumes

Costumes have always been a major element in the theatrical experience. They are vehicles for the "dressing-up" that actors and audiences alike have always considered a requirement for theatrical satisfaction.

THE FUNCTIONS OF COSTUME

Costumes serve both ceremonial and illustrative functions. The first theatrical costumes were essentially ceremonial: the *himation* (a gownlike costume) of an original performer in Greek tragedy was derived from the garment worn by the leader of the ancient choral performance of the dithyramb; the comic and satyr-play costumes, with their use of phalluses and goatskins, were likewise derived from more primitive god-centered rites. The priests who first enacted the *Quem Queritis* trope (a brief, sung liturgical text) in medieval Europe simply wore their sacred albs, hooded to indicate an outdoor scene but otherwise unaltered. The actors of the classic Japanese noh drama also wore—and wear today—costumes that relate more to spiritual sources than to secular life. These ancient uses of costuming served primarily to separate the actors from the audience and elevate them to a quasi-divine status. They became indeed larger than life in the fourth century B.C.E. Greek theatre, where principal actors wore thick-soled footwear called *kothurnoi* to stand much taller than ordinary humans—a literal dressing-up that gave their characters a superhuman magnitude.

By the time of the Renaissance, the ceremonial costuming of the ancient theatre had given way, at least in the West, to costumes designed to distinguish individual characters and historical periods. The Italian commedia dell'arte boasted dazzling, highly distinctive costumes so each of its traditional characters—such as Arlecchino with his multicolored patches, Pantalone with his red tights and slippers, and Il Dottore with his black cap and ankle-length black coat—could be instantly identified by what they wore. Elizabethan actors were often favored by their

Plays often indicate design colors for symbolic importance. In this 2002 production of Tennessee Williams's *A Streetcar Named Desire,* Glenn Close plays the role of Blanche—French for "white"—who is dressed in a white dress, white lace, and a white hat—with white rosebuds. *©Andy Butterton/PA Images/Getty Images*

patrons with the gift of their cast-off but still elegantly detailed garments. Such costumes reflected the value of distinction over historical accuracy: for example, while a 1595 drawing of an Elizabethan production of Shakespeare's *Titus Andronicus* shows the ancient Roman general wearing a toga appropriate to his historical era, it also portrays other male characters wearing standard Elizabethan attire.

Modern costuming, however, is based on an overall design plan. This plan became important during the eighteenth and nineteenth centuries, as realism began to arrive in Western theatre. Realism led to an interest in historical accuracy in design, which required consistency, and by the early 1800s, painstaking efforts would be made to ensure that the design of every costume in a play (along with every prop and set piece) was accurate to the era of its dramatic action. Thus a production of *Julius Caesar* would recreate the exact clothing worn in first century B.C.E. Rome, a *Hamlet* production would mirror the dress and architecture of medieval Denmark, and a costumer for *Romeo and Juliet* would seek to make garments just like those worn in Renaissance Verona.

The passion for historical accuracy no longer dominates the world of costume design, but it helped pave the way for a more conceptual and holistic approach to a show's overall design. Such an approach is no longer historical but *stylistic*. It communicates attitudes, themes, feelings, and ideas rather than historical pictures. And, when historicity is involved, it may be of a period unrelated to the one set by the author: *King Lear,* for example, has been played as variously taking place in medieval Japan, the Iran-Iraq War, and provincial India. Costume design in the twenty-first century is generally a more imaginative art that conveys not just a historical period or group of characters but a view of the world of the play.

Modern costume design serves four separate functions. First, it retains at least a hint of the ceremonial magic once conjured by ancient priests and shamans. Even today, costume demonstrates a primordial theatricality. As Theoni Aldredge said of the clothes she designed for the hit musical *A Chorus Line*, they "had to look real and yet theatrical enough for an audience to say, 'Okay, I'm in the theatre now.'"

Second, the costumes of a play show us what sort of world we are asked to enter, not only in terms of historical place and period but also social and cultural values. The word *costume* has the same root as *custom* and *customary*; as such it indicates the "customary" wearing apparel (or the "habitual habit") of persons living in a particular place and time. For example, the Mexican American characters in Luis Valdez's *Zoot Suit*, set in the 1940s, are seen as virtual extensions of the overly long pegged trousers and looping watch chains referenced by the play's title. Plays often indicate design colors for symbolic importance. For example, Tennessee Williams, in *A Streetcar Named Desire*, specifically directs the poker players to wear shirts of "bright primary colors" to contrast their primary sexuality with that of Blanche DuBois's deceased gay husband, whom the dramatist named "Allan Grey." The ensemble of costumes in a dramatic production reveals the social and cultural environment of its collective characters.

Third, the costumes can express the specific individuality of each character's role. They may reveal at a glance, for example, the character's profession, wealth, age, class status, tastes, and self-image. More subtly, costume can suggest the character's vices, virtues, and hidden hopes

Sometimes the costuming literally comes to life, as it does here in *The Suit* (2013), an adaptation of a short story by Can Themba. Pictured here is Nonhlanhla Kheswa, who caresses—and semi-embodies—the suit left by a fleeing lover. ©*Geraint Lewis*

and fears. Through the judicious use of color and shape, and even the movement and sound of the fabric, costume designers can imbue each character with distinct qualities that contrast that character to the others in the play. When Hamlet insists on wearing his "inky cloak" and "suits of solemn black" in his uncle's presence, for example, he signifies his continued act of grieving his father's death—and as such his refusal to accept the authority of his uncle, the king, who has asked for an end to mourning for his brother. The garments therefore become both a mark of Hamlet's character and a reflection of the play's action. The connection of character to costume becomes supremely realized in Peter Brook's 2013 adaptation of Can Themba's story *The Suit,* where a costume *becomes* an actual character, of sorts, in the play. After a jealous husband finds a suit belonging to his wife's lover, he demands that his spouse carry the suit with her everywhere.

Red, white, and black—surrounded by a hall of mirrors—make startling design patterns of love, life, and death in this Australian production of Jean Genet's *The Maids*, with both costumes and scenery designed by Alice Babidge and lighting by Nick Schlieper for this 2014 performance in New York. A petty thief, prostitute, and frequent prisoner, Genet was a shocking avant-garde novelist and playwright of the second half of the twentieth century. His maids are shown here planning to assassinate their mistress—if they don't kill each other first. Cate Blanchett (*foreground, with back to the mirror*) and Isabelle Huppert play the title roles. *©Ruby Washington/The New York Times/Redux*

Characters address the suit, caress it, and otherwise treat it like a person; its presence and emptiness becomes a potent and haunting symbol in the play's setting of apartheid South Africa.

Finally, and perhaps most practically, the costume serves as wearable clothing for the actor. A costume, after all, is a form of clothing; it must be functional as well as meaningful and aesthetic. Actors do not model costumes; they walk sit, duel, dance, and tumble down stairs in them. Indeed, unless the character is a prisoner or a pauper, we are supposed to believe that the character actually chose the costume and really wants to wear it! The wearability of a costume can also have an impact on the character being portrayed. Oftentimes actors will rehearse with certain costume items early in the process to see how their physicality is affected, which can become internalized as psychological components of their characters. The costume must also be able to change in accordance with the evolving interpretations of actors and directors. Thus the costume designer does not simply draw pictures on paper but must design workable, danceable, and actable clothing that can be cut, stitched, and changed quickly. For this reason, costume designers generally collaborate very closely with the actors they dress.

THE COSTUME DESIGNER AT WORK

The costume designer begins, as all designers do, with ideas about the play's action, themes, historical setting, and theatrical style. Collaboration with the director, who ordinarily takes a leading role from the start, and with the other designers is important even at this early stage, as ideas begin to be translated into decisions on fabrics, colors, shapes, and time periods.

Fabrics exist in many textures and weaves and can be cut, shaped, stitched, colored, and draped in innumerable ways. Fabrics can also be altered by adding leather, armor, jewelry, feathers, fur, hair (real or simulated), metallic ornamentation—in fact, any material known to exist. The designer selects and oversees the acquisition of all materials. Often costumes are acquired whole. For contemporary plays with modern settings, some or all costumes may be selected from the actors' own wardrobes, purchased from thrift shops, or bought at clothing stores. Costumes have even been solicited as gifts. In a celebrated instance, Louis Jouvet appealed to the citizens of Paris after World War II to donate their fancy prewar clothing to provide costumes for the premiere of Jean Giraudoux's *The Madwoman of Chaillot*. The spectacular garments that poured into the Athénée theatre for that brilliant 1945 Parisian production signaled to the world that France had survived the scourge of Nazi occupation with its devotion to the arts intact.

It is, however, the production designed and built entirely from scratch that fully tests the measure of the costume designer's imagination and ability. In such productions, the designer can create a unique design and demonstrate originality in bringing the text to life. The comprehensive design for such a production moves from the conceptual stage to a developmental one. The designer usually compiles a portfolio of images gathered from research, creates a series of quick sketches, sometimes called "roughs," and assembles various palettes of possible color samples, all in the service of giving the director and the entire design team a quick idea of the design's direction. Once this basic direction is approved by the director, and is seen to harmonize with the work of the entire design team (and the show's budget), the designer proceeds to create actual designs. Generally they take the form of drawings, first in black-and-white and then in color, known as renderings. Designers supplement these renderings with notes about each costume's accessories, hairstyles, and construction details. Enlarged drawings provide information about items too small to show in a single head-to-toe illustration.

The acquisition of fabrics—the basic medium of the costumer's art—is the crucial next stage. Designers consider each fabric's texture, weight, color, suppleness, and response to draping, dyeing, folding, crushing, twirling, and twisting. Velvet, silks, and woolens are the costumer's luxury fabrics; cottons, felt, burlap, and painted canvas are less expensive and often very effective for theatrical use. Contemporary designers, particularly in nonrealistic productions, may also turn to unique and surprising materials: Dean Mogle, for example, adapted hundreds of beer

Robert Wilson's *Les Fables de La Fontaine* is a hugely imaginative and sumptuously costumed re-creation of the stories of France's greatest fabulist. Here a masked Bakary Sangaré plays the Lion and Céline Samie is Circé in "The Lion in Love." The 2005–2006 Comédie-Française production, directed and designed by Wilson, was immensely popular with both adults and children at this historic theatre.
©Laurencine Lot

bottle caps into his costumes for a Utah Shakespeare Festival production of *Macbeth*.

These fabrics can be drastically altered, as well. Design teams can distress the material to make it appear old and used; detail and color the fabric with dyes, appliqués, and embroidery; and employ creative methods to have less expensive fabric emulate more expensive material—for example, the costume designers known collectively as Motley simulated leather by rubbing thick felt with moist yellow soap and spraying it down with brown paints. Before large quantities of fabric are ordered, samples or swatches can be pinned to the renderings to forestall the purchase of material at odds with the desired "look."

Costume accessories greatly affect the impact of the basic design. Jewelry, hats, sashes, purses, muffs, and

Photo Essay: Costume Designer Catherine Zuber

With fifty Broadway shows glimmering on her résumé, along with over a hundred off-Broadway and regional productions around the country and abroad, Catherine Zuber is currently one of the most active costume designers in the United States. Her productions have netted her nine Tony Awards (*The King and I, The Royal Family, South Pacific, Awake and Sing, The Light in the Piazza*, all three parts of *The Coast of Utopia*, and a 2018 revival of *My Fair Lady*), as well as seven additional Tony Award nominations (*War Paint, Golden Boy, Born Yesterday, How to Succeed in Business Without Really Trying, Seascape, Dinner at Eight*, and *Twelfth Night*) and a host of other awards and tributes.

1. Catherine Zuber shows your author some of the research pictures she has collected for her current design of *Impressionism* in the "costume space" allocated to her in the basement of the Broadway theatre where the play is in technical rehearsals. On the table below the pictures, you can see her black-and-white rendering of the costumes being readied for dress rehearsal. ©*Robert Cohen*

2. Zuber and First Costume Design Assistant Nikki Moody discuss which of the newly purchased costume items could best be added to the design at this point. ©*Robert Cohen*

3. Going over their collection of fabric swatches for the show, Zuber and Assistant Designer Patrick Bevilacqua are delighted to come up with a swatch they both like. "Patrick and I have a great relationship," Zuber explained. "It's a collaboration: I show him a sketch and he interprets it. And when really great assistant designers like Patrick take it a step further, it becomes a great collaboration!"
©*Robert Cohen*

1.

2.

3.

4. In the basement of the theatre, Zuber and Bevilacqua test whether a new skirt goes with the already selected jacket. ©*Robert Cohen*

5. The Irishness of John Patrick Shanley's *Outside Mullingar*, a play about his own father, his farm, and what Shanley called the "amazing language" of the Irish Midlands, was matched by Catherine Zuber's strikingly accurate Irish costuming for the Irish actors—from left to right Peter Maloney, Brian F. O'Byrne, and Dearbhla Molloy—in the play's 2014 Broadway production. ©*Sara Krulwich/ The New York Times/Redux*

Robert Cohen met with Zuber in the tiny basement costume shop of the Shoenfeld Theatre on 45th Street, where she was making final adjustments to Jeremy Irons's costume for *Impressionism*. This wasn't her only obligation on this day, however. She had just come from a final dress rehearsal of *The Winter's Tale* at the Brooklyn Academy of Music and was about to head to Lincoln Center, where she was designing a gala performance celebrating the Metropolitan Opera's 125th anniversary.

Zuber explained that she had come to her profession from an undergraduate background in art, with a major in photography. But after college graduation and a subsequent move to New Haven, Connecticut, she met up with several Yale theatre students who, admiring the vintage clothes she liked to wear, encouraged her to design costumes for their extracurricular productions staged at Yale's undergraduate colleges. "I just loved doing this," Zuber exulted, and after a year of designing such shows she assembled a portfolio of her designs and applied to the Yale School of Drama for graduate professional training in the field. Jane Greenwood, a veteran designer who then headed the Yale costume program, was enthusiastic, and Zuber was admitted. "I also had a photo portfolio," she added. "Being a costume designer is not about costumes alone! Learning photography proved extremely helpful because it taught me how to compose an entire image—a picture of the set with characters wearing my costumes in it. Composing such images taught me how to design a show so that my costumed people would appear to belong in that world, to hold their own within it rather than disappearing into the scenery. Costumes then become an ensemble of characters within a rectangular image, not just clothes on a rack."

Zuber now moves easily between classic verse dramas (*Macbeth, Twelfth Night, The Winter's Tale*), revivals of modern comedies (*Born Yesterday, The Royal Family*), musicals (*The Bridges of Madison County, How to Succeed . . . , South Pacific*), historical dramas (*A Man for All Seasons, Coast of Utopia*), and new plays set in modern times (*Outside Mullingar, Impressionism, Doubt*). "I enjoy going from one style to the other," she said. Though with contemporary plays, she noted, "It's sometimes harder to convince the actors to wear certain things, as they all have their own ideas of how they should dress. And that's natural because in a modern realistic play the actors need to stay connected to who they are. But in a period show,

6.

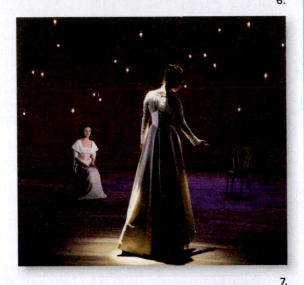

7.

8.

6. Sometimes costume uniformity is required, as in the case of "uniforms." In *South Pacific*, Zuber has given each sailor a measure of individuality by the way he wears his uniform: with his blue shirt buttoned or unbuttoned and with or without a name or initials printed on it; with his metal dog tags worn or abandoned; with his white hat brim turned up or rolled up or rolled down, or with his hat taken off entirely; and, in the case of one actor (Andrew Samonsky), with a plain white undershirt that stands out in the otherwise "uniform" naval brigade. Lifted by the men and holding a grass skirt is Loretta Ables Sayre as "Bloody Mary," a Polynesian native seller of exotic local products who wears layered garments and exotic jewelry—all sharply contrasting with the bold masculinity of the sailors. ©*Joan Marcus*

7. & 8. Every costume designer faces a challenge in Shakespeare's *The Winter's Tale* because the play takes place in two very different locales: the gloom-ridden court of Sicilia and the joyous festival of Bohemia. **7.** In Sicilia, young princess Perdita (Morven Cristie) sees what she thinks is a statue of her long-dead mother, Hermione (Rebecca Hall); Zuber has dressed each in silky white flowing dresses against the black background of the joyless kingdom. **8.** In Bohemia, Zuber has costumed the Bohemian country revelers in rough-textured, earth-colored, and multilayered fabrics that play brilliantly against the scenic background of dark blue sky and red, white, and blue balloons. Ethan Hawke (*center*) plays the shifty but entertaining tradesman Autolycus in a mismatched ensemble of shirt, vest, and trousers; a black hat with a bright yellow flower; tall leather boots, one strapped up to his knee; and doubly dark sunglasses, and with hair that straggles down to his shirt pockets. His friends strum their guitars in even more casual garb, and the women, under their loosely tied country aprons, wear rugged red, green, and orange skirts that reach the floor in this 2009 production at the Brooklyn Academy of Music.

7. ©*Joan Marcus*; **8.** ©*Geraint Lewis*

9. Zuber's exuberant 1940s lounging wear for Harry Brock (Jim Belushi) and Billie Dawn (Nina Arianda) in Garson Kanin's 1946 *Born Yesterday*, revived on Broadway in 2011, earned her an eleventh Tony nomination. ©*Carol Rosegg*

actors are more trusting of the designer: there's enough distance from where they are in their everyday life, and who they are playing as a character." Zuber particularly loves designing fantasy plays: "I [love] a project that must come mainly from my imagination, and where I can therefore go more 'over the top.' That's absolutely thrilling!"

But designers never work wholly on their own, and Zuber is quick to point out that costume design is a "real collaboration" with those technicians who actually pattern, cut, drape, and sew the costumes that she draws: "Costume designers are very dependent on the people who make the clothes. We show them the sketch and they interpret and build it—and the really great ones take it a step further."

Technology has come to the aid of costume designers as it has all the design arts, and Zuber now finds her process greatly enhanced by Photoshop in particular. She explained, "I sketch freehand, then scan it into the computer, and then add color—and if the director doesn't like the color I can change it right away. After that, I can manipulate it any way I want. I can put all the costumes together on one page, and if I see that one character stands out inappropriately, or doesn't stand out enough, I can change this very quickly. When I was designing the last act of *Cherry Orchard* [at the Brooklyn Academy of Music in 2008], I could show the director all the characters onstage together just as they would be in the play. And on a separate page I can trace each individual character's journey so the director can see the character's trajectory through the play, so the director can say, 'This character should be messier here,' or something like that. Photoshop is a fantastic tool to show what the designs will look like onstage in all these formats."

Zuber adores her profession: "I love being a costume designer! You're learning something new with each show, meeting new people. And the greatest thing is that it leaves beautiful, indelible memories. Of course, it's a lot of hard work, and while some people coming to New York may have stars in their eyes, they should know it's not very glamorous. Sometimes we have to laugh at how ridiculous our work conditions can be—just look at this room [referring to the cluttered basement workplace] for instance! But if you really have a love for it, and a passion, there's absolutely nothing like it!"

———————————

Courtesy of Catherine Zuber.

other adornments have considerable storytelling impact: they display to the play's audience a character's rank or role in society. Even the shoes, if unwisely chosen, can destroy the artistry of a production by being unsuitable for the character or by being so badly fitted that the actor's posture or gait is altered.

Whether arrived at through design and fabrication or through careful selection from a thrift store, good costume design creates a sense of character, period, style, and theatricality out of wearable garments. In harmony with scenery, makeup, lighting, and the play's interpretation, costumes can subtly underline the play's meaning and the characters' personalities, or they can loudly vie for attention—and sometimes even become the star of the show. But even in productions of purely naturalistic drama, well-designed and well-chosen costumes can exert a magical theatrical force and lend a special magnitude to the actors' and the playwright's art. Much like lighting—and all other design elements—costuming can be most effective when it seems invisible but is in fact contributing to create the seamless impression of an entire world.

Makeup

Makeup, which is essentially the design of the actor's face and hair, occupies an undervalued position in much contemporary theatre, where it tends to be the last design field to be considered. In amateur theatre, makeup is often applied for the first time at the final dress rehearsal—and sometimes not until just before the opening performance. Indeed, makeup is the only major design element whose planning and execution are often left entirely to the actor's discretion.

Makeup, however, is one of the elemental arts of the theatre, quite probably the first of the theatre's design arts, and it was absolutely fundamental to the origins of drama. The earliest chanters of the dithyramb, like the spiritual leaders of indigenous tribes today, invariably made themselves up—probably by smearing their faces with blood or the dregs of wine—in preparation for the performance of their holy rites. Their resulting makeup subsequently inspired the Greek tragic and comic masks that are today the universal symbols of theatre itself. The ancient art of face painting remains crucial to Chinese xiqu, as well as to other traditional Asian, African, and Native American theatre forms.

Makeup, like costuming, serves both illustrative and ceremonial functions. The illustrative function of makeup is unquestionably the more obvious one today—so much so that we often forget its ceremonial role entirely. Illustrative makeup is the means by which the actor changes her

or his appearance to resemble that of the character. Makeup of this sort is particularly useful in helping make a young actor look older or an old one look younger and in making an actor of any age resemble a known historical figure or a fictitious character whose appearance is already set in the public imagination. Makeup gives Cyrano his great nose and Falstaff his red one; it reddens Macbeth's "bleeding captain" and whitens the ghost of Banquo; it turns the college sophomore into the aged Prospero, the Broadway dancer into a lion cub. Makeup design can create endless variations in the human face: artificial scars, deformities, bruises, beards, wigs, moustaches, sunburn, frostbite, and scores of other facial embellishments, textures, and shadings can all contribute significantly to the depth of individual characterization.

A subtler use of makeup, still within the realistic mode, is aimed at the evocation of psychological traits through physical clues: the modern makeup artist may try to suggest character by exaggerating or distorting the actor's natural eye placement, the size and shape of the mouth, the angularity of the nose, or the tilt of the eyebrows. There can be no question that we form impressions of a character's inner state on the basis of observable characteristics—as the title character of Shakespeare's *Julius Caesar* nervously notices Cassius's "lean and hungry look," so do we. And the skilled makeup artist can go far in enhancing the psychological texture of a play by the imaginative use of facial shaping and shading.

Another realistic use of makeup seeks merely to enhance the actor's features in order to make them distinct and expressive to every member of the audience. This is known as creating a face that "reads" to the house—that is, one that conveys its fullest expression over a great distance. To achieve this effect, the makeup artist exaggerates highlights and shadows and sharply defines specific features such as wrinkles, eyelashes, eyebrows, and jawlines. Such simplified, emboldened, and subtly exaggerated makeup, combined with stage lighting, creates an impression of realism far greater than any that could be achieved by makeup or lighting alone.

Ceremonial makeup goes beyond realism altogether. This category includes makeup that is stylized or represents the actor as a superhuman presence. The face painting of the traditional Chinese xiqu actor, for example, like the mask of the Japanese noh performer, can endow the person applying it with the illusion and, perhaps, the inner feeling of spiritual transcendence. Like the war paint applied in ancient rituals, ceremonial makeup allows the audience to imagine the performer becoming larger than life—a divine ascendant to a higher world. This apparent enhancement of the actor may even be thought of as the "up" in "makeup."

Brian d'Arcy James required ninety minutes to put on his makeup to play the title role in *Shrek* when he starred in the 2008 family friendly Broadway musical. ©Sara Krulwich/The New York Times/Redux

Duelist and would-be lover Cyrano de Bergerac has a large nose—indeed, that's the axis on which the entire plot of Edmond Rostand's Romantic era play of the same name turns. But most actors don't have giant noses, so makeup artists need to be experts in prosthesis—the artificial extension or replacement of human body parts. Here Stephen Rea sports a skillfully created prosthetic proboscis, as created by costume designer John Bright, in a 2004 production of the play at England's National Theatre. ©Robbie Jack/Corbis Entertainment/Getty Images

Some obvious examples of such traditional makeup and "making up" are still evident, particularly in European and Asian theatre. The makeup of the circus and the classic mime, two formats that developed in Europe out of the masked commedia dell'arte of the sixteenth century, both use bold colors: white, black, and sometimes red for the mime and an even wider spectrum for the circus clown. Avant-garde and expressionist playwrights also frequently utilize similar sorts of abstracted makeup, while Asian theatre has always relied on the often dazzling facial coloring (and mane-like wigs and beards) of certain characters in Japanese kabuki, Indian kathakali, and Chinese xiqu.

No matter how it is used, makeup serves a primal function: to transform the actor into a performer. In this way, it serves both the realistic and symbolic functions of theatre. Even the most stylized makeup is based on the human form, and even the most realistic makeup conveys some theatricality. The theatre, after all, is never so immersed in the ordinary that it could—or should—be wholly mistaken as everyday life. So when actors sitting at a makeup table open their makeup kit, with its bottles and tubes, brushes, and eyebrow pencils, more is going on than simple, practical face-making. Powerful forces are at work in this moment that link the actor to the celebrants who in ages past painted their faces to assure the world that they were leaving their temporal bodies and boldly venturing into the exalted domain of the gods.

Makeup reflects ancient roots. These young Yacouba women have applied bold geometric face paint in a centuries-old design for their performance of a traditional dance-drama of the Ivory Coast based on an ancient hunting ritual. The design, originally intended not merely to entertain an audience but to suggest a magical transformation into the spirit realm, continues to carry at least the resonance of that meaning today. ©*MyLoupe/UIG/Getty Images*

Stagecraft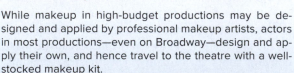

The Makeup Kit

While makeup in high-budget productions may be designed and applied by professional makeup artists, actors in most productions—even on Broadway—design and apply their own, and hence travel to the theatre with a well-stocked makeup kit.

The foundation is a basic color applied thinly and evenly to the face and neck and sometimes to other parts of the body as well. Cream makeup, formerly (and still commonly) known as greasepaint, is a highly opaque and relatively inexpensive skin coloring that comes in a variety of shades. Cake makeup, or pancake, is less messy than cream but also less flexible. Cake makeup comes in small plastic cases and is applied with a damp sponge.

Color shading defines the facial structure and exaggerates its dimensions to give the face a sculptured appearance from a distance; ordinarily, the least imposing characteristics of the face are put in shadow and the prominent features are

highlighted. Contour colors, known as liners, come in both cream and cake form and are usually chosen to harmonize with the foundation color, as well as with the color of the actor's costume and the color of the lighting. Shadows are made with darker colors and highlights with lighter ones; both are applied with small brushes and blended into the foundation. Rouge, a special color application used to redden lips and cheeks, is usually applied along with the shading colors. When greasepaints are used, the makeup must be dusted with makeup powder to "set" it and prevent running. A makeup pencil is regularly used to darken eyebrows and also to accentuate eyes and facial wrinkles.

Special applications may include false eyelashes or heavy mascara; facial hair (beards and mustaches, ordinarily made from crepe wool); nose putty and various other prosthetic materials; and various treatments for aging, wrinkling, scarring, and otherwise disfiguring the skin. A well-equipped actor has a makeup kit stocked with glue (spirit gum and liquid latex), solvents, synthetic hair, wax (to mask eyebrows), and hair whiteners—in addition to the standard foundation and shading colors—to create a wide variety of makeup effects.

Sound Design

Music and sound effects have been in use in the theatre since ancient times. Aristotle considered music one of the six essential components of tragedy, and offstage thunder, trumpet "flourishes" and "tuckets," and "the noise of a sea-fight" are all called for in Shakespeare's stage directions. Before the electronic age, theatres were routinely equipped with such devices as rain drums (barrels filled with pebbles or dried seeds that made rain sounds when revolved), thunder sheets (hanging sheets of tin that rumbled ominously when rattled), and thunder runs (sloping wooden troughs down which cannonballs rolled and eventually crashed). Since 1900, most theatres have also used an electric telephone ringer (a battery-powered bell mounted on a piece of wood) and a door slammer (a miniature doorframe and door, complete with latch) to simulate the sounds of domestic life. All of these sound effects were ordinarily created by an assistant stage manager, but the rapid development of audio recording and playback technologies starting in the 1970s and 1980s has led to a virtual revolution in the area of sound design and the emergence of an officially designated sound designer in theatres around the world. Like musical scoring in cinema and sound engineering in rock concerts, theatre sound is now almost entirely an electronic art.

Theatrical performances frequently augment the sounds that occur naturally in a production. Almost all musicals and many "straight" (nonmusical) plays employ electronic sound enhancement that reinforces the actors' voices and creates a "louder than life" sonic ambience. In such cases the actors usually wear miniature wireless microphones—often concealed. The use of live or recorded offstage sounds may establish locale (such as fog-horns), time of day (midnight chimes), time of year (birdsong), weather (thunder and rain), and onstage or offstage events (a ringing telephone, an arriving taxi, an angel crashing through the ceiling). Stage sounds can be realistic (an ambulance siren), stylized (an amplified, accelerating heartbeat), stereophonically localized (an airplane heard

The Midas XL8 audio mixer is one of the newest and most elaborate sound consoles on the market, providing user-friendly desk operation for the most complex sound-scored productions and concerts, including the 2009 Nobel Prize Ceremony in Oslo and Depeche Mode's "Tour of the Universe," which played worldwide to audiences of up to eighty-five thousand in 2009–2010. ©Simon Lees/Future Music Magazine/Getty Images

The Encounter, from 2016, is surely one of the odder productions to grace the Broadway stage. Audience members wear headphones that help create a rich sonic environment as they see—or more accurately *hear*—a complex story about a *National Geographic* photographer traveling down the Amazon River. Simon McBurney, pictured here, controls the soundscape with live recordings and subtly manipulated monologues. ©*Joan Marcus*

as crossing overhead from left to right), or pervasive and "in-your-head" (a buzzing mosquito, electronic static, a thousand ringing cell phones).

One recent production demonstrated how sound can create an entire theatrical world. For *The Encounter,* a 2016 play created and performed by Simon McBurney, each audience member was provided a set of headphones. McBurney, onstage, manipulated microphones that transmitted sounds directly into audience members' ears—all while the sound designer played prerecorded atmospheres and speeches that coincided with the live action. The sound, here, is not simply one design element: it is largely the design itself, and the success of this play attests to the power of sound to affect our perception of reality.

Music, as well as sound effects, often evokes a mood, supports an emotion, intensifies an action, or provides a transition into or between scenes. Music accompanying a play can be composed for the production or derived from

recordings; it can be played live during the performance, often in full sight of the audience, or it can be played back through a sound system or onstage "prop" speakers, such as a radio. Naturally, many combinations are possible. The director John Doyle has specialized in staging plays in which performers also play various instruments, thereby scoring their own action—and blurring the line between performer and musician. Even in these cases, though, the sound designer designs and oversees the implementation of all of these elements.

Sound design has rapidly escalated in importance over the past two decades as playwrights and directors incorporate the new technologies that have swiftly expanded theatrical potential, first with audio recording and now with highly complex digital recording, editing, processing, and playback technologies. However, contemporary sound design is not without its detractors. Controversially, the administration of the Tony Awards elected, in 2014, to

Photo Essay: Sound Designer Scott Lehrer

When Scott Lehrer received the Tony Award in Sound Design for *South Pacific* in 2008, it was an honor not only for him but also for sound design itself, as his award was the first Tony ever awarded in this blossoming field. He has designed forty plays on Broadway, including 2018's revival of *Carousel,* 2017's *Hello, Dolly!, The Front Page, Fiddler on the Roof, Dames at Sea, The King and I, Death of a Salesman, South Pacific, Angels in America, A Streetcar Named Desire,* and *The Heidi Chronicles.* Lehrer acknowledged in an interview with Robert Cohen that the Tony was "something of a culmination after working in the mines for many years," but he was also insistent that there have been many other sound design pioneers who should be recognized. "I was just lucky enough to be doing a show the year they initiated these," he modestly declared.

Lehrer practiced and studied music when he went to college at Sarah Lawrence in the mid-1970s, first expanding his early love of rock, folk, and jazz and then "getting weird sounds out of synthesizers." Soon he was deep into electronic music, picking up bits of "found sound" and creating sound collages for classmate directors and choreographers to go with their performances. "I became fascinated by the entire world of sound," he explained. "It was all quite new and wonderful." Not limiting himself to drama or dance productions, he created sound for giant public events such as New York's SummerStage in Central Park with 100,000 attendees, along with museum exhibitions, live industrial shows, and corporate media. But theatre beckoned strongly when he took a job as the sound engineer for the Colonnades Theatre Lab, an avant-garde off-off-Broadway theatre on New York's Lower East Side. "We all worked together there," he recalled, "blending multichannel 'surround sound' into the rehearsals so that the actors would get used to hearing sounds while rehearsing and would respond to those sounds like they responded to the other actors. Sound simply became part of their

1. Sound designer Scott Lehrer, in the professional sound studio he has built in his apartment in lower Manhattan, builds up possible cues for a new production.
©Robert Cohen

world." At the time, Lehrer didn't realize how unusual this was, but in the days when offstage sound was mainly created by stage managers operating wooden, handheld "door-slamming" devices or executing "needle drops" on long-playing records played over a loudspeaker, he and his colleagues were innovating truly revolutionary techniques.

By 1980, Lehrer had moved up the ladder to off-Broadway, where he worked at many of the finest companies: Circle Repertory, Manhattan Theatre Club, the American Place, and, mainly, Playwrights Horizons, where he described himself as "almost in residence" for many years. "We were still in the Stone Age as far as equipment was concerned," Lehrer recalled. "We had to be really creative, figure out how to do things with very little money, invent new ways of working."

No theatre technology has advanced as rapidly in the past decades as sound. Lehrer said: "Young people coming into this field today have little idea how new it all is. In just the time I've been doing all this, we've gone from records to tape decks to samplers to digital sound and music sequencers. The speed with which we can create sound design, and the level of control we have over it, have increased almost beyond belief." To

create the sound of road construction that director Susan Stroman had thought of adding into her production of *Happiness,* at New York's Lincoln Center, for example, Lehrer sent his assistant out to record the jackhammers then hammering away on the street outside. "I handed him my recorder at 10:00, at 10:15 I plugged the recorder into my Pro Tools [digital audio system], by 10:30 I had cleaned it up, and by 10:45 I had it in my QLab [sound software] ready to go into the show. Just a few years ago this would have taken three days!"

By the end of the 1980s, Lehrer was on Broadway, first with Wendy Wasserstein's *The Heidi Chronicles,* which received the Pulitzer Prize and the Tony Award for best play of the year, and soon thereafter designing sound for Tony Kushner's landmark play *Angels in America.*

What, aside from a mastery of technology, does it take to be a sound designer? Lehrer does not pretend to have a single aesthetic style. Instead, he considers himself something of a chameleon and frames his designs in

2. At his piano, Lehrer composes a new melody that might be inserted into his design. ©*Robert Cohen*

close concert with the context of the play and the perspective of the director. Working with the playwright/director Richard Nelson, for example, who asks for the sound "to be a part of the storytelling, to be another character in the play," he investigates the sonic ambience of the text. For Nelson's *Franny's Way,* set in an apartment above a jazz club, Lehrer described his challenge as creating the unseen people downstairs: "What would they be listening to? Jazz, of course, but what kind of jazz? What tempo? Cool or hot, ballad or up-tempo? Saxophone, yes, but Dexter Gordon or John Coltrane? I tried to find the musical style that would convey the ambient emotional feel Nelson wanted." For Terrence McNally's *A Perfect Ganesh,* two older American women are traveling through India. "What sort of music do they hear?" Lehrer asked himself. "There are many regions in India and many local musical forms, and it would

be disrespectful to the culture not to represent this. So I have to be an amateur musicologist; I have to listen to everything from the locale, the era, and the culture that the play is seeking to represent."

Lehrer considers sound design a perfect marriage of art and technology: "You have to have something to say. Sound design is not just technical, but you absolutely have to have the skills to do it. While you can't let the technique get in the way, you also have to make it work for you. Sound design takes place in real time. When you're in technical rehearsals, if you don't know the technology you can't keep up with the speed of the rehearsal, and if that happens you simply can't realize your art. You have to control the technology; you can't let the technology control you."

———————————

Courtesy of Scott Lehrer.

3. In the Mitzi Newhouse Theatre in Lincoln Center, technical rehearsals are about to get started for the world premiere of *Happiness,* with Lehrer as sound designer. A "sound table" has been placed in the theatre's auditorium where Lehrer and Drew Levy, his assistant, have set up their computers and audio equipment to create the sound cues that will be executed—and adjusted—for this afternoon's rehearsal. ©*Robert Cohen*

4. Now, in the theatre's light booth from which the sound will be operated during actual performances, Lehrer confirms that the sound operating system—with the GO button the technician will use to execute the individual cues—is properly set up. ©*Robert Cohen*

eliminate the Tony Award for sound design altogether—a decision that led to much pushback and criticism from designers and other theatre artists. After a few years, the Tony administration agreed with the critics and reinstated the award for the 2017–2018 season. This decision helped cement something sound designers and many other theatre artists have long known: sound is absolutely fundamental to the production of today's theatre around the globe and is quite definitely here to stay.

Puppets and Projections

In the spring of 2011, the Broadway production of *War Horse* won Tony Awards for best play, direction, scenery, costume, and sound design—but took no awards for what everyone left the theatre talking about: its magnificent puppets and projections. These are currently the two fastest-growing design areas in theatre, and each has seized an important space in today's theatrical design; clearly, further recognition will soon be coming. We will look at them separately.

PUPPETS

Puppet theatre began in China two thousand years ago and has long been used in the Japanese bunraku and Indonesian wayang kulit shadow puppetry, as well as for supernatural effects in medieval and Renaissance drama. But increasingly, puppets are used to represent live dramatic characters in major contemporary plays, such as young adults in the long-running *Avenue Q*, animals in Julie Taymor's *The Lion King,* and horses in *War Horse.* Those horses—designed, fabricated, and directed by Basil Jones and Adrian Kohler of the Handspring Puppet Company—are controlled by expertly trained crews operating from within skeletal frames, which are seen to prance, gallop, whinny, and rise up on their back feet throughout the production. The effect is certainly spectacular, but what is particularly surprising is that after a few minutes of admiring the technology, the audience settles back and begins to forget that the "horses" are puppets and imagines them instead as real animals. They then empathize with their feelings, and with the feelings of the characters who love

War Horse astonished audiences in London in 2007, and then in New York in 2011, with the giant projections of World War I battlefields designed by 59 Productions, and by the amazing, full-size, puppet horses created by Basil Jones and Adrian Kohler. ©*Simon Annand*

them. When the horses "die" at the end of the play, many grown adults in the audience wipe tears from their eyes.

Puppets have been employed in both big Broadway shows—like *War Horse*—and more experimental productions, as with the celebrated company Manual Cinema, which uses handmade paper puppets, coupled with vintage overhead projectors, to startling and often profound effect. Their *Mementos Mori,* in 2015, employed over 100 puppets to tell a haunting story of death and technology. Whatever their use, though, puppets have proven to be more than an addition or feature of theatre: they tap into one of the art form's deepest powers—the ability for an audience to treat a clearly artificial construction as a deeply human reality. Puppets help us discover that an open display of theatrical mechanics can heighten, rather than distract from, the intellectual and emotional thrust of the play being performed.

PROJECTIONS

Projections were not possible until the development of the steady beam of focused, incandescent, electric light in the late 1800s. But by the 1920s, German designer Erwin Piscator was experimenting with projected images as part of his scenic design, while his colleague Bertolt Brecht projected titles on screens to indicate the location (for example, "A highway cutting through barren fields" in his *Mother Courage*) or projected supplementary material (for example, historical maps and documents in his *Galileo*). In America, Tennessee Williams called for "a screen on which were projected magic-lantern slides bearing images or titles" to be used in the production of his 1944 play *The Glass Menagerie* "to give accent to certain values for each scene." (The play's first director, Eddie Dowling, decided not to use this device, but many subsequent directors of the play have done so.)

Today, led by the trend away from strict realism as well as new technological developments, such as digital imaging, video recording, and computer-designed animation, both image and video projections have frequently become integral to theatrical design. As a result, the projection designer, sometimes called the image designer or video designer, has become a new member of theatrical design

Projections are the main—and almost the only—scenery in *The Curious Incident of the Dog in the Night-Time,* a prize-winning play about an autistic but brilliant fifteen-year-old boy who hates being touched. The set was designed by Bunny Christie, but the ever-changing video design, which dominated the stage at all times and reflected Boon's mind, was by Finn Ross. Graham Butler plays the boy (shown here) in the 2014 production at London's Gielgud Theatre; the play won many awards. It opened on Broadway later that year and won five Tony Awards, including Best Play and Best Director. ©Geraint Lewis/Alamy Stock Photo

teams around the world. Wendall K. Harrington has been a particularly important leader in this field, having been credited as projection designer (or video designer or multi-image designer) thirty-five times on Broadway since his work on *They're Playing Our Song* in 1979, and having created the country's first projection design program at the Yale School of Drama in 2010.

In a landmark moment in the development of projection design, Timothy Bird and the Knifedge Creative Network earned the first-ever Drama Desk Award for outstanding projections and video design for their work on the 2008 Broadway revival of *Sunday in the Park with George*, the celebrated musical about French artist Georges Seurat and his influence on modern art. In *Sunday*'s 1984 premiere, the first act was staged in front of a large painted canvas of Seurat's famous painting that shares the play's title, with the costumed actors taking the positions of the artist's human figures. The twenty-first-century design, however, projected shifting images on an LED wall at the rear of the stage. The effect allowed the audience to see the painting created from completely blank canvas to finished masterpiece during the act. Moreover, the videos created an overall visual design from thousands of tiny dots of color—a brilliant replication of Seurat's style of painting. More recently, 2017's hit Broadway musical *Anastasia*—which also won the Drama Desk Award for projection design—used the technology to create ghostly effects, such as phantomlike dancers who mingle with the flesh-and-blood actors in one sequence set in a ballroom. The dance exists in one character's memory, and as such the projections help create a sense of surreal, hazy reminiscence—a psychological truth, not simply a spectacle for its own sake.

Projections—both realistic and abstract—are certainly growing as almost routine theatrical components. Their critical reception has become more positive, and the public has rapidly acclimated to their integration into the theatrical experience. Like sound and lighting design before it, projection design is becoming less a "feature" and more an artistic component that demonstrates ideas, not just flashy techniques.

Projections on huge movable screens is at the heart of the Cloud Eye Control theatre collective in Los Angeles, seen here in its 2015 production of *Half Life* at the REDCAT theatre. Inspired by the Fukushima nuclear meltdown after the 2011 tsunami in Japan, this short play—with two actors, two onstage musicians, and no real plot—is mesmerizing due to its abstract portrayal of a fantasy life among schools of fish, flocks of birds and butterflies, growing vegetation, and skies filled with stars and clouds. ©*Marcus Yam/Los Angeles Times/Getty Images*

Re-Animator: The Musical is a semi-operatic farce staged by Stuart Gordon (who also directed the film of that name) that capitalizes on bizarre magical effects created by effects designer John Naulin and costume designer Joe Kucharski. The play premiered at the Steve Allen Theater in Hollywood in 2011; the now-headless Professor Hill is played by Jesse Merlin, who is staring at the body of his Dean's daughter (Rachel Avery), while the Dean, played by George Wendt, looks on from behind. ©*Thomas Hargis*

Special Effects

Theatre "magic" often entails special effects not easily described as simply lighting or sound. These include fire, explosions, fog, smoke, wind, rain, snow, lightning, spurts of blood, and mysterious arrivals and disappearances, such as what stage directions in Shakespeare's *The Tempest* describe as the goddess Juno descending from Mount Olympus and certain nymphs who "heavily vanish" after "a strange hollow and confused noise." Commercial devices can help theatre technicians achieve these effects, but each bit of magic requires its own on-the-spot ingenuity to be both credible and effective. In 2017, the Royal Shakespeare Company took on *The Tempest* using motion-capture technology, a form of technology that had been, up until then, reserved for the cinema. When the sprite Ariel reminisces on his past, in which he was imprisoned in a tree by a witch, the actor contorts his body—thus manipulating a towering, three-dimensional digital image of his memory, complete with gnarled bark and twisting branches, that reflects his every movement. Later, when he transforms into a harpy—a mythical creature with the body of a bird and head of a woman—to serve his master, Prospero, he once again has his movements reflected on a giant digital avatar of himself

In what is surely the cutting edge of contemporary theatre technology, motion-capture sensors in this 2017 production of William Shakespeare's *The Tempest,* at the Royal Shakespeare Company, translate the real-time movements of an actor to a three-dimensional image. Pictured here are Simon Russell Beale in the role of Prospero, and a fantastic projection created by Mark Quartley as the magical sprite Ariel. *Photo by Topher McGrillis ©RSC 2016*

Live fire is one of the theatre's main—but also most dangerous—effects; it was what burned down Shakespeare's Globe Theatre (via an offstage cannon shot) in 1613. Here it is used safely in *Dara,* a Pakistani production set in 1659 and brought to London's National Theatre in 2015, which portrays two brothers fighting each other to rule the Muslim empire. ©*Geraint Lewis*

as this beast. We are truly on the forefront of a new hybrid form of theatre, one that mixes media with bodily acting.

Of course, there are still minimal, special-effects-free versions of *The Tempest,* and there always will be. Special effects in the theatre are not necessarily a positive or negative development; like all other design elements, they ultimately must serve the play, rather than provide their own purpose for existence. But when they do work with the other aspects of the play, they clearly can offer a distinct kind of stage magic.

Digital Technologies in Theatre Design

Today's theatre designers have a vast array of digital programs at their fingertips. These programs are only the most recent in a long list of technological tools used by visual artists, however. For centuries, designers have worked with such basic implements as charcoal, colored paints, rulers, squares, and drafting tables. These ancient

devices are surely forms of technology, and while they may seem more rudimentary, they can still lead to work of subtlety and precision. Complicated "drawing machines" came into play during the Renaissance: Leonardo da Vinci invented a device known as a perspectograph to help artists transform their perceived earthly realities into two-dimensional sketches and engravings in the early 1500s, and Canaletto's detailed paintings of eighteenth-century Venice were executed with the aid of a room-size camera obscura.

What does digital design offer that pencil and paper do not? Computers, of course, cannot analyze a text with the critical imagination of a human. Nor can they suggest a costume, conceive a style, or make an audience laugh. But what digital technology *can* do is aid and accelerate the process of artists who do these things. Computers have the capacity to digitally combine and configure (and then reconfigure) ideas, angles, shapes, colors, spaces, perspectives, and measurements. This ability makes possible the execution of a range of experimental and aesthetic possibilities with the speed of light and the assurance of a mathematician. Perhaps no other era of theatre history has seen a technological innovation so successfully balance reality's hard facts with the artist's free-floating imagination.

Digital design has become invaluable to contemporary designers on a variety of levels. First, computer-aided-design (CAD) programs can assist with or even replace much of the drudgery of sheer drawing mechanics. With a click of the mouse, straight lines, angles, circles, shapes, colors, and typefaces can be selected from a menu of choices and placed where desired. Moreover, all of these can be shifted in an instant: colors can be changed, lines lengthened, walls thickened, floors raised, furniture moved, sight lines adjusted, and dimensions measured. Individual design elements can be instantly replicated: an elaborately drawn banister post can become a dozen posts in a flash. Whole drawings can be rescaled and zoomed in or out, individual elements can be rotated or relocated freely about the page, and the resulting drawings can be shared instantly with design team members working anywhere around the world (as designers often do). Global collaboration has become not merely possible in the digital age, it has become routine.

Digital storage allows designers to draw upon vast visual databases. A designer can, for example, dip into virtual art catalogues of eighteenth-century chandeliers, Victorian drapery, Roman togas—all digitized for computer retrieval and available (subject to copyright considerations) for incorporation into stage designs. And digitized cutting and pasting allows the designer to combine virtual forms. A costume designer can thus virtually sew the sleeves of one digitized garment onto another or even virtually dress one digitized actor with a digital costume, giving a view of a fully costumed character without buying a single inch of fabric. Dedicated database programs also save lighting and sound technicians innumerable hours of storing, sorting, and printing the dozens of dimmer schedules, cue sheets, and loudspeaker assignments needed in multiproduction repertory assignments.

Furthermore, in many theatres digitized scenographic modeling has supplemented traditional drawings by creating, on a computer screen, three-dimensional models of the stage set that can demonstrate perspectives from any vantage: the left, right, or center of the house; or from a bird's-eye position that may clarify lighting and off-stage storage positions. Designers, directors, and actors can now walk through the set while it exists solely as a virtual reality, and they can light the scenery in a variety of ways before anything is built—or even before a theatre is rented. The opportunity to digitally storyboard scenery, costumes, and lighting, together with text and music and sound, is an extraordinary advance in the art of production planning wherever time and money are involved, as they almost always are.

Finally, of course, digital technology is not merely a preparatory tool for the designer; it is now the very medium by which sound, lighting, and projections are routinely transmitted to the audience. The music and sound that emanate from house speakers have been fully digitized, the still or moving images projected onto screens or LED walls are now pixelated, and the intensity of the lighting instruments—and increasingly their colors and movements as well—are executed today with the aid of highly specialized computer software. Additionally, the cues for these operations are, in many theatres, now called from digital promptbooks. Theatre has definitely entered the digital age.

The Technical Production Team

Far outnumbering all the other members of the theatre staff—the actors, designers, writers, and directors—are the artisans and technicians who get the production organized, built, installed, lit, and ready to open, and who then make it run.

Because of their numbers, theatrical technicians are ordinarily organized in a hierarchical structure, headed by stage, house, and production managers, technical directors, and shop supervisors, all of whom are charged with guiding and overseeing the work of a virtual army of craftspersons. This section provides a typical breakdown of these functions, which you might also find detailed in the theatre program of any major theatre.

The *production stage manager (PSM)*—usually known simply as the stage manager—is a role that has existed at least since the eighteenth century. The PSM coordinates the scheduling, staffing, and budgeting of every element of the production, including the acting rehearsals and the building, loading in, and operation of all the design and technical elements. An expert in legal codes, safety procedures, and accounting policies, and sensitive to the varying artistic needs of actors, directors, designers, and technicians, the PSM wrestles with the complex problems of integrating the play's disparate elements—determining, for example, whether the lights should be hung and focused before or after the scenery is installed (there can be reasons for going either way on this) and anticipating how long it will take to train the stage crew or to set the light cues.

The PSM coordinates the director's work with that of the actors and the technical and design departments. At the beginning of rehearsals, the PSM is involved primarily in organizational matters: scheduling calls and appointments; recording the blocking of actors; anticipating technical problems of quick costume changes, set shifts, and the like; and organizing the basic "calling" of the show—that is, the system by which lighting, sound, actor-entrance, and scene-shift cues are initiated.

During the performance, the PSM is in full charge of the show, observing it (directly from a booth above the audience, from the side of the stage, or through one or more video monitors) and physically calling each lighting, sound, and scene-moving cue—normally through an electronic intercom system. The PSM may also signal actor entrances, usually by means of cue-lights, which are tiny backstage lights the PSM triggers—a crucial task when an entrance must be timed to an onstage physical action that the actor cannot see from backstage. It is the job and, more important, the art of the PSM to precisely time these cues to create the theatrical impact intended by the director, while also making adjustments for unexpected interruptions such as sustained audience laughter or applause, electrical outages, or actor or technician accidents onstage.

The PSM also maintains the production after its opening performance by conducting understudy and replacement rehearsals when needed; arranging for the cleaning, repair, or replacement of costumes, props, and stage machinery; and in other ways assuming the functions of the director, who, in most professional productions, is no longer present on a regular basis. Many professional stage directors (including Robert Cohen, one of your authors) and film directors (including Stephen Spielberg) began their theatrical careers by stage managing their high school or college productions.

Working for the PSM is one or more assistant stage managers (ASMs). In rehearsals, ASMs typically set out props, follow the script, prompt actors who are off book (no longer rehearsing with script in hand) when they forget their lines, take line notes when actors recite lines incorrectly, and substitute for actors who may be temporarily away from the rehearsal hall. During the performance, as the PSM calls the show from a fixed offstage position, the ASMs—on two-way headset connections—implement the PSM's calls to the actors and crew chiefs, often transmitting them as visual "go" signs for scene shifts, actor entrances, and effect cues. ASMs also serve as the backstage eyes and ears of the PSM, who is always watching the stage.

Technical director (TD) is a term that dates from early in the twentieth century, when a person holding that title was responsible for the scenery, lighting, sound, stage machinery, and just about everything "technical" that was designed to operate onstage. Although the title is still used, the TD is usually now only in charge of the building

and operation of scenery and stage machinery. The position requires great knowledge and skill in engineering, drafting, construction, budgeting, and team management (of shops and crews). But it is a high art as well, for every construction and operation the TD oversees is a one-of-a-kind project and must be completed in most cases on an exactly fixed schedule—no small order, given the massive technical complexities of theatre today.

The TD's first task is to receive the scenic designs—which may simply be drawings augmented by overall dimensions, perhaps supplemented by three-dimensional models—and figure out how their various elements will be constructed. Dozens of factors must be considered and, much of the time, traded off: the cost of materials and labor must be carefully reconciled with the available budget; scenery meant to look light and airy must be engineered with critical concerns for stability and safety; and scenery meant to look heavy and gargantuan often must be built to roll or fly offstage at lightning speed—or in a choreography of alternating acceleration and deceleration. During this phase the TD drafts the working drawings for the scenery's construction and exact placement and consults, often daily, with the designer and director as to whether the working drawings will lead to the intended look of the set and yield scenery that works in the manner each of them has imagined.

Once the scenery is built, the TD oversees its load-in and establishes the manner in which scenery is to be shifted, either by manual pushing and pulling or by computerized mechanical devices. At the end of the play's run, the TD organizes the strike—the speedy removal of scenery into storage or a local dumpster.

During final rehearsals and actual productions, technical crews, working under the PSM and trained by the TD, hoist, lower, and push scenery pieces exactly on cue to precisely predetermined locations. They shift props and furniture to the right places at the right times. They pull the curtain (if there is one) up and down when cued by the PSM or ASM. In general, they make the carefully preplanned scene changes, prop appearances, and actor entrances appear to flow effortlessly. The technical crews' skills ensure that the audience concentrates on the play's action rather than on the theatre's mechanics. One particularly special "tech" assignment is flying actors through the air, which is usually done by only a few professional companies with patented equipment and expertly trained personnel; the crash-landing of a *Spider-Man* actor during Broadway previews in 2010 was a reminder of the potential danger in this field. (Fortunately, the actor survived his thirty-foot fall and returned to the show five months later.)

📷Photo Essay: Broadway Stage Manager Lisa Iacucci

1. Lisa Iacucci © *Lorna Cohen*

2. Lisa checks out the position of an onstage car before the show. © *Lorna Cohen*

musical *Head Over Heels.* This book's coauthor, Robert Cohen, interviewed her backstage before a 2014 performance of *Hedwig and the Angry Inch.*

"I'm from Queens," she began. "I was a pre-med and philosophy major at Franklin and Marshall College, but I've always gone to the theatre. My parents were into culture, often taking me to the theatre and opera, and I thought 'Let me just see what this would be like.' So, with zero experience (I had never acted or studied theatre in high school or college) I applied for a bunch of internships. By chance, a small-theatre recruiter told me, "Our stage management team needs a PA [production assistant]. Do you want to do that?' and I said 'Yes!'

"It was an amazing education. I knew literally nothing, and so every day was interesting. I made the coffee, I swept, I did props and whatever they asked; it was the most exciting summer I ever had. And then I started to work my way up, from college to the Manhattan Theatre Club to Lincoln Center and then onto the Big White Way.

"My duties are intense. I 'live' behind my PSM podium on stage right, behind a piece of Plexiglas that helps buffer the sound to limit me from losing my hearing. (The show is a very loud rock and roll musical.) I wear earplugs to deal with this, and the actors have earplugs too—in-ear monitors, actually—through which they can hear the band, and hear me, and hear themselves. So each actor has a personal mix, and can decide what they want to hear—how much of themselves or other people on stage. They can also hear me speaking from my podium.

"I call all the cues from my headset: lights, sound, scene shifts, and whatever crew actions are necessary. I keep the production book. I write down all the blocking, a complete and accurate account of every move the characters make, since it's all very specific, and when I am training understudies, there are things that simply have to be exactly the same, so every move on stage must be carefully noted. After every show, I write a report and then I go home.

Lisa Iacucci has been working backstage in professional theatres in New York since 1990 and has climbed Broadway's stage managerial ladder since 1998—first as an assistant stage manager for Susan Stroman's *Contact* and the National Theatre's *War Horse,* and more recently as a production stage manager (PSM) for On a *Clear Day You Can See Forever, Hedwig and the Angry Inch,* Michael Moore's 2017 one-man show *The Terms of My Surrender,* John Leguizamo's 2017 *Latin History for Morons,* and the 2018

3. Lisa Iacucci at her backstage PSM (production stage manager) desk, an hour prior to a 2014 performance of *Hedwig and the Angry Inch* at Broadway's Belasco Theatre. The performance area is forward of her left; the monitors in front of her and across the stage show her the critical areas of backstage, onstage, and the front rows of the audience seating area. The closed "rehearsal book" on her desk will soon become her open "production book," which will indicate, line by line, the cues she will be "calling" to the actors, her assistants, and/or to the conductor before the show—first the "get-ready" cues through her headset, followed by the "Now!" indications transmitted by the twelve cue lights in front of the production book. ©*Lorna Cohen*

"I also do a huge amount of scheduling. I help 'maintain' the show by watching it every night: if I see something wrong, as when an actor is in the wrong light, or there is something dramatic that's not happening, it is my responsibility to say something, because it's the actor's relationship with the audience that's primary, and I and my associate have to take charge of that.

"You have to have passion for this job. You have to really feel it's what you want to do. I am aware of this when I interview potential PAs. Many come in with a sense of entitlement. Perhaps they graduated at the head of their class and now realize they'll have to start back at the bottom. But they *are* at the bottom! I have to tell them, 'Look, if I'm sharpening the pencils,

you're *not* sharpening them—but then I'm being taken away from a far *more important* task that you're not yet trained to do!' So they have to be continually 'present' in the room.

"And that's for me too. We *all* have to be present, and proactive, and do whatever's necessary, and do it with a smile. The director should never look over at any of us and see us texting on our smartphones. I'm talking about my whole team now, because I need to be present, as do they. They have to learn to be responsible, but as PSM, I'm the boss, and I'm finally responsible, for better or for worse. I'm happy to share the credit when it's deserved, but if anything bad happens, it's my responsibility!"

"Responsibility" seems to be Iacucci's chief concern when she's working and, indeed, it must be every stage manager's chief concern. Everything that happens in a show— every actor's entrance, every shift of scenery, every light and sound cue, every prop location, every cover of an accident or prompt of a dropped line—are all under the PSM's oversight, and each action, shift, cover, or cue must be carefully and precisely executed. As she and I talked during this pre-show interview, Iacucci had at least one eye on the stage—and another on her many colleagues—at least 90 percent of the time. And this was still an hour before *Hedwig's* curtain time.

Working in the scene shop—normally under the TD, a shop supervisor, or a scenery supervisor—are production carpenters (and master carpenters) and scenic artists (painters). They are joined by welders when steel—commonly used today for weight-bearing constructions—needs to be joined and shaped.

A wider array of specialists is required in the costume shop, though many costume designers and technologists assume more than one of these roles:

- Costume directors (or costume shop managers) coordinate the entire operation, supervising personnel, work spaces, and schedules.

- Dyers dye fabrics to the color specified by the design and may also be skilled at fabric painting, aging, distressing, and other fabric modifications.

- Drapers drape fabrics on actors or mannequins, testing and choosing the way the fabric falls to create the desired look of the eventual garment both at rest and on a moving (and possibly dancing, tumbling, or fencing) actor.

- Cutters cut the fabric according to the selected grain direction, either from a flat paper pattern or with no pattern at all, often first creating a cheap muslin prototype. (Most often today, draping and cutting are performed by the same person, a draper/cutter.)

- First hands work directly for the cutter and correct the pattern after the muslin prototype has been fitted to the actor and then "hand off" the work to stitchers.

- Stitchers sew the garment.

- Craft specialists make costumes or costume elements involving more than fabric—armor, belts, masks, and so forth. Some plays use specific specialists, such as milliners to make hats and cobblers to make shoes. Other specialists may be involved in distressing costume elements (making them look older and well used) or adding decorations, such as badges, military ribbons, and gold braid.

- Hairstylists and wig-makers coif the actors as the designers specify.

- Wardrobe supervisors ensure that costumes are cleaned and maintained during the run of a show and delivered to the appropriate backstage areas during dress rehearsals and performances. Wardrobe (or storage) supervisors and technicians also oversee the costume storage area and help determine which existing costumes can be taken from storage and rebuilt to serve a new design.

- Dressers work backstage during dress rehearsals and performances, helping the actors when necessary with quick changes between scenes.

In the area of lighting, electricians and *master electricians (MEs)* hang, focus, and "gel" (put color media in) lighting instruments prior to and during technical rehearsals and maintain the lighting technology during the run of a show. Lighting-board and follow-spot operators execute the lighting cues called by the PSM. For the sound department, one or more sound engineers work with the sound designer in recording the sound cues and placing the speakers, and a soundboard operator executes the cues during technical and dress rehearsals and performances. And in the makeup room, makeup artists may provide assistance to actors requiring it, or they may apply full makeup to the actors as specified by the designers.

Each of these backstage technicians plays an absolutely crucial role in theatrical presentation. The stage fright of the actor playing Hamlet is not necessarily greater than the nervousness of the stagehand who pulls the curtain: backstage work, though technical, is never merely mechanical. Every stage production poses a host of problems and situations that are new to the people who deal with them (and sometimes new to the theatre itself). Technological innovation takes place when sound knowledge of craft combines with creative imagination in the face of unanticipated problems. The technical artists of the theatre have always manifested impressive ingenuity at meeting unprecedented challenges in creative ways. Each of the theatre's shops—scene, costume, prop, and makeup—is both a creative artistic studio and a teaching laboratory for all its members.

When follow-spot operators and stage managers are placed in direct public view, sound operators and their consoles are plopped in the midst of the audience, and puppeteers are seen visibly manipulating their puppets on the stage, the theatre's technicians themselves are increasingly drawn into direct public awareness—and in some cases are invited to take onstage curtain calls with the rest of the cast. Popular fascination with technology, combined with diminishing interest in realism, has led to a scenography that deliberately incorporates technology as a visible aesthetic component of the theatre itself. Given this trend and the theatre's increasing use of the most recent technical innovations—superhydraulics, lasers and holograms, air casters, wall-size video, moving lights, and projections, to name but a few—theatre technologists are becoming widely recognized not merely as implementers but as full-fledged stage artists and creators.

Chapter

6

The Director

©Robert Cohen

T HE ROOM IS ALREADY FILLED with people when she enters, a bit distracted, with a bundle of books and papers under her arm. Expectation, tension, and even a hint of panic lurk behind the muffled greetings, loose laughter, and choked conversation prompted by her arrival.

She sits, and an assistant arranges chairs. Gradually, the others seat themselves at the other end of what has suddenly become "her" table. An edgy silence descends. Where are they going? What experiences lie ahead? What risks, what challenges are to be demanded? What abstract ideas and feelings, in the coming weeks and months, are going to become a poignant reality?

Only she knows—and if she doesn't, no one does. In this silence, tender with hope and fear, the director breaks ground for the production. Her plan begins to become work and her imagination begins to become art. It is the peak moment of directing—and of the director.

That is an idealized scenario, to be sure. There are many down-to-earth directors who deliberately avoid invoking an impression of "mystique" and whose primary efforts are directed toward dispelling awe, dread, or any form of personal tension among their associates. Nonetheless, the picture holds a measure of truth for every theatrical production. The art of directing is an exercise in leadership, imagination, and control; and in the director's hands rest the aspirations, neuroses, skills, and ideas of the entire theatrical company.

Directing is an art whose product is the most ambiguous, perhaps the most mysterious, in the theatre. The direction of a play is not visible like scenery or costumes, and unlike the actor's voice or the playwright's text, it cannot be directly heard or sensed. If you witness a stunning moment onstage, you might express awe at the power of the performers or designers—but how would you know the director's role? One paradox of directors is that their touch is everywhere and nowhere: it is connected to each aspect of the play, but is invisible and undetectable. Stranger still, the goal

Director Gábor Tompa's 2011 staging of Georg Büchner's nineteenth-century comic political satire *Leonce and Lena* set the play in a ruined eighteenth-century chateau and stylized the actors' movements in a brilliant pastiche of aristocratic buffoonery that implied the innate idiocy of royal rule. The production opened at the Hungarian Theatre in Cluj, Romania, and went on to tour in Hungary, France, Germany, Croatia, and Colombia. The stunning scenery and costumes were designed by Carmencita Brojboiu. ©István Biró/Hungarian State Theatre of Cluj

of direction is, in one sense, to attain this level of invisibility. Direction resides not within one part of the play but instead in the nearly infinite and hopefully seamless connections among its different parts. Utterly absorbed by the theatrical experience, direction animates and defines that experience. An entire class of theatrical artists in our time have reached international eminence in this elusive art. But what, exactly, is involved?

At the technical level, directors organize the production. They schedule the work process and supervise the acting, designing, staging, and technical operation of the play. This is usually the easiest part of the director's job.

At the more fundamental and artistic level, though, directors inspire a creation of theatre with each production. They conceptualize the play, give it purpose—both social and aesthetic—and inspire the company of artists to join together in collaboration. This is the hard part. It is also the part by which directors earn their reputations.

Directors fuse together the technical and the artistic aspects of the theatre to create—through a synthesis of text, materials, and available talent—a unique and vivid experience.

A Historical Overview

Although playwrights since the time of Aeschylus have been known to stage their own plays, the idea of an independent "director" did not even exist until the nineteenth century. Even then, the director, as we understand the role today, was not a universally accepted member of the artistic team. Now, however, the role of the director has become so significant that many critics and theatregoers speak of the current stage as a "director's theatre," and many directors have become celebrities more famous than the actors they direct.

How did we get here? The director's evolution is not simply the story of one member of the production ensemble breaking free. The emergence of the director resulted from the stylistic growth of the theatre itself—particularly the advent of two major movements, realism and antirealism (see the chapter "The Modern Theatre"). With the arrival of realism, directors transformed from administrative functionaries to artists in their own right who were capable of unifying acting styles into a cohesive and lifelike whole. And when realism gave way to antirealism, directors' artistic potential expanded even more to encompass abstract interpretations that governed all other theatrical elements, including scene design, sounds, lights, costume, and acting styles. In other words, the progression of the theatre from pre-modern to realistic to antirealistic saw with it the progression of directors from managers to artists among peers to primary artists in charge of a play's overall meaning.

TEACHER-DIRECTORS

In the earliest days of the theatre, directing was considered a matter of instruction. The Greeks called the director the *didaskalos*, which means "teacher," and in medieval times the director's designation, in all the various European languages, was "master." The underlying assumption of this early phase of directing was that the (almost certainly male) teacher had already mastered his subject and was simply required to teach the current conventions of acting and design to his less-experienced colleagues. The earliest directors basically passed along the "correct" performance techniques within a given style. These directors didn't impose their own interpretations, nor did they care about the emotional, psychological, or thematic effects of their productions. Instead, they were craftsmen who were in charge of transferring skills into new hands.

Early on, the director did not occupy a separate, independent role in the artistic team. Often the playwrights themselves served as directors: in Molière's play *The Rehearsal at Versailles*, for example, the seventeenth-century playwright-director depicts himself staging one of his own plays. But this changed in the eighteenth and the early nineteenth centuries, partly in response to the remarkable fascination of those times with natural philosophy (what we would now call science) and empirical research. The same dedication to rationalism that fostered a profusion of libraries and museums also emphasized accuracy and consistency in the arts. Theatre audiences demanded historically accurate revivals of classic plays whose authors were no longer around to direct them. Producing these works would require research, organization, and comprehensive coordination. These teacher-directors were still, essentially, copyists and fact-checkers who made sure

their productions were consistent and reflected historical correctness: a Greek tragedy would have ancient Greek costumes, for instance.

With only a few exceptions, directors before the twentieth century received as little public recognition for their efforts as do present-day museum directors for creating historical dioramas. Sometimes the directing was attributed to a famous acting star, such as the Englishman Charles Kean or the American Edwin Booth, when in fact the work was often done by a lesser functionary. These teacher-directors who labored largely in the shadows began the art of directing as we know it today: they dedicated themselves to creating unified and coherent theatrical works by corralling an ensemble of actors, designers, and technicians toward established ends.

DIRECTORS OF REALISM

The second phase in the development of modern-day directing began at the end of the nineteenth century. Realism took hold as a dominant theatrical style, and now mere historical accuracy wouldn't do: plays had to reflect realistic human behavior. A new wave of directors who studied the conventions of realism strove to make their play productions more lifelike than those of past eras. George II, Duke of Saxe-Meiningen (1826–1914), was among the first of this breed and is now known as the first modern director. The duke, who headed a provincial troupe of actors in his rural duchy, presented a series of premieres and classical revivals in the late 1870s and 1880s that dazzled the German public with their carefully harmonized acting, staging, and scenery. The duke's productions focused less on a star performer and more on a total ensemble of actors who all appeared to be behaving naturally and individually. The Meiningen theatre style became acclaimed throughout Europe as the troupe toured the continent. By the 1890s, the position of a director was firmly established: a person who would organize and rehearse an entire company toward a complexly and comprehensively fashioned theatrical presentation.

In 1887 André Antoine began a movement of even greater realism in Paris with his Théâtre Libre, and in 1898 Russian actor-director Konstantin Stanislavski initiated his Moscow Art Theatre, which eventually became the international model of realistic ensemble acting (see the chapter "The Actor"). Both of these directors, who were amateurs at the outset of their careers, went on to develop innovative techniques in acting and actor-coaching. Both also sought to make the theatre a powerful social instrument for the expression of truth. Realism, after all, was a political movement, not just an artistic one: it sought to reflect society back to itself, warts and all. Antoine and Stanislavski, like

Saxe-Meiningen, were not content simply to coordinate the many aspects of a theatre production. They were true artists—and directing was now considered an art.

DIRECTORS OF ANTIREALISM

The rise of realism in the theatre of the late nineteenth century soon gave way to the rise of antirealism in the twentieth, which in turn further accelerated the importance of the modern director. The new breed of antirealistic directors, unrestrained from any charge to depict human behavior with accuracy, aimed instead toward the more abstract goals of originality, theatricality, and style. Their goal was to create sheer theatrical brilliance, beauty, and excitement, and to lead their collaborators in explorations of pure theatre and theatrical imagination.

Antirealistic directors were often reactionary. Paul Fort, one of the first of these third-phase directors, launched his Théâtre d'Art in Paris in 1890 as a direct assault upon the realist principles espoused by Antoine. In Russia, Vsevolod Meyerhold, a one-time disciple of Stanislavski, combated his former teacher's philosophy with what he called "biomechanical constructivism," an acting method characterized by bold gestures and rapid, near-acrobatic movement. The styles of these innovators and others like them introduced new elements to the director's role: lyricism and symbolism, expressive and abstract uses of design, and intentionally contrived (and decidedly nonrealistic) methods of acting.

The unbounded creativity of the antirealistic director led to its increased prominence in the artistic staff. Perhaps the most influential proponent of the antirealistic director, however, was not a director at all but an eminent designer and theorist. In a seminal essay titled "The Art of the Theatre" (1905), Edward Gordon Craig, known for creating expressive and abstract scenery, compared the director of a play to the captain of a ship: an absolutely indispensable leader whose rule, maintained by strict discipline, extends over every last facet of the enterprise. "Until discipline is understood in a theatre to be willing and reliant obedience to the manager [director] or captain," wrote Craig, "no supreme achievement can be accomplished." Craig's essay was aimed at a full-scale "Renaissance of the Art of the Theatre," in which a "systematic progression" of reform would overtake all the theatre arts—"acting, scenery, costuming, lighting, carpentering, singing, dancing, etc."—under the complete control and organizing genius of this singular newcomer to the ranks of theatrical artistry, the independent director. The idea Craig expresses here is an essentially antirealist one: what matters most is not fidelity to history or the script, but to the director's all-encompassing vision.

GLOBAL DIRECTORS

The notion of a director as an artistic guide, one who creates a more conceptual understanding of a play, has been largely an innovation in the West. This is not to say that theatrical leaders failed to emerge in non-Western contexts, however. As we discuss in the chapter "Theatre Traditions," theatrical troupes in Japan, for example, were helmed by well-known figures, such as the Japanese noh master Zeami. But Zeami's responsibility was not necessarily to interpret the text in new ways; he was called on to handle more logistical matters. Once the more conceptual understanding of directing gained prominence in the West during the modern era, however, it had a profound impact on the development of theatre in Asia, Africa, and Latin America. Non-Western theatres adopted the Western idea of a director. For instance, the rise of Chinese *huaju*, a "spoken-word drama" modeled after Western realism, saw a concurrent rise in the role of a director's vision. And this emergence brought with it a way to apply both European and Chinese sensibilities, as with a celebrated 1924 production of *Lady Windemere's Fan,* Oscar Wilde's light Victorian comedy of manners, that used elements of traditional Chinese opera.

This influence cut both ways. Western directors were deeply affected by theatrical traditions in other cultures. In the early twentieth century, the well-known French director Charles Dullin witnessed the Japanese noh performances of Tsutsui Tokujirō's company, which was touring Europe at the time. As a result, Dullin went on to advocate for a more physical and vital approach to staging plays. (One of Dullin's pupils, Antonin Artaud, would take this approach to a profound extreme in his own theatrical philosophy, as discussed in the chapter "The Modern Theatre.") Bertolt Brecht, whose historical impact on the theatre is truly immeasurable, borrowed many ideas and techniques from Chinese opera, most prominently those of the brilliant performer Mei Lanfang. And in the 1960s, the English director Peter Brook reportedly stated, after witnessing a performance of a ta'ziyeh "mourning play" in Iran, that "this is what has been missing from the Western theatre for a long time." Struck by the immediacy of the play, and by the deep emotional investment of its audience, Brook sought to infuse his own theatre productions with a newfound sense of urgency and public engagement.

In other words, while the full understanding of a director, as we are using the term, may have initially been a modern-era Western innovation, its expansion and development were certainly international. Today's theatre is, as a result, a profoundly global one, whose productions often incorporate directorial visions from all over the world.

Perhaps no single director better embodies the global theatre than Peter Brook. In 2016's *Battlefield* (pictured here), Brook—at the age of 91—created a sequel of sorts to his 1985 adaptation of *The Mahabharata,* the great Sanskrit epic poem. In the 65-minute-long *Battlefield,* however, Brook aims for elegance and minimalism, as opposed to the nine-hour grandeur of *The Mahabharata:* simple props and a nearly bare stage provide a backdrop for a diverse cast to find universal themes in ancient stories.
©Geraint Lewis/Alamy Stock Photo

The work of William Shakespeare has long invited cross-cultural interpretation. Here, a performer from a Chinese opera troupe poses in front of a cutout in Stratford-upon-Avon (Shakespeare's birthplace) while visiting in 2016 to commemorate the 400th anniversary of Shakespeare's death. ©Leon Neal/AFP/Getty Images

Robert Wilson has both designed and directed over eighty stage productions since 1959, and many have been considered—at least by his admirers—close to miraculous. His specialties are extravagance, physical surprise, and truly brilliant color combinations. This production of Johann von Goethe's Romantic epic *Faust* premiered in Berlin in 2015. ©David Baltzer/Zenit/laif/Redux

CONTEMPORARY DIRECTORS

Today, Craig's hoped-for renaissance has surely arrived. This indeed is the age of the director, in which the directorial function is fully established as the art of synthesizing script, design, and performance into a unique and splendid theatrical event. If, as performance theorist J. L. Styan says, "the theatre persists in communicating by simultaneity of sensory impressions," it is above all the director who is charged with inspiring these impressions and ensuring their simultaneity.

Today's director understands realism and antirealism and feels free to mix the two with impunity. At the beginning of a production, the director faces a completely blank canvas: not a single gesture has been notated, not one design element has been decided upon, and no line has yet been spoken by an actor. The play lives wholly in the imagination of the director, and the tools at the director's disposal for translating this imagination into reality are nearly infinite: not only the underlying conventions of the time but also all those of the past, which can be revived for novel effects and stunning juxtapositions. The theatre of today allows for varieties of artistic and historical combinations. Shakespeare can be presented as a modern chamber piece, Greek tragedy as a kabuki spectacle, the theatre of the absurd as vaudevillian buffoonery, and romantic melodrama as campy satire. Actors can play multiple parts in a play, and their scenes can be performed on stilts or in water-filled fish tanks. Nothing, in short, is taken for granted.

One curious effect of the expansion of directorial possibilities is, at times, the diminishment of the director as a sole figure of authority. In many cases, the director's job has become less to impose a strict framework onto a production—although many such directors still exist!—and instead to create an atmosphere in which the whole ensemble can feel free to make their own contributions to the overall understanding of the play. This approach occurs often on the level of devised theatre (see the chapter "The Playwright"), in which the play originates not from a piece of text but from collaborative improvisation and research. Companies such as Forced Entertainment, from England, create works with a collective, not solitary, artistic approach. Directors can be deeply collaborative in more traditional settings, too. The celebrated director Anne Bogart is renowned for her ability to generate and guide innovative work that results from the improvised movements of her performers. And Thomas Kail, the director of Broadway's *Hamilton*, has received accolades for his deeply generous and cooperative method of staging work.

Sometimes a play has no all-powerful visionary director. Such is the case with the work of the English company Forced Entertainment, whose members have long devised work collaboratively. Pictured here is the company's 2017 work *Real Magic*, which follows contestants in an absurd game show that is impossible to win. Like all of its work, it was conceived by the company: the work results from a long process of communally generating ideas. ©*Hugo Glendinning*

📷 Photo Essay: Director Susan Stroman

No director-choreographer has captured Broadway audiences and critics of musical theatre at the turn of the twenty-first century better than Susan Stroman, who won Tony Awards for both her direction and choreography of *The Producers* in 2001 and Tony nominations in both of those categories for *The Scottsboro Boys* in 2011—along with three Tony Awards and five nominations for her earlier work in *Crazy for You, Showboat, Contact, Steel Pier, The Music Man, Oklahoma!,* and *Young Frankenstein.* Recent Broadway credits include the adaptations of the films *Big Fish* and *Bullets Over Broadway.* In 2015 she branched out to opera with a well-reviewed production of *The Merry Widow.* In 2018, Stroman once again received critical acclaim for *The Beast in the Jungle,* a stage adaptation of the Henry James novella. It is quite a set of achievements for a Wilmington, Delaware, girl who hit the ground running—or at least dancing—immediately after her college graduation.

Coauthor Robert Cohen met up with Stroman in Las Vegas, where she was restaging her Broadway production of *The Producers*—which won a staggering twelve Tony Awards—for the Paris Hotel and Casino. The show had begun its preview performances the evening before, and Stroman was working with a few actors prior to the full rehearsal, which was to begin in the following hour.

RC: When did you start thinking of being a choreographer?

SS: Always. I'm not one of the people who dance-dance-dances and then decides to try choreography. Ever since I was a little girl, whether it was classical or rock and roll or an old standard, I visualized music. My father was a wonderful piano player. He would play the piano and I would dance around the living room, but in my head I would be imagining loads of people dancing with lights, sets, and costumes. When I came to New York, I knew I couldn't just

1. Directing and choreographing a musical involves close personal interaction, plus great attention to the details of both script and musical score. Here Stroman (*center*) gathers members of her *Producers* cast around the orchestral score, which she has laid on the stage in the convenient spotlight so all can see it (and her) clearly. From left to right behind her are Associate Choreographer Bill Burns and performers Matthew J. Vargo, Shari Jordan, Katrina Loncaric, and Patrick Boyd. ©*Robert Cohen*

"take over"—I would have to come as a song-and-dance gal because I could sing and dance—but I did so always with the idea of going to the other side of the table. So I started to choreograph and direct industrial shows and club acts in small venues—just dabbling in it to see if I could compete. But at a certain point I had to stop being known as a performer, because in New York you have to be either one thing or another. You have to focus on what you want to be. So I stopped performing and decided to go for it. I was in a Broadway show called *Musical Chairs,* and with me was another aspiring fellow, Scott Ellis, who also wanted to be on the other side of the table. We both knew [the musical Broadway team of composer John] Kander and [lyricist Fred] Ebb, and we decided to go to them and ask if they would allow us to mount an off-Broadway production of their

Flora the Red Menace. This is a good lesson because in any business you need to ask yourself, "What's the worst that can happen?" They can say "no" or they can say "yes," but you won't get anywhere unless you ask the question. So Scott and I went to Kander and Ebb and they said yes! We mounted a production of *Flora,* which developed a cult following and launched our careers. I think we made about three hundred dollars that entire summer. Of course we starved to death, but we had made the leap to the other side. And we have never gone back. It was a wonderful combination of believing in the show, adoring Kander and Ebb, and asking "the question" that led us to get that one really good break. Coincidentally, Kander and Ebb wrote a song in that show called "All I Need Is One Good Break."

That was when things really opened up for me. Hal Prince asked me to choreograph *Don Giovanni* at the New York City Opera, and then we collaborated on the Broadway show *Showboat.* Liza [Minnelli] also saw *Flora.* She asked me to choreograph her show *Stepping Out* at Radio City Music Hall. The key is really to be ready for that break when it happens.

RC: How did you then make your transition to directing?

SS: The transition to directing was very natural. Being a theatre choreographer is very different from being a ballet or modern dance choreographer (although I have done these too—for the New York City Ballet and the Martha Graham company). For choreographing theatre, you have to acknowledge the lyric. Everything must center on the plot; your role is to push the plot forward through the choreography. Plus you have to create time period, geographical area, and rich characters. Because of all this, the choreographer is right there with the director from beginning to end. It's not like one job starts where the other one finishes; you're trying to make a total vision together. So it was a very natural transition for me.

The first Broadway show that I directed was *The Music Man,* and that was perfect for me because I love that show. Love it, love it! I grew up in a house filled with music. My father was my real Music Man: he was a salesman and he played the piano. There's a wonderful line in the show where the little boy accuses Harold Hill of lying about being the leader of a band. Harold Hill says, "I always think there's a band, kid." For musical comedy people, that line resonates because we grow up thinking that there's always a band—we're always hoping our band is coming around the corner. So for *The Music Man* to be the first Broadway show I directed was very meaningful. The movement in *Music Man* is a very important aspect. When you first meet the

characters in Iowa they're very stiff, they don't move at all, but by the end, the entire town is dancing the "Shipoopee." And it's all because Harold Hill has introduced the town to rhythm and music.

RC: How did you come up with the terrific ending?

SS: Closing the book after one of my readings of the script during rehearsals I thought, "Well what is this town doing now? What *could* they be doing? Well, perhaps they all took trombone lessons?" So for the curtain call I decided the entire company should play the trombone. What did I have to lose? I'll hire a trombone teacher, they'll either learn it or they won't, and if they don't they'll just come out and bow. After the second week of rehearsal they sounded like a moose herd, and I thought this is never going to happen. And then *I* became the music man! All of a sudden, they had become my kids, and they were playing seventy-six trombones and it sounded beautiful. I was so pleased and proud! And that's how it ended up as the curtain call.

RC: What do you like about directing?

SS: It gives me great pleasure to be in the back of the house and see something I've created affect an audience. Whether it makes them laugh from something they saw in *The Producers,* or makes them cry from a moment in *Contact,* or—in *Crazy for You*—the audience puts their arms around one another (*laughs*). Even last night at the first preview of our Vegas production of *The Producers,* I saw a lady doubled over with laughter and tumbling into the aisle at the sight of the walker dance with the little old ladies. It gave me such joy to see her laugh.

RC: How do you conceive of some of the darker themes you explore, as in *Contact*?

SS: Oh, I have a million stories in my head. Being allowed to do something like *Contact* was amazing. Lincoln Center is the only place you can do something like that: take an idea and build it into a show. My production of *Steel Pier*

2. Directing often takes the form of one-on-one coaching. Here Stroman works with Burns on the "Ball and Chain" prison number in the final act. ©*Robert Cohen*

3. Studying the script, Stroman and Vargo go over dialogue. ©*Robert Cohen*

only lasted about six months on Broadway, but [Lincoln Center's artistic director] André Bishop saw it and called me. He loved the choreography and said, "If you have an idea I will help you

4. Stroman works individually with the actors as they rehearse, fine-tuning choreographic gestures, expressions, and focus points (where actors are to look). ©*Robert Cohen*

develop it." And to hear those words from a producer is like hearing a beautiful melody! It's unheard of. Usually, they just want you to do a revival, or something safe. And I said, "Well, as a matter of fact I *do* have an idea." A few weeks before I had been to a dance club in NYC's Meatpacking District, a swing club where everybody wore black. Out of this sea of black stepped a girl in a yellow dress. I got obsessed watching her, and I thought to myself, "She's going to change some man's life tonight." I thought she was quite bold—a New Yorker wearing yellow—so when André asked if I had an idea, I said, "I absolutely have an idea," and so I started to develop a story about the girl in the yellow dress. I called my friend John Weidman, who wrote *Assassins and Pacific Overtures*. We went into the rehearsal rooms of Lincoln Center with eighteen dancers, and we created a story about someone who, if he doesn't make contact that night, will die. It was remarkable to have the opportunity to develop this work from the

visuals and concepts in my mind. Before it opened, I thought, "Well, there'll be a handful of people that will get this," but it took the city by storm. The girl in the yellow dress was on every bus in Manhattan! It clearly has a very universal theme.

RC: Do you have any advice for a young person aspiring to be a director?

SS: You have to really have a passion and a drive, and you can't be afraid to take chances. You can't just wait around for someone to hire you; you've got to create your own work. And that's the way it should be. There is a collaborative passion in the theatre that I don't think exists in any other business. All of us are in a swimming pool together, and we either drown together or we win an Olympic medal together. It is passion and drive that make a show work. And the drive toward an opening night: there is nothing like it, nothing like people coming together with a goal to move an audience. It's an amazing feeling. I am very fortunate to be in the theatre. I love the theatre so much!

5. All directors have individual ways of communicating with actors. Stroman's signature style is to write down individual cast notes on index cards and then pass them out to the actors—Patrick and Katrina in this case—after each rehearsal unit concludes. ©*Robert Cohen*

Courtesy of Susan Stroman.

We should not, however, conclude that the collaborative director is any less potent an artist force as a result. Turning an ensemble's ideas into a cohesive play is itself a daunting task: the director is responsible for making an atmosphere in which everyone feels comfortable enough to pitch in—and for knowing what to keep and what to discard. Perhaps the most fateful words a director can utter in these occasions are "keep it"—the decision to retain one choice (a gesture, movement, concept, or line reading, for instance) and, by implication, not select any other options. Collaborative directors are no less decisive than the authoritarian ones. They are still responsible for the play's vision—its most powerful and elusive quality.

The Directing Process: Step by Step

Directing a play is a long process and does not begin when the director walks into the rehearsal room for the first time.

The director may spend a year or more preparing and staging a production, and then more years restaging it in different theatres, in cases where the production begins in one theatre and then moves on to others. Take, for instance, the recent critical Broadway hit *Natasha, Pierre & the Great Comet of 1812.* The play premiered in 2012 at the relatively small Ars Nova, a theatre in the Hell's Kitchen neighborhood of New York City. It moved to a temporary structure built in the Meatpacking District of New York City in 2013, then to the esteemed American Repertory Theater (A.R.T.) in Cambridge, Massachusetts, from 2015 to 2016, before finally opening on Broadway from late 2016 into 2017. That's a total of five years of development, during which the way the play refined its staging, changed its cast, altered its overall concept (it began as an immersive dinner club and had to change to a more traditional proscenium-stage presentation), and adapted to changes in the script. But all along the way it had the same director—Rachel Chavkin, who was nominated for a Tony for the play—at the helm.

This example is typical. The process of directing a play is a long one and has two distinct periods. The first, and ordinarily the longest, is the *preparation period.* The second, normally shorter, is the *implementation period.* We shall look at these in the rough order that they take place—"rough" because the ordering of events may be different from one director to another, and from one production (or theatre organization) to another.

THE PRE-PREPARATION PERIOD

During the pre-preparation period, directors become compelled, in some way, by a play. They read and re-read it, and begin to conceptualize a production, first dramaturgically (What is the story that I want to tell?), then intellectually (What are the ideas I want to promote?), aesthetically (How do I want this play to look, sound, and feel?), and personally (Who do I think might be spectacular in these roles?). At this point, a director might begin to think, Who might produce it?

The *producer* is basically somebody who can turn the play into a performance. Producers may have the money—or perhaps know the people who might be able to provide the money—that would help acquire a theatre space, some designers, actors, crews, and, if needed, the legal rights to perform the particular script. The producer may be the head of a college theatre department, or the artistic director of a regional theatre or theatre festival, or even a professional Broadway producer; the producer might even be the person who had proposed the play to the director. In any event, the pre-preparation consists mainly of discussions—normally not in a theatre but more often in homes and offices, in email exchanges and telephone conversations, and at meetings in coffee shops, restaurants, and theatre lobbies—between the would-be director and would-be producer until an agreement, tentative or solid, has been reached. And then the preparation itself begins.

THE PREPARATION PERIOD

The preparation begins with the director re-reading the play and taking notes. Many of these notes come from the pre-preparation thoughts and discussions but many incorporate what has already been determined: the expected theatre, the anticipated budget, the potential actors and designers who might be interested and pursued.

Once the play has been chosen, the next steps will focus on developing its working text. In many cases, and certainly if the play is still under copyright, the text is simply the author's version as published and licensed. (Currently, American copyright law covers an author's work until seventy years after the content creator's death.) If the play is not under copyright, however, it is in what is called the public domain, and the director is free to make any textual changes as desired, such as cutting, adding, or revising lines for the new production. This process is particularly prevalent in the current era, when the average length of stage productions is closer to two hours than the two-and-a-half to three hours that was common in the past century.

There are probably hundreds of *Hamlet*s produced every year, but very few (if any) will include all of its 4,072 lines, which would take at least four hours to present in its entirety. The vast majority of today's Shakespearean productions are therefore cut, usually by 5 to 15 percent of their original length. (In one striking example, the famous Shakespeare director Peter Brook cut one-third of *Hamlet* to produce a lean, two-hour-and-twenty-minute version.) Older texts are altered in other ways, too: archaic words may be replaced with more commonly understood ones, scenes may be rearranged or eliminated altogether, and characters may be combined to reduce cast size. These revisions hold the potential danger that audience members familiar with the play may consider such productions distortions of what they had come to see, but general audiences rarely notice them and, when they do, may be more grateful than disappointed.

Along with changing the script, directors may change fundamental aspects of a play's dramaturgy—sometimes with shocking results. Indeed, more slimmed-down and radical adaptations of classics are becoming almost common. The director Charles Marowitz led this movement in London and Los Angeles in the 1970s and 1980s with his drastically revised version of Shakespeare's *The Taming of the Shrew*. Paring the title to simply *Shrew*, Marowitz deleted two-thirds of the text, added a few scenes of his own, and winnowed Shakespeare's cast to merely five characters—Kate, the strong-willed "shrew" of the title, and four men, who not only taunt and domesticate her, as in Shakespeare's original, but also brutally terrorize and sexually assault her, which drives her insane.

Many other such radical revisions of classical texts abound. Phyllida Lloyd's production of *Julius Caesar*, which arrived in New York in 2013, was set in a women's prison—and as such had an all-woman cast. John Tiffany and Andrew Goldberg's *Macbeth* played on Broadway, also in 2013, with Alan Cumming playing 15 roles in Shakespeare's tragedy, which was set in a mental institution—the title character enacted the entire play as a way of exorcising his own violent and traumatic history. In 2015, the legendary downtown New York theatre Café La Mama hosted three productions of *The Tempest* that displayed a range of directorial revision: Karin Coonrod's more traditional staging; Tae-Suk Oh's adaptation, set in fifth-century Korea and interspersed with scenes from that country's ancient folklore; and, most radically, a version by Motus, an Italian company, in which Prospero was played by a strobe light, a video displayed scenes of protest against the mistreatment of immigrants, and actors reminisced about their own histories.

Today, directors have an absolutely gigantic sweep of potential adaptations and conceptions that they may create while staging even a classic play. While some might stage a straightforward rendering of the text, others might use the text as a starting point, a prompt to consider other ideas that might interest them. The treatment of the text, in other words, is closely connected to the next step—the development of the play's concepts.

CONCEPTUALIZING THE PRODUCTION

More has been written in modern times about the step of conceptualizing the production than about any other directorial task; entire books are devoted to the creation of a central concept that focuses and unifies an entire production. There are two different sorts of directorial concept, however: the *core concept* and the *high concept*. All plays require the first; not all require the second.

The Core Concept   The core concept is the director's determination of the most important of the many images, ideas, and emotions that should emerge from the play. This idea might seem overly limiting: Why should there be only one core concept when every play, when read, presents a multiplicity of important images, ideas, and emotions? Anton Chekhov's *The Three Sisters*, for example, is about love, ambition, sisterhood, despair, the oppression of women, rivalry between social classes, the social freedom of professional men, the oppression of rural Russian domesticity, the agony of unfulfilled hope, the corruption of provincial czarist bureaucracy, and the seeds of a coming revolution. It is also a play that can be, and has been, staged as a comedy, tragedy, or romance. But a director who tries to give equal weight to all those themes and styles would create a mess—a production that is unfocused and all over the place. While a director's vision may ultimately incorporate many of the play's possible themes, they must be prioritized, and one of them should be given the highest priority. That highest-priority image, idea, style, or emotion becomes the core principle that will give the production shape, meaning, importance, and momentum. It will help audience members clarify what the production is "about," and what it "means."

How does a director decide on a single core principle? There is no universally correct answer to that question. Although research is important, the decision making is essentially a creative task. One helpful exercise is to ask, What should a poster for this production look like? Should a poster of *Three Sisters* show the image of Masha's final embrace with her lover? the sisters

Some productions prepare their scripts by pruning and trimming them; others rip it out, root and branch, and use it to fashion something entirely new. The Italian company Motus certainly fell into the latter camp with its 2015 adaptation of *The Tempest* called *Nella Tempesta* ("In the Tempest"), which radically reimagined Shakespeare's play as a multimedia piece that incorporated scenes of visceral movement—as with the scene pictured here, in which characters violently struggle over a blanket. ©*Tiziana Tomasulo*

abandoned by the soldiers at the final curtain? Natasha hiding in shame from the sisters gossiping about her in the next room? a birthday party of gaily laughing women and military officers, with the image of Lenin smirking at them from above? And should the poster's typeface be old-fashioned or modern? Should a few Cyrillic (Russian) letters be used to emphasize the play's Russian setting? Should the colors be primary or pastel, earth-toned or black-and-white, distressed, fragmentary, or faded? Should the design of the poster be clean or grimy, bold or subtle, abstracted or detailed? Should the mood be hopeful or despairing, the style elegant or grim? Answers to these questions point the director toward a possible core concept.

A tagline can also be helpful by condensing the concept to a single, direct statement. A tagline may be social ("a play about tyranny") or philosophical ("a play about

self-knowledge"). It may signal a specific interpretation ("a play about a man who cannot make up his mind") or invoke an invented dramatic genre ("a revenge melodrama"). A director may state the core concept in terms that are psychological ("a primitive ritual of puberty"), historical ("a play about fratricide in the Middle Ages"), imagistic ("a play about swords, sables, and skulls"), or metatheatrical ("a play about playing"). And sometimes the director can define a basic tone, such as sad, heroic, or royal, or a basic texture, such as rich, cerebral, or stark. As diverse as these examples may seem, they all fall within the range of possibilities for conceptualizing the same play: Shakespeare's *Hamlet*.

The High Concept   A high concept is another matter altogether. When a director uses a high concept, the entire play is placed within a context not hinted at in the script.

(This is the case with the aforementioned production of *The Tempest* by Motus.) By doing so, a contemporary director can make a familiar play surprising—even astonishing—by introducing highly unexpected insights into character, story, or style. In its simplest form, a high concept may mean nothing more than moving a play out of the period in which it is set and placing it into another: for example, resetting Molière's seventeenth-century *Tartuffe* from Catholic France into the contemporary Middle East (as French director Arianne Mnouchkine did in 1995); or producing Shakespeare's dark comedy *Measure for Measure* as a 1940s era screwball farce set in an office building (as Elevator Repair Service did in 2017); or staging Chekhov's *The Cherry Orchard* not as a story of Tsarist Russia transitioning into a more modern era, but as a Virginia plantation transitioning into post-bellum life (as Claire Beckman did in 2017).

Physical relocation alone, however, is not enough to make a play astonishing or even surprising. High concepts can alter the play in a more abstract way, as well, as when a director "deconstructs" a work by highlighting its artifice and focusing on a few expressive elements rather than a unified whole. (This is a similar philosophy to "postmodernism," as discussed in the chapter "Designers and Technicians.") Ivo van Hove, for instance, has become a master of such high concepts. His 2015 production of *A View From the Bridge* ended with blood raining down onto the characters from above—surely not something Arthur Miller intended to happen when he wrote his script in 1955. But van Hove's gesture did more than simply inject a dash of boldness into the proceedings. It connected the play to a deep, visceral sense of tragedy, one that similarly infused the bloody works that mark the first Western dramas. (For more on van Hove, see the chapter "Theatre Today.")

In a stirring example of high-concept direction, Claire Beckman's adaptation of Anton Chekhov's *The Cherry Orchard,* which originally took place in turn-of-the-century Russia, relocates the dramatic action to the post–Civil War American South. While the location is different, the power of Chekhov's psychological insight remains, and in fact is enhanced by the stirring resonance between these two eras. ©*Doug Barron*

Like it or not (and there are many who do not), audiences and critics today are much more likely to admire and remember productions by high-concept visionaries who aim for unique and revelatory revisions of major theatrical works, such as Robert Wilson and Peter Sellars (American); Peter Brook and Katie Mitchell (English); Ariane Mnouchkine and Dominique Serrand (French); Xu Xiaozhong and Tian Qinxin (Chinese); Peter Stein, Thomas Ostermeier, and Frank Castorf (German); Romeo Castellucci (Italian); Denise Stoklosà (Brazilian); and Andrei Serban, Mihai Maniutiu, Silviu Purcarete, and Gábor Tompa (Romanian).

Such productions captivate audiences worldwide by transcending conventions and presenting profound, moving theatricalizations. High-concept theatre also avoids the potentially museum-like traditions of realistic staging. A director known for brilliant high concepts will also discourage prospective attendees from declining to see his or her latest production of, say, *King Lear* on the grounds that "I've already seen it," since they can be pretty sure they will never have seen anything like *this* production of it.

Most productions of classic plays in the twenty-first century, not just in experimental theatre but also in mainstream theatre, seek high concepts. Directors and directing students are inevitably drawn to them, and audiences and critics, though sometimes skeptical, are almost always intrigued. These days, "What is your concept?" is very likely to be the first question a colleague or a reporter asks a director engaging in a new production of a well-known play.

Arriving at a high concept is no easy task. Once selected, the concept must "work" for the entire play. If

Flemish director Ivo van Hove is one of the twenty-first century's most celebrated directors. His production of *A View From the Bridge,* above, balanced high-concept experimentation—the play takes place on a bare, coolly minimal set—with raw, emotional power. It proved a smash hit in London and transferred to Broadway in 2015. ©*Geraint Lewis*

Othello is set in World War II, what does the actor (or the property designer) do with Othello's "Keep up your bright swords" line? How much can freshness add to a show without diminishing—or even obliterating—it? And how does the high concept actually improve the play, at least for its intended audience? What new ideas, readings of the text for the actors, and images for the designers does the high concept arouse? A concept should never exist purely for its own sake. It must always serve the play. Serious research and a comprehensive knowledge of the entire script are essential for the director trying to come up with an effective, workable, and genuinely inspiring high-concept production.

The formation of both core and high concepts takes place at conscious and unconscious levels. It begins when the director first hears of a certain play, and it grows and develops as the director reads the play, considers producing it, imagines its effects on an audience, and mentally experiments with possible modes of staging. Either sort of directorial concept is a product not only of the director's intelligence and vision but also of personal experiences that relate to the matters portrayed by the play. Core and high concepts also call into play the director's personal likes and loves, appreciations and philosophical leanings, and hopes for the audience's and critics' reactions to the final product. A great directorial concept is ultimately personal; it represents the director's studied and unique vision. It is also mysterious. It leads the actors and directors to impressive dramatic action.

Consulting the Dramaturg   Many directors and producers today engage special theatre artists to assist the director in this conceptualizing period (and often in the play selection period as well). The usual title for this position is a *dramaturg* (sometimes spelled "dramaturge"), although it is sometimes referred to as literary adviser or research assistant.

A dramaturg is essentially a specialist in dramatic analysis who serves as a bridge between the director and the text. In some cases, if the play is a new one, the dramaturg may have already assisted the playwright in preparing the manuscript for production. The dramaturg may also help the director (and sometimes the actors) research the play and conceptualize the directorial approach. Oftentimes the dramaturg serves as an in-house critic who closely views the rehearsal process to let the director know how the production relates to the play's history and the director's own stated vision. The dramaturg's contributions are always advisory, but a well-trained and well-schooled dramaturg's advice often makes the difference between a bad production and a good one, and between a good one and a great one.

IMPLEMENTATION PERIOD

As the production segues from preparation to implementation, the next task, if it has not already been initiated, is the assembling of a complete artistic team that will collaborate in the creation of the production. This will include, in addition to a dramaturg who may already be on board, the production's designers, stage managers, casting directors, actors, chief technicians, and various other personnel.

The director becomes the active head of this artistic team and bears the responsibility of sharing with the team the production's conception, thereby giving their work a point of focus (a "direction," quite literally) and motivating the team to move toward it. From this time forward, the tasks of a play director are not unlike those of a corporate manager or chief executive: to set goals, establish priorities, facilitate communication, maintain the schedule, monitor progress, heighten the stakes, build team morale, and inspire excellence from everyone. No two directors will fulfill these functions in the same way or to the same degree, but, for most, a confident, natural, inspirational, and collaborative way of working with these teammates is at least as important as mastery of staging techniques. Artistic sensitivity, interpersonal skills, and eagerness to accept responsibility—along with exercising needed authority—are always expected of professional play directors.

The steps of implementing the production's direction are many. Most are discussed in the following sections. Bear in mind, however, that in practice they are less clearly segmented than they appear here, as each of the separate elements (acting, lights, scenery, costumes, makeup) affects each of the others. And once abstract concepts are turned into an actual physical existence, they often generate an unexpected impact on a production's other elements—for good or bad—and therefore on the production as a whole. A director may want to have a pile of sand onstage, for instance, but once this becomes a reality, many obstacles become a reality as well—suddenly, there's sand in the costumes, actors are slipping on the stage, and the crew must appear early to make sure the sand is properly dry. Idealistic choices have realistic repercussions, so the sequence you are about to read is rarely as smoothly executed as it is described.

○Spotlight

Dramaturg Jerry Patch

One of America's leading and longtime dramaturgs, Jerry Patch has played a role in the development of four Pulitzer Prize–winning plays (David Lindsay Abaire's *Rabbit Hole*, Donald Margulies's *Dinner with Friends*, Margaret Edson's *Wit*, and Lynn Nottage's *Ruined*), four Pulitzer-nominated plays (Amy Freed's *Freedomland*, Richard Greenberg's *Three Days of Rain*, and Donald Margulies's *Sight Unseen* and *Collected Stories*), and about 150 others.

Most of this work took place in his three-plus decades as head dramaturg at South Coast Repertory in Southern California, but he also spent eight seasons as artistic director of the Sundance Theatre Program in Utah, which includes the noted Sundance Playwrights Laboratory. He was also co–artistic director of San Diego's Old Globe Theatre for three years until, in 2008, he was invited to New York to assume the post of director of artistic development at the distinguished Manhattan Theatre Club (MTC), where one of your authors, Robert Cohen, interviewed him for this profile.

One of Patch's greatest successes was discovering Margaret Edson's *Wit* in the mid-1990s. It was one of the hundreds of plays submitted annually "over the transom" (unsolicited, unrepresented by an agent, and written by a beginning playwright unknown to the theatre's management) to South Coast Repertory.

"When we got it," Patch said, "its core was there, but elements in the first draft showed the playwright's inexperience. I knew there was an intelligence there, and the story that moved me was very human, and I was impressed that for all of Vivian Bering's [the lead character's] intelligence, she was most comforted by the nurse giving her a Popsicle. For a woman in her twenties to write this work was pretty amazing, so even though it wasn't seaworthy at that time, it was full of potential. So we took a couple of years—maybe three—working with Maggie to get the play to where it made sense for us to produce it. During that time we gave her regular dramaturgical feedback, we gave it a public reading, and finally we put it into rehearsal, during which we encouraged her to trim it from two acts and over two hours to a ninety-minute one-act—a very different structure. It was absolutely amazing, and she's an amazing woman."

Wit has enjoyed enduring success: it opened in New York in 1998, won the Pulitzer Prize in 1999, and made its Broadway premiere, starring Cynthia Nixon, in 2012. You can see an excerpt of the script in the chapter titled "The Playwright."

Patch acknowledges that today's New York theatre is at least as much about star actors as it is about new plays. He says it was difficult to get Lynn Nottage's *Ruined* produced in New York because it had "no stars, and, with eleven actors and understudies and a couple of musicians, it was not a cheap show to put on." He added, "And what's it about? A woman who gets raped in the Congo! So at first we had to

Dramaturgs don't always work in theatres! Here, over a couple of beers, dramaturg Jerry Patch (*left*) and playwright Donald Margulies (*right*) talk through a moment in Margulies's *Time Stands Still*, which the Manhattan Theatre Club brought to Broadway in 2010, where it enjoyed a year's run and won a Tony nomination. ©*South Coast Repertory Theatre*

paper the hell out of the house [give away free tickets] to get audiences. But once people saw it, they became its advocates. The play became a grand event and we extended it several times; nearly everyone who saw it recommended it."

Patch had worked with Nottage before, at Sundance on her earlier *Crumbs from the Table of Joy* and then at South Coast for the co-premiere (in a coproduction with Baltimore's Centerstage) of her *Intimate Apparel*. The latter won "every critics' prize that year except the Pulitzer," Patch said wistfully.

Ruined first opened at Chicago's Goodman Theatre, where it remained in development until its New York debut at MTC. Before its MTC opening, Patch—along with his MTC colleague Mandy Greenfield—"mostly just went to the rehearsals and gave notes." He continued, "We just asked questions, such as 'This is what I'm getting—is it what you want?' and 'Could this be shorter?' Lynn took it from there, and the play went all the way." In all, *Ruined* received thirteen best-play awards—including the Drama Desk, New York Critics, Outer Critics, and Obie Awards, as well as the 2009 Pulitzer Prize.

Patch well remembers being told at the start of his career, "No kid ever dreamed of growing up to be a dramaturg." With the enormous contribution dramaturgs now make to the American theatre—and, indeed, to American culture—it is not surprising that students around the country are now contradicting that observation.

———

Courtesy of Jerry Patch.

Selecting the Designers The concept is the director's own creation, but its refinement and realization rest equally in the hands of designers, whose personal inclination inevitably plays an enormous role in the shape and impact of the final product. Hence the selection of these individuals is by no means a mechanical or arbitrary task; it is a central directorial concern of great artistic consequence.

Ordinarily directors make every effort to work with designers with whom they feel not only personal compatibility but also mutual respect and an overlap of artistic and intellectual vision. Like all true collaborations, the most effective director-designer relationships result in a give-and-take of ideas, plans, and feelings—a sense of sharing and support.

Collaborating with the Designers Designing a production marks the first step toward transforming vision into actuality: at this stage, people turn ideas into concrete visual realizations. The director's role in the design process is generally indirect and suggestive; the level of success in this delicate task is highly dependent on the personalities of the individuals involved. In theory, the director's and designers' goals are identical: an actable space, wearable costumes, and a clear understanding of the vision as a whole. In practice, though, each of the principals has an independent perspective on what is actable, what is memorable, and what is visionary. Each may also have a different sense of the importance of sometimes contradictory values. A costume designer, for example, may place a higher value on the appearance of a garment than does the director, who may be more concerned with the actor's ability to move in it. A lighting designer may be greatly interested in evoking a sense of murkiness, whereas the director may be more concerned that an actor's face be clearly seen at a particular moment. These are the sorts of artistic perspectives that must be reconciled in the design process, which is less about finding the "right" or "wrong" solution and more a matter of subjective choice.

Production design normally takes place in a series of personal conferences between director and designers, sometimes on a one-on-one basis and sometimes in group meetings. (Increasingly, in America's regional professional theatres, many of these conferences take place online via live video conferences, because a production's freelance director and designers may be working in different parts of the country—or world.) These are give-and-take affairs, for the most part, with the director doing most of the giving at the beginning and the designers taking over shortly thereafter. Often the first step is a collective meeting—the first design conference—where the director discusses her concept in detail and suggests some possibilities for its visual realization.

In the ensuing conferences, designers normally present their own conceptions and eventually provide the director with a progressive series of concrete visualizations: sketches, drawings, renderings, models, ground plans, working drawings, fabrics, technical details, and devices. During these conferences the design evolves through a collaborative sharing in which the director's involvement may range from minimal to maximal, depending on how well the initial concept and the developing design seem to be cohering.

The director's function at this stage of design is to approve or reject, as well as to suggest. As the person who sits at the top of the artistic hierarchy, the director has the last word on design matters, but that does not mean it's possible to simply command the show into being. Theatre design, like any creative process, cannot be summoned forth like an obedient servant. Moreover, the rejection of a designer's work after the initial stages inevitably involves serious time loss and budgetary waste—not to mention the risk of angering your artistic team before clocking even

King Lear (Philippe Girard) is covered by skeletons in Olivier Py's horrific production of *King Lear* at the 2015 Avignon Theatre Festival.
©Anne-Christine Poujoulat/Getty Images

one rehearsal. For these reasons, the directorial effort must be committed from the outset to sound collaborative principles. Once under way, the director-designer collaboration must take the form of shared responsibility in a developing enterprise, not confrontation between warring artists attempting to seize control.

Casting the Actors   The time has come to cast the play with actors. An old cliché states that "casting is 90 percent of directing," and while certainly a simplification, it contains more than a germ of truth. Actors not only attract more audience attention than any other aspect of the play, but they also represent what the audience cares about and will remember the next day. They certainly garner much of the interest an audience devotes to a play, and if they squander that interest they can destroy the effectiveness of any theatrical presentation.

The theatre historian Brian Eugenio Herrera has called the language that surrounds casting "mystical," and indeed, many play reviews bear out this claim by speaking of "inspired" or even "magical" decisions to have a particular actor in a role. This kind of wording often obscures the incredible amount of labor, ideology, and pragmatic decision making that goes into the actual practice of casting, which is far from simply a magical process of a director being struck with divine inspiration.

However, similar to the notion of casting being 90 percent of directing, there is some truth to this mysticism. Oftentimes directors pursue their intuition, rather than their intellect, in selecting a particular performer. And oftentimes that decision seems counterintuitive to others. To take some classic examples, the burlesque and comic performer Bert Lahr—known most famously for playing the blustering Cowardly Lion in the film *The Wizard of Oz*—originated, in 1956, the role of Estragon in Samuel Beckett's absurdist masterpiece *Waiting for Godot*. The assumption may have been that a play deemed by many as intellectual, dense, and inaccessible should not have had such a comic performer. Yet while even Lahr himself claimed not to understand the play fully, his performance wholly realized the desperation and humanity of Beckett's work. More recently, in 2015, the director Brian Mertes staged Tennessee Williams's *The Glass Menagerie* at Trinity Repertory Theatre with Brian McEleney, an actor in his sixties, filling the role of Tom Wingfield—a character described by Williams as in his twenties. Here, too, we find something more than simply "stunt" casting. *The Glass Menagerie* is about a man looking back on and reenacting the memories of his youth. To have an older man actually embody those memories adds a haunting, moving quality to the production. And in 2016, Karin Coonrod—who

had directed one of the versions of *The Tempest* mentioned earlier in the section on preparing the text—cast *five* actors in the single role of Shylock, the Jewish moneylender in Shakespeare's *The Merchant of Venice*. The five performers ranged in race and gender, and when they all appeared onstage in the play's final moments, the effect is profound—the predicament of Shakespeare's complex, persecuting character takes on a sense of universality.

Casting relies on a simple truism: actors are people. And as people, they are individuals. The audience, being human itself, is particularly attuned to the actor's human and idiosyncratic uniqueness. The actor's personality, physical and vocal characteristics, technical abilities, and presence weigh mightily in the final realization of every individual performance and in every ensemble of performances. In professional theatre, initial casting decisions are often made by a casting director, who seeks potential actors for the parts being cast and often considers submissions (mainly photos and résumés) from actors who wish to be considered for one or more of the roles. The actual casting then takes place during a series of auditions in which the actors—either by their own application or on the recommendation of a casting director—can be seen and heard by the director, either in a reading of material from the play to be produced, or in a previously prepared dramatic monologue. The director's ability to detect an incipiently brilliant performance in either of these contrived formats is a critical factor in effective casting.

Depending on the specific demands of the play and the rehearsal situation, the director and casting director may, in this first audition, pay special attention to the actor's training and experience, physical characteristics and vocal technique, suitability for the style of the play, perceived ability to impersonate a specific character in the play, personality traits that seem fitted to the material at hand, ability to understand the play's history and genre, personal liveliness and apparent stage presence, past record of achievement, and apparent cooperativeness in the context of an acting ensemble. And the director might well be looking for a great many other things besides.

Actors who survive the first audition then read for the part again—sometimes several times, alongside other performers who have been, or may be, cast—and at this stage the director is involved more and more in the audition process, often coaching the actors to determine how rapidly they can acquire the qualities needed. Such callbacks can go on for days and even weeks in the professional theatre, and are limited only by requirement of Actors' Equity Association, the labor union for American stage performers, that all actors receive their full union pay.

The part of Tom, in Tennessee Williams's groundbreaking play *The Glass Menagerie,* is written to be a young man—yet a recent 2015 Trinity Repertory Theatre production (pictured here) cast Brian McEleney, a man in his sixties (*standing*) in the role. Rather than simply being "stunt casting," however, this choice proved to be haunting—and proved a critical success. ©*Mark Turek*

Sometimes a performer taking on a part is the primary motivation for that play's production in the first place. A recent ad for the award-winning 2017 Broadway revival of *Hello, Dolly!* added only two words—"Bette Midler"—after the play's title to make a successful bid for theatregoers' attention. And the participation of the Oscar-winning actor Lupita Nyong'o in the 2015 production of *Eclipsed,* a harrowing account of sexual slavery in Liberia, was the main reason for that play's staging—and of its transfer from off-Broadway to Broadway in 2016, where Nyong'o earned a Tony Award nomination.

Casting in many cases can certainly prove controversial. At times, celebrities appear onstage to great acclaim, as with Oscar Isaac in *Hamlet* at the Public in 2017, or Bryan Cranston in *All the Way* on Broadway in 2014. The success of celebrity casting can be mercurial, as well. Audiences flocked to see the bestselling singer Josh Groban in the 2017 Broadway premiere of *Natasha, Pierre & the Great Comet of 1812;* but later, after he dropped out, ticket sales plummeted—despite the play's critical raves. The play's producers' attempted to save the play by cutting short the contract of Groban's replacement, Okieriete Onaodowan, to make way for the Broadway mega-star Mandy Patinkin—only to face a social media backlash due to charges of racism for stopping the Nigerian American Onaodowan's run with the white Patinkin. Patinkin agreed with this view and pulled out, and the show closed prematurely. (For more on the topic of race and casting, see the Spotlight "Casting and Diversity.")

Clearly, the casting of a celebrity can be a play's savior, but it may also backfire. Either way, the selection of an actor for a role is clearly one of the most important decisions a director will have to make.

Sometimes star power alone is enough to get a play produced. Such was the case with the Oscar-winning Lupita Nyong'o (*center*) who campaigned for Danai Gurira's *Eclipsed* (pictured here) to be staged. The play follows the divergent survival strategies of a group of women forced into sexual servitude in Liberia. Nyong'o's advocacy proved fruitful: *Eclipsed* was nominated for five Tony Awards. ©*Joan Marcus*

The international megastar Josh Groban (pictured here), known primarily as a recording artist, no doubt surprised many of his fans when he opted to star on Broadway in *Natasha, Pierre & the Great Comet of 1812,* an adaptation of a section of Tolstoy's *War and Peace.* The role Groban played—the titular Pierre—is far from flashy, and the play's plot is thorny and complex. And yet Groban's presence was enough to draw in sellout crowds and make the play a hit—until he left, at which point ticket sales plummeted despite rave reviews. ©*Sara Krulwich/ The New York Times/Redux*

○ Spotlight

Diversity and Casting

Casting is a crucial step in producing a play. It is also a highly sensitive one.

Even though actors make many important choices about how their characters behave and look, some aspects of their identity cannot help but become part of their performance. Some of these qualities are relatively innocuous. For instance, in 2013, a forty-six-year-old Paul Giamatti played the young and impetuous Prince Hamlet at Yale Repertory Theatre. Critics took note of Giamatti's age, but no one was offended.

But what about when an actor's race, sex, or gender becomes part of a character's identity? If a black actor is cast in a role that traditionally has been played by white actors, does this change our view of the character? What if, for instance, a black man played Willy Loman, the white protagonist of Arthur Miller's classic *Death of a Salesman*? This was, in fact, precisely the question asked by the acclaimed black playwright August Wilson in a famous speech in 1996. Wilson's answer is that to cast black actors as white characters like Willy "robs us of our humanity." Instead, Wilson argued, black theatre artists should celebrate and cultivate a rich tradition of art that portrays specifically black identity.

The critic and director Robert Brustein answered with an essay that makes the opposite point: theatre is universal and casting only actors of the same race as their characters is equivalent to segregation. What Brustein suggests doing is called *color-blind casting*. This idea remains controversial. Recently, a production of Edward Albee's play *Who's Afraid of Virginia Woolf?* was shut down by the Albee estate because it planned to feature a black actor as Nick, a character written as a white, blond man. And *Harry Potter and the Cursed Child*, the play based on the blockbuster series of books and movies, cast a black woman in the role of Hermione in its London premiere. In this case, the author of the *Harry Potter* books, J. K. Rowling, approved, but the casting decision was noteworthy enough to make headlines around the world. Why do some people expect performers to require a certain racial background to play these parts? Brustein, one imagines, would approve of these casting choices.

However, Wilson's point also resonates today. If we ignore the race of performers, aren't we erasing an important part of their identity? And isn't it important to have different races and cultures represented in popular art forms like theatre? What about plays like Wilson's own *Fences* or *Joe Turner's Come and Gone* or *The Piano Lesson*, all of which very specifically portray the history of black America? The history of race and theatre in the United States also informs these decisions. After the blackface performances of minstrelsy and early musical theatre, in which white actors embodied racist stereotypes of black culture, can we ever truly be "color-blind"?

Some plays knowingly address these questions. At times the results are intentionally confusing. Branden Jacobs-Jenkins's *An Octoroon,* for instance, features black actors portraying characters from the nineteenth-century melodrama *The Octoroon* by the white playwright Dion Boucicault. These characters were originally played by white actors in blackface. And the biggest hit on Broadway, *Hamilton,* has actors of color portray America's founding fathers—historical figures who were all white. Should these choices go unnoticed, or are they part of the play's artistic vision?

The same questions pertain to gender. While women have taken on men's roles in plays by Shakespeare, could we have a woman play Willy Loman? We have had female Hamlets and Lears, and male Violas and Juliets; audiences have generally been more accepting of cross-gender casting in Shakespeare's works. Perhaps this is because he is the most-produced playwright in the world and we are more comfortable experimenting with how his characters are portrayed. Perhaps it is because women were forbidden from acting in Renaissance England, so Shakespeare's plays originally had boys play roles written for women. The relative absence of women taking on men's roles in more modern plays, however, indicates some reluctance in pushing the boundaries of cross-gender casting too far.

Recently, casting debates have centered on characters written as transgender—that is, someone whose gender identity differs from the gender assigned at birth. Can a non-transgender actor portray a transgender character? This question came up recently in a production of the musical *Southern Comfort* at the Public Theater in New York City. The play's main character is a transgender man. But he was played by a woman, Annette O'Toole. This casting choice prompted protest from the transgender community. This incident is notable because the ability of the performer was never in question: O'Toole was roundly praised. Instead, the casting became the focus. Is casting an opportunity to give equal representation for different marginalized populations? Or is it simply a matter of finding actors who will do a great job, no matter how they identify?

When we see layer upon layer of identities onstage, we confront these difficult questions. It can be difficult to determine where the actor ends and the character begins. Casting, in other words, is a delicate and complicated process, one that gets to the heart of what makes theatre such a special art form: it is both artificial and real. As a result, it gives us a fascinating look at our current day's attitudes and values. In a time of debate and discussion over issues of identity, perhaps we can turn to the theatre to find a reflection of who we really are.

📷 Photo Essay: Casting Director James Calleri

How can a professional director choose a cast from the more than 200,000 professional actors in the United States with any accuracy—much less seek out newcomers from the even larger number of student actors hoping to enter the professional world? A casting director helps sort through this colossal and potentially overwhelming task.

Casting directors became a vital part of the theatre and film worlds of New York and Los Angeles in the latter half of the twentieth century. They now operate within theatre companies and in independent offices. The basic job of the casting director is to study scripts going into production, meet with producers and directors to assess what types of actors they're looking for, and, through interviews and preliminary tryouts, assemble a pool of outstanding performers to audition for the directors and producers. James Calleri, founding president of Calleri Casting in New York, has cast dozens of Broadway, off-Broadway, and regional theatre productions, as well as hundreds of film and television roles. His recent credits include Broadway's *Hughie,* in 2016, and *Fool for Love* in 2015. One of your authors, Robert Cohen, asked him for his thoughts in 2009, soon after he had cast *33 Variations* on Broadway with Jane Fonda and, off-Broadway, *The Seagull* with Dianne Wiest and Alan Cumming. By this edition's time of writing, he has won twelve Artios Awards for outstanding achievement in casting from the Casting Association of America.

"My interest in casting started when I was in grad school," Calleri began. "I tended to be somewhat opinionated, and a little bossy with my teachers about who should be playing what roles (particularly when I didn't like somebody in something), and I remember speaking up about it. I thought somebody must know how to do this better, and so I packed up my car and moved to New York the day after I graduated. I didn't know anybody when I first got there, but I was lucky to get a job as an assistant at a talent agency, and that

1. James Calleri, founding president of Calleri Casting in New York, in the informal interview room of his Lower Manhattan office. ©*Robert Cohen*

2. With assistant Katya Zarolinski, Calleri looks through headshot photographs of actors he is considering for a new off-Broadway production. ©*Robert Cohen*

3. Most of the submissions from actors and agents now come through the Internet. Here Calleri examines one of hundreds of digital headshots of actors under consideration for the show's initial auditions. ©*Robert Cohen*

put me in the middle of everything. I developed a great relationship with the casting directors I met, and pretty soon I went to work for them, first sweeping floors and filing pictures and soon casting shows myself.

"What do I look for in an actor? Of course, I want to see a person who's terrific in his or her craft, but I'm also hoping to see a fascinating personality, a mystique, a unique point of view about life. Equate this to dating: What is it about a person that keeps him or her in your mind? What drives you to ask that person for a second date? Well, an actor having that quality makes me confident that an audience will want to spend two to three hours watching him or her onstage or in multiple episodes of a TV series. For camera media, particularly TV, I'm looking primarily for personality. With theatre casting, it's much more about where you went to school, who you've worked with, what shows you've done, what theatres you've performed in, what type of roles you've played, what your voice is like and your body's like—all those things.

And of course on Broadway, name recognition in the cast is pretty crucial. A play doesn't get to Broadway today unless the producers have a name they can hitch it to."

How can a beginning actor break into New York theatre? "You have to try to find work," Calleri advised. "Join a company, do a show that our agency would cover, perhaps in the fringe festival [an annual array of low-budget productions mounted around the city in late August], or a showcase, or a downtown theatre company that we frequent. That's where we find most people."

How has modern technology changed the business of casting? According to Calleri, "We do a lot more looking at an actor's reels [short compilations of video clips of the actor's performance distributed on DVDs or via the Internet] these days, and we share video clips of our New York auditions with the producers and directors in other cities. When I started at ABC, we would tape our auditions in New York and then ship the reels overnight to our colleagues at the studios in Los Angeles. Now we record them digitally and have them uploaded, edited, and sent out right to the L.A. set, where the producers can go into their trailers, watch the clips on their iPhones, and (we hope) say, 'Yes, that's exactly who I want!'"

How does Calleri like his job? "Casting? I love it," he exclaimed. "It's great, it's always different, it's always challenging, it never gets old."

Courtesy of James Calleri.

REHEARSALS

With the play selected and conceptualized, with the designers chosen and the designs under way, and with the actors auditioned and cast, the production begins to take physical, emotional, and above all dramatic shape. This is the period of *rehearsal*. During the coming weeks, the play will be read aloud, memorized, staged, and rehearsed, often in a room with makeshift rehearsal furniture and the walls of the set indicated by taped marks on the floor. The actual sets, costumes, and props will be designed and built in shops available for those purposes. Sound, lighting, and special effect cues will be created and eventually worked into the rehearsals. The acting will be coached, detailed, and drilled into the actors' muscle memories. While these elements may change in previews (performances before opening night that give the artistic team the chance to finalize the production), or even during the run of the play, the foundation of the play becomes established, first and foremost, in rehearsal.

The director's ability to maintain both leadership and creative inspiration through this period becomes more crucial with each passing day. From the time of that first company meeting, the director controls the focus and consciousness of the entire cast and staff. As the head of an ambitious and emotionally consuming enterprise, the director will be the repository of the company's collective artistic hopes—and the focal point for the company's collective frustration, anxiety, and, on occasion, despair. The director is the company's shield against the intrusions of an outside world, as well as the spokesperson for the enterprise to which the company has collectively dedicated itself. Directorial power or influence cannot be substantially altered by any attempt the director may make to cultivate or repudiate it—it simply comes with the job and with the need for every theatrical company to have focus and, quite literally, direction. The manner in which directors use that power, and the sensitivity with which they bring the production into being, determines the nature of each director's individual brand of artistry.

Staging   Positioning the actors on the set and having them move about in a theatrically effective manner is the most obvious of directorial functions. Directorial composition, as it is sometimes called, is the one thing directors are always expected to do and to do well, and it is the one they are most often seen doing; it is no wonder traditional textbooks on directing tend to be largely devoted to this function.

The medium of staging is the actor in space and time—with the space defined by the acting area and settings and the time defined by the duration of the theatrical event

Theatre does not always happen in a theatre. Kenneth Branagh codirected (with Rob Ashford) and also played the title role of *Macbeth* in this production, which originated in a rain-filled and mud-floored deconsecrated church in Manchester, England, in 2013, as seen here, before coming to New York's Park Avenue Armory the following year. ©Johan Persson/ArenaPAL

and the dynamics of its dramatic structure. Staging should aim to create focus for the play's themes, lend credibility to the play's characters, generate interest in the play's actions, unify the play's appearance, provoke suspenseful involvement in the play's events, and, in general, stimulate a fulfilling level of engagement for the entire production.

The basic structure of staging is called *blocking*, which refers to the timing and placement of a character's entrances, exits, rises, crosses, embraces, and other major movements of all sorts. The pattern that results from the interaction of characters in motion provides the framework of an overall staging; it is also the physical foundation of the actors' performance. Many actors have difficulty memorizing their lines until they know the blocking that will be associated with them.

Staging sometimes begins with a reformulation of the nature of the playing space itself. Today's directors may completely redefine the relationship between audience and actor, either by placing the audience on the stage and the actors in the "audience" or by making other variations on the conventional theatrical arrangement. In Mihai Maniutiu's 2007 *Job Experiment*, for example, which the director adapted from the Old Testament Book of Job, the play's actors—perhaps echoing Satan's biblical question to God, "Have you not put a fence around him and his house?"—are surrounded by a closed-in polygonal wall (codesigned by Maniutiu and Christian Rusu) that is pierced by forty-four windows through which audience members, one to a window, peer in on the action. Here Job (*kneeling, right*) is in anguish as an angel of death kills his herd of cattle, represented by gold balloons. Maniutiu explained his goal was "not to bring old rites to life but to create a ritual fiction." The production was presented at the 2008 Romanian National Theatre Festival in Bucharest. *©Pierre Borasci*

The director may block a play either by preplanning the movements (preblocking) on paper or by allowing the actors to improvise movement on a rehearsal set and then fixing the blocking sometime before the first performance. Often a combination of these methods is employed, with the director favoring one method or the other depending on the specific demands of the play, the rehearsal schedule, rapport with the acting company, or the director's own stage of preparation. Complex or stylized plays and settings and short rehearsal periods usually dictate a great deal of preblocking; simple domestic plays and experienced acting ensembles are often afforded more room for improvisation. Each method can produce highly commendable results in the right hands and at the right time.

Likewise, both can present serious problems if misapplied or ineptly handled.

For the most part, the blocking of a play is hidden in the play's action; it tends to be effective insofar as it is not noticed. Blocking should simply bring other values into play and focus the audience's attention on significant aspects of the drama. By physically enhancing the dramatic action and adding variety to the play's visual presentation, a good blocking pattern can play a large role in creating theatrical life and excitement. Indeed, there are often moments when inspired blocking choices can create truly astonishing theatrical effects. Such a dynamite moment was achieved, for example, by director Peter Brook in his celebrated 1962 production of *King Lear*, when Paul

Fight scenes are not always duels or military battles. Here actors Roger Allam and Jodhi May have at each other with ordinary office chairs, as staged by Fight Director Malcolm Ranson in David Harrower's *Blackbird,* an intense drama about pedophilia and its horrific aftermath. The play, directed by the acclaimed German director Peter Stein, was performed at the Edinburgh Festival in 2006. *©Geraint Lewis*

Scofield, as Lear, suddenly rose and, with one violent sweep of his arm, overturned the huge oak dining table at which he had been seated, sending pewter mugs crashing to the floor as he raged at his daughter Goneril's treachery. This stunning action (though it might seem almost timid today) led to a reevaluation of the character of both Lear and Goneril and of the relationship between this tempestuous and sporadically vulgar father and his socially ambitious daughter. It also instantly established Brook as one of England's greatest living directors and is still talked about to this day.

Some plays require specialized blocking for particularly raucous or dramatic movements. The Broadway hit *The Play That Goes Wrong*—a transfer from London, where it similarly proved a smash success—features collapsing sets, falling props, and actors flying through walls. Other plays feature even more dynamic movements, such as the flying effects in *Peter Pan.* Such scenes require

particularly skilled direction and coaching, so the director may wish to engage a choreographer, fight director, or flying specialist to create the highly detailed moment-to-moment movements that scenes such as these require. Such specialized dramatic situations are hardly rare. Actors in Renaissance England most likely finished their performances with a dance (some remnants of these dances still exist in the play texts, as with Shakespeare's *Much Ado About Nothing*). And almost every play written before the nineteenth century includes a dance, a duel, a battle, or some combination of all of them. The ability to create or at least to oversee a captivating dance number or an exciting battle or flying scene is clearly requisite for any director aspiring to work beyond the strictly modern-realistic mode.

Business is a theatre term that refers to the small-scale movements a character performs within the larger pattern of entrances, crosses, and exits. Mixing a cocktail, answering

The smash hit *The Play That Goes Wrong* details a hapless group of actors who attempt to put on a play in which, indeed, everything goes wrong. Ironically, for the actual production everything has to go *right* with surgical precision: in order to appear as if mistakes happen, the technical and artistic team need to rehearse rigorously every last second of action. ©*Markus Scholz/picture-alliance/dpa/AP Images*

a telephone, adjusting a tie, shaking hands, fiddling with a pencil, winking an eye, and drumming on a tabletop are all bits of business that can lend a character credibility, depth, and fascination. Much of the stage business in a performance is originated by the actor—usually spontaneously over the course of rehearsal—although it may be stimulated by a directorial suggestion or request. The director acts as an editor of the actors' business, ultimately selecting from among the rehearsal inventions to determine what will become a part of the finished performance. When this determination is made, bits of business become part of the blocking plan.

Staging, then, in the broadest sense, includes both hidden and bold blocking effects, specialized movements, and small idiosyncratic behaviors, all combined into a complex pattern that creates meaning, impact, and style. From a subtle nervous tic to a grand entrance on a flying trapeze, every movement onstage counts as staging—and all ultimately result from the director's decisions. Skillful staging unites the design elements of a production with the acting, creating an omni-dynamic spatial interaction between actors, costumes, scenery, and audience, and infusing the stage with life. Getting a play on its feet, as the

theatrical jargon puts it, is usually the first step in allowing the actors to experience the full human vitality of the playwright's characters, both in the actions they take and the words they utter.

Actor-Coaching   The director is the actor's coach who initiates and leads the various activities—discussions, improvisations, games, exercises, lectures, research, blocking, and polishing—that will occupy the actors during each rehearsal. Like an athletic coach, the director seeks to stimulate proactive teamwork among the players, as well as develop their individual craft excellence and artistry. Because the work of the theatre inevitably demands of the actor a good measure of emotional, psychological, and even spiritual investment, the director has an opportunity (if not an obligation) to provide an atmosphere in which actors can feel free to liberate their powers of sensitivity and creativity. Good directors lead their casts; great directors inspire them.

Guiding the actors through the script may be important in the early stages of rehearsal, particularly if the language is complex, the historical period unfamiliar, or the play's characters unlike persons known to the actors themselves.

One of the major problems in staging realistic plays is letting the audience see the expressions of important characters—and hence the faces of the actors playing them—while still maintaining the credibility of those characters, who are (supposedly) talking to each other and not to the audience. Director Guy Masterson solves this by having all actors focus on a key prop in this jury-room scene in Reginald Rose's *12 Angry Men*, produced at the Edinburgh Festival in 2003. ©*Geraint Lewis*

Wilfried Minks's 2008 production of *A Streetcar Named Desire* indicates the isolation of its protagonist, Blanche, by foregrounding her during this scene. We can see her wince in pain, but the oblivious men behind her cannot. ©*Aris/Sueddeutsche Zeitung Photo/Alamy Stock Photo*

Stagecraft

"This Is How It's Done!"

Publicity photographs taken in rehearsal frequently show a director onstage with a few actors, demonstrating a bit of business and "showing them how it's done." This kind of publicity has probably fostered a certain misunderstanding of the director's role among the general public, for demonstration is only a part of directing, and a distinctly small part at that. Indeed, some directors scrupulously avoid it altogether.

Demonstration as a way of teaching an actor a role has a long history in the theatre and was a particularly common practice in those periods when directing was carried out chiefly by retired actors. Even today, young actors rehearsing for classical plays at the Comédie-Française (founded in France in 1680) are expected to learn their parts by mimicking the performance of their elders down to the last detail of inflection, tone, gesture, and timing. And many contemporary American directors occasionally give "line readings" to an actor or demonstrate the precise manner of gesturing, moving, sitting, or handling a prop if they perceive that a specific desired behavior might not come naturally.

However, demonstration as an *exclusive* method of coaching an actor in a role is very much a thing of the past. Most contemporary directors make far greater use of discussion, suggestion, and improvisation. These methods seek to address the inner actor and to encourage the individual to distill the performance out of self-motivated passions and enthusiasms. Because they know that a purely imitative performance is all too likely to be a mechanical performance, today's directors tend to rely on methods more creative than "getting up there and showing how it's done."

Sometimes the director will invite the dramaturg, if one is on the artistic team, to provide appropriate research or give a company lecture on the more elusive points of the text. The director may also ask voice coaches, dance and fight choreographers, and others to provide assistance where specialized performance techniques are desired.

The ways that directors coach actors are various and probably more dependent on personality than on planning. Some directors are largely passive; they either "block and run," in the jargon of commercial theatre, or function primarily as a sounding board for actors' decisions about intention, action, or business. Conversely, there are directors closer to the popular stereotype, fanatics whose approaches at times turn them into dictators: they cajole, bully, plead, storm, and rage at their actors; involve themselves in every detail of motive and characterization; and turn every rehearsal into a mixture of acting class, group therapy session, and religious experience. Both methods, as experience teaches, can produce theatrical wizardry, and both can fail utterly. Probably the determining factors either way are the strength of the director's ideas and the extent to which the cast is willing to accept directorial authority.

Too little direction can be as stultifying to actors as too much. The passive director runs the risk of defeating the actors' performances by withholding constructive response. Similarly, the extremely active director may, in a whirlwind of passion, overwhelm the actors' own creativity and squelch their efforts to build a sensitive performance, thereby condemning the production to oppressive dullness. For these and other reasons, most directors today strive to find a middle ground, somewhere between task mastery and suggestion, from which they can provide actors with both a goal and a disciplined path toward it while maintaining an atmosphere of creative freedom.

Directors need not be actors themselves, but they must understand the complexities of acting if they are to help their cast fashion powerful performances. The greatest acting braves the unknown and flirts continuously with danger of exposure, failure, transparency, and artifice. The director must give the actors a careful balance of freedom and guidance to foster the confidence that leads to that kind of acting. Directors who are insensitive to this requirement—no matter how colorful their storming and coaxing or how rational their discussions of the playwright's vision—are almost certain to forfeit the performance rewards that arise from the great actor-director collaborations.

Pacing   The pace of a play is perhaps the only aspect for which general audiences and theatre critics alike are certain to hold the director accountable. Frequently, newspaper reviews of productions devote whole paragraphs of praise or blame to the actors and designers and evaluate the director's contribution solely in terms of the play's pace: "well paced" and "well directed" are almost interchangeable comments in the theatre critic's lexicon. When critics pronounce a play "slow" or "dragging," everyone understands they are firing a barrage at the director.

To the novice director (or critic), however, pace appears to be simply a function of the rate at which lines are said; hence a great many beginning directors attempt to make their productions more lively simply by instructing everyone to speak and move at a fast clip: "Give it more energy!" "Make it happen faster!" But dramatic pace is not determined solely by a stopwatch. Rather, it is created on the basis of a complex and composite time structure that incorporates many variables: credibility, suspense, mood, and style. The pacing of a play also incorporates the natural rhythms of life, such as heartbeat, respiration, the duration of a spontaneous sob, and the suddenness of an unexpected laugh. How much time is properly consumed, for example, by a moment of panic? a pregnant pause? a flash of remembrance? an agonized glance? a quick retort? And what are the patterns of those rhythms?

Knowing the play's genre helps answer that question. In a farce, the audience needs almost no time to synthesize information; therefore, farce generally is propelled rapidly, with information coming as fast as the actors can get it out. Political drama, on the other hand, demands of us a critical inquiry into our own societies, and demands time for the audience to linger over certain well-poised questions before moving on to speedier scenes as the play's arguments escalate toward climaxes. Deeply psychological dramas present a third pattern, often profiting by an even slower pace that fosters the audience's deeper understanding of the play's characters and their issues. Sympathy in these plays is more likely to be engendered when audience members have an opportunity to compare the characters' lives with their own, and are able to put themselves in the characters' situations to ponder the subtle meanings that emerge from the onstage actions.

But there is no one-size-fits-all pace for each genre; no pace is simply mechanical or unvaried. Just as a symphony is composed of several movements, a well-paced theatrical

Directing comedy is an art in itself, and Nicholas Hytner scored a brilliant success in 2011 with a modern-day adaptation of an eighteenth-century Italian commedia play. Richard Bean's *One Man, Two Guvnors,* which updates Carlo Goldoni's 1743 *The Servant of Two Masters*, began at the National Theatre in London in 2011 and transferred to Broadway a year later. James Corden—as the titular man torn between two bosses—gave a virtuosic performance of physical clowning. Pictured here is a typically strenuous bit of clowning by Corden, who won a Tony Award for Best Actor in a Play.
©Sara Krulwich/The New York Times/Redux

production inevitably has its range of tempos, from a stately march to a frantic waltz. Faster tempos tend to excite, bedazzle, and sharpen audience attention; slower ones give audience members a chance to consider and to augment the play's actions and ideas with their own reflections. Often directors speak about "setting up" an audience with a rapid pace and then delivering a "payoff" with a powerful, more deliberately paced dramatic catharsis. The sheer mechanics of theatrical pacing demand the greatest skill and concentration from both actor and director, and for both, the perfection of dramatic timing (and most notably comic timing) is a mark of great theatrical artistry.

Directors vary in their manner of pacing plays. Some wait until final rehearsals and then stamp out rhythms on the stage floor with a stick or clap their hands at the back of the house. Some experiment with different patterns in the early rehearsals and explore them in great detail with the actors. Directorial intervention of some sort is almost always present in the achievement of an excellent dramatic pace; it rarely occurs spontaneously. Actors trained in the realist manner often tend to work through material too slowly; actors trained in a more technical manner tend to proceed so quickly they leave the audience lost; and when a variety of actors, trained in different schools, come together in production for the first time, they can create such a confusing collection of paces that the play becomes unintelligible until the director steps in to guide them.

Coordinating   In the final rehearsals the director's responsibility becomes focused on coordinating different elements of the production: the concept and the designs, the acting and the staging, the pace and the performance. Now all the production elements that were developed separately must be judged, adjusted, polished, and perfected. Costumes must be seen under lights, staging must be seen against scenery, pacing must include the shifting of sets, acting must incorporate sound amplification and the size of the performance space, and the original concept must be reexamined in light of the actual production that has emerged. Crucial questions must be answered: Is the theme coming across? Are the actions clear? Can the actors be heard and understood? Do the costumes read? Is the play focused? Is the play interesting? Do we care about the characters? about the themes? about anything?

Timing and *unity* are governing concepts in this final coordinating phase of production. A play's timing is the overall effect of the individual paces that the director and actors have hammered out. In assessing the play's overall timing, the director must be prepared to judge the play's duration and to modify or eliminate those parts of the production that muddy the play's potential for communicating

information, feelings, or ideas. Last-minute cutting is always a painful process—much labor and creative spirit have gone into the parts that will be cut—but many a production has been vastly improved by judicious pruning at this time. In the interest of providing unity—the more conceptual quality that gives a play a sense of visionary wholeness—the best and bravest directors are willing in these final moments to eliminate elements that fail to cohere with the play's overall appearance and significance. Often these elements hold a special meaning for directors; they may even have figured into their earliest conception of the production. But now, directors have to think more coldly and analytically. As the common saying goes, they must be willing to "kill their darlings"—the parts of the play that they may love, but that do not contribute to the production as a whole. What was fun and engaging in rehearsal may rather look painfully like directorial indulgence or extraneous showing off. The best directors are those who can be most rigorous with themselves at this stage. They must realize a universal truth—the play is bigger than any one person.

In the *technical rehearsals,* when scenery, lighting, and sound are added, and dress rehearsals, when the actors don costumes and makeup for the first time, directors arrive at a crossroads: though remaining responsible for every final decision about the timing and wholeness of theatrical elements, they must now "give over" the core of the production to the actors and technicians who will execute it. Though they have pored over every moment of the play, they no longer have as much control as in those early days of exploration. In these final rehearsals the director's role becomes more a matter of finessing the show's details, delivered to the cast and staff in hundreds of last-minute notes, rather than general concepts or inspirational speeches. Yet it is in just these minute details that a production develops the refinement that distinguishes the outstanding from the mediocre.

What an extraordinary exchange of power has taken place between the first meeting of the cast and director and these final days! Whereas earlier the entire production was in the director's head and the cast waited in awe and expectation, now the actors hold the play in their heads and everyone confronts the unknowns of the play's reception. The actors have a new master now: the audience. In these days even the most experienced actors confront their fundamental vulnerability. They must face the audience with nothing to shield them save their costumes, characters, and lines. To the actor, the director is no longer a leader but a partner, no longer a parent but a friend.

Presenting   A popular proverb of the theatre states that nobody is more useless on opening night than the director. If all has progressed without major catastrophe and the production has successfully been given over to those who will execute it, the director's task on opening night consists chiefly in seeing and evaluating the production. The days leading up to this time may have been filled with last-minute decisions, however. During previews, the director has had the responsibility to evaluate the production in terms of its audience response, and institute changes where desirable—including cuts and changes in the text if it's a new play and the playwright is on hand and willing—right up to the opening performance. The director may invite the dramaturg, if one is on the team, to provide comments throughout this final period and spot moments that may not be coming through as strongly as they could be. The dramaturg may also, in the final days of preparation, write the dramaturgical notes on the play that will be printed in the program. These notes may allude to historical context and thematic resonances that would guide the audience as to what they might want to look for in the performance they are about to see.

Although in professional theatre a director's contract normally terminates on opening night, most directors try to see performances periodically during the run, and may follow up their visits with notes to the actors—either to encourage them to maintain spontaneity or to discourage them from revising the original directorial plan. One perhaps mythical show-business story has it that the American director George Abbott once posted a rehearsal call late in a play's run in order to "take out the improvements."

Just as the actor might feel abandoned in those empty moments prior to the opening performance, the director might feel a twinge of isolation at the applause that follows it. In that curtain-call ovation, the audience takes over the director's function and the director is consigned to invisibility. The actors, heady with the applause, suddenly remember that they provide the essential ingredient of theatre, while the director, cheering the ensemble from the back of the house, suddenly feels like just another face in the crowd. Only directors who can derive genuine satisfaction from creating art out of the medium of others' performance will thrive and prosper in directorial pursuits. Those who aspire to public acclaim and adulation will most likely face perpetual frustration as practitioners of this all-encompassing, all-consuming craft.

The Training of a Director

Traditionally, directors have come to their profession from a great many areas, usually after achieving distinction in another theatrical discipline: for example, Elia Kazan was first an actor, Susan Stroman a choreographer, Harold Prince a producer, Kwame Kwei-Armah a playwright and actor, Peter Hunt a lighting designer, Franco Zeffirelli a scenic designer, Robert Brustein a drama critic, and Mike Nichols an improvisational comedian. In addition to a specialty, most of these directors have brought to their art a comprehensive knowledge of the theatre in its various aspects. Having distinction in one field is important chiefly insofar as it gives directors a certain confidence and authority—and it gives others confidence in their exercise of that authority. But it is comprehensive knowledge that enables directors to collaborate successfully with actors, designers, managers, playwrights, and technicians with knowledge and enthusiasm.

Directors entering the profession today are more likely than not to have been trained in a dramatic graduate program or conservatory—and often they have supplemented this training with an apprenticeship at a repertory theatre. One of the most remarkable recent developments in the American theatre has been the emergence of a cadre of expertly trained directors with a broad understanding of the theatre and a disciplined approach to directorial creativity.

Well-trained directors will possess—in addition to the craft mastery of staging, actor-coaching, pacing, and production coordinating—a strong literary imagination and an ability to conceptualize intellectually and visually. They will be sensitive to interpersonal relationships, which play an important role in the onstage and offstage collaborations under their control. They will have a thorough working knowledge of the history of the theatre, the various styles and masterworks of dramatic literature, the potential of various theatre technologies, and the design possibilities inherent in the use of theatrical space. They will have at their command resources in music, art, literature, and history; they will be able to research and closely analyze plays to investigate production possibilities without starting at absolute zero; and they will be able to base ideas and conceptions on sound social, psychological, and aesthetic understandings. And while the accumulation of knowledge is crucial, the development of a more conceptual skill is also fundamental: the ability to be open to the world. Well-trained directors should seek the extraordinary but also find limitless potential in the ordinary. Like practitioners of every other theatrical craft, directors must be excellent listeners and observers.

All of these advanced skills can be effectively taught in a first-rate drama program. For that reason, today's top-flight theatre directors, more than any other group of stage artists, are likely to have studied in one or another of the many rigorous programs found in schools all over the world. The accomplished director is perhaps the one all-around "expert" of the theatre. Nothing is truly irrelevant to the training of a director, for almost every field of knowledge can be brought to bear upon theatre production.

📷 Photo Essay: *The Tempest*

In the summer of 2017, Professor Eli Simon directed Shakespeare's *The Tempest* as part of the New Swan Shakespeare Festival in Irvine, California. Like all plays in the festival, *The Tempest* employed professional actors, technicians, directors, professors, and graduate and undergraduate students. Also like all plays in the festival, *The*

Tempest was staged at the New Swan Theatre, a portable, 16-ton, 130-seat miniature version of an Elizabethan playhouse that was assembled on the campus of the University of California, Irvine (UCI).

Simon normally oversees his entire theatre season and personally directs one play of his own choosing. *The*

Tempest is a particularly difficult Shakespearean work, a peculiar masterpiece that mixes comedy, tragedy, romance, and fantasy in equal amounts. The photos included here help us go behind the scenes to see how this production—and many like it—came to be, from its early meetings to its final curtain call.

1. *Creating the Company.* It may take a year or even more to hire and engage the full staff needed for a production: actors, directors, designers, scene builders, lighting technicians, assistants, understudies, publicists, promoters, vocal coaches, fight choreographers, and dramaturgs—to name just a few. Here, the actors and creative team meet for the first time. Everybody introduces themselves, Simon explains his basic plan for the show, and the designers show their initial ideas. The actors then have a first "read-through" of the play, speaking their roles in the scripts provided them. ©*Robert Cohen*

2. *Rehearsing.* Actors rarely, if ever, rehearse a play on the stage where it will be mounted. For *The Tempest,* the performers began rehearsing their scenes in a studio at the university. With swords drawn, the actors Deshawn Mitchel (*left*), playing Sebastian, and Grace Morrison (*right*), playing Antonia ("Antonio" in Shakespeare's original), threaten their enemies on the floor. In the background, Greg Ungar, who plays the lead role of Prospero, reads and memorizes his lines in preparation for his own scene work, which will begin shortly. ©*Robert Cohen*

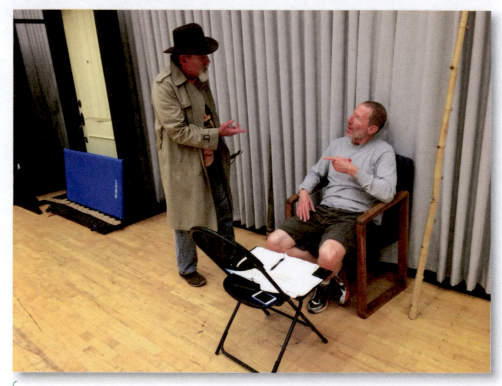

3. *Actor Coaching with Other Actors.* Also in Studio Five, the actors—David Golbeck (*left*) as the old councilor Gonzalo and Greg Ungar (*right*) as Prospero, now coach each other, as they will become important partners onstage. ©*Robert Cohen*

4. *Building the Set.* In the scene shop, theatre students Fuchi Thao (*left*) and Geronimo Guzman (*right*) paint a twenty-two-foot tower. The students are surrounded by the shop's working tools, saws, wires, and pipes. On the wall behind them hang a painting and fake crocodile from earlier productions at the university. (The crocodile is from a production of Mozart's opera *The Magic Flute* directed by your author Robert Cohen in 1989!) ©*Robert Cohen*

5. *Scene Building.* Keith Bangs, the UCI Drama Department's production manager and technical director, is in charge of the scene shop. Here, with the assistance of student Fuchi Thao, he builds the ship's mast for *The Tempest*'s first scene. ©*Robert Cohen*

6. *Making the Costumes.*
In another building,
a costume room is filled
with fabrics, garments, and
various clothing items that
will be designed, sewn,
and created by
the production's costume
department, including
Kathyrn Wilson (*left*) and
Jessica VanKempen (*right*).
©*Robert Cohen*

7. *Touching up the Costume
Design.* Kathryn Wilson
checks her hand-drawn
costume design against the
actual costume. Wilson has
designed for the New Swan
for all six of its seasons to
date and now teaches
costume design full time at
California State University,
Fullerton. ©*Robert Cohen*

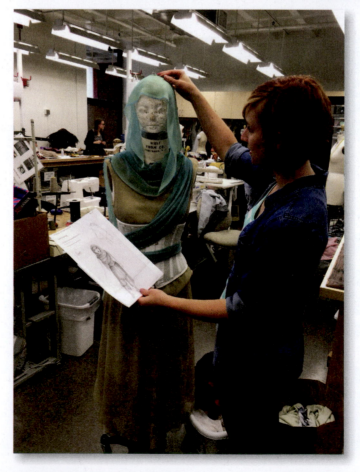

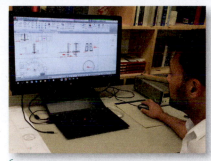

8. *Adjusting the Scenic Design.* UCI Drama Professor Dipu Gupta has designed sets for theatre and opera throughout the United States and Mexico. In his office, he studies his design of the mast and sail that will be at the center of the stage at the New Swan Theatre. *©Robert Cohen*

9.

10.

9. *Painting the Set.* Back in the scene shop, Chris Holmes paints the sail onto the cloth held up by the mast. *©Robert Cohen*

10. *Composing the Music.* Vincent Olivieri, a professor at UCI and professional sound designer, plays his marimba in his studio. For *The Tempest,* Olivieri not only created the soundscape but also composed the music that backs up the dramatic action. Like Simon and Gupta, Olivieri has worked around the United States, both on Broadway and in regional theatres, and abroad, in Romania, Italy, China, South Korea, and the Czech Republic. *©Robert Cohen*

11. *Actor Coaching from the Director.* Back in Studio Five, Simon coaches his actors on specific lines in the play and suggests attitudes, expressions, movements, and speeds for their actions. *©Robert Cohen*

11.

12. *Reviewing the Set with Production Manager and Technical Director.* Keith Bangs (*left*) orchestrates the annual transfer of the New Swan Theatre from the storage room next to the scene shop to a concrete patio outside the campus library. Like many public theatres during the Renaissance, the New Swan is circular. It holds 105 seats, and actors are able to run onto the set from several entrances and exits. With his colleague Cody Gummerman, Keith is indicating what still needs to be done in the upper gallery. ©*Robert Cohen*

13.

14.

13. *Collaborating.* Keith Bangs (*left*) and Dipu Gupta (*right*) discuss the coordination of Gupta's set and Bangs's theatre building. ©*Robert Cohen*

14. *Mounting Stage Lights.* Lighting technician Chris Gummerman mounts different stage lights onto the high poles that encircle the stage. ©*Robert Cohen*

15. *Putting Down the Flooring.* The floor has to be screwed onto supports to create slightly elevated levels above the theatre's permanent concrete bottom. Here Matt Eisenmann screws the supporting pieces into the appropriate places prior to covering them with the final floor. ©*Robert Cohen*

16. *Setting the Lights.* Karyn D. Lawrence (*right*) has designed lighting throughout the United States and in Italy, Poland, Romania, and the Czech Republic. Here she arranges hundreds of precisely timed lighting cues that will be carried out during each performance by the light board operator, Nita Mendoza (*on Lawrence's left*). ©*Robert Cohen*

17. *Moving In.* Finally moving into the now erected outdoor theatre where the play will be presented, the company meets to plan the transition into this new space. The actors, now in costume, will learn to perform in their new environment with complete assurance and safety. The first rehearsals of the play, which have helped the cast memorize their lines and general movements, must now make way for technical rehearsals, which require the actors to precisely perform their movements, entrances, exits, sword fights, and leaps around the actual stage, steps, ladders, balcony, and props—all of which will soon be surrounded by a full-house audience inches away from the action.
©Robert Cohen

18. *Practicing Onstage.* Thomas Varga, as the monstrous Caliban, and Grace Theobald, as the lovely and elegant spirit Ariel, practice an interaction they will perform in daytime and in costume, while Simon (*behind them*) gives movement instructions to a hooded Druid. Because of the darkness in which the play will actually be performed, the actors have to learn to drill these physical actions in absolute safety and with absolute accuracy.
©Robert Cohen

19. *Managing the Production.* Miriam Mendoza, the stage manager, sits in the highest seat above the stage and prepares to call actor entrances, along with light, sound, and special effects, during the nighttime show. Tucked away in the top rows, she will be unseen by the audience. ©*Robert Cohen*

20. *Running the Sound.* During an afternoon rehearsal, Vincent Olivieri, the composer, determines the specific beginnings, endings, and volumes of his recorded music. ©*Robert Cohen*

21. *Changing Costumes.* Greg Ungar is aided in putting on his final costume as Prospero. ©*Robert Cohen*

22. *Applying Makeup.* Grace Theobald, who plays Ariel, has her makeup adjusted by Katelin Phillips. ©*Eli Simon*

23. *Getting the Right Light.* In the dark, lighting technician Wesley Charles Chew focuses the lights onto the precise position on the stage as determined by the lighting designer. ©*Robert Cohen*

24. *Readying the Puppets.* The mounting of this gigantic creature, the Goddess Juno—part of Prospero's "masque," or spectacular presentation—takes place in the daytime rehearsal to ensure that it will be mounted effectively in the nighttime performance. ©*Robert Cohen*

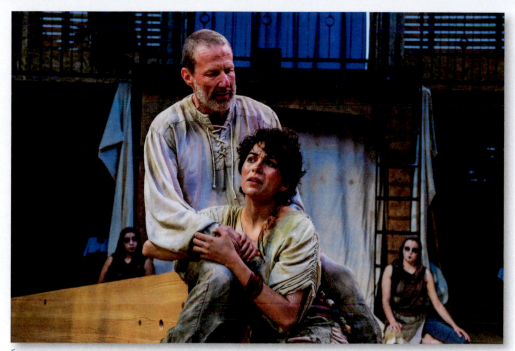

25. *Rehearsing at Night.* The play is now being rehearsed for the first time in the evening, as Greg Ungar as Prospero explains his life to his daughter, Miranda, played here by Anita Abdinezhad. At nighttime, actors and technicians gain a more accurate sense of the conditions of the performance. ©*Paul Kennedy*

26. *Putting on the Show.* Now all the elements—design, acting, direction—come together for the actual production. Here, airy druids and spirits, cloaked and belted, perform for a live audience. ©*Paul Kennedy*

27. *Resolving the Plot.* In the final moments of a live performance, the play reaches a resolution: The major villain Alonso, the King of Naples (Adrian Alita, *left*), blesses the forthcoming marriage of Miranda and the gentle Ferdinand, played by Eric Flores. ©*Paul Kennedy*

28. *Documenting the Play.* Paul Kennedy, the publicity photographer for this production, takes photos of the actors in action. These images will be used for marketing materials and for the professional portfolios of the artists who collaborated on the play. ©*Robert Cohen*

Chapter

7

Theatre Traditions

©Pei Hung Hsu

WHEN YOU WITNESS AN ACTOR playing a well-known part, you are hearing words that have rung out thousands of times before, all over the world, in a nearly infinite variety of settings. Yet you are seeing this actor on *this* stage, at *this* moment: the play exists completely in the present even as it recalls centuries of history. It is both ephemeral and permanent, fleeting and memorable. Old plays aren't entirely old, and new plays aren't entirely new—they inevitably get compared to earlier works. Theatre is a living art but also a living tradition.

Some plays travel through time effortlessly, reappearing in new guises at dozens of points throughout history. *The Lot Drawers*, a fourth century B.C.E. Greek comedy by Diphilos concerning an old man foolishly in love with a young girl, was revised a century later by the

Roman Plautus as *Casina*—and a thousand years later Plautus's version was revised by the Italian playwright Niccolò Machiavelli as *Clizia*. Nor did it end there: scenes and gags from *Clizia* later appeared in the plays of Shakespeare and Molière and continue to be seen in American comedies onstage, in films, and on television right up to the present day.

Indeed, many of the world's greatest plays are closely based on preceding ones. The Indian dance-drama known as *kathakali,* developed in the mid-seventeenth century, uses and re-uses stories from ancient Sanskrit epics. (New kathakali plays continue to be written occasionally, however, as in 2013 when *Karnnaparithyagam,* or "The Abandoning of Karna," made its debut.) Similarly, many eighteenth-century Japanese *kabuki* dramas are based on ancient Japanese folklore, often bearing the same titles as the old tales—many of which also serve as the basis of ancient noh and kyogen plays. French tragedies of the seventeenth century, as well as comedies of the twentieth century, were often based on Greek and Roman models more than two thousand years old. Many of William Shakespeare's best-known plays—*King Lear, Hamlet, Measure for Measure,* and *The Taming of the Shrew*, for example—were revisions of earlier English plays. Shakespeare's plays, in turn, have been a source for literally hundreds of modern dramas, including Tom Stoppard's *Rosencrantz and Guildenstern Are Dead*, Lee Blessing's *Fortinbras*, Paul Rudnick's *I Hate Hamlet*, Richard Nelson's *Two Shakespearean Actors*, Ann-Marie McDonald's *Goodnight Desdemona (Good Morning Juliet)*, Amy Freed's *The Beard of Avon*, Stephen Sondheim's *West Side Story*, Punchdrunk's 2011 *Sleep No More*, Rolin Jones and Billy Joe Armstrong's *These Paper Bullets*, La Fille du Lautier's 2017 *Macbeth Muet,* and Taylor Mac's 2019 *Gary: A Sequel to Titus Andronicus,* all of which parody or creatively alter portions of Shakespeare's plays. Shakespeare is the most prominent example, but the theatre as a whole continually resurrects its past traditions, just as it always seeks to extend and surpass them.

Therefore it is helpful, when looking at the theatre of today, to look to the traditions of the theatre in the past. For the sake of our organization, we will divide our overview into "West" (Europe and the Americas) and "East" (Asia and the Indian subcontinent), even though—as this and subsequent chapters will make clear—the borders that separate these cultures often become blurred. What follows is an overview of theatre's origins and a capsule history of eleven important theatre traditions—Greek, Roman, medieval, Renaissance, Royal, and Romantic in the Western world, and Sanskrit, kathakali, xiqu, noh, and kabuki in the East—that together outline the major world developments prior to the start of the modern theatre in the nineteenth century. All of these traditions are alive today, either in the form of regular and careful revivals or by a continuous tradition of performance. And all of these traditions have influenced the modern theatre, as we will see in the chapter "The Modern Theatre."

The Origins of Theatre

How did theatre begin?

No one knows for sure, but the theatre, along with human civilization itself, almost certainly began in Africa. The first known theatrical presentations occurred in northern Africa, alongside the Nile River in ancient Egypt, as much as five thousand years ago, possibly as early as 3300 B.C.E.

But there are indications of possible tribal performances from even earlier, as far back as 6000 B.C.E. Although we know very little about such performances—which, unlike the arts of painting and sculpture, left behind no permanent records—it is very likely they resembled tribal performances widely performed in rural Africa today. From such present-day performances, we can see two possible foundations of the theatre as it has been known and enjoyed throughout the course of human civilization: ritual and storytelling. Both have existed since ancient times, and both remain apparent—though in different forms—wherever theatre is performed today.

RITUAL

Ritual is the theatre's distant cousin. A ritual is a collective ceremony, performed by members of a society, normally for religious or cultural reasons. The most ancient rituals were primarily intended to summon gods and influence nature, as with rain dances and healing ceremonies. But tribal rituals also arose to observe important life events, such as the changing of the seasons, and to provide public witness to life passages such as birth, death, marriage, and coming of age. Contemporary Christian baptism and Jewish bar mitzvah (coming-of-age) rituals, along with funeral rites in nearly all cultures, are descendants of these ancient tribal ceremonies. Other rituals reenact defining moments of a culture's religious history—such as the birth, death, or resurrection of divine beings—thus allowing adherents to directly experience the passion of their culture's sacred heritage. Regardless of purpose, rituals all imbue bodily movements and objects with symbolic power. In a ritual, everything becomes heightened with meaning.

Of course we should be hesitant to call such ritual "theatre." Ritual, like theatre, creates a sense of order out of life, and it does so in ways that can be spectacular. And ritual has occasionally connected itself historically with theatre, as when the medieval Catholic Church began implementing theatrical devices into its liturgy. But there is no "smoking gun" that shows a direct evolution of theatre out of ritual, even though such a narrative held scholarly sway for generations. While ritual certainly had—and still has—an important relationship to theatre, it is not necessarily one of its predecessors; as such, we can take note of ritualistic *similarities* rather than outright claims of artistic parenthood.

Early tribal rituals incorporated many elements we would now consider essential to the theatrical event, such as staging, costuming, masks, makeup, music, dance, formalized speech, chanting, singing, and specific physical

DNA studies have shown that the San people, seen here in a ritual trance-dance in their native Botswana, are direct descendants of the first evolved *Homo sapiens* from more than 100,000 years ago. The San remain hunter-gatherers; after a kill, the whole group chants and dances in a prehistoric desert ritual, summoning spiritual powers into each person's stomach to heal both physical and psychological illnesses. *©Art Wolfe/Iconica/Getty Images*

props, such as staffs, spears, and skulls, which could contain totemic or spiritual properties. Unlike theatre, these rituals did not present themselves to an audience. Rather, they were used solely for the collective worship of the participants themselves—there were no simple witnesses or bystanders, as there are in much of theatre today.

Not all rituals are based in religion, of course. Secular rituals exist in Western society today that give a spiritual or larger-than-life dimension to more culturally significant events. Elements of secular rituals include the black robes of courtroom judges, the precisely choreographed changing of the guard at the Tomb of the Unknown Soldier, the daily recitation of the Pledge of Allegiance in many American classrooms, and even the lowering of the ball in New York's Times Square on New Year's Eve.

Perhaps the wedding ceremony is the most common collective ritual in Western culture, with its costumes (tuxedo or T-shirt), elevated language (psalms or sonnets), symbolic gift exchanges (ring or rings), and traditional music (Brahms or Beatles). And the slow march down the aisle retains the ancient symbolism of father figures giving away their children to new partners. Here too we see echoes of theatre, if not outright influence. Marriage—like other contemporary rituals—is an act of participants re-creating, intensifying, and making meaningful the beliefs and traditions common to their collective lives.

STORYTELLING

Storytelling is, as you might suspect, the act of conveying a narrative. It began as an oral tradition: long before people could write, they imparted myths and legends through speech. Storytelling allowed tribal identity to survive by imparting structure: much like theatre, it streamlines and elevates life into chronicle. Of course, we cannot know those stories that predate writing, but traces of them survive in ancient artifacts, such as cave paintings, that may have recorded (or even assisted in) the recitation of tales.

Storytelling is more personal than collective ritual performance because it generally relies on a single voice—and therefore a single point of view. While rituals may not have an audience, storytelling requires one: every tale must, by definition, have listener-spectators who either don't know the story being told or are eager to hear it again. Storytelling

Asaro Mudmen of the South Pacific, isolated from the rest of the world until the twentieth century, still cover their bodies in mud and wear homemade clay masks for their ancient hunting ritual, performed in their villages and also, as shown here, at a biannual September gathering of tribes in the town of Goroka. *©Marc Dozier/Corbis Documentary/ Getty Images*

thus generates elements of character without utilizing impersonation. When reciting a story, the teller can create voices, gestures, and facial expressions that reflect the personalities of the individuals described, but the storyteller does not *become* the characters described.

Storytelling also seeks to entertain, and therefore provides a structured narrative rather than a random series of observations, which in turn helps encourage audience engagement through a calculated momentum of escalating events. These elements of structured action, in drama, combine to become the plot. Storytelling is thus one important element of drama, stripped down to its essence: all that is required is a teller, a tale, and a witness.

One ancient example of storytelling is the recitation of epic poems, such as *The Iliad* or *The Odyssey*. In Aristotle's major treatise on classical Greek theatre, the *Poetics*, he contrasts the medium of theatre with epic storytelling. Theatre, Aristotle claims, mimics real life: actors take on the roles assigned to them. Conversely, the epic storyteller describes the action as a narrator, not as someone directly involved in the action being described. Even though storytelling does not employ a strictly imitative sense of character—the storyteller remains the teller and does not seek to "disappear" into a role—its content is still personal and affecting. The distinction between epic and theatre would later be utilized by the German theatre modernist Bertolt Brecht, who sought to combine elements of both forms to develop an "epic theatre." Brecht's new form of theatre sought to integrate storytelling's more detached method of engagement with a more traditional understanding of theatre as a collection of actors pretending to be their characters. In Brecht's epic theatre, actors would suddenly stop pretending to be their characters and talk to the audience directly as themselves. Or they would "spoil" the scene they were about to enact by explaining what was going to happen—just as Homer would foreshadow events in his epics. (See the chapter "The Modern Theatre" for more on Brecht.)

Storytelling, an art more ancient than theatre, is still practiced as a public performance form, nowhere more successfully than at the annual Jonesborough, Tennessee, storytelling festival. Seen here is storyteller Donald Davis spinning a tale. ©*Alexia Elejalde-Ruiz/Chicago Tribune/MCT/Getty Images*

Storytelling, in other words, has both key similarities and differences to theatre. For example, they share features of the development of a plot and use of a live audience, but theatre goes a step further with the impersonation of characters by actors and a deeper level of emotional realism.

SHAMANISM, TRANCE, AND MAGIC

The ancient form of theatre known as dance-drama appeared first on the African continent and afterward in tribal cultures around the world. Dance-dramas continue to be performed in, among other places, Siberia, South America, Southeast Asia, Australia, and many countries in Africa, including Nigeria and South Africa. Many Native American communities continue to practice the form as well. Storytelling provides these performances with audience-attracting narratives and details taken from familiar elements of daily human life, and ritual provides

the intensity of the celebrants who commit, body and soul, to the impersonation of divine spirits and the reenactment of otherworldly events. Belief in the power of such spirits to animate objects has been called animism, a catchall term describing the basic religious impulse of tribal culture in prehistory. Humans who assume an animist role to mediate between spirit and earthly realities are—in a similarly general way—called shamans.

Shamans have been identified in the tribal cultures of the Upper Paleolithic era since at least 13,000 B.C.E. and possibly even earlier. In the eyes of his community, the shaman (almost always male in the ancient world) can cure the sick, aid the hunter, conjure the rain, and help the crops grow. Shamans may also appear as mediums, taking the forms of unearthly spirits, often animal or demonic. In most shamanic practices, the shaman performs in a state of trance, a level of consciousness beyond everyday awareness.

By existing on the border of one world and the other, shamans exist in a liminal space, neither within society nor outside of it. As the performance scholar Richard Schechner has noted, this in-between state is similar to that of the present-day actor, since when we see the famous Shakespearean actor Laurence Olivier play Hamlet, we realize that "Olivier is not Hamlet, but he is also not not Hamlet." The shaman is not a spirit, nor is he not *not* a spirit.

Unlike Olivier, though, shamans are believed to have magical abilities, such as entering otherworldly realms. As a result, their performances take on a magical appearance. Ecstatic dancing and rapturous chanting are often primary features of shamanism, usually climaxing in violent shaking. Acrobatic feats are common: in the *pegele* dance of Nigeria, shamans leap high in the air, spin around horizontally, and then come down far from where they left the ground. Sleight of hand may be involved in this "magic," as when the Formosan shaman "stabs" himself but really only pierces a blood-filled animal bladder hidden beneath his clothes.

Costumes, body paint, headdresses, and—above all—masks disguise the shaman-performer, sometimes completely, marking him as a spiritual presence. Masks, common in almost all tribal cultures, initially adapted themselves from the ecstatic contortion of the shaman's face during trance and subsequently served to represent the spirit that the trance-liberated shaman inhabited. But the mask has outlived the rituals that spawned it. Today, it remains a prominent symbol of drama around the world.

Dogon performers of the *dana* ritual, dancing on six-foot stilts, represent larger-than-life forces in the most literal way: by being double human size. ©*Bruno Morandi/robertharding/Getty Images*

THE BEGINNINGS OF TRADITIONAL DRAMA

Many shamanistic rituals incorporate dialogue, along with impersonation. In doing so, they begin to contain "dramatic" elements. For instance, the Sri Lankan *Sanni-yakuma*, a traditional, all-night curing ceremony of drumming and "devil dancing," includes a scene of a suffering patient who seeks exorcism of the devil and includes this exchange:

YAKKA (demon): What is going on here? What does this noise mean?

DRUMMER: Somebody has fallen ill.

YAKKA: What are you going to do about it?

DRUMMER: We will give him a medicine.

YAKKA: That will not be of any use! Give me twelve presents and I will cure him.

While this brief dialogue may not have directly led to the development of theatre as we think of it today, it has many of the theatre's elements: it uses imitation to create suspense, conflict, danger, and action.

TRADITIONAL DRAMA IN SUB-SAHARAN AFRICA

In Sub-Saharan Africa, one can still see today a vast variety of traditional performances in which ritual and storytelling continually interweave. More than 1,000 languages are spoken here, and each language represents a culture with roots in the past and social community in the present. Many of these cultures have long-standing traditions of dance-dramas. The Dogon performers of Mali are celebrated for their stilt walking and brightly colored masks. The Senufo of Ivory Coast and Burkina Faso have animal masks to frighten witches—with the tusks of wild boars, the teeth of alligators, and the horns of antelopes—and brightly colored masks for certain women characters

The Senufo Lo Hunter society of Burkina Faso perform at a funeral for a deceased hunter. The dance reenacts a hunt; the performer here wears a mask that represents the antelope. *©H. Christoph/ullstein bild/Getty Images*

(played by men). Such masks feature arched eyebrows, visible teeth, and scar marks on the cheeks, and the characters' hand props often include horsetail whisks. In the Yacouba country of Ivory Coast, traditional performers may wear elaborate beaded headdresses and full-face makeup instead of masks, or, as in the panther dance-drama, cover their entire heads in painted cloth with panther ears. Acrobatics feature in Burundi performances; rain-dance rituals are common in Botswana.

EGYPTIAN DRAMA

For many theatre historians, a ceremonial rite in Egypt known as the *Abydos Passion Play* marks the first "traditional" drama in the West. Little is known of this ritual; the only historical record that survives is the Ikhernofret Stela, an engraved stone slab that contains the testimony

of a companion to Pharaoh Senusret II. It is impossible to determine, based on this evidence, whether this ceremony (apparently a festival that lasted days) contained any trace of impersonation, or if it led to any further development of drama in Egypt or elsewhere. Indeed, the name contemporary historians have given it—the "passion play"—is not quite appropriate, since "passion plays" are more commonly thought of as reenactments, in medieval Europe, of the last days of Jesus Christ.

The stela describes a festival that celebrates a foundational myth in ancient Egypt: the murder of Osiris, an ancient divine king, by Set, his brother; the lamentation by Osiris's wife, Isis, and the goddess Neptys; the tearing asunder of Osiris's body; Osiris's resurrection and the birth of his son, Horus; and the fierce combat between Horus and Set. The basic rhythms of this story in turn echo even more ancient ritualized reenactments of the coming of spring that celebrated the rebirth of vegetation in the fields. For instance, one Babylonian ceremony tells the story of the god Baal dying, traveling to the equivalent of Purgatory, and rising again on the same day. These ritualistic enactments, performed in the springtime, are ultimately joyous, not sad. The deaths of Osiris and Baal are not permanent; after Osiris's death, he will be revived—as will the coming year's wheat crop after its seeds are scattered by the wind and submerged in the annual flooding of the Nile. The tragedy of death, therefore, yields life, and the tears of lamentation become nourishment for the seeds of life's renewal. However painful, such tragedy brings with it rejuvenation and hope.

Theatre in the West

Theatre in the West began in ancient Greece. In the middle of the first millenium B.C.E., there arose a spectacular theatre in the city-state of Athens, which over the course of 150 years—mere moments in the timeline of civilization—produced four of the greatest playwrights and the most important dramatic theorist in the theatre's long history. Greek drama established the formal foundations of Western theatre by shaping and defining essential concepts—such as tragedy, comedy, characters, and plotlines—that remain essential to Western drama as we know it today.

GREEK DRAMA

The drama of Athens in the fifth century B.C.E. still stands as one of the greatest bodies—some would say *the* greatest body—of theatrical creation of all time. A magnificent blend of myth, legend, philosophy, social commentary,

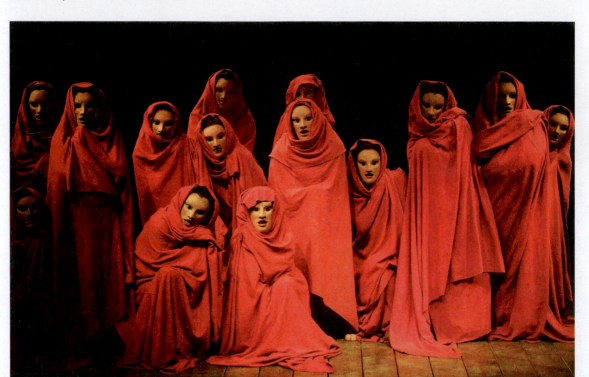

Peter Hall's production of Euripides' *The Bacchae* played at England's National Theatre in 2002, and then to an audience of eleven thousand at the ancient theatre of Epidaurus in Greece. Hall and his designers employed bold and uniform colors—blood orange and sea green—to emphasize the masklike uniformity of members of the chorus as they collectively, not individually, wrestle with the play's giant spiritual themes. ©ArenaPal/Topham/The Image Works

poetry, dance, music, public participation, and visual splendor, Athenian drama created the fundamental genres of tragedy and comedy. Its characters have become cultural archetypes in successive eras, laying the foundation not only of future Western drama but also of continuing debates as to how—and to what purposes—life should be lived.

Aristotle and later scholars tell us Greek tragedy derived from *dithyrambs*, ancient choral hymns that celebrated Dionysus, the demigod of fertility and wine. According to one account—by no means definitive, as evidence is scant—this chorus became theatrical when a performer named Thespis introduced acting into the ritual. Rather than be one among fifty or so anonymous singers, Thespis impersonated a specific person. Here we have the basic structure of Greek tragedy: the creation and development of individual characters in relation to a mass of other actors who comprise the chorus. Dionysus continued to be the presiding divinity: when classic Greek dramas came to be staged on the Athenian acropolis by the latter part of the sixth century B.C.E., it was at the Great Theatre of Dionysus, during the annual springtime festival known as the *City Dionysia* (or Great Dionysia). Dionysus has, ever since, been considered the founding deity of Western drama.

By the end of the fifth century B.C.E. three great tragedians—Aeschylus, Sophocles, and Euripides—had written and produced close to 300 tragedies. Thirty-three have come down to us, and most of them are on every theatre scholar's list of the world's greatest dramatic masterpieces. Furthermore, there was a brilliant author of comic dramas—Aristophanes—from whom eleven plays survive, one of which (*The Frogs*) is a biting and vastly informative satire about the three great tragedians who shared his times. Other authors of Greek comedy, including Menander, and literary theorists, including Aristotle, whose *Poetics* provided the West's most fundamental treatise on dramatic theory, flourished in the century that followed. The small portion of surviving texts we have count among the richest bodies of dramatic work ever known.

Greek tragedies explore the social, psychological, and religious meanings of the ancient gods and heroes of

In the dithyrambs that preceded ancient Greek tragedy, there was a chorus of fifty performers. Romanian director Silviu Purcarete, at the National Theatre of Craiova, employed a chorus of double that number—fifty men and fifty women—in his innovative production of *Les Danaïdes*, adapted from Aeschylus's war tetralogy, *The Suppliants*. Purcarete's highly stylized production, performed (in French) in Manhattan's Damrosch Park as part of the Lincoln Center Theatre Festival in 1997, had clear overtones of then-current problems in eastern Europe and the Balkans and a strong emphasis on political terrorism, sexual assault, and the ambiguity of gender and cultural identity. ©*Stephanie Berger*

Greek history and myth; the comedies satirize issues contemporary to the time of their creation. Both types of drama were first staged in a simple wheat-threshing area on the ground (the *orchestra*), with a dressing hut (*skene*) behind it; the audience was seated on an adjacent hillside (the *theatron*). As Greek culture expanded, however, huge amphitheatres—the largest of which seated upward of fifteen thousand people—were built, first in Athens and subsequently throughout the growing Greek empire. Many of those theatres remain today, in various stages of ruin and renovation, not just in parts of Greece but also in Italy and Turkey. And words remain, as well—or at least, their English adaptions: *orchestra, scene,* and *theatre* all derive from their Greek forbears.

All ancient Greek actors were male. They performed in masks, partly to indicate the age, gender, personality, and social standing of the characters they were playing and partly to amplify their voices. (The word "person" derives from the Latin *per sonum*, or "for sound," which initially referred to the amplification of the actor's voice and later became the root of the term *dramatis personae*, or "cast of characters.") Each tragic actor wore elevated shoes (*kothurnoi*), an elaborate headdress (*onkos*), and a long colorful gown (*himation*) with a tunic (*chlamys*) over it. The ornate costumes and props helped enhance the larger-than-life struggles depicted in the drama—no ordinary-looking characters could so do. Plays were performed with only two (later three) principal actors, who, by changing masks, could play several parts each during the course of a play. The actors were supported by a chorus of twelve or fifteen singer-dancers (usually representing the local populace) who, like the dithyrambs from which they originated, chanted their lines in unison. When the skene became an elevated stage for the principal

The work of the theatre company Démodocos utilizes ancient Greek dramatic techniques; pictured here is a performer with traditional mask and garb appearing in its 2017 production of Sophocles' great tragedy *Antigone*. ©Laurencine Lot

actors, the chorus members remained in the orchestra below, separated from the main interactions.

Greek tragedy was chanted or sung, not spoken. Unfortunately, the music has not survived. And the chorus danced, as it did in the dithyrambic ceremonies, sometimes formally, sometimes with wild abandon. Greek tragedy, therefore, is the foundation not merely of Western drama but also of Western musical theatre, including opera. Greek comedy, in contrast, provided the foundation of today's burlesque, satire, and television sitcoms. The plays of Aristophanes, referred to as Old Comedy, are filled with broad physical humor, gross sexual gags and innuendos, and brilliant wordplay and repartee, often at the expense of contemporary politicians and celebrities. The later plays of Menander, known as New Comedy, gave rise to "stock characters" (such as the bumbling suitor and the timid warrior) and comic plot devices (such

as mistaken identity) that would go on to supply the elements of comedies in the Renaissance and beyond—many of today's television shows still rely on comedic "types," just as Menander's plays did.

The City Dionysia was a weeklong festival of celebrations and dramatic competitions. On the first day, during introductory ceremonies, each playwright introduced his cast and announced the theme of his work. The second day featured processions, sacrifices, and the presentation of ten dithyrambs; on the third day, five comedies were played. On the fourth, fifth, and sixth days, the three competing playwrights presented—each on a separate day—three related tragedies (a *trilogy*), followed by a comic variation or parody (a *satyr play*) on the same theme. The authors served as the directors of their works. On the seventh, and final, day, judging took place and prizes for the best play and best leading actor were awarded. It appears that the entire population of freeborn men, and perhaps of freeborn women (it's not known for certain), attended these performances and rooted for their favorites; judging by later commentaries, outstanding dramatists and actors were as famous then as are today's best-known film directors and movie stars. Clearly the City Dionysia of fifth-century Athens was a monumental and glorious undertaking that led to some of the most thrilling dramas and theatrical spectacles in history.

ROMAN DRAMA

Greek civilization, battered by internal wars, had lost its vitality by the end of the fifth century B.C.E., and the power balance in the Mediterranean shifted, in succeeding centuries, to the growing Roman Empire. Excelling in architecture and engineering more than in dramatic creativity, the Romans created many astonishing stage buildings, of which more than two hundred (most dating from the first centuries C.E.) survive to the present day. Roman architects dispensed with the Greek hillside theatron and threshing-circle orchestra and designed a theatre that was an entirely integrated structure set on a level plain. They also cut the orchestra in half and created tunnel entrances (*vomitoria*) on both sides. The simple Greek skene became an elaborate three-story wall (the *frons scaenae*) decorated by dozens of statues.

Roman dramatists often drew upon Greek sources for their work; many Roman plays are about Greek characters and Greek struggles. The Roman comic playwrights Plautus and Terence, popular in their time, frequently adapted Menander's works of New Comedy. Many of their works survive and are performed occasionally today, as are (albeit more rarely) the chamber tragedies of Seneca, a

The Greek theatre of Priene, in modern-day Turkey, dates from about 300 B.C.E. Unlike most Greek theatres, Priene was never rebuilt by the Romans and thus remains one of the best examples of a hillside Greek theatron. The standing row of columns and connecting lintel once made up the front of the stone skene, or stagehouse. ©Robert Cohen

mentor (and ultimately victim) of Emperor Nero. All three of these Roman dramatists, in fact, were very popular and much admired by writers and audiences during the European Renaissance. Together, Greek and Roman drama form a classical foundation for Western drama right up to the present day.

MEDIEVAL DRAMA

The fall of Rome (around the middle of the first millennium C.E.) brought the classical era of theatre to an end. The early Christian religion seems to have had a complicated relationship with theatre: many rituals and services incorporated processions, songs, and traces of impersonation, yet the Church also found theatrical imitation to be potentially heretical. Church officials thus attempted to regulate the use of theatre in its ministry, and we have today some surviving decrees that sought to prescribe very careful rules for just how "dramatic" services could be. One such early dramatization of that period was a brief moment, known as a *trope,* in the church's Easter service. This trope, known as the "Quem Quaeritis," featured a reenactment of the apocryphal biblical story of the Three Marys visiting the tomb of Jesus. "Whom seek ye?" (*Quem quaeritis?*) an angel asks. "Jesus of Nazareth," reply the Marys, whereupon they are told, "He is not here, He has risen." They then break into a chorus of hallelujahs. Because we only have traces of evidence of this trope, and because many of those traces had a political agenda—they sought to regulate the drama, not encourage it—we are unsure today just how the early Church used theatrical techniques, but we do know of hundreds of church-sponsored dramatizations that depicted and celebrated traditional Judeo-Christian stories, from the Creation of the Universe and Adam and Eve to Doomsday and the Harrowing of Hell.

The Oberammergau Passion Play, which depicts the trial and crucifixion of Jesus, is certainly the most attended medieval play in the world today, as it has been produced in that southern Bavarian city every ten years (with a few exceptions) since 1634, where it is viewed by tens of thousands of mainly foreign visitors. Here Frederik Mayet, one of the 2,000 Oberammergau residents that take part in the production, plays Jesus speaking his last words to God in the 2010 production directed by Christian Stückl. ©*Johannes Simon/ Stringer/Getty Images*

Adam and Eve (Alessandro Mastrobuono and Erin Jellison) take their instructions from God (Tom Fitzpatrick) in Brian Kulick's 2003 *The Mysteries* in the Actors' Gang production in Los Angeles. The actors would probably have worn flesh-colored body stockings in medieval times, but contemporary theatre is able, on this occasion, to express their innocence before the fall more literally. ©*Ray Micksha/The Actors' Gang*

Medieval drama remained in church liturgy for nearly two centuries, but by about 1250, Bible-based drama had moved outdoors, first to churchyards and then to public streets throughout Europe. By this time the medieval *mystery plays*, as they were then called, were performed in the common languages of French, English, Spanish, German, and Italian rather than Latin, and they included scenes that were more secular than purely religious, often with contemporary political overtones. The actors were no longer monks but ordinary citizens; the term "mystery play" may derive from the Latin *ministerium,* or "guild," in reference to the different organizations that sponsored different plays. Mystery plays were grand spectacles but were also rooted in the local culture of the towns in which they were staged. Town clergy would purchase a generic script and adapt its specifics to the local culture. The scripts themselves were adaptations of the formal text of the Bible, changed into the stuff of robust, gripping drama: comic interplay, jesting repartee, swashbuckling bluster, and harrowing tragedy. One of the most popular types of mystery play was the *passion play*, which depicted (oftentimes in graphic detail) the suffering of Jesus Christ.

Entire festivals of such plays, numbering in the dozens, were presented in hundreds of European towns every spring and attracted rural audiences from all around. On the European continent, such drama festivals lasted for many days or even weeks, with huge casts performing on a series of stages (known as *mansions*) set up next to each other in the town plaza or marketplace. Audiences could stroll from one play to the next as they were performed in sequence. In England, the plays were performed on wagon-mounted stages, one for each play, which were wheeled from one audience site to another during a day-long springtime festival known as Corpus Christi.

At first glance, these mystery plays may appear stylistically simple, at least in contrast to the splendor of the classic Greek tragedies, but twenty-first-century productions have demonstrated their tremendous dramatic impact, even to today's religiously diverse audiences. The scale of medieval theatre production—with its mansions, rolling stages, and casts of hundreds—was simply astonishing. Like the great Gothic cathedrals—also created anonymously and at roughly the same time—the Bible-based medieval theatre was a monumental enterprise that affected the lives of the entire culture that created and experienced it.

RENAISSANCE DRAMA

Medieval drama was created in ignorance of its classical predecessors, but when, in the High Middle Ages, Roman and then Greek texts began to be translated, their influence—on all arts and culture, not merely the theatre—proved overwhelming. This period in which ancient culture was "reborn" and fused, sometimes uneasily, with the medieval and Gothic forms that had been dominant for centuries is called the Renaissance.

An eighteenth-century illustration of Italian commedia dell'arte.
©*Bettmann/Getty Images*

The Renaissance English playwright Christopher Marlowe's *Tamburlaine the Great* here features John Douglas Thompson, as the title character, forcing his conquered rivals to pull his chariot; the production was a great success in Michael Boyd's 2014 off-Broadway production of both Parts I and II at the Theatre for a New Audience in Brooklyn, New York. *©Sara Krulwich/The New York Times/Redux*

By most reckonings, the drama of the Renaissance began in Italy, where the plays of Plautus and Seneca were first translated in the 1470s. Amateur productions of these Italian versions soon became popular, giving rise to freer adaptations, which are now known as *commedia erudita*, or "learned comedies." By the 1520s, the Florentine diplomat and essayist Niccolò Machiavelli was famous throughout Italy for his learned comedies based on—and expanding upon—Roman drama. By the middle of the sixteenth century, groups of itinerant professional actors began performing a semi-improvised variation of this commedia erudita, which soon became known as *commedia dell'arte* as it spread in popularity throughout the Italian peninsula and beyond. Soon both commedia dell'arte and scripted plays in modern European languages—based on classic or current themes rather than biblical ones—became common throughout Europe.

It was in England that the Renaissance brought forth the dramatic masterpieces of William Shakespeare (1564–1616). The England of Shakespeare's day witnessed the rise of a vibrant theatrical culture with palatial court theatres, freestanding outdoor public theatres (and at least one indoor one), and companies of traveling professional actors who entertained in court and for the public. The theatre of the Renaissance featured dozens of playwrights whose works remain popular today. While Christopher Marlowe, Ben Jonson, and John Webster are three of Shakespeare's most prominent contemporaries, and brilliant authors in their own right, none compare to Shakespeare's impact on global literature and culture. Shakespeare's work has been praised for its mastery of different genres: comedy, history, satire, tragedy, and romance. Four centuries after they were written (from approximately 1580 to 1610),

Like its predecessor, the modern Globe Theatre replica in London schedules performances by daylight, come rain or shine. As in Shakespeare's day, a sizable portion of the audience (the "groundlings," as they were called in Elizabethan times) observes from a standing-room pit in front of the stage; everyone else sits on hard wooden benches in the surrounding galleries. Shown here, the concluding dance of The Globe's 1998 *As You Like It* enchants the audience on all sides of the stage, which is thrust into their midst. ©*Robert Cohen*

One of the hottest tickets in New York for the 2016–2017 season was a stripped-down production of *Hamlet* directed by Sam Gold and starring Oscar Isaac (*center*) in the title role and Keegan-Michael Key (*right*) as his friend Horatio. In a small theatre, audiences could appreciate the subtle, lived-in performances and intimate drama—eternally appealing qualities of Shakespeare's most famous work. ©*Carol Rosegg*

A Midsummer Night's Dream remains one of Shakespeare's most beloved comedies, and with good reason: its dramaturgy combines magic, spectacle, romance, and farcical whimsy to great effect. Erica Whyman, the director of this 2016 production at the Royal Shakespeare Company, enhanced the play's themes by incorporating elements of Hindu ceremony, postwar jazz, and British music hall comedy. Pictured here is Ayesha Dharker as the fairy queen Titania and David Mears as the hapless craftsman. ©Geraint Lewis

his plays are the most-produced dramas in theatres around the world and comprise the primary repertoires of more than one hundred theatre companies named after him.

Shakespeare was not only an author; he was also an actor and part owner of his own theatre company, the King's Men, and of The Globe Theatre, which his company built and operated. A new Globe has now been built near the original site and, since its 1997 opening, has been used for the presentation of Shakespearean-era plays. With its thrust stage and standing-room "pit" open to the sky and surrounded by thatched-roof seating galleries on three levels, the modern restored Globe helps us better understand the power of Shakespearean-era staging and the potential of his drama to electrify a large and diverse audience. Shakespeare's plays are well known to literary scholars for their poetic brilliance,

relentless investigation of the human condition, and deeply penetrating character portrayals; but they are also filled with music, dancing, ribaldry, puns, satire, pageantry, and humor, which only performance truly brings to life. They are both great dramatic art and magnificent theatrical entertainment.

THE ROYAL THEATRE

The energy that characterized the Renaissance became consolidated and refined in the era that followed. This age, too, was characterized by a passion for understanding the wider world through historical study, natural observation, and global exploration. However, now these ideas became more focused and ordered. The Royal era, as it is sometimes known, emphasized empirical science and rational philosophy. It also, as its name implies, saw the

◐ Spotlight

Did Shakespeare Write Shakespeare?

Students occasionally wonder about the so-called authorship question, which challenges the commonly accepted belief that Shakespeare's plays were written by Shakespeare. Although several books have argued against Shakespeare's authorship, and some distinguished thinkers (among them Mark Twain and Sigmund Freud) have shared their doubts as well, there is simply no question to be posed. The evidence that Shakespeare wrote Shakespeare's plays is absolutely overwhelming. Not a single prominent Elizabethan scholar has accepted the "anti-Stratfordian" (as proponents of other authors are called) argument, which one of America's most noted Shakespearean scholars, Harold Bloom, simply dismisses as "lunacy."

Shakespeare's name appears as author on the title pages of thirty-seven editions of plays published between 1598 and 1622, far more frequently than that of any other poet or dramatist of this period. Eleven of his plays are cited (and praised) in a book published when he was thirty-four. He is credited as the author of the First Folio in its title *Mr. William Shakespeare's Comedies, Histories, and Tragedies*, published just seven years after his death. The Folio's editors were his acting colleagues, who describe Shakespeare in the preface as fellow actor, author, and friend. Their preface also includes four poems—one by dramatist Ben Jonson—each unequivocally referring to Shakespeare as the author of its plays. Surviving records show him performing in his plays at the courts of both Queen Elizabeth and King James, and he was buried, along with his wife, daughter, and son-in-law, in the place of greatest honor at his hometown church. An inscribed funeral monument shows him with pen in hand, looking down at his own grave. Birth, marriage, death, heraldic, and other legal records, plus dozens of citations during and shortly after his life, tell us more information about dramatist William Shakespeare than we have collected for all but a few common-born citizens of his era.

So, what is left to argue? Anti-Stratfordians maintain that the evidence doesn't paint the picture we should expect of such a magnificent playwright: he apparently didn't go to college; his name was spelled in several different ways and sometimes hyphenated; his signatures indicate poor handwriting; his wife and daughters were probably illiterate; he didn't leave any books in his will; no ceremony marked his death; he never traveled to Italy, where many of his plays were set; and an early engraving of the Stratford monument looks different—lacking its pen—than the monument does now.

Little of this is provable, however, and even if true, the evidence does not add up to a definitive account. Aeschylus, Euripides, Henrik Ibsen, and George Bernard Shaw didn't go to college, either. Shakespeare's knowledge of Italy is nothing an intelligent person couldn't have picked up in the extensive travel literature and gossip of the era—and it wasn't even geographically accurate (Shakespeare writes of one who could "lose the tide" sailing from Verona to Milan—where no water route exists). Many people have unreadable signatures, and in Shakespeare's day neither spelling nor hyphenation was standardized, nor was literacy a norm. That we don't know of a memorial ceremony doesn't mean there wasn't one, and evidence clearly indicates the engraving of a penless monument was simply one of many errors in a hastily prepared book. Finally, if Shakespeare maintained a library, he could simply have given it to his son-in-law (a doctor) before his death or left it to be passed on to his wife along with his house and furnishings, or perhaps he kept books in a private office at The Globe Theatre in London, which burned to the ground three years before his death.

What is perhaps most troubling about the anti-Stratfordian position, though, is that its outrageous claims obscure more interesting ways that Shakespeare's work legitimately challenges our contemporary understandings of authorship. In other words, while there was certainly no vast conspiracy to cover up a secret author of Shakespeare's works, there are many aspects of his writing process that would seem suspect in our current day. Shakespeare frequently borrowed from other writers, at times copying passages nearly verbatim. And many scholars believe that some of his plays—perhaps as many as fourteen—were written collaboratively, with help from peers such as Christopher Marlowe, Thomas Nashe, Ben Jonson, and others. But these revelations should not lead us to believe Shakespeare was a fraud. Collaborative writing and creative borrowing were common practices in his day. The more we learn of how Shakespeare's work is not the product of a single author, the more we are reminded of how different playwriting and publishing were during the Renaissance. The man himself remains a towering figure, and the work itself remains an unparalleled body of insightful and brilliant art.

---

increasing importance of European royalty. Much of the seventeenth-century European theatre enjoyed powerful support from the monarchy: the dramas of Pedro Calderón de la Barca at the court of King Philip IV in Spain, the tragedies of Jean Racine and Pierre Corneille and the comedies of Molière under the patronage of King Louis XIV in France, and the Restoration comedies of William Wycherley and William Congreve under King Charles II in England.

Though the era saw the rise of amateur theatre companies, burlesque entertainers, and play-reading groups, the main dramatic output of the time was generally aimed more at the aristocracy than at the general populace and, as such, reflected the gentility of the seemingly refined

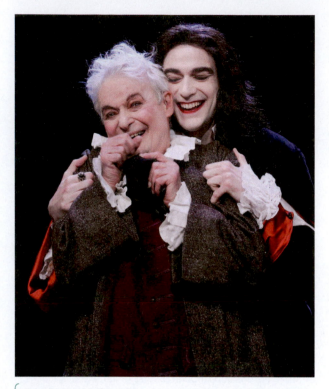

Jean-Baptiste Molière is France's greatest playwright of all time, and his 1665 sexual comedy, *Dom Juan*, is certainly a classical masterpiece, along with its foreign descendants, Byron's *Don Juan* and Mozart's *Don Giovanni*. Here Arnaud Denis (*right*) directs and plays the title role of Juan, while Jean-Pierre Leroux (*left*) is his loyal and comic servant, Sganerelle, to whom the Dom happily explains the joys of love. Presented in Paris at Theatre 14 in 2014, with captivating period costumes by Virginia Houdinière. ©*Laurencine Lot*

taste of courtly patrons. Rational sensibility dominated the times: theories of drama, adapted—often incorrectly—from Aristotle and hence called "neoclassical," sought to regulate dramatic structure so that all of a play's events would take place in one location and occur over the course of one day. These neoclassical theories also established rules that eliminated onstage depictions of physical violence. Indoor theatres, lit by candles instead of sunlight, replaced the outdoor public theatres of earlier times, providing more intimate and comfortable surroundings for an increasingly well-dressed audience. Furthermore, protection from wind and weather permitted elaborately painted scenery and stage machinery. Style, wit, grace, and class distinction became not merely the framework of drama but its chief subject, and aristocratic items such as the fan and the snuffbox became signature props. This was also the Western world's first era of extensive theatrical commentary and thus the first from which we have detailed reports and evidence—both textual and visual—of the era's dramatic repertoires, acting styles, artists' lives, and manifestos that attempt to define the art of drama. The era also saw women first grace the stage as performers in the English theatre—previously, only men and boys (often dressed up as women) had been allowed to act.

THE ROMANTIC THEATRE

Every era in theatre, to some extent, rebels against the previous one, and the Romantic theatre of the eighteenth and nineteenth centuries was no exception. Gone was the

Michel Vuillermoz plays Cyrano, the famously hook-nosed poet-warrior in Edmond Rostand's romantic 1897 masterpiece *Cyrano de Bergerac*, here shown kneeling above his young friend Christian (Éric Ruf), who is dying in the arms of Roxanne (Françoise Gillard), a woman tragically fated to love them both. This 2006 Comédie-Française production was directed by Denis Podalydès in 2006; Ruf also served as the scene designer. ©*Laurencine Lot*

Royal era's emphasis on decorum and rationality. Romanticism, in contrast, celebrated florid expressiveness over dignified restraint, and believed wholeheartedly in the vital spirit of the individual rather than the social organization of class, court, or academy. Compassion, rather than style and wit, was central to the Romantic creed, and authors such as Johann Wolfgang von Goethe and Friedrich von Schiller, in Germany, and Victor Hugo, in France, intrigued audiences with their deep humanitarian concerns in plays that dealt with grand, larger-than-life characters: devils and monsters, robbers and priests, hunchbacks and heroes.

The excesses of romanticism gave rise to melodrama and grand opera, which in turn supplied much of the inspiration for early American drama, as it coincided with the colonization of the American continent. Moreover, the Romantic quest for the foreign and exotic represented Western drama's first serious reengagement—deeply problematic though it was—with the theatre of the East. This, then, is a good point at which to return to drama's earlier years—to the Eastern traditions of theatre that sprang from Egyptian and Canaanite beginnings and soon resurfaced on the Indian subcontinent and later throughout Asia.

Theatre in the East

There is no singular "Asian theatre." There is instead a sprawling array of Asian theatre cultures and tradition, each as distinct as the cultures that produce them. And each tradition is itself marked with multiple cultural influences and changes over time. Asia, after all—with nearly two-thirds of the world's population—comprises dozens of countries, hundreds of languages, and, as a result, thousands of theatre forms. These forms employ many principles that are markedly different from Western traditions; we list here a few examples to help situate the reader unfamiliar with Asian theatre:

- Asian drama is often danced, chanted, mimed, and sung.

- Asian dramatic language is, as a result, frequently rhythmic and melodic and is appreciated for its sounds and tones.

- Asian theatre is more commonly experienced in performance than it is read. (In this way it is similar to many theatre traditions in the West.) When we speak of "Asian drama" we are not just speaking of scripts, but also of the modes of performance that bring the drama to life: dance, song, mime, gesture, acrobatics, puppetry, music, sound, costume, and makeup.

- Asian theatre has a strong emphasis on storytelling, myth, and music, but it does not have a sense of "plot" as it has developed in Western cultures. There are rarely escalating incidents, reversals, climaxes, or elaborate plot closures in Asian plays. (Likewise, much Western drama lacks elements crucial to Asian theatre traditions.)

- Actors train in traditional Asian dramatic forms through an intense apprentice system that begins in early childhood and lasts into early middle age.

- Asian theatre is deeply traditional and often contains deep associations with folk history, ancient religions, and cultural myths.

INDIAN SANSKRIT DRAMA

Asian drama probably began in India. India's oldest dramatic form is Sanskrit dance-theatre, which seems to have been created around the second century B.C.E. and remained popular for more than a thousand years thereafter. Sanskrit plays survive from about 100 C.E., and a comprehensive book of dramatic theory, the *Natyasastra*, or "rules of drama," ascribed to Bharata Muni, dates from somewhere between 200 B.C.E. and 200 C.E. The most comprehensive study of theatre that survives from the ancient world, the *Natyasastra* contains detailed analyses of Sanskrit dramatic texts, theatre buildings, acting, staging, music, gesture, dance, and even theatre-company organization. The treatise describes ten major genres of Sanskrit drama, including two primary ones: the *nataka*, based on well-known heroic stories of kings or sages, and the *prakarana*, based on the theme of love. The greatest Sanskrit poet Kalidasa wrote his masterpiece, *Sakuntala and the Ring of Recollection*, in the nataka style somewhere around the fifth century. *The Little Clay Cart*, attributed to Sudraka, is the best known of two surviving examples of prakarana.

Sanskrit theatre, as far as we can tell (no ruins or drawings survive), was performed indoors, within roofed buildings. Rectangular in structure and fitted with a stage of about forty-eight by twenty-four feet, these buildings could seat somewhere between two hundred and five hundred spectators. Two doors, with an onstage orchestra between them, provided access to the dressing area behind the stage, and four columns held up the roof or an upper pavilion. Carved wooden elephants, tigers, and snakes adorned the pillars and perhaps the ceiling. The performers, all from priestly castes and trained from early childhood, danced and acted with an onstage instrumental and percussive accompaniment.

In the Indian kathakali dance-drama, royal characters wear an elaborate *kiritam*, or crown, which frames the actor's eye movements—one of the most intensively studied skills of kathakali performers. ©*Grigory Kubatyan/Shutterstock*

Sanskrit drama died out around the tenth century, when the Hindu court culture fragmented in the wake of repeated Mongol invasions. In succeeding centuries, an abundance of provincial theatre forms became popular throughout the subcontinent, such as the *ankiya nat* of the state of Assam and the *bhavai* of Gujarat. A vast number of these forms remain in the present day; the most well-known of these post-Sanskrit forms is the kathakali ("story play").

INDIAN KATHAKALI

Originating in rural villages in the province of Kerala in the seventeenth century, kathakali is currently performed in many urban centers in India and abroad. Its stories come from three great Indian epics, *Ramayana, Mahabharata,* and *Bhagavata Purana*. Kathakali performance can be somewhat of an epic itself, beginning at ten in the evening and lasting well past dawn of the following day. Audience members are free to leave, take naps, and eat during these performances, and in modern times,

kathakali performances are more commonly confined to more manageable three-hour evening time blocks.

In kathakali, the text is sung—to a percussion accompaniment of gongs, drums, and cymbals—by two singers seated at the side. Performances often begin in a public place, and once an audience has gathered, lamps are lit and a drumbeat introduces the first verses of the play. Actors dance and pantomime the dramatic action with precise and elaborate hand gestures, footwork patterns, distinctive eye movements, and bodily contortions. Yet while kathakali thrives on precision, it also celebrates playfulness—one of the recurrent themes of its works is *lila*, the Hindu concept of the "play of the gods" that suggests our earthly reality is the outcome of divine whimsy. At times, traces of storytelling culture remain, as when performers sing descriptions of a scene before it begins. Much of kathakali resides in the physical performances more than any text; the performers' bodies reveal subtleties of meaning and characterization that are barely suggested by the written words. Consequently, actors train rigorously for kathakali performance from early

The Monkey King—a ferocious scamp—is the most enduring character in xiqu; he is always dressed in yellow, as shown here in this Qi Shu Fan Peking Opera Company production of *Journey to the West* in 2008. Ding Meikui (*center*) plays the Monkey King. ©*Jack Vartoogian/Archive Photos/Getty Images*

childhood, achieving mastery only by about age forty. Highly stylized makeup and costuming also convey characterization and attitude: red- or black-bearded characters represent evil, white-bearded ones the divine. No scenery is used in kathakali, as plays are presented in various sites with four simple poles to define the acting area.

CHINESE XIQU

China is Asia's largest nation and its oldest continuous culture. It is also where the oldest known theatre performances in Asia took place, approximately 2,000 years ago. Like all Asian drama, Chinese theatre is more sung than spoken; indeed, traditional Chinese theatre is known by the umbrella term *xiqu* (Chinese for "tuneful theatre"), which has been translated to English as "Chinese opera."

Although forms of xiqu existed in China before the first century C.E., the first well-defined Chinese opera form, known as *zaju* ("various plays"), appeared in China during the Song dynasty in the tenth century and reached its golden age in the thirteenth century under the Mongol emperor Kublai Khan. Zaju was a comedic music-dance-drama, with acrobatics and clowning; it was so popular that a single amusement park in thirteenth-century Keifeng (then China's northern capital) featured at least fifty indoor zaju theatres, the largest of which held several thousand people. As this dramatic form became more popular, its rules became more regimented: it had four acts and each scene had to feature a character singing an emotional climax.

The tightening of zaju's structure led to the rise of a more stately, aristocratic, and poetic opera form known as *kunqu*, which originated from the town of Kunshan in the sixteenth century. Soon thereafter, kunqu became the favored theatre entertainment of the Chinese court; it is still performed today. Another popular theatre form developed around the same time in the form of a boisterous "clapper opera," characterized by the furious rhythmic beating of drumsticks on a hardwood block. Subsequent years saw the rise of other regional theatre styles, influenced by the zaju, kunqu, and clapper-opera forms. As a

Professional-level acrobatics are a fundamental part of all kunqu, and indeed of all Chinese opera. Here, in Hell, a devil leaps high over Du Liniang to terrorize her in the Suzhou Kun Opera production of *The Peony Pavilion* at the University of California–Irvine in 2006.
©Pei Hung Hsu

result of all this intermixing, China today sports as many as 360 variations of Chinese opera, most of them—such as Cantonese opera, Sichuan opera, and Hui opera—known by their regional origins.

The most famous Chinese opera in modern times is Beijing (Peking) opera, which is known in Chinese as *jingju*, or "theatre of the capital." Jingju was founded in 1790, when, in celebration of the emperor's eightieth birthday, a group of actors from the mountains of Anhui came to Beijing and amazed the court with their innovative acrobatic styles. Chinese opera, which had previously been more physically restrained, gained a new sense of dynamic movement. A new "capital" style arose as local actors assimilated the Anhui physical style with their own local opera forms. This new genre reached its current form around 1850, by which time it had become the dominant popular theatre throughout China.

The stories and plots of Chinese opera are normally ancient and well known, so their productions often alter or adapt aspects of the staging—much like popular musical theatre in the West often plays with familiar plots and devices. Chinese opera's staging also becomes a celebration of performers' individual skills; in particular, actors must master the classic fourfold combination of singing (*chang*), speech (*nian*), acting and movement (*zuo*), and martial arts and acrobatics (*da*). Nearly all Chinese opera performers are proficient in all four of these arts; the greatest performing artists—who are famous throughout the country and, in the case of the renowned master Mei Lanfang, the world—have mastered each of them to virtuoso standards. Indeed, it might be said that the equivalent of a great Chinese actor in the West would be someone who could perform ballet, opera, Shakespearean drama, and circus gymnastics—all on the same evening!

Chinese opera offers a spectacular visual feast, with dazzling costumes, huge glittery headdresses, and brilliantly colorful face painting. Actors of both sexes wear multilayered gowns in bold primary colors; many of them have long, flowing "water-sleeves" that fall all the way to the floor. Chinese opera singing, much of it in an extreme falsetto (originally employed, according to traditional accounts, so that actors could be heard over the din of people talking during the performance), is accompanied by the percussive ringing of gongs and cymbals, clapper claps, and drumbeats and the furious strumming of various two-stringed fiddles. Movement skills include a rapid heel-to-toe walk, contorted body-bending maneuvers, sudden jerks and freezes, and thrilling displays of full-stage acrobatics. Back-springing performers bound across the stage, and in battle scenes combatants repel spear thrusts— sixteen at a time, all from different directions—with both hands and both feet. Chinese opera has never been dependent on scenery. Instead, entire worlds are conjured through the simple manipulation of props: an actor who enters holding a paddle behind him is on a boat; an actor entering with a riding crop is on horseback. All in all, its innovative storytelling conventions and its spectacular displays offer audiences one of the world's most thrilling and magnificent theatrical experiences.

JAPANESE NOH

Japan has created two major theatre forms, *noh* and *kabuki*. (One other form is worth noting: *kyogen,* the short comical plays that complement noh performances,

Many contemporary directors fuse Asian and Western theatrical styles, as with a production of Henrik Ibsen's *Hedda Gabler* (pictured here) that used Chinese opera techniques. Retitled *Hedda, or Aspiration Sky High*, this production was directed by Sun Huizhu, Fei Chunfang, and Liu Lingzhi, and was produced by the Hangzhou Yueju Opera Company in Zhanjiang Gang in 2008; it also played in Germany, India, and Norway. Zhou Yujun (*left*) plays Hedda, looking over the manuscript of her would-be lover as her husband, played by Chen Xueping (*right*), looks on. ©*William Huizhu Sun, PhD*

much like satyr plays punctuated the performance of tragedy in ancient Greece.) Each tradition complements the other: noh is austere and metaphysical where kabuki is spontaneous and rambunctious. Each also gives the audience insight into traditions that go back centuries.

Noh is Japan's most revered and cerebral theatre. It is also the oldest continuously performed style of theatre in the world. In the fourteenth century, noh rose to prominence when a young performer named Zeami performed with his family in front of the shogun (the ruler of feudal Japan). Zeami was singled out by a shogun for his skill and brought to court to further his studies. He began to write plays—the exact number is unknown though is probably somewhere around 50 or 60—along with treatises on noh performance. His acting and theories of aesthetics became renowned throughout Japan.

Noh is a highly ceremonial drama that almost always portrays supernatural events and characters. All noh plays center on a single figure, the *shite* (pronounced "she-tay" and meaning "doer"), who is interrogated, prompted, and challenged by a secondary character, called the *waki*. Whereas waki characters are always living male humans—usually ministers, commoners, or priests—shite characters may be gods, ghosts, women, animals, or warriors. The shite, unlike the waki, wears a mask. Noh actors train for only one of these role types and then perform them throughout their careers. Extensive training provides actors with the precise choreography and musical notations required of their danced and chanted performances.

The actual noh stage is a square of highly polished Japanese cypress flooring, about eighteen feet across, supported from below by large earthenware jars that resonate with the actors' foot-stompings. A bridgelike runway (*hashigakari*) allows for solemn entrances and exits; an ornate, curved roof sits atop four wooden pillars, each with its own name and historic dramatic function. A wooden "mirror wall" at the rear of the stage reverberates the sounds of music and singing to the audience. This wall depicts a painted pine tree, which provides the only scenery. Four musicians—on flute, small and large hand drums, and stick drum—provide continuous musical accompaniment at the rear of the stage, and six to ten singer-chanters stand on a platform. The absolute precision of the performance elements gives noh a ceremonial and mysterious quality unique in world drama.

Noh's language is poetic but also elliptical and at times obscure. The cast is small, the action relatively static, and the pace, by the breakneck standards of contemporary culture, nearly glacial: the basic noh walk, said to be derived from tramping through rice paddies, is a deliberate slip-slide shuffle, with the feet barely leaving the ground. The actors are trained to keep their faces immobile and expressionless at all times. Certainly noh is produced today more for enthusiasts than for the general public, but the number of such enthusiasts—at least in Japan—is currently growing, not falling. Like the studies of martial arts, flower arranging, and the tea

The Kanze Noh Theatre, one of the world's most prestigious noh companies, presented works to great acclaim at the Lincoln Center Festival in 2016. The elegant set design befits the austerity of this ancient dramatic form.
©Stephanie Berger

ceremony, noh remains a Japanese national passion. Its sublime mystery and serenity—reflective of deep Buddhist and Shinto values—resonate profoundly in contemporary Japanese life and have proven increasingly influential to Japanese as well as Western dramatists of the current era.

JAPANESE KABUKI

Kabuki theatre emerged two hundred years after noh and offered a more spectacular and accessible form of entertainment. Whereas noh is refined, dignified, and designed for small, studious audiences, kabuki is gaudy and exhilarating. From its earliest days, kabuki sought to delight large crowds of merchants, traders, courtesans, and ordinary city dwellers. Instead of the minimal acting styles of noh, kabuki performers present an extravaganza of dazzling effects. Actors flamboyantly dance and recite their lines with passionate emotion. Elaborate stage machinery adds riotous spectacle to the proceedings, and the audiences contribute to the overall energy by shouting their favorite actors' names or other words of encouragement at key moments in the play.

Kabuki was created in Kyoto around 1600 by the legendary shrine maiden Izumo Okuni, whose showy and dramatic style of dancing became hugely popular in Kyoto's brothels and teahouses. Okuni began to employ actors who had been rejected from professional theatre companies. Her theatre became known as *kabuku*, meaning "outlaw," due to its itinerant nature and use of unprofessional performers. Okuni also cast men and women in her productions—another offense in the eyes of the authorities. This casting changed as the government passed a series of laws to forbid female actors, and the stories became more complex as they drew on the themes of traditional myths, historical incidents, and even noh drama. One popular subgenre was the "overnight pickle play," which would address a recent scandal—sometimes the very next day after the scandal broke! As this new theatrical form evolved, it changed its name from "kabuku" to "kabuki," a term that combined three separate words: ka ("song"), bu ("dance"), and ki ("skill").

By the eighteenth century, elements of kabuki became more formalized. The staging began incorporating curtains and scenery, playwrights' names were printed in kabuki programs, and star actors had emerged. Two such

Kabuki's famous dance-drama *Kagami Jishi* (*The Lion Dance*) features the fantastically arrayed title character, traditionally portrayed with a long white mane and gold and black robes. *©Education Images/UIG/Getty Images*

In this bunraku production of *Yoshitsune and the Thousand Cherry Trees* in Osaka, Japan, two unmasked but silent and expressionless puppeteers operate the principal "characters" while other operators, completely covered in black robes, assist them from beside and below. Musicians and chanters on and around the stage provide the music and songlike spoken texts. *©Werner Forman/Universal Images Group/Getty Images*

stars gave birth to two principal kabuki acting styles: *wagoto* (the elegant and naturalistic "soft style" of actor Sakata Tōjūrō, from Kyoto) and *aragoto* (the thundering "rough style" of Ichikawa Danjūrō, from Edo, now Tokyo). The traditions of both these actors remain central to kabuki in the modern era. In fact, all current kabuki actors can trace their lineage—familial and professional—back to their kabuki-performing ancestors. The contemporary star Ichikawa Ebizō XI, for example, is the great-great-great-great-great-great-great-great-grandson of Ichikawa Ebizō I, born in 1673; the celebrated family style has been directly passed, father to son, down through the centuries.

There are many types of kabuki dramas, but the major works fall generally into two categories: history plays (*jidaimono*, or "period things") and domestic plays (*sewamono*, or "common things"). The history plays dramatize—usually in spectacular fashion—major political events of the remote past. Often, however, the historical setting offers a protective cover for playwrights and actors to depict controversial political issues in their own time. Domestic plays, in contrast, deal with the affairs of the townspeople, merchants, lovers, and courtesans of the playwright's era, often focusing on the conflicts between affairs of the heart and the call of duty. A great many domestic plays end in suicide (many, in fact, in double suicides), with the lovers vowing to meet again in the world to come.

Kabuki is mainly an actor's theatre; many of its plays are of unknown authorship and have been augmented over the centuries by actors' additions. One notable exception, however, is the kabuki author Chikamatsu Monzaemon (1653–1725). Considered the greatest Japanese dramatist of all time, Chikamatsu was also a famous playwright of bunraku, the Japanese puppet-theatre founded in 1684 and particularly popular in its hometown of Osaka.

Chapter

8

The Modern Theatre

©István Biró/Hungarian State Theatre of Cluj

WHEN WE CALL SOMETHING "MODERN," we usually mean that it's new or cutting edge. We talk of a device's "sleek, modern look" or of people being "modern" in their views. However, when we use a similar word, "modernism," we mean something else: a critical attitude taken toward the assumptions of the previous eras. "Modernism" is a historical and artistic term. It is historical because it refers to a specific time period—although the exact parameters of that time period are debatable—and it is artistic because it refers to an attitude taken to the creation of new work across different media: painting, writing, and of course theatre.

Some scholars claim that modernism began after the advent of nuclear weapons. Others will say that modernism began at the turn of the century. And others still will say that it began long before that—in fact, many scholars refer to the Renaissance as the "early modern" period, as if to suggest that modernism is actually quite

old. Modernism began at different *places,* as well. By the time modernist innovations came to American art, those same inventions had become passé back in Europe. And—as we will discuss shortly—modernism isn't necessarily only a Western (European and American) idea. It is now thought of as global.

Some clarity, then, is needed. For the purposes of this book, we will define modern drama geographically as two related, but distinct, phenomena: Western modern drama and global modern drama. And we will define it as historically as beginning in the late nineteenth century.

Why that particular time? For the West, it is because modern drama's roots lie deep in the social and political upheavals in the eighteenth and nineteenth centuries, a time characterized by revolution. Revolutions in the United States and Europe, along with the more global shift to industrial economic systems, deeply changed

the political, social, and economic structures of the Western world. In the wake of these developments came an explosion of public communication and transportation; a tremendous expansion of literacy, democracy, and public and private wealth; and a general shift from countryside to city. Simultaneously, an intellectual revolution—in philosophy, science, social understanding, and religion—altered fundamental ideas of our place in the world. The accepted wisdom of the previous eras became riddled with doubt: Is there really a divine power? Are we even in control of our own destinies? Is there even such a thing as destiny, or is life simply random?

Global modernism also began at this time because different cultures reckoned, in distinct ways, with their colonial pasts and presents. In Japan, China, India, Iran, and other countries occupied by Western powers, modernism refers to the ambivalent relationship drama forged with the artistic legacies of the invading cultures. In other words, modernism referred to the way they both adopted and rejected aspects of Western modernism, oftentimes merging them with their traditional forms of theatre.

Some historical factors affected modernism all over the world. The innovations of Charles Darwin, for instance, altered the entire course of scientific and philosophical thought. Darwin argued that we *Homo sapiens* are directly linked to other mammals—descended not from Adam and Eve or pagan demigods but from prehistoric apes. The work of Sigmund Freud posited the existence of the unconscious, a dark and lurking inner self filled with infantile urges, fantasies, and suppressed fears and desires. The writings of Karl Marx contended that economic and political structures make us economic prisoners without us even realizing it.

These and scores of other serious challenges to traditional thinking were accompanied everywhere by public debate and dispute. Some believed humankind was no longer free and that, in the traditional sense, humankind wasn't even really human. Rather, we are all chained to our classes, our genetics, and our emotions.

The modern theatre—both in the West and more globally—has its roots in these political, social, and intellectual revolutions. Ever since its outset it has been a theatre of challenge, a theatre of experimentation. It has never been a theatre of rules or simple messages, nor has it been a theatre of gods, heroes, or villains. It has reflected, to a certain degree, the confusions of its times, but it has also struggled to clarify and to illuminate, to document and explore human destiny in a complex universe.

We will first examine global modern drama, which is a more recent concept; for much of theatre history, modernism was thought to be a strictly Western affair. We will then look at the realism and antirealism movements of Western modern drama, the field typically thought of as more traditionally modernist.

Global Modern Drama

Recently, historians of theatre have sought to define modernism as a global, rather than solely Western, movement. What, then, is global modernism? While there are no generalizations to be made for Indian *and* Japanese *and* Chinese *and* Middle Eastern theatrical development, all of these cultures share a struggle, if not an artistic principle: they have all grappled with the legacy of the West. It is this struggle that defines global modern drama.

This is not to say that these cultures simply replicated the styles of Western modern drama. Instead, they merged the artistic methods of outsider Western cultures with their native forms of theatre. For instance, when England ruled over India in the late nineteenth century, many Indian schoolchildren were educated in English schools and read English plays, primarily Shakespeare. In fact, the first educational editions of Shakespeare ever published were done so with the express purpose of teaching Indian children. As a result, adaptations of Shakespeare's works in Hindi combined with Indian traditions of dance-drama gained popularity.

However, this absorption of English culture led, perhaps inevitably, to a forceful rejection of its influence. The Indian People's Theatre Association (IPTA), founded in 1942, produced plays that actively critiqued British colonial practices. Yet they did so within a Marxist framework. The IPTA, in fact, remains the official theatre company of the Communist Party of India. With this rejection of one facet of the West, then, we also find the acceptance of another.

In the late nineteenth century, Japan also found itself wrestling with Western influences. Japanese theatre artists toured Europe and would often bring back innovative ideas. The result was new forms of older theatre genres, such as *shin-kabuki* ("new kabuki"), a version of the lively Japanese drama with a focus on psychological realism. Likewise, European artists found themselves moved and challenged by Japanese theatre forms, such as the kabuki on display by the teacher and civil rights leader Fukuzawa Yukichi, who with his wife performed more accessible versions of Japanese drama throughout Europe.

China merged its operatic styles with some of the West's more straightforwardly realistic approaches. Many theatre historians pinpoint the first instance of this mixture as an adaptation of *Uncle Tom's Cabin*—the popular American novel by Harriet Beecher Stowe—called "Black

Slave's Cry to Heaven." In this startling production, the struggles of the African American slave in the United States found a parallel in the contemporary struggles of the Chinese people, who were in the wake of a war and faced internal and external divisions. (Strikingly, a similar adaptation of *Uncle Tom's Cabin* occurs in the Rodgers and Hammerstein musical *The King and I,* when a slave girl stages a Siamese ballet based on the novel.)

Finally, one fascinating example of global modernism occurs in the Arab world, which saw increasing urbanization and trade at the turn of the twentieth century. The period known as Al-Nahda, which roughly translates to "Renaissance," saw a simultaneous revival of the considerable past achievements of Islam and a forward-looking impulse known as *iqtibās*, or "the process of lighting one's fire from that of another." The other "fire" in this case was—as it was with other non-Western cultures—the West. Cairo and other hubs of trade between the Middle East and Europe became hubs of cultural exchange as well. The dramatic trends that emerged, which blended Middle Eastern and Western influences, would lead to even more forthright versions of Western realistic drama and a resurgent and flourishing theatrical culture. The preeminent dramatist of this synthesized style is the Egyptian Tawfiq al-Hakim, whose 1966 play *Fate of a Cockroach* became an international hit and continues to be produced to this day.

Globally, then, the legacy of Western modernism was at times contested and at times embraced. But what was this legacy, exactly? What were these styles that became so influential that they forced a worldwide reckoning? In the next section, we will survey the West's considerable history of modernism, from its realistic and antirealistic beginnings to its eventual splintering into countless styles.

Realism

Thus far, the movement that has had the most pervasive and long-lived effect on the modern Western theatre is, beyond question, realism. Realism has sought to create a drama without conventions or abstractions. *Likeness to life* is realism's goal, and in pursuit of that goal it has renounced aspects of the drama that preceded it: no more idealized settings, stylized verse, contrived endings, ornate costumes, or exaggerated performance styles.

Realism is a difficult aesthetic philosophy to define. In a way, the theatre has always taken "real life" as its fundamental subject, so realism seems at first glance to be the perfect style with which to approach the reality of existence. Instead of having actors represent characters, the realists would say, let us have the actors *be* those characters. Instead of having dialogue stand for conversation, let

us have dialogue that is conversation. Instead of having scenery and costumes that convey a sense of time and place and atmosphere, let us have scenery that is genuinely inhabitable and costumes that are real clothes.

But, of course, realism has its limits: any dramatic piece must inevitably involve a certain stylization, no matter how lifelike its effects, and advocates of theatrical realism are well aware of this fact. Realism might seem like the rejection of style, but realism is also itself a style, as careful and deliberate as any other. Realist artists pushed the limits of realism's stylization and ideology during the last years of the nineteenth century and the first years of the twentieth. The results of these artists continually challenging themselves to create a more lifelike style have formed a meaningful body of theatre that remains enormously significant today.

A LABORATORY

In essence, the realistic theatre aspired to be a laboratory in which the nature of relationships or the ills of society are "objectively" set down for the final judgment of an audience of impartial observers. In its purest form, realistic theatre should strictly adhere to the "scientific method" of the laboratory. Nothing must ring false. The setting must resemble the prescribed locale of the play as closely as possible, even if that means the scenery comes from a real-life environment and is simply transported onto the stage. Characters' costumes in the realistic theatre follow the dress of "real" people of similar societal status; dialogue recreates the cadences and expressions of daily life.

Early in the realist movement, the proscenium stage of the Romantic era was modified to accommodate scenery constructed in *box sets*: three fully visible walls that featured real bookcases, windows, fireplaces, swinging doors, and so forth, built just as they are in a house interior. The audience felt as if they were eavesdropping and witnessing interactions within an actual private home. In the same vein, realistic acting was judged effective insofar as it drew from the behavior of life and insofar as the actors seemed to be genuinely speaking to each other instead of playing to the audience. A new aesthetic principle had spawned: the "theatre of the fourth wall removed," in which the life onstage was conceived to be the same as life in a real-world setting, except that, in the case of the stage, one wall—the proscenium opening—had been removed. Thus the theatre was like a laboratory microscope and the stage like a biologist's slide: a living environment presented for careful inspection by curious observers.

Realism presents its audience with an abundance of seemingly real-life "evidence" and permits spectators

Brian Dennehy (*left*) and Nathan Lane (*right*) are two of America's greatest modern actors, each having won two Tony Awards to date. Here they are shown arguing in a barroom—the play's only setting—in Eugene O'Neill's powerful *The Iceman Cometh*, written in 1939. Restaged on Broadway by Robert Falls in 2015 (following his 2012 production at Chicago's Goodman Theatre), the play lasted nearly five hours and received rapturous reviews and responses from critics and audiences. ©*Sara Krulwich/The New York Times/Redux*

to arrive at their own conclusions. There is some shaping of this evidence by author and performer alike, to be sure, but much of the excitement of the realistic theatre is occasioned by the genuine interpretive freedom it allows the audience and by the accessibility of its characters.

Yet while characters were familiar, they were also complex—much like we all are in real life. In presenting its evidence from the surface of life, realism encourages us to delve into the mystery that lies beneath it. Realism's characters are defined by detail rather than by symbol or abstract idealization: like people we know, they are ultimately unpredictable—humanly messy rather than clear-cut. As such, while realism does not inherently advocate one straightforward position, its works inevitably have political repercussions. The exposure of society's suppressed secrets can be potentially scandalous—but also, as history shows, extremely popular.

The success of realism is well established; it remains one of the dominant modes of drama to this day. At its most profound, when crafted and performed by consummately skilled artists, realistic theatre can generate extremely powerful audience empathy by virtue of the insight and clarity it brings to real-world moments. In giving us characters, the realistic playwright also gives us companions—fellow travelers on the voyage of human discovery with whom we can compare our thoughts and feelings.

PIONEERS OF REALISM

The realistic theatre had its beginnings in the four-year period that saw the premieres of three shocking plays by Norwegian playwright Henrik Ibsen: *A Doll's House* (1867), *Ghosts* (1881), and *An Enemy of the People* (1882). Already famous for historical and poetic dramas, including the magnificent *Peer Gynt* (1867), Ibsen (1828–1906),

Lee Breuer's celebrated production of *Dollhouse* with the Mabou Mines company, which he co-heads in New York, was remarkable for casting all the male roles in this adaptation of Ibsen's play (usually translated as *A Doll's House*) with actors four feet tall or less, and with the play's women towering two feet above them. The setting (by Narelle Sisson) was also a "doll house," with miniature walls and furniture. Maude Mitchell plays Nora in this performance, seen at the 2007 Edinburgh Festival, with Mark Povinelli as her husband, Torvald. ©*Geraint Lewis/Alamy Stock Photo*

soon to be known as the "father of dramatic realism," turned his attention in these works to more contemporary and everyday themes: the role of women in society, hereditary disease, mercy killing, and political hypocrisy. Ordinary people populate Ibsen's realistic world, and they face recognizable issues played out in the interiors of ordinary homes. Controversial in their own time, these plays retain their pertinence today and still have the power to inform, move, and even shock. The reason for their lasting impact lies in Ibsen's choice of issues and his skill at showing conflicting sides through brilliantly captured psychological detail.

The realistic theatre spread rapidly throughout Europe as other writers, inspired by Ibsen, followed suit. The result was a proliferation of "problem plays," as they were sometimes called, which focused genuine social concern through realistic dramatic portrayals. In Germany, Gerhart Hauptmann (1862–1946) explored the plight of the middle and proletarian classes in several works, most notably in his masterpiece *The Weavers* (1892). In England, Irish-born George Bernard Shaw (1856–1950) created an intellectual brand of comedy through which he addressed issues such as slum ownership (in *Widowers' Houses*, 1892), prostitution (in *Mrs. Warren's Profession*, 1902), and urban poverty (in *Major Barbara*, 1905). In France, André Antoine (1858–1943) created his Théâtre Libre in 1887 to encourage stagings of realistic dramas, including Ibsen's *Ghosts* and *The Wild Duck*, Hauptmann's *Weavers*, and the French plays of Eugène Brieux (1858–1932), including *Damaged Goods* (1902), about syphilis, and *Maternity* (1903), about birth control. By the turn of the century, realism was virtually the standard dramatic form in Europe.

The realistic theatre came to prominence with the plays of Ibsen and continued to establish its legacy in the

The three sisters of Anton Chekhov's *Three Sisters* display their grief—and familial bonds—at the end of this 1901 masterpiece, directed here by Claire Lasne Darcueil at the Théâtre de la Tempète in Paris in 2014.
©Laurencine Lot

major works of Anton Chekhov (1860–1904). Chekhov was a physician by training and a writer of fiction by vocation. Toward the end of his career, in association with realist director Konstantin Stanislavski (see the chapter "The Actor") and the Moscow Art Theatre, Chekhov also achieved success as a playwright through four plays that portray the last decades of the czarist era in Russia with astonishing force and subtlety: *The Seagull* (1896), *Uncle Vanya* (1899), *Three Sisters* (1901), and *The Cherry Orchard* (1904). The intricate craftsmanship of these plays makes them seem more like lived-in worlds than artistic works. Even the minor characters seem to breathe the same air we do.

Chekhov's technique was to create deeply complex relationships among his characters and to develop his plots and themes more or less between the lines. Every Chekhovian character is filled with secrets that the dialogue never fully reveals. For an example of Chekhov's realist style, examine the dialogue in the following scene from *Three Sisters*. In this scene, Vershinin, an army colonel, meets Masha and her sisters, Irina and Olga, whom Vershinin dimly remembers from past years in Moscow:

VERSHININ: I have the honor to introduce myself, my name is Vershinin. I am very, very glad to be in your house at last. How you have grown up! Aie-aie!

IRINA: Please sit down. We are delighted to see you.

In 2017, the brilliant young playwright Lucas Hnath wrote a "sequel" to Henrik Ibsen's modernist masterpiece *A Doll's House*—cheekily called *A Doll's House, Part 2*—in which Ibsen's protagonist, Nora, returns to the family from which she triumphantly departed in the closing moments of the first play. Laurie Metcalf (*right*), pictured here with Jayne Houdyshell (*left*), received raves and a Tony Award for her portrayal of Nora.
©Sara Krulwich/The New York Times/Redux

Realistic plays do not necessarily require realistic scenery. In Alfred Uhry's *Driving Miss Daisy*, an elderly southern Jewish woman (Vanessa Redgrave) is driven around town by her African American chauffeur (James Earl Jones). Over the years, they develop a profound, though mostly unstated, emotional relationship. It would be impossible to stage the moving car realistically, so this vital element must simply be mimed, as in the 2011 Broadway production shown here. However, the costumes, dialogue, and acting are acutely realistic. ©*Geraint Lewis/Alamy Stock Photo*

VERSHININ: (*with animation*) How glad I am, how glad I am! But there are three of you sisters. I remember—three little girls. I don't remember your faces, but that your father, Colonel Prozorov, had three little girls I remember perfectly. How time passes! Hey-ho, how it passes! . . .

IRINA: From Moscow? You have come from Moscow?

VERSHININ: Yes. Your father was in command of a battery there, and I was an officer in the same brigade. (*To Masha*) Your face, now, I seem to remember.

MASHA: I don't remember you.

VERSHININ: So you are Olga, the eldest—and you are Masha—and you are Irina, the youngest—

OLGA: You come from Moscow?

VERSHININ: Yes. I studied in Moscow. . . . used to visit you in Moscow.

Masha and Vershinin's deepening, largely unspoken communion will provide one of the most haunting undercurrents to the play. And how lifelike is the awkwardness of their first encounter! Vershinin's enthusiastic clichés ("How time passes!") and interjections ("Aie-aie!") are the stilted stuff of everyday conversation; the news that he comes from Moscow is repeated so that it becomes amusing rather than informative, a revelation of character rather than of plot.

Masha's first exchange with Vershinin gives no direct indication of the future of their relationship. Theirs is a crossed communication in which one character refuses to share in the other's memory. Is this a slight insult, or a flirtatious provocation? The acting, not simply the text, must establish their developing rapport. The love between Vershinin and Masha will demand that the actors who play them express deep feeling and subtle nuance, through the gestures, glances, tones of voice, shared understandings, and sympathetic rhythms that distinguish lovers everywhere. It is a theme that strongly affects the mood of the play but is rarely explicit in the dialogue.

One of the seminal plays of midcentury American realism was Clifford Odets's *Awake and Sing*. First produced by the Group Theatre in 1935, this drama popularized a down-to-earth, gritty style of both playwriting and acting. The play focuses on Jewish immigrants during the Great Depression and dominated the American theatre long after its debut. Pictured here are Mark Ruffalo (*left*) and Lauren Ambrose (*right*) in a 2006 Broadway revival. ©*Sara Krulwich/The New York Times/Redux*

NATURALISM

Naturalism represents an extreme attempt to dramatize human reality without any appearance of dramatic form. The naturalists flourished primarily in France during the late nineteenth century. Émile Zola (1840–1902) was their philosopher-in-chief. The naturalists based their artistic principles on nature, particularly Darwin's understanding of humanity's place in the natural environment. To the naturalist, human beings were no more than animals whose behavior was determined entirely by genetic and social circumstances. To portray a character as a hero, or even as a credible force for change in society, was anathema to the naturalists, who despised neat dramatic conclusions or climaxes. Whereas realist plays at that time tended to deal with well-defined social issues—women's rights, inheritance laws, worker's pensions, and the like—naturalist plays offered nothing more than a "slice of life." The characters of the play were the play's entire subject. Any topical issues that arose served merely as a result of the characters' situations, frustrations, and hopes.

● Spotlight

Interview with Oskar Eustis

What do *Angels in America*, *Fun Home*, and *Hamilton* have in common? For one, all three of these plays have in some way altered the landscape of American theatre by redefining the form: *Angels* with its four-hour-plus running-time, grand magical realism, and historical scope; *Fun Home* with its expansion of the musical genre; and *Hamilton* with its status as not simply a great work of theatre but also as a once-in-a-generation cultural phenomenon. All three also share recognition in the form of scads of prizes—a combined 21 Tony Awards.

These works share something else in common in their histories—something less heralded, perhaps, but just as crucial: all were developed under the eye of one of the preeminent artistic directors in the United States, Oskar Eustis. Eustis commissioned *Angels* while he worked at the Eureka Theatre in San Francisco, and he developed *Fun Home* and *Hamilton* while working at the Public Theater in New York, a position he has held since 2005.

At the Public, Eustis has seen this venerable institution expand its ambitions and successes. The Public, with its five theatres, nightclub, and famous Shakespeare in the Park series over the summer, is constantly nurturing and producing new work. And like Eustis, it is never content; it always seeks to honor the legacy of its founder, Joseph Papp, while also responding to the world around it. The theatre is the only of its kind in New York—a place where Shakespeare and the avant-garde are equally at home, where new work and old are afforded the same attention and dignity. To be in the lobby of the Public on a weekend evening is to feel the buzz of theatre evolving in real time: all around you, in different ways, new work is redefining the field. As Eustis says, "We are modeling history and we are existing in history."

Eustis's role is itself the product of relatively recent history. While theatre troupes have long had managers and individual plays have long had directors, the role of an artistic director—an overall leader who oversees all aspects of a company's artistic production—emerged during the modern era.

In 2017, one of your authors, Donovan Sherman, sat down with Eustis to talk about his work and the mission of the Public—and of theatre and democracy more broadly.

DS: How would you describe the role of the artistic director? What does it mean to you?

OE: It's my job to realize the mission of the theatre through the shows and programs we do. Selecting the artists that we work with—the actors, the directors, and the designers—and creating the programs that are off the main stage are the purest reflections of our mission and values.

At any given point we have somewhere between 50 and 70 projects in development here. And in

Oskar Eustis, in his office at the Public. ©*Lorna Cohen*

development its simplest form can be that we've commissioned a playwright to write a play and we haven't seen a word yet; its more complex form is that we have a musical that we've been working on for three years and we've gone to two workshops.

DS: I love that you have a dramaturgical background. Is that something that still informs your work today?

OE: It leads the work I do today. I'm an artistic director like the dramaturg I am. That's always the leading artistic principle for me. It's the reason why all artistic directors should be dramaturgs, because the core of dramaturgy is trying to recognize and support somebody else's vision. It's trying to understand, in its simplest terms, the ideal version of the play that the playwright is writing and trying to help them get them there.

DS: What is a moment when you just could sense something about a new work? Is it intuitive?

OE: The vast majority of pieces that I respond to, I respond to quickly and intuitively. But of course, the intuition is made up of everything we thought and know.

(continued)

What is common is the process of being in dialogue with artists (sometimes for years), watching something start to take shape, and then seeing the way it catches fire. And you realize, "Oh that's really gonna be special." The process from there to the finish line can be grueling. I think about *Fun Home*, which won the Best Play Tony a couple of years ago and was the most unlikely musical to ever win it. . . . [W]e had to really rip it apart and put it together. But I'm incredibly proud of what it was, and Jenine [Tesori, who wrote the music] and Lisa [Kron, who wrote the book] turned out to have a genius for rewriting that is absolutely essential if you're going to succeed in this business.

DS: You are in some ways the face of this institution, and yet to hear you talk about it you're the person shepherding and listening. You're not front row center.

OE: My job is to continually explain to all of our stakeholders what we're doing, why the Public Theater is important, what our mission is, and how does all that translate. And I feel like I'm doing that to artists and donors and audiences and to the cultural community as a whole, and that process is actually really important. It's really important to be repeating over and over in different ways: "This is what we stand for. This is what our values are. This is why we're somewhat different from some of our sister theatres."

DS: I'm really intrigued by the way the Public is a distinctly American institution, and yet you're really informed by a lot of European traditions. Is that a kind of peaceful relationship or is there tension?

OE: I think it's primarily peaceful. I had this huge advantage which is when I was 19 and I moved to Switzerland. And between nineteen and twenty-one I lived in Switzerland and worked in the German-speaking world and retained very close ties there. But at the age of twentyish I made this very firm decision that I was going back. I actually had a moment where I said, "I could be an expatriate, I could work in the German state theatre system." And I really decided I'm not going to do that. So as a result I've been able to take an enormous amount of what I learned in particularly the German speaking world but also England.

And of course the theatre, however influenced it is by other traditions, is always by definition a local enterprise. It's always happening. And I will say the American theatre is incredibly myopic about its foreign roots. We're very happy to brag about the Provincetown players and Eugene O'Neill, but what nobody talks about is the Moscow Art Theatre touring here in 1923 through '24, which is the other great root of the American theatre. It was the Chariot of the Gods! The Russians came in for eighteen months and then left and affected a generation of theatre artists.

DS: The first line of the mission statement of the Public is that it is "of, by, and for the people." Can you elaborate on what that means to you?

OE: What it expresses is that the core value of the theatre aligns with the core value of the country, which is democracy. Namely, the idea that everybody deserves a place at the table. Everybody's story is important and that we are made stronger by understanding the diversity of each other's stories. And that principle that I believe is expressed in the Declaration of Independence and has partial manifestation in the Constitution. What it means is that we can never be satisfied because we never are speaking to everybody. We have never given everybody a voice, but we can continually be prodded by that mission to keep pushing boundaries and keep thinking of new ways to bring more people to the table, more people into the conversation in the room. Which you know I think is the good part of what America does.

DS: You've been behind some major milestones for the Public and also for American theatre. Do you know in the moment when you have something on your hands like *Hamilton* or *Angels in America*? Are you aware it's going to be a historical event and not just another play?

OE: Along the development of *Angels* or *Hamilton*, there were moments where you exposed it to an audience in some way. But nobody could have predicted what happened with *Angels*. No way could we have predicted what happened with *Hamilton*. It was clear we set a bomb off and we knew from then it was something special. Nobody knew it would have the kind of impact that it would have.

DS: This leads to a more fundamental question: When you're developing your work, do you think of the audience at all? Or are you so in the world of this play, you think, "It is what it is and we can't account for the audience"?

OE: You always think about concentric circles. One of the things I think is great about the theatre is that it encompasses every possible phase of socialization. Writers have to be alone in their room facing that blank screen and write something. They then have to show it to directors and dramaturgs who comment on it. Then they show it to actors and do a reading of it. Then you get the designers and, along the way, you're expanding the degree of socialization. So in the best possible, system, you're slowly exposing your piece to more and more people. And each time there's a feedback loop, each time increasing the feedback, the amount of information you're taking, and that helps you refine what you've got.

DS: You've taught classes on collaboration and it seems to be a kind of motif through a lot of your career, both in the micro level of the artistic act but also the grander public vision of democracy. What are a few things you've learned about collaboration that perhaps our readers could benefit to hear?

OE: Theatre and democracy were born in the same decade because they both depend on the same belief system: that nobody owns the truth and the truth is only to be discovered in the opposition of different viewpoints. That's the only way to discover the truth.

Any good artistic collaboration leads to two or four or fifty people working together and trying to figure out what is actually essential. It's about trying to create a field where everybody flourishes, where the best of everybody can go forward. You get in a rehearsal room and rehearsal gets going and you're better than you are when you're by yourself. You're less petty, less egotistical, less vengeful and envious and angry and competitive. You actually get lifted up and you become your better self in the company of others. And that's something that I believe is a deep truth about theatre.

The naturalists sought to eliminate every trace of dramatic convention: "All the great successes of the stage are triumphs over convention," declared Zola. Their efforts in this direction are exemplified by the Swedish playwright August Strindberg's (1849–1912) elimination of the time-passing intermission in *Miss Julie*. Instead of a traditional gap of time, a group of peasants, otherwise irrelevant to the plot, enter the kitchen setting between acts and dance to fill the time Miss Julie is spending in the offstage bedroom of Jean, her servant. The Austrian playwright Arthur Schnitzler (1862–1931) similarly eliminated conventional scene beginnings, endings, and climaxes in the interlocking series of love affairs that constitute the action of his *La Ronde*.

In the United States, the early work of Eugene O'Neill (1888–1953) adapted the naturalistic style popularized in Europe to the more industrial and gritty milieu of American society. He would return to naturalism in his later autobiographical masterpiece, *Long Day's Journey into Night*—a play so true to life that O'Neill forbade its production or publication until many years after his death. In subsequent years, the dramas of Arthur Miller, Lorraine Hansbury, Tennessee Williams, August Wilson, Wendy Wasserstein, Theresa Rebeck, Ayad Akhtar, and Annie Baker are all strongly influenced by both realism and naturalism, which continue to have a commanding presence on the American stage.

Antirealism

Realism and naturalism were not the only new movements of the late nineteenth century to make themselves strongly felt in the modern Western theatre. A reactionary force, equally powerful, was to emerge. First manifest in the movement known as symbolism, this counterforce evolved and expanded into what we will call antirealistic theatre.

As its name suggests, *antirealism* arose in reaction to realism—a rebellion against a rebellion.

THE SYMBOLIST REBELLION

The symbolist movement began in Paris during the 1880s as a joint venture of artists, playwrights, essayists, critics, sculptors, and poets. If realism is the art of depicting reality as ordinary men and women might see it, symbolism sought to explore—by means of images and metaphors—the inner realities that cannot be directly or literally perceived. "Symbolic" characters, therefore, would not represent real human beings but instead would symbolize philosophical ideas or warring internal forces in the human soul.

Symbolism had another goal as well: to crush what its adherents deemed to be a spiritually bankrupt realism and replace it with traditional artistic values—poetry, imagery, novelty, fantasy, extravagance, profundity, audacity, charm, and superhuman magnitude. United in their hatred for literal detail and for all they considered mundane or ordinary, the symbolists demanded abstraction, enlargement, and innovation. The symbolist spirit soared in poetic speeches, outsized dramatic gestures, fantastical visual effects, and sudden plot departures. Purity of vision, rather than accuracy of observation, was the symbolists' aim, and self-conscious creative innovation was to become their primary accomplishment.

The first symbolist theatre, founded in 1890 by Parisian poet Paul Fort (1872–1960), was intended as a direct attack on the naturalistic Théâtre Libre of André Antoine, founded three years earlier. In some ways, the theatres of Antoine and Fort had much in common: both were amateur, gained considerable notoriety, and served as centers for "schools" of artistic ideology that attracted as much attention and controversy as any of their theatrical offerings. But the two theatres were openly at war. While Antoine presented premieres of naturalistic and realistic dramas by August Strindberg, Émile Zola, and Henrik Ibsen, Fort presented the staged poems and poetic plays of both contemporary and earlier writers, such as the French Arthur Rimbaud and Paul Verlaine, the Belgian Maurice Maeterlinck, and the American Edgar Allan Poe. Whereas Antoine would go to great lengths to create realistic scenery for his plays (for example, he displayed real sides of beef hung from meat hooks for his presentation of *The Butchers*), Fort prevailed upon leading impressionist painters—including Pierre Bonnard, Maurice Denis, and Odilon Redon—to dress his stylized stage. Silver angels, translucent veils, and sheets of crumpled wrapping paper were among the decors that backed the symbolist works at the Théâtre d'Art.

Fort's theatre created an immediate sensation in Paris. With the stunning success in 1890 of *The Intruder*, a mysterious and poetic fantasy by Maeterlinck, the antirealist movement was fully engaged and, as Fort recalls in his memoirs, "the cries and applause of the students, poets, and artists overwhelmed the huge disapproval of the bourgeoisie."

The movement spread quickly as authors and designers alike awakened to the possibilities of a theatre wholly freed from the constraints of verisimilitude. Realism, critics concluded, would never raise the commonplace to the level of art; it would only drag art down into the muck of the mundane. As such, the symbolists reasoned, realism ran counter to all that the theatre had stood for in the past; it throttled the potential of artistic creativity. In fact, such naturalistic and realistic authors as Henrik Ibsen, August Strindberg, Gerhart Hauptmann, and George Bernard Shaw soon came under the symbolist influence and abandoned their social preoccupations and environmental exactitude to seek a new dramatic vocabulary. As an added element, at about this time Sigmund Freud's research was being published and discussed, and his theories concerning dream images and the worlds of the unconscious provided new source material for the stage.

By the turn of the century, the counterforce of theatrical stylization set in motion by the symbolists was established on all fronts; indeed, the half decade on either side of 1900 represents one of the richest periods of experimentation in the history of dramatic writing. Out of that period came Hauptmann's archetypal fairytale *The Sunken Bell* (Germany, 1896), Alfred Jarry's outrageously cartoonish *Ubu Roi* (France, 1898), Ibsen's haunting ode to individualism *When We Dead Awaken* (Norway, 1899), Strindberg's imagistic *A Dream Play* (Sweden, 1902),

William Butler Yeats's evocative poetic fable *Cathleen ni Houlihan* (Ireland, 1903), Shaw's philosophical allegory *Don Juan in Hell* (England, 1903), and James Barrie's whimsical and buoyant fantasy *Peter Pan* (England, 1904). Almost every dramatic innovation that has followed since that time has been at least in part anticipated by one or more of these seminal works.

The realist-versus-symbolist confrontation affected every aspect of theatre production in Europe. Symbolist-inspired directors and designers, side by side with the playwrights, drastically altered the arts of staging and decor to accommodate the new dramaturgies that surged into the theatre. Realist directors such as Antoine and Stanislavski suddenly found themselves challenged by scores of adversaries and renegades. A school of symbolist and poetic directors rose in France, and a former disciple of Stanislavski, Vsevolod Meyerhold (1874–1940), broke with the Russian master to create a "biomechanical" style of acting that viewed the performing body as a machine whose parts needed to be tuned with precision. At first, Meyerhold's techniques stood in sharp contrast to the more realistic styles established at Stanislavski's Moscow Art Theatre, but by 1904 that theatre featured Stanislavski himself producing the symbolist plays of Maeterlinck.

The advent of electrical stage lighting, too, created new opportunities for stylization: the technology enabled the modern director to create vivid stage effects, starkly unrealistic in appearance, through the judicious use of spotlighting, shadowing, and shading. Technology, in addition to trends in modern art that were well established in Europe by 1900, led to scenery and costume designs that departed radically from realism. Exoticism, fantasy, sheer sensual delight, and aesthetic purity became the prime objectives of designers who joined the antirealist rebellion.

In some respects, the symbolist aim succeeded perhaps beyond the dreams of its originators. Fort's Théâtre d'Art, although it lasted only two years, now has spiritual descendants in every city in the Western world where theatre is performed.

THE ERA OF ISMS

The symbolist movement itself was short-lived, at least under that name. Within years of its birth, symbolism as a movement was deserted by founders and followers alike. Where did they go? Off to found newer movements: futurism, dadaism, idealism, impressionism, expressionism, constructivism, surrealism, and perhaps a hundred other ism-labeled movements now lost to time.

Director Robert Wilson and costume designer John Conklin co-designed the scenery for this dreamlike American Repertory Theater production of Ibsen's *When We Dead Awaken* in 1991. ©*Richard Feldman*

The first third of the twentieth century was an era of theatrical isms, rich with continued experimentation by movements self-consciously seeking to redefine theatrical art. Ism theatres sprang up like mushrooms, each with its own manifesto, each promising a better art, or even a better world. It was a vibrant era for the theatre. Out of this explosion of isms, dramatic art took on new social and political significance in the cultural capitals of Europe and the United States. A successful play was not merely a play but also a forum for a belief, and behind that belief was a group of zealous supporters and adherents who shared a deep commitment.

The Western world doesn't necessarily have isms anymore—at least, not the way that it did a century ago. In fact, one of the most prominent theatre movements in recent history, *postmodernism*, might be thought of as promoting "the death of isms" rather than as a specific ism

itself. Instead of communicating a unified sense of artistic vision, postmodernist works combine various styles without attempting to connect them. A postmodernist play could incorporate elements of melodrama, naturalism, and symbolism—all at the same time. As such, while postmodernism promotes some antirealist ideas—most notably a failure of communication, a break from recognizable reality, and an awareness of its status as theatre—it also abandons any attempt to ask the profound questions that characterized movements such as symbolism. A recent production of Shakespeare's *Troilus and Cressida*, renamed "Cry, Trojans!" by the postmodern theatre company The Wooster Group, exemplifies this style: actors wore costumes that evoked, at times stereotypically, Native American dress, while movie screens displayed selections from the early 1960s American melodrama *Splendor in the Grass*. What did this all mean? What do these

Willem Dafoe as "The Idiot" and a friendly "Duck" tease the audience in Richard Foreman's postmodernist *Idiot Savant*, presented by Foreman's Ontological-Hysteric Company performing at the New York Public Theater in 2009. ©*Sara Krulwich/The New York Times/Redux*

choices have to do with Shakespeare's work? We are given no answers. Similarly, Mabou Mines—another stalwart of downtown Manhattan—mixed and merged different preexisting texts in its 2017 *Glass Guignol: The Brother and Sister Play*, which patched together sections from the writing of Tennessee Williams and Mary Shelley to create, in their words, a "rabbit hole" of different scenes, characters, and events. Rather than connecting each segment of these plays in a traditional Aristotelian sense, or working to create a cohesive whole, Mabou Mines gives us instead a fragmentary, unconnected look at preexisting works. "Nothing is new under the sun," these productions seem to say—the age of modernist discovery is over. Instead all we can do is reconnect the same old elements, over and over.

Isms have not completely vanished, however. They may have new names and be directed to new aims, but today's theatre movements retain the fundamental spirit of the artistic exploration of the isms. The experiments and discoveries of those early days of the twentieth century and the nonrealistic spirit of symbolism itself survive under a variety of formats such as ritual theatre, poetic theatre, holy theatre, theatre of cruelty, existentialist theatre,

art theatre, avant-garde theatre, theatre of the absurd, epic theatre, contemporary allegory, domestic realism, dance-theatre, and immersive theatre. These present-day groupings, unlike the early isms, are critic-defined rather than artist-defined. Most theatre artists today reject any "grouping" nomenclature whatsoever. However difficult it may be to pin down their specific characteristics, though, the thriving and diverse artists that continue to move beyond realism can all trace their origins back to the drive in the late nineteenth century to rebel against convention, challenge traditional theatrical representation, and expand the potential of theatrical language. That expansion has come in a variety of contemporary antirealistic stylizations, as we'll discuss in the next section.

Stylized Theatre

Although endlessly diverse, antirealist theatre artists all insist on transforming reality into a larger-than-life theatrical experience. We can thus refer to the entire spectrum of antirealist theatre as *stylized*. Of course, theatre of all eras have had distinctive styles, but those in earlier times were largely imposed by then-current conventions while more recent dramatists have consciously selected and created styles to satisfy their aesthetic theories, their social principles, or simply their desire for novelty and innovation.

The techniques of the modern theatre come from anywhere and everywhere: from the past, from distant cultures, and from present and futuristic technologies. As the inheritors of antirealist modernism, present-day theatre artists have unprecedented sources to draw upon and are generally unconstrained by political, religious, or artistic traditions. Almost anything can now be put on a stage, and in the twenty-first century it seems that almost everything is.

In the stylized theatre, characters usually represent more than individual persons or personality types. Like medieval allegories, modern stylized plays often involve figures who represent forces of nature, moral positions, human instincts, and the like—entities such as death, fate, idealism, the life force, the earth mother, the tyrant father, or the prodigal son. The conflicts associated with these forces, unlike the conflicts of realism, do not reflect human behavior. More often than not, they represent permanent discords in the human condition. The stylized theatre resonates with tension and frustration in the face of irreconcilable demands.

But that is not to say the many stylized forms of antirealist theatre are inevitably grim. On the contrary, they often use whimsy and wit. To help us understand the diversity of stylized theatre that results from modernism, we will examine brief examples from plays written over the past hundred-plus years.

SURREALISM AND THE AVANT-GARDE: *UBU ROI*

The opening of Alfred Jarry's *Ubu Roi* (King Ubu) at the Théâtre de l'Oeuvre in Paris on December 10, 1896, was perhaps the most violent dramatic premiere in theatre history. The audience shouted, whistled, hooted, cheered, threw things, and shook their fists at the stage. Duels even broke out after subsequent performances. The *avant-garde* was born.

The term "avant-garde" comes from the military, where it refers to the advance battalion, or the "shock troops" that initiate a major assault. In France the term initially described the wave of French playwrights and directors who openly and boldly assaulted realism in the first four decades of the twentieth century. Today the term is used worldwide to describe any adventurous, experimental, and nontraditional artistic effort.

Alfred Jarry (1873–1907), a rebellious artist ("eccentric to the point of mania and lucid to the point of hallucination," says critic Roger Shattuck), unleashed his radical shock troops from the moment the curtain rose. Jarry had called for an outrageously antirealistic stage—painted scenery depicting a bed with a bare tree at its foot, palm trees with a coiled boa constrictor around one of them, a gallows with a hanging skeleton, and falling snow. Costumes, in Jarry's words, were "divorced as far as possible from [realistic] color or chronology." Characters entered through a painted fireplace, and the title character stepped forward to begin the play with a semi-vulgar word that quickly became immortal: "Merdre!" or "Shrit!"

Vulgar epithets, common enough in the works of Aristophanes and Shakespeare, had been pruned from the theatre in the Royal era and abolished entirely in the lofty spirit of romanticism; far from trying to sneak them back in, Jarry simply threw them up in the face of the astonished audience. The added *r* in "merdre" (or, in translation, the added *r* in "shrit"), far from "cleansing" the offending obscenity, only called more attention to it and to its deliberate intrusion onto the Parisian stage.

Ubu Roi was, in fact, quite literally a schoolboy play; Jarry wrote the first version at the age of fifteen as a lampoon of his high school physics teacher. Jarry was only twenty-three years old when the play astounded its Parisian audiences, and the juvenile aspects of the play's origins were evident throughout the finished product, which proved to be Jarry's sole complete play. In this savage and often ludicrous satire on the theme of power in which

Father (later King) Ubu—an overweight, foul-mouthed, venal, amoral, and pompous Polish assassin—Jarry had written one of the stage's greatest creations. The play's thirty-three scenes are often just crude skits barely linked by plot, but the interplay of farce and violence is inspired, as in the famous dinner scene:

FATHER UBU, MOTHER UBU, CAPTAIN BORDURE and their followers enter the dining room.

CAPTAIN BORDURE: Hey, Mother Ubu! What delicacies have you for us today?

MOTHER UBU: Here's the menu: Polish soup, rat chops, veal, chicken, dachshund pâté, turkey butt, charlotte russe . . .

FATHER UBU: Hey, that's enough!

MOTHER UBU: No, there's more! Iced cannonball, fruit salad, boiled artichokes, cauliflower à la shrit.

FATHER UBU: Hey, what do you think I am, the Emperor of Japan?

MOTHER UBU: (*to the others*) Don't listen to him; he's an imbecile!

FATHER UBU: Hah! I'll sharpen my teeth on your ankles!

MOTHER UBU: Eat this instead, Father Ubu. Good Polish soup!

FATHER UBU: (*sips a mouthful and spits it out*) Crap! That's terrible.

CAPTAIN BORDURE: Pretty awful, no?

MOTHER UBU: What's wrong with it, you pigs?

FATHER UBU: (*striking his forehead*) I know what to do! Back in a minute! (*He leaves.*)

MOTHER UBU: Gentlemen, it's veal time!

CAPTAIN BORDURE: It looks OK, but I'm all done!

MOTHER UBU: Turkey butt, then!

CAPTAIN BORDURE: Now that's terrific! Exquisite! Long live Mother Ubu. (*He leads the others in a cheer.*)

EVERYONE: Long live Mother Ubu!!!

FATHER UBU: (*returning furiously, waving a toilet brush in his hand*): You'll soon be crying, "Long live Father Ubu!" (*He throws the toilet brush onto the meat platter and stirs the food with it.*)

MOTHER UBU: You horrible man! What are you doing?

FATHER UBU: Go on! Taste it! (*Everyone takes a bite and falls down, poisoned.*) OK, Mother Ubu, gimme those rat chops, so I can hand 'em out.

MOTHER UBU: (*handing them over*) Here you go.

FATHER UBU: Captain Bordure, I need to talk to you. The rest of you, head for the door!

THE OTHERS: But we haven't finished our dinner!

FATHER UBU: You haven't? Why not? To the door! Not you, Bordure. (*No one moves.*) By my green candle, take your rat chops and get out of here! (*He starts throwing the rat chops and the rest of the food at them all.*)

French director Alain Timar directed and designed this adaptation of *Ubu Roi* at the Hungarian Theatre of Cluj (Romania) in 2011. The twelve actors wear identical cream-colored long underwear and alternate in the roles of Mother and Father Ubu while clothing themselves, and/or stuffing their costumes, with great sheaves of white paper torn from a giant roll at the rear of the stage. ©*István Bíró/Hungarian State Theatre of Cluj*

EVERYONE: Oh! Ouch! Help! Save us! I've been hit! I'm dying!

FATHER UBU: Shrit! Shrit! Shrit! Out the door! (to his wife) See? I did it!

EVERYONE: Save yourselves! That horrible Father Ubu! He's a traitor! A rascal! A rogue!

FATHER UBU: At last! They're gone. I can breathe again. But what a terrible dinner! Let's go, Bordure.

They leave with MOTHER UBU.

We are far from the rarefied style of romanticism—or, for that matter, the vaunted rationalism of the Royal era. Jarry's play creates a riotous sense of overturning social and artistic convention in real time; its enduring popularity testifies to its perpetual capacity to shock and excite.

EXPRESSIONISM: *MACHINAL*

Expressionism might be a familiar term to you because it is also used to describe a similar movement in the visual arts. In both painting and drama, expressionism focuses on externalizing and exaggerating ideas and internal states. In expressionist works, emotions become luridly on display, ideas take grotesque physical form, and interior struggles turn into exterior conflict. The theatrical form of expressionism that was much in vogue in Germany during the first decades of the twentieth century, particularly in the 1920s, boldly exaggerated its theatrical elements to reflect emotional, rather than objective, truths. These early works featured angular scenery, piercing sounds, glaring lights, and bold symbols; dramaturgically, German expressionist works linked together short scenes that built to a powerful climax.

In America, expressionist writers addressed the growing concern that the country's rapid industrial and financial successes were crushing human freedom—and human nature itself. During the 1920s, in the boldly expressionist dramas *Subway*, *The Adding Machine*, and *Street Scene*, Elmer Rice (1892–1967) angrily attacked what he considered the

The British actor Rebecca Hall (the daughter of the famed Shakespeare director Peter Hall) received critical raves for her performance as the "Young Woman" in this 2013 revival of Sophie Treadwell's expressionist masterpiece *Machinal*. Here, in a rare moment of human connection, she speaks with a young man with whom she is having an affair. ©*Sara Krulwich/The New York Times/Redux*

dehumanization of modern American life. And Eugene O'Neill, who had begun as a realistic playwright in the previous decades, wrote a play in 1921, *The Hairy Ape,* that became a landmark of expressionist theatre.

The American playwright and journalist Sophie Treadwell (1885–1970) found in expressionism a powerful medium for calling attention to the oppression of women. Her 1928 masterpiece *Machinal*—originally titled *The Life Machine*—presents episodes from the life of a young woman (whose name, we learn, is Helen, though the play, like the society around her, refers to her only as "Young Woman") as she works in a lifeless office, marries her boss, is abandoned by her young lover, has a child, and finally—in an act based on a real-life case—murders her husband in a bloody act of attempted liberation. These acts are portrayed like modern-day stations of the cross, except that instead of salvation, Helen finds only condemnation and cruelty.

In this early scene, Treadwell brilliantly captures many expressionist elements, such as the machine-like quality of the woman's surroundings and—in the contrast of exaggerated and repetitive dialogue with Helen's more singular voice—a mingling of the naturalistic with the artificial. In a drab "office scene" with "the sound of machines" ringing in the air and the back-and-forth dialogue of the secretary pool echoing their machines' clatter, the young woman enters, belatedly.

Enter YOUNG WOMAN. Goes behind telephone booth to desk right.

STENOGRAPHER: You're late!

FILING CLERK: You're late.

ADDING CLERK: You're late.

STENOGRAPHER: And yesterday!

FILING CLERK: The day before.

ADDING CLERK: And the day before.

Elmer Rice's *The Adding Machine* (1923) is one of America's most important expressionist plays, showing the dehumanization of employees trapped in a corporate accounting department. Anne Bogart directed this rambunctious version for the 1995 Classics in Context festival at Actors Theatre of Louisville. *©Richard C. Trigg/Actors Theatre of Louisville*

STENOGRAPHER: You'll lose your job!

YOUNG WOMAN: No!

STENOGRAPHER: No?

The workers exchange glances.

YOUNG WOMAN: I can't!

STENOGRAPHER: Can't?

Same business.

FILING CLERK: Rent—bills—installments—miscellaneous.

ADDING CLERK: A dollar ten—ninety-five—3.40—35—12.60.

STENOGRAPHER: Then why are you late?

YOUNG WOMAN: Why?

STENOGRAPHER: Excuse!

FILING CLERK: Excuse.

TELEPHONE GIRL: Excuse it, please.

STENOGRAPHER: Why?

YOUNG WOMAN: The subway?

TELEPHONE GIRL: Long distance?

FILING CLERK: Old stuff!

ADDING CLERK: That stall!

STENOGRAPHER: Stall?

YOUNG WOMAN: No—

STENOGRAPHER: What?

YOUNG WOMAN: I had to get out!

The nonrealistic dialogue of the scene relies on the dulling repetition of the same clichés and phrases, yet Helen's words ring out, forcing the other workers to pause—like a machine breaking, temporarily—before resuming their judgment and ceaseless patter. The play was a smash hit on Broadway when it premiered, featuring a young Clark Gable, and has proven to be a perennial favorite in professional theatre, including a revival at London's Almeida Theatre in 2018.

METATHEATRE: *SIX CHARACTERS IN SEARCH OF AN AUTHOR*

First produced in 1921, *Six Characters in Search of an Author* expresses from its famous title onward a *metatheatrical* motif by which the theatre itself becomes part of the content, not merely the vehicle, of the play's production. Shakespeare may have announced, "All the world's a stage," but in this play Luigi Pirandello (1867–1936) explores how the stage is also a world—and how the stage and the world, illusion and reality, relate to and often blur with each other. In this still-stunning work, a family of dramatic "characters"—a father, his stepdaughter, a mother, and her children—appear as if by magic on the "stage" of a provincial theatre where a "new play" by

A director attempts to direct a family that wishes to rewrite his play's script in this French production of Luigi Pirandello's *Six Characters in Search of an Author*, as staged by the Théâtre de la Ville at Moscow's Pushkin Drama Theatre in 2017. ©*Artyom Geodakyan/TASS/Getty Images*

Pirandello is being rehearsed. The "characters," claiming they have an unfinished play in them, beg the director to stage their lives so they may bring a satisfactory climax to their "drama." The audiences—the one onstage and the actual audience watching Pirandello's play—must keep shifting their perceptions. Which is the real play and which is real life? There are actors playing actors, actors playing "characters," and actors playing "actors-playing-characters"; there are also scenes when the actors playing "characters" are making fun of the actors playing "actors-playing-characters." It is no wonder most audiences give up trying to untangle the planes of reality Pirandello creates in this play; they are simply too difficult to comprehend except as a dazzle of suggestive theatricality.

Pirandello contrasts the passionate story of the "characters"—whose drama concerns a broken family, adultery, and the suggestion of incest—with the artifice of the stage and its simulations. In the course of this exposition Pirandello's performers discuss the theatricality of life, the life of theatricality, and the eternal confusions between appearance and reality:

THE FATHER: What I'm inviting you to do is to quit this foolish playing at art—this acting and pretending—and seriously answer my question: WHO ARE YOU?

THE DIRECTOR: (*amazed but irritated, to his actors*) What extraordinary impudence! This so-called character wants to know who I am?

THE FATHER: (*with calm dignity*) Signore, a character may always ask a "man" who he is. For a character has a true life, defined by his characteristics—he is always, at the least, a "somebody." But a man—now, don't take this personally—a man is generalized beyond identity—he's a nobody!

THE DIRECTOR: Ah, but me, me—I am the Director! The Producer! You understand?

THE FATHER: Signore—think of how you used to feel about yourself, long ago, all the illusions you used to have about the world, and about your place in it: those illusions were real for you then, they were *quite real*—but now, with hindsight, they prove to be nothing, they are nothing to you now but an embarrassment. Well, signore, that is what your present reality is today—just a set of illusions that you will discard tomorrow. Can't you feel it? I'm not speaking of the planks of this stage we stand on, I'm speaking of the very earth under our feet. It's sinking under you—by tomorrow, today's entire reality will have become just one more illusion. You see?

THE DIRECTOR: (*confused but amazed*) Well? So what? What does all that prove?

THE FATHER: Ah, nothing, signore. Only to show that if, beyond our illusions (*indicating the other characters*), we have no ultimate reality, so your reality as well—your reality that touches and feels and breathes today—will be unmasked tomorrow as nothing but yesterday's illusion!

These lines illustrate Pirandello's use of paradox, irony, and the theatre as metaphors to create a multilayered drama about human identity and human destiny. By contrasting the passion of his "characters" with the frivolity of his "actors," Pirandello establishes a provocative juxtaposition of human behavior and its theatricalization—all within a theatrical format.

POSTMODERN FARCE: *CLOUD NINE*

The title page of a printed copy of *Cloud Nine* will surely say it is by Caryl Churchill, but the work actually emerged from improvisations with the Joint Stock Theatre Company in the late 1970s. It is thus a devised work of theatre that emerged from a group vision, and this collective philosophy is reflected in the play's unique dramaturgy. The first act presents a melodramatic, satirical, and at times shockingly explicit comedy of manners in a Victorian-era British African colony. What seems to be an idyllic, Platonic family is in fact an artificial front that disguises repressed sexual desires. The second act takes place in contemporary (1970s) London, with the same characters—except they have aged only twenty-five years, rather than over one hundred.

This chronological confusion is underlined by Churchill's bold decision to have many of the characters in the first act played by actors of the opposite gender. So while Clive, the colonial father-figure, is played by a man, his son is played by a woman, his wife by a man, and so on. Furthermore, his African slave, Joshua, is portrayed by a white man, and his daughter is played by a ventriloquist's dummy. In the second act, actors play characters that match their identities—except for the actor playing Clive, who now portrays a baby.

Confused? Anyone would be; that, it seems, is part of the play's point. In true postmodern style, identity is shown to be a collection of masks and performances rather than a stable essence—no one really is who they pretend to be, and that includes the actors! Furthermore, Churchill draws on the tradition of metatheatre in pointing out how theatrical acting is not that different from the everyday acts we put on in asserting that we have a "self." However, for the play to work, it must play briskly, like a traditional *farce*—a vigorous and physical comedic genre popularized by playwrights such as the British Alan Ayckbourn and the American Neil Simon.

These many elements are on display in the following scene, from the end of the frenetic first act, which finds the patriarchal Clive attempting to comfort his friend Harry—who has, unbeknownst to Clive, been struggling with repressed same-sex desires—only to find his gestures misinterpreted:

CLIVE: There is something dark about women, that threatens what is best in us. Between men that light burns brightly.

HARRY: I didn't know you felt like that.

CLIVE: Women are irrational, demanding, inconsistent, treacherous, lustful, and they smell different from us.

HARRY: Clive—

CLIVE: Think of the comradeship of men, Harry, sharing adventures, sharing danger, risking their lives together.

(*HARRY takes hold of CLIVE.*)

CLIVE: What are you doing?

HARRY: Well, you said—

CLIVE: I said what?

HARRY: Between men. (*CLIVE is speechless.*) I'm sorry, I misunderstood, I would never have dreamt, I thought—

CLIVE: My God, Harry, how disgusting.

HARRY: You will not betray my confidence.

CLIVE: I feel contaminated.

HARRY: I struggle against it. You cannot imagine the shame. I have tried everything to save myself.

CLIVE: The most revolting perversion. Rome fell, Harry, and this sin can destroy an empire.

HARRY: It is not a sin, it is a disease.

CLIVE: A disease more dangerous than diphtheria. Effeminacy is contagious. How I have been deceived. Your face does not look degenerate. Oh Harry, how did you sink to this?

HARRY: Clive, help me, what am I to do?

CLIVE: You have been away from England too long.

HARRY: Where can I go except into the jungle to hide?

CLIVE: You don't do it with the natives, Harry? My God, what a betrayal of the queen.

The dialogue ends with Clive advising Harry to marry a woman, to which Harry responds, "I suppose

Caryl Churchill's gender- and genre-bending 1979 farce *Cloud Nine* still has the power to shock and delight: pictured here is the 2015 Atlantic Theatre Company production directed by James MacDonald, where the stereotypically ideal Victorian family at the heart of the play's first act has some characters played by actors of opposite genders (and in the case of the baby, by a doll). ©*Doug Hamilton*

getting married wouldn't be any worse than killing myself." Here Churchill satirizes the stereotype of the "stiff upper lip" British explorer while asking bold questions about identity and sexuality, particularly the expectations of proper gender behavior. All the while she builds a careful thesis about how masculinity can turn toxic in its relation to perceived femininity and nonwhite identity. (After all, according to Clive, Harry's "betrayal" in having sex with native men is not against the natives but against the queen!) *Cloud Nine* was the play that placed Churchill on the world stage; she would go on to produce several other critically acclaimed works ranging in genre but always showing a modernist's commitment to surprise and disturb us, even when we laugh.

THEATRE OF CRUELTY: *JET OF BLOOD*

Antonin Artaud (1896–1948) was one of drama's greatest revolutionaries, although his importance lies more in his ideas and influence than in his actual theatrical achievements. A stage and film actor in Paris during the 1920s, he founded the Théâtre Alfred Jarry in 1926 and produced, among other works, Strindberg's surrealist *A Dream Play* and, in 1935, an adaptation of Shelley's dramatic poem *The Cenci*. His essays, profoundly influential in the theatre today, were collected and published in 1938 in a hugely influential book titled *The Theatre and Its Double.*

The theatre Artaud envisioned was a self-declared theatre of cruelty, for, in his words, "Without an element of cruelty at the root of every performance, the theatre is not possible." This cruelty does not necessarily mean *bodily* cruelty, though it often had elements of violence. Instead, Artaud proposed a cruelty against forms—representations, stand-ins, and fakery. The "cruel" theatre would flourish, Artaud predicted, by providing the spectator with the *true* sources of theatre's visions by creating an absolute sense of presence without pretense.

If this sounds impossible, it is. Artaud's legacy is not as a pragmatic innovator but as an inspirer. His vivid prose captivated entire generations of theatre artists. In a famous metaphor, Artaud compared the theatre to the great medieval plague, noting that both plague and theatre had the capacity to liberate human possibilities and illuminate human potential:

> If the essential theatre is like the plague, it is not because it is contagious, but because like the plague it is the revelation, the bringing forth, the exteriorization of a depth of latent cruelty by means of which all the perverse possibilities of the mind, whether of an individual or a people, are localized.

Artaud's ideas were radical, and his essays were incendiary; his power to shock and inspire is undiminished today, and many influential twentieth-century theatre artists can claim an Artaudian heritage. But, perhaps not surprisingly, Artaud's own productions were failures; he was formally "expelled" from the surrealist movement, and he spent most of his later life abroad in mental institutions. His one published play, *Jet of Blood* (1925), illustrates both the radically antirealistic nature of his dramaturgy and the difficulties that would be encountered in its production. This is the opening of the play:

THE YOUNG MAN: I love you and everything is beautiful.

THE YOUNG GIRL: (*with a strong tremolo*) You love me and everything is beautiful.

THE YOUNG MAN: (*in an even lower voice*) I love you and everything is beautiful.

THE YOUNG GIRL: (in an even lower voice than his) You love me and everything is beautiful.

THE YOUNG MAN: (*leaving her brusquely*) I love you.

(*A silence.*) Look me in the face.

THE YOUNG GIRL: (*playing the game, she faces him*) There!

THE YOUNG MAN: (*in a sharp, exalted voice*) I love you, I am great, I am articulate, I am complete, I am strong.

THE YOUNG GIRL: (*in the same sharp voice*) We love each other.

THE YOUNG MAN: Intensely! Ah, how well-created is this world.

SILENCE. *We hear what seems to be an immense windmill blowing air: it soon becomes a hurricane. Two stars collide. A mass of legs falls from the sky. along with feet, hands, hair, masks, columns, porticos, temples, followed by three scorpions and a frog and a beetle that come down slowly and vomit. Enter a knight from the Middle Ages . . . followed by a nurse holding her breasts in both hands. . . .*

Artaud's apocalyptic vision has stimulated many subsequent theatre artists, including Jean-Louis Barrault and Roger Blin in France, Peter Brook in England, Jerzy Grotowski in Poland, and Judith Malina in America; his influence can also be seen in the plays of Sarah Kane and even popular music—Jim Morrison, of the 1960s psychedelic band The Doors, was a big fan. Artaud's notion of a theatre of cruelty, though not fully realized onstage in his lifetime, has been more closely approached by each of these artists and may still be achieved.

THEATRE OF THE ABSURD: *WAITING FOR GODOT*

The term *theatre of the absurd*, coined by English critic Martin Esslin in his 1962 book of that name, applies to a grouping of plays that share certain common structures and styles and are tied together by the theory of *absurdism* as formulated by French essayist and playwright Albert Camus (1913–1960). Camus likened the human condition to that of the mythological King Sisyphus, who was condemned eternally in the afterlife to roll a boulder up a hill—only to have it roll back down upon nearing the top. Camus saw the modern individual as similarly engaged in an eternally futile task: the absurdity of searching for some meaning or purpose or order in human life. To Camus, the inescapable irrationality of the universe is what makes this task absurd. For an absurdist, the fundamental question of humanity is not the traditional "what is the meaning of life?" but instead, in facing the fact of life's meaninglessness, the far bleaker "is life worth living?"

The plays that constitute the theatre of the absurd are obsessed with the futility of all action and the pointlessness of all direction. These themes are developed theatrically through a deliberate and self-conscious flaunting of a sense of the ridiculous. Going beyond the use of symbols and the fantasy and poetry of other antirealists, the absurdists distinguish themselves by fully embodying the meaninglessness of life without explaining it. In the theatre of the absurd, characters are helplessly trapped without any clear awareness—and so, too, is the audience.

The theatre of the absurd includes mid-twentieth-century works by Jean Genet (French), Eugène Ionesco (Romanian), Friedrich Dürrenmatt (Swiss), Harold Pinter (English), Gertrude Stein (American), and Fernando Arrabal (Spanish); contemporary inheritors include Suzan-Lori Parks (American) and María Irene Fornés (Cuban-born American).

The towering figure of absurdist theatre is, however, the Irish poet, playwright, and novelist Samuel Beckett. Beckett (1906–1989), the unquestioned leader of the absurdist writers, eschewed all realism, romanticism, and rationalism to create relentlessly unenlightening works that are indeed committed to a final obscurity. "Art has nothing to do with clarity, does not dabble in the clear, and does not make clear," argued Beckett in one of his earliest works. His theatre was based on the thesis that humans are and will remain ignorant regarding all matters of importance.

Beckett's play *Waiting for Godot* first brought him worldwide attention. *Godot* is a parable without a message. On a small mound at the base of a tree, beside a country road, two elderly men in bowler hats—"Gogo" and "Didi"—wait for a "Mr. Godot," with whom they have presumably made an appointment. They believe that when Godot comes they will be "saved"; however, they are not at all certain Godot has agreed to meet with them or if this is the right place or the right day or whether they will even recognize him if he comes. During each of the two acts, which seem to be set in late afternoon on two successive days (although nobody can be sure of that), the men are visited by passersby—first by two men, a master (Pozzo) and his slave (Lucky), and subsequently by a young, unnamed boy who tells them that Mr. Godot "cannot come today but surely tomorrow." Gogo and Didi continue to wait as the curtain falls.

What Beckett has drawn here is clearly an absurdist model of the human condition: an ongoing life cycle of vegetation serving as the background to human decay,

Shown here from left to right are the celebrated British actors Ian McKellen (left) as Estragon and Patrick Stewart (right) as Vladimir, raucously dancing in the 2013 Broadway production of *Waiting for Godot*.
©Sara Krulwich/The New York Times/Redux

hope, and ignorance. But Beckett's tone is whimsical, not bleak. Gogo and Didi play enchanting word games with each other; they amuse each other with songs, accounts of dreams, exercises, and vaudevillian antics; and in general they make the best of a basically hopeless situation. Here, in one exchange, the two tramps demonstrate Beckett's impeccable ability to balance comedy and despair:

VLADIMIR: You're a hard man to get on with, Gogo.

ESTRAGON: It'd be better if we parted.

VLADIMIR: You always say that and you always come crawling back.

ESTRAGON: The best thing would be to kill me, like the other.

VLADIMIR: What other? (*pause*) What other?

ESTRAGON: Like billions of others.

VLADIMIR: (*sententious*) To every man his little cross. (*He sighs.*) Till he dies. (*Afterthought.*) And is forgotten.

ESTRAGON: In the meantime let us try and converse calmly, since we are incapable of keeping silent.

VLADIMIR: You're right, we're inexhaustible.

ESTRAGON: It's so we won't think.

VLADIMIR: It's so we won't hear.

ESTRAGON: We have our reasons.

VLADIMIR: All the dead voices.

The rhythm of these lines recalls the back-and-forth of trained clowns or comedians, and yet the topics they touch on, such as death, sacrifice, and the fear of silence, are anything but light. We in the audience may laugh, but we may also feel compelled, or even disturbed, by the hints of darkness. Such is Beckett's enduring genius: a mixture of the profound and comic that serves as a perfect epitome of the absurd condition.

CONTEMPORARY ALLEGORY: *DUTCHMAN*

Amiri Baraka's *Dutchman* (1964) is in some ways a small play; it clocks in, typically, at under an hour. Yet its impact is still being felt. With stunning economy, Baraka (1934–2014) presents a scene familiar to anyone even dimly aware of Western religion: a seductive woman entrances a man in a quiet, secluded space; she offers him an apple, begging him to bite. But the Eve-like woman is white and the Adam, here, is black; the time is the late 1960s, and instead of a garden, they meet in a subway car that hurtles through subterranean Manhattan—or, as Baraka puts it in the stage directions: "*In the flying underbelly of the city.*"

The setting is at the same time realistic (the man reads a newspaper, wears a suit) and allegorical, almost mythical: the subway car is desolate, deep in the "underbelly"—perhaps even the subconscious—of the city. Baraka's Garden of Eden is decidedly not a story of redemption, either: Lula, the Eve figure, tempts Clay (his name hinting at the clay with which God sculpted humankind) with increasingly uncomfortable racial taunts, provoking the mild-mannered man to finally burst out with pent-up furor. Lula finally stabs him in an act of ritualistic murder, with other passengers appearing to take up Clay's body and carry him out. The play ends with Lula perching next to a new victim.

Along with his plays, Baraka has also published controversial (and at times deeply offensive) poetry, along with passionate essays on art. His involvement with many mid-century avant-garde groups, most notably the Black Arts Movement, put him in contact with many other artists across diverse media. And while we can trace many European modernist traditions that Baraka engaged with—the theatre of cruelty, expressionism, metatheatre—his idiom was distinctly American. Witness the following passage of *Dutchman*, where we find rhythms of everyday urban life interspersed with mythical incantation:

CLAY: You act like you're on television already.

LULA: That's because I'm an actress.

CLAY: I thought so.

LULA: Well, you're wrong. I'm no actress. I told you I always lie. I'm nothing, honey, and don't you ever forget it. (*Lighter*) Although my mother was a Communist. The only person in my family ever to amount to anything.

CLAY: My mother was a Republican.

LULA: And your father voted for the man rather than the party.

CLAY: Right!

LULA: Yea for him. Yea, yea for him.

CLAY: Yea!

LULA: And yea for both your parents who even though they differ about so crucial a matter as the body politic still forged a union of love and sacrifice that was destined to flower at the birth of the noble Clay . . . what's your middle name?

CLAY: Clay.

LULA: A union of love and sacrifice that was destined to flower at the birth of the noble Clay Clay Williams. Yea! And most of all yea yea for you, Clay Clay. The Black Baudelaire! Yes! (*And with knifelike cynicism*) My Christ. My Christ.

CLAY: Thank you, ma'am.

LULA: May the people accept you as a ghost of the future. And love you, that you might not kill them when you can.

At the climax of Amriri Baraka's furious 1964 one-act play *Dutchman,* the seductive Lula stabs Clay—a symbol of the era's simmering racism boiling over into violence. The play continues to find resonance; pictured here is a 2014 revival by the National Black Theatre and the Classical Theatre of Harlem. Lula is played by Ambien Mitchell and Clay by Sharif Atkins. *©Christine Jean Chambers*

CLAY: What?

LULA: You're a murderer, Clay, and you know it. (*Her voice darkening with significance.*) You know goddam well what I mean.

Some of these lines sound like the kind of awkward, slightly flirtatious discussion two people might have on the subway, filled with earnest banalities ("your father voted for the man rather than the party") and Clay's cautiously polite interjections ("Yes, ma'am"). But Lula's increasingly dark and complex language creates an undercurrent of unease. Especially ominous is her pronouncement that Clay is a "ghost of the future" who might kill "the people" if they don't love him—as if she has sensed reserves of violence and rage that even Clay can't sense. With both its resolutely symbolic language and attention to the realistic textures of speech, Baraka's play creates a vital allegory of his time—and, perhaps, ours as well.

THEATRE OF ALIENATION: *THE GOOD PERSON OF SZECHUAN*

Contrasting vividly with the theatre of the absurd is the theatre of alienation (a term based on the German word *Verfremdung*, or "distancing"). As the name suggests, the theatre of alienation seeks to distance, rather than engage, its audience through effects that call attention to its artifice. Whereas the self-contained plays of absurdism highlight the essential futility of human endeavors, the sprawling, socially engaged "epic" theatre of alienation concentrates on humanity's potential for growth and society's capacity to effect change. The guiding genius of the theatre of alienation was Bertolt Brecht (1898–1956), a theorist, dramatist, and director whose impact on modern theatre remains overwhelming. Brecht brought to the theatre practices that openly defied many of the principles in use since the days of Aristotle, and in so doing he

Many of Bertolt Brecht's "distancing" theatrical techniques—an onstage band, bright colors, actors looking and singing directly to the audience, obviously fake scenery—were exemplified by the 2013 Foundry Theatre production of *The Good Person of Szechwan*. Shen Te (in red) is a woman who, during the play, fools her enemies by pretending to be Shen Te's brother, Shui Ta, and punishing them. The celebrated drag performer Taylor Mac, the actor playing Shen Te, takes the play's sexual fluidity to another level. ©*Richard Termine/The New York Times/Redux*

invigorated postwar theatre with an abrasive humanism that reawakened the audience's sense of social responsibility and awareness of the theatre's capacity to mold public issues and events.

Brecht, who was born in Germany, emerged from World War I a dedicated Marxist and pacifist. Using poems, songs, and eventually the theatre to promote his ideals following Germany's defeat, Brecht vividly portrayed his country during the Weimar Republic as caught in the grips of four powerful and malevolent forces: the military, capitalism, industrialization, and imperialism. For example, his *Rise and Fall of the City of Mahagonny*, an "epic opera" of 1930, proved an immensely popular blending of satire and propaganda, of music and expressionist theatricality, and of social idealism and lyric poetry. It was produced all over Germany and throughout most of Europe in the early 1930s as a depiction of a rapacious international capitalism evolving toward fascism.

Brecht's theatre draws on a potpourri of theatrical conventions, some derived from the ancients, some from Eastern drama—notably in collaboration with the famous Chinese opera artist Mei Lanfang—and some from the German expressionist movement in which Brecht himself played a part in his early years. In addition, he and his company, the Berliner Ensemble, developed many conventions of their own: lantern-slide projections with printed captions, speeches in which actors deliberately stepped out of character to comment on the action, and procedures aimed at demystifying theatrical techniques (for example, lowering the lights so the pipes and wires would be displayed). All of these innovations created the separation of the audience from involvement in the dramatic action.

His innovations extended to acting, as well. In Brecht's view, ideal actors wouldn't "become" their characters but would instead view them with critical objectivity. By looking dispassionately, actors could discover their characters' social functions and political commitments, rather than their inner emotional landscapes. In attempting to repudiate the "magic" of the theatre, Brecht demanded it be made to seem nothing more than a place for workers to present a meaningful parable of life, and he in no way wished to disguise the labor of the actors and stagehands. In every way possible, Brecht attempted to achieve audience distance, preventing his spectators from becoming swept up in an emotional wave of feelings: his goal was to keep the audience, like the actors, separated from the literal events the play depicted so they would be free to concentrate on the larger social and political issues the play generated and reflected.

Brecht's theories were to have a staggering impact on the modern theatre. He provided a new dramaturgy that encouraged playwrights, directors, and designers to tackle social issues directly rather than through contrived dramatic situations. Combining the technologies and styles of other media—the lecture hall, the slide show, the public meeting, the cinema, the cabaret, the rehearsal—Brecht fashioned a vastly expanded arena for his social arguments.

No play better illustrates Brecht's dramatic theory and method than *The Good Person of Szechuan* (1943). This play, set in western China, concerns a kindhearted prostitute, Shen Te, who is astounded to receive a gift of money from three itinerant gods. Elated by her good fortune, Shen Te uses the money to start a tobacco business. She is, however, quickly beset by petty officials seeking to impose local regulations, by self-proclaimed creditors demanding payment, and by a host of hangers-on who simply prey upon her good nature. At the point of financial ruin, Shen Te leaves her tobacco shop to enlist the aid of her male cousin Shui Ta, who strides imperiously into the tobacco shop and rousts the predators, making it safe for Shen Te to return. But the predators come back, and Shen Te again has to call on the tyrannical Shui Ta to save her. A simple story—but Brecht's stroke of genius is to make Shui Ta and Shen Te the same character: Shui Ta is simply Shen Te in disguise! The aim of the play is not to show there are kind-hearted people and successful people but that a person must choose to be one or the other. What kind of society is it, Brecht asks, that forces us to make this sort of choice? And, as audience members, what choices do we face every day about being good in our own societies—choices, perhaps, we may not have even realized are choices at all? At the end of the play, the actor playing Shen Te and Shui Ta addresses the audience:

> Ladies and gentlemen, don't feel let down
> We know this ending makes some people frown.
> We had in mind a sort of golden myth
> Then found the finish had been tampered with.
> Indeed it is a curious way of coping:
> To close the play, leaving the issue open.
> Especially since we live by your enjoyment.
> Frustrated audiences mean unemployment.
> [...] There's only one solution that we know:
> That you should now consider as you go
> What sort of measures you would recommend
> To help good people to a happy end.
> Ladies and gentlemen, in you we trust:
> There must be happy endings, must, must must!

Here, Brecht characteristically points out a conflict but does not presume to solve it. The problems Brecht's works address are to be solved not on the stage but in the world itself: the audience, not the fictional characters, must find the appropriate balance between morality and greed and between individualism and social responsibility. This vibrant call to action has resonated in politically-minded theatre ever since Brecht came onto the scene; artists all over the world, including American playwright Tony Kushner (who adapted Brecht's *Mother Courage and Her Children*) and the Brazilian innovator Augusto Boal (who created the Theatre of the Oppressed movement to combat oppression through "invisible" street theatre), credit Brecht as an influence.

Chapter

9

Musical Theatre

Musical theatre is a form of theatre that, as its name suggests, incorporates music in its dramatic construction. More than simply having music as ornamentation or incidental sound, however, musical theatre features music as a fundamental part of its production. The music is *needed* for the play to happen: characters sing and oftentimes dance, and live musicians accompany the dramatic action.

In the chapter "The Modern Theatre," we learned how antirealistic theatre rebelled against the realistic conventions of its forerunners. In a sense, musical theatre—the subject of this chapter—is, like those modernist rebels, antirealistic. People don't suddenly burst into song in the middle of daily life, nor do public crowds start dancing in perfectly coordinated unison (though we might wish they did!). But the musical theatre is, for the most part, far from rebellious. No riots have erupted at the premieres of musicals. The genre of musical theatre was created as its own unique style, rather than as a rejection of a previous one.

Most musical theatre came about in the twentieth and twenty-first centuries in the United States. Of course, other cultures have theatrical traditions that incorporate music into their productions, but in America, musical theatre is its own distinct genre, with its own conventions and history, in contrast to nonmusical or "straight" drama. Musical theatre is one of the top cultural exports of the United States, which makes it a popular genre all over the world. Hence our focus in this chapter will be on the American musical, rather than music and theatre more broadly.

The Role of Music in Theatre History

Drama has always been at least partly musical. As we saw in the chapter titled "What Is a Play?" Aristotle considered music to be the fifth component of tragedy (by which he meant all serious drama). Classic Greek tragedy had song and dance and was accompanied by the *aulos* (flute) and other instruments. Aeschylus, who directed his own plays, was particularly noted for his skill in choreographing the chorus's entrance. Most Renaissance and commedia dell'arte plays included songs and instrumental music, and twenty-five of Shakespeare's thirty-eight plays contain at least some singing (*The Tempest* alone has nine scripted songs). Moreover, evidence suggests that many of Shakespeare's comedies, as well as those of his contemporaries, ended with full-stage company dances.

In the seventeenth century, English dramatist Ben Jonson wrote musical *masques*—brief, spectacular pieces that featured lively movement and music—for the court of King James I, and in France, Molière wrote *comédie* ballets for King Louis XIV. Each of the five acts of Molière's *The Bourgeois Gentleman,* for example, ends with a fully orchestrated and choreographed mini-opera. The eighteenth-century European Age of Enlightenment, despite or because of its focus on rationality and reason, saw the rise of theatre works that focused on the marvelous and supernatural—oftentimes with music to match. And as mentioned earlier, virtually all major Asian dramatic forms involve singing, dancing, and instrumental music— sometimes continuously throughout the performance.

While spoken text predominates in modern Western drama, singing and dancing make frequent appearances there, too, especially in the antirealistic theatre. Most of the plays in Bertolt Brecht's theatre of alienation involve songs, most notably his collaborations with the composer Kurt Weill (*The Threepenny Opera, Happy End*, and *The Rise and Fall of the City of Mahagonny*), and brief songs are included in the texts of Samuel Beckett's absurdist dramas *Waiting for Godot* and *Happy Days*. (For more on the theatre of alienation and the theatre of the absurd, see the chapter "The Modern Theatre.")

How, then, is the genre of musical theatre different from these many examples of theatrical styles that incorporate music? First, the musical does not use music incidentally, like Greek dramas and Beckett's plays. In other words, the music is not simply there to fill the silences between scenes or to play underneath the spoken dialogue. It is essential to the play's production: if you took it away, the play would not make sense. On the other hand, musicals do not rely *entirely* on music, as operas do. Musicals have scenes of spoken dialogue interspersed with sung lyrics, whereas most operas have nearly every line sung. There are exceptions, though: some musicals, like *Les Misérables,* are "sung through" like operas: their characters sing every line. So what makes *Les Misérables* a musical and not an opera? Even though every line is sung, it is ultimately focused on words, whereas operas are ultimately focused on music. Opera audiences are moved by the tones and textures of the vocals and instrumentation, even if they do not understand the language that is sung. Whereas musicals, even sung-through ones, rely on communicating through words. The music is needed, but it is there to support the lyrics.

The musical, then, uses music more fundamentally than plays that incorporate music as mere decoration. On the other hand, musicals—even musicals that have music playing at every moment—are focused on communicating through words, in distinction to opera.

Musical theatre as a distinct genre, though, has gained popularity over the last century in the American theatre. Its creation was calculated—at first, anyway—to provoke audience merriment. The original incarnation of musical theatre absorbed elements of light opera, operetta, ballet, and, even more significantly, nineteenth-century entertainments such as England's music hall acts and America's minstrel and variety shows. Today's American musical theatre has become its own unique—and immensely popular—form that brings to the stage a sense of exciting entertainment with a truly global commercial appeal.

Nowhere is that commercial and entertainment success better known than in the Broadway district in New York, which remains the international capital of the world's musical theatre—although London, Toronto, and Sydney are currently hot competitors. Over the past two decades, as much as 80 percent of Broadway's box-office income has been derived from musical theatre alone. Several musicals (*Hamilton, Phantom of the Opera, Chicago, The Lion King, Mamma Mia*, and *Wicked* among them) seem all but permanently installed in the theatres where they play eight times a week. Overall, at the current time of writing, twenty-eight musicals grace Broadway stages, with many more performed off-Broadway and in America's regional, touring, and university theatres.

The American musical theatre, in particular, has also become a staple of major theatres abroad, including government-subsidized theatres such as the National Theatre, in England, which in the past three decades has become a major producer and re-interpreter of American musicals (*Follies, Guys and Dolls, Carousel, Oklahoma!,* and *Anything Goes,* to name a few). Up to a third of the main

Claude-Michel Schönberg and Alain Boublil's *Les Misérables* has proven to be one of the most durable Broadway musicals of all time, both adored and lampooned in equal measure. Here, the cast of a 2014 Broadway revival, directed by Cameron Mackintosh, sings a showstopper during that year's Tony Awards ceremony. ©*Sara Krulwich/The New York Times/Redux*

theatres in Berlin, Budapest, London, Tokyo, Seoul, Sydney, and Stockholm are at any given time hosting engagements of such world-popular American musicals as *Rent, Chicago, Jersey Boys, Miss Saigon, The Book of Mormon, The Lion King*, and *The Sound of Music*. (Occasionally musicals that flopped on Broadway find a second life overseas, as with *Tarzan,* which fizzled in New York but continues to be a hit in Germany.) Such musical theatre engagements can form the commercial backbone of an entire theatre community's offerings.

But commercial appeal is hardly the sum of the American musical theatre's international importance. Such theatre is a dramatic form of great variety, vitality, and—on many occasions—creative significance. The Pulitzer Prize has been awarded to nine American musicals to date (*Of Thee I Sing, South Pacific, Fiorello!, How to Succeed in Business Without Really Trying, A Chorus Line, Sunday in the Park with George, Rent, Next to Normal,* and *Hamilton*). Combining themes and ideas as old and

rarified as Greek tragedy with the rough-and-tumble energy of popular entertainment, musical theatre authors and artists have created both artistic innovations and social impact through brilliantly integrated disciplines of melody, cadence, choreography, and rhyme.

The Broadway Musical

What we now know as the Broadway musical has roots deep in the nineteenth century, beginning with singing and dancing shows known as *extravaganzas*, such as *The Seven Sisters*, marketed as a "Grand Operatic, Spectacular, Musical, Terpsichorean, Diabolical, Farcical Burletta" when it premiered in 1860 at the fabled Niblo's Garden in downtown Manhattan. Such lavish extravaganzas were soon joined by increasingly popular *vaudeville* entertainments (collections of musical and variety acts, originally performed in brothels and drinking parlors but increasingly more widely performed) and *burlesques* (broadly comedic parodies of serious musical works). All of these forms led to a rapidly growing profession of musical performers adept at singing, dancing, acting, and comedy.

Burlesque and vaudeville lasted well into the twentieth century. Florenz Ziegfeld became one of America's great showmen with his annual Ziegfeld Follies—a musical revue dedicated to "Glorifying the American Girl" that combined elements of burlesque and vaudeville. But the play that is now regarded as America's first true musical premiered in 1866: *The Black Crook* began as an ordinary melodrama until its producer, William Wheatley decided to add a French ballet company, which was stranded in the city, to give the show extra entertainment value. Wheatley also added original music, and the play evolved into something more than a set of unrelated scenes of dance, music, and acting. *The Black Crook* was not just a revue of individual sketches and songs but a unified musical entertainment.

The popularity of staged musical entertainments grew by leaps during the nineteenth and early twentieth centuries. Challenging the old custom of white actors performing in *blackface* (in which white actors portray a racist stereotype of a black person by darkening their faces with burnt-cork makeup) for minstrel shows, a new black musical comedy arose that employed the emerging ragtime musical styles of earlier black vaudeville reviews (that is, jaunty and precisely syncopated rhythms, primarily in piano compositions). Bob Cole's 1898 *A Trip to Coontown* (the title refers to the highly racist term "coon" as well as the tradition of "coon songs," in which a white performer in blackface parodied black musical traditions) was one of the most successful: a full-length black musical comedy written and performed by African Americans (some in whiteface), it played to large mixed-race audiences in New York. Though an unapologetic farce—with coarse ethnic humor, erotically charged dance numbers, and semi-operatic interludes—Cole's play included at least one song of direct social protest: "No Coons Allowed!" tells of a young man unable to bring his date to the "swellest place in town" because of the club's racist policy.

By the end of the nineteenth century, New York also proved a hospitable site for comic operatic works from abroad. The highly witty and still-popular satirical light operas of the English duo W. S. Gilbert and Arthur Sullivan (*H.M.S. Pinafore, The Mikado,* and *The Pirates of Penzance,* which even premiered in New York City), the *opéra bouffe* (satirical comic opera) of French composer Jacques Offenbach (*La Périchole, La belle Hélène,* and *Orpheus in the Underworld*), and the Viennese operetta of Franz Lehár (*The Merry Widow*) all demonstrated to New York theatregoers that theatre could employ music to tell

a story in a delightfully appealing way. Audiences flocked to these continental productions, while American writers and composers created homegrown products that could compete with these imports. Irish-born Victor Herbert, an *émigré* to the United States at twenty-seven, became America's first great composer for the stage. Herbert's major hits, *Babes in Toyland* (1903) and *Naughty Marietta* (1910), proved immensely successful. More composers joined in the action when Rhode Island–born vaudevillian George M. Cohan's *Little Johnny Jones* (1904), in which Cohan also starred, provided what became his—and some of America's—signature songs: "I'm a Yankee Doodle Dandy" and "Give My Regards to Broadway." By the first decade of the new century, American musical theatre was becoming the world leader in a newly defined theatrical form: musical comedy.

MUSICAL COMEDY

The first third of the twentieth century was the great age of musical comedy—a genre that emphasized comedy as well as singing but also portrayed youthful romance. It featured choruses of women, liberal doses of patriotic jingoism, and, in response to the "dance craze" of the early 1900s, spectacular dancing—including the new, flashy style known as "tap"—to a jazzy or ragtime beat.

By the 1920s and 1930s, American musical comedy had dozens of starring composers, lyricists, and performers. The loosely strung-together revues of the early century were slowly cohering into more thematically unified works. Tourists from all over the country flocked to midtown Manhattan to see such musical works as the brothers George (music) and Ira (lyrics) Gershwin's *Lady Be Good, Oh, Kay!, Funny Face,* and *Girl Crazy*; Vincent Youmans's sweetly romantic *Hit the Deck* and *No, No, Nanette* (which featured the song "Tea for Two"); Jerome Kern's bouncy *Very Good Eddie and Sunny*; Cole Porter's witty *Anything Goes* and *DuBarry Was a Lady*; and a series of especially droll and delightful musical comedies by Richard Rodgers (music) and Lorenz Hart (lyrics), including *A Connecticut Yankee, On Your Toes,* and *Babes in Arms*. These works shared some similar qualities: a simple plot, a cast composed of romantic and comedic characters, a wholly unchallenging theme, lots of revealing costumes, and abundantly cheerful singing and dancing that had little or no connection to the narrative. Although these works were often frivolous, the music transcended the flimsiness of the drama. Many Gershwin songs ("Embraceable You," "But Not for Me," and "Bidin' My Time"), along with those of Rodgers and Hart ("The Lady Is a Tramp," "Small Hotel," and "Bewitched, Bothered and

Bewildered"), have entered the American songbook, and the shows they come from have been regularly revived.

Meanwhile, in Harlem, Bert Williams and J. Leubrie Hill drew large mixed-race audiences for their *Darktown Follies* of 1914 (introducing the hit number "After the Ball"). And in 1921 a black musical dominated a full Broadway season for the first time: composer Eubie Blake and lyricist Noble Sissle's wildly successful *Shuffle Along* ran more than five hundred performances and introduced such songs as "In Honeysuckle Time" and "I'm Just Wild about Harry." This landmark musical followed black characters modeled after those in more traditionally white plays; rather than portray the horrific stereotypes that filled the stage elsewhere, *Shuffle Along* showed people of color embodying more realistic and three-dimensional characters.

Black musicals also featured more straightforward showcases for dance and musical talents, as well. Popular high-stepping, side-slapping "black-bottom" dancing was a feature of many black musicals of the 1920s, as was the Charleston, a generation-defining dance craze. Introduced in the 1923 black musical *How Come?* (composed by Maceo Pinkard), the Charleston started a national craze in the hit show *Runnin' Wild* (by James P. Johnson and Cecil Mack) later that year.

A GOLDEN AGE

By 1925 the American musical was beginning to dominate cultural life in the United States. That September, four great musicals opened on Broadway in four days: Youmans's *No, No, Nanette;* Rudolf Friml's *The Vagabond King;* Jerome Kern and Oscar Hammerstein II's *Sunny;* and Rodgers and Hart's *Dearest Enemy.* Each of these shows was wildly popular and went on to run for hundreds of performances and well into the following year. What is widely considered a "golden age of musicals" had begun.

The golden age ushered in a new genre—*musical drama*—characterized by increasingly serious *books* (the spoken texts) and sophisticated musical treatments. *Show Boat*, written by Jerome Kern (music) and Oscar Hammerstein II (book and lyrics) in 1927, was an early masterpiece of musical drama. It represents one of the great pieces of fully acted—and not just sung—vocal literature in the American theatre. Adapted from a gritty novel by Edna Ferber, the play has a complex plot that is carried by the music and dancing as well as by the work's spoken dialogue. The musical also touches significantly on race relations in America, as with the poignant song "Ol' Man River," in which a black dockworker laments the racism he faces with equal parts resilience and lamentation.

Meanwhile, the Gershwin brothers' *Strike Up the Band* and *Of Thee I Sing* moved them into the arena of political satire and proved so successful that the latter production received the 1932 Pulitzer Prize—the first musical to do so. The Gershwins followed with *Porgy and Bess* (1935), which remains a staple of both international opera companies and American theatres today and was revived to great acclaim on Broadway in 2012.

The second serious phase of the musical's golden age came into full flower with Rodgers and Hart's startling *Pal Joey* (1940), adapted from grimly ironic and sophisticated *New Yorker* stories by John O'Hara and featuring an amoral gigolo and his often unsavory companions in the contemporary urban nightclub scene. While certainly tame by today's standards, *Joey* shocked prewar audiences with its suggestive lyrics about sexual infidelity and shady business ethics and with a show-stopping song ("Zip!") belted out by an exotic dancer who sang out her thoughts while doing her act.

Many serious musicals followed. Marc Blitzstein's *The Cradle Will Rock* (1938), which concerns the struggle to organize a union of steelworkers in "Steel-town" against the opposition of Mr. Mister, the town's leading capitalist, was canceled an hour before its New York opening by U.S. government officials who objected to the play's "left-wing propaganda." The play was performed later that night at another theatre without scenery or costumes to tremendous enthusiasm—as memorialized in Tim Robbins's 1999 film *Cradle Will Rock.* And *Lady in the Dark* (1941)—with a book by dramatist Moss Hart, lyrics by Ira Gershwin, and music by Kurt Weill—concerns itself with psychology, dream analysis, and the perilous situation of a career woman, Liza Elliott, in a world dominated by old-fashioned ideas of marriage and women's roles. *Lady's* musical numbers all took place in the abstract space of Liza's dreams.

After the United States entered World War II in December 1941, seriously themed Broadway musicals became the norm for the commercial American theatre. *Oklahoma!* (1943), with music by Richard Rodgers and lyrics by Oscar Hammerstein II, addresses social and sexual tensions in the frontier of the western states. This important work marked a key historical moment in the genre's development: it was the first *integrated* musical theatre piece, which means that it was the first to advance its plot through its musical numbers. Music and dance were no longer superfluous—they were essential to the dramaturgy. Dispensing with accepted conventions, *Oklahoma!* ran for five years and featured balletic choreography by Agnes de Mille that treated its historical subject, which included an onstage killing and the quick

The Gershwins' Porgy and Bess is the revised title of this 2012 musical theatre version (by playwright Suzan-Lori Parks and director Diane Paulus) of George and Ira Gershwin's 1935 American opera, set in Charleston, South Carolina, in the 1930s. Audra McDonald, in red, is Bess, with her friends on Charleston's fictitious "Catfish Row." The production won the Best Revival of a Musical Tony Award for the year, and McDonald received the Tony for Best Performance by an Actress in a Leading Role in a Musical. ©Sara Krulwich/The New York Times/Redux

dispensing of frontier justice, with romantic passion and a new level of social intensity. Rodgers and Hammerstein followed *Oklahoma!* with one success after another, each balancing solemn subject matter with joyous celebration: *Carousel* (1945) deals with spousal abuse, *South Pacific* (1949) with racial prejudice, *The King and I* (1951) with gender discrimination and ethnocentricity, *Flower Drum Song* (1958) with the tensions associated with assimilation, and *The Sound of Music* (1959) with the rise of Nazism. These works all feature social and intercultural conflict, richly romantic settings and songs, beautiful solo numbers and love duets, and thrilling performance ensembles.

Additionally, Leonard Bernstein, one of America's leading orchestral conductors and composers, left a considerable mark on the musical's golden age with his *On the Town* (1945), about World War II sailors on leave in Manhattan, and *West Side Story* (1957, with lyrics by Stephen Sondheim), a powerfully emotional retelling of Shakespeare's *Romeo and Juliet* with a Polish American Romeo

and Puerto Rican American Juliet. And in 1964, Jerry Bock and Sheldon Harnick conveyed a profoundly moving version of Jewish shtetl life in tsarist Russia with *Fiddler on the Roof*.

Not all musicals were deeply sober and serious, of course. More lighthearted and satirical musicals of the 1940s and 1950s—first-rate works that still featured well-integrated plots, characters, themes, and musical styles—included Frank Loesser's *Guys and Dolls* (1950), based on the urban stories of Damon Runyon; Cole Porter's *Kiss Me Kate* (1948), based on a backstage romance during a tour of Shakespeare's *The Taming of the Shrew*; and Irving Berlin's *Annie Get Your Gun* (1946), based on the life of American folk heroine Annie Oakley. Richard Adler and Jerry Ross's *The Pajama Game* (1954), about union organizing in a pajama factory, and *Damn Yankees* (1955), a tale about baseball and the devil, both featured superlative jazz dancing choreographed by Bob Fosse. Alan Jay Lerner (book and lyrics) and Frederick Loewe (music) first successfully collaborated on the fantasy *Brigadoon* (1947), about a mythical Scottish village, and then followed with *My Fair Lady* (1956), a brilliant musical revision of George Bernard Shaw's play *Pygmalion* that wittily explores the heroine Eliza Doolittle's entrance into high British society.

The hits of Broadway's golden age were commercially successful beyond anything in theatre's previous history. Successful plays ran not for weeks or months, as before, but for years. They were, indeed, more than just plays; they were world-renowned cultural phenomena. For the first time, theatre tickets were sold as far as six months in advance, and travelers would trek hundreds of miles to Manhattan solely to catch a play, returning home to provide a full report on the latest musicals in town. Touring companies brought the best of these shows to the rest of the country: first-class national tours, with the actual Broadway stars, and, subsequently, "bus and truck" tours, with less-familiar performers filling in, traveled around the nation. It is likely that most Americans during these years first experienced live theatre in the form of a road version of a Broadway musical. Songs from the best musicals—and even from some mediocre ones—routinely made the radio "hit parade" (forerunner of the "top forty" listings of today) and gained an instant national audience. Film versions of many musicals—*Oklahoma!, Carousel, My Fair Lady, Guys and Dolls, The Sound of Music, West Side Story*—became widely popular. And the stars of Broadway golden-age musicals—Jimmy Durante, Eddie Cantor, Mary Martin, Ethel Merman, Julie Andrews, Carol Channing, Pearl Bailey, Bob Hope, and John Raitt—achieved national celebrity status; many became the pioneer performers on America's new entertainment medium, television. It is certain that the theatre had never played such a central role in American popular culture before.

The Contemporary Musical

While the golden age did not last forever, it irrevocably changed theatrical—and American—culture. Today, the bulk of musicals produced in America, on Broadway and the amateur stage alike, are revivals of the great musicals of mid-twentieth-century America. However, a new and more contemporary musical theater, at once less sentimental and more ironic, has recently come onto the scene.

THE EMERGENCE OF CHOREOGRAPHER-DIRECTORS

Since the 1960s, there has been a tremendous escalation in the importance of choreography in American musicals.

Agnes de Mille, as previously mentioned, was instrumental in initiating this movement with her plot-advancing dance numbers in Rodgers and Hammerstein's *Oklahoma!* However, later years saw the emergence of several choreographers who became more widely known than the directors they worked with—and who, indeed, became their productions' directors.

Jerome Robbins (1918–1998), trained in both ballet and acting, was the first of these. His "Small House of Uncle Thomas" ballet—a deliberately quaint, intimate version of the novel *Uncle Tom's Cabin* in *The King and I,* along with his vigorous teenage "street rumble" dances in 1957's *West Side Story*, earned him national critical fame. Robbins went on to combine directorial and choreographic chores in the seriocomic Broadway musicals *Gypsy* (1959), about the burlesque performer Gypsy Rose Lee and her mother, and in *Fiddler on the Roof*, about Jewish life in prerevolutionary Russia. In 1989 Robbins put together a retrospective collection of his dances in *Jerome Robbins' Broadway*, which won the Tony Award for best musical.

Gower Champion (1921–1980) and Bob Fosse (1927–1987) were of Robbins's generation but utterly unlike him, or each other. Champion, a veteran dancer (with his wife, Marge) in many Broadway shows and Hollywood films, returned to the stage in 1960 to both stage and choreograph the energetic, crowd-pleasing *Bye Bye Birdie* (1960). He followed this up with the romantic *Carnival* (1961) and the brashly entertaining *Hello, Dolly!* (1964). In each case, dance was at the center of the dramatic entertainment. Champion's final show—he tragically died on its opening night—was *42nd Street* (1980), a valentine to the Broadway theatre and particularly to tap dancing. The show enjoyed a long run after its opening and was brought back in a Tony Award–winning revival twenty years later. Fosse, also a golden-age choreographer (*The Pajama Game* and *Damn Yankees*, 1954 and 1955, respectively), went on to develop a highly distinctive style—quick, brisk motion that suddenly gives way to slow, sinuous gestures—in, particularly, *Chicago* (1975) and *Dancin'* (1978), as well as in the film of *Cabaret* (1972) and his own filmed autobiography, *All That Jazz* (1979). A posthumous retrospective of Fosse's dances, simply titled *Fosse*, opened on Broadway in 1999, ran for two years, and won the Tony Award for Best Musical.

Michael Bennett (1943–1987) was of a later generation, and his artistic goals were somewhat more conceptual: his masterwork was *A Chorus Line* (1975), a musical about musicals that Bennett conceived, staged, and choreographed. Taking place in a dance audition, and consisting largely of dances interspersed with "interviews" of the auditioning

The iconic "musical about musicals" is Michael Bennett's *A Chorus Line* (1975), which portrays New York musical performers auditioning for a show—in part created from true stories told to Bennett by such performers. This 2006 Broadway revival was directed by Bob Avian (the original production's choreographer); the costumes were designed by Theoni V. Aldredge, who also designed the original costumes. *©Paul Kolnik*

dancers, it was initially developed off-Broadway with a series of improvisations with selected performers, many of whom appeared in the Broadway production. *A Chorus Line* became, at the time, Broadway's longest-running show, lasting for fifteen years and 6,137 performances.

At the top of the twenty-first century, the choreographer-director Susan Stroman practically seized control of the Broadway musical stage, winning every award in sight for her extraordinary direction and choreography of the hit Broadway production of Mel Brooks's *The Producers*, which won a record-shattering twelve Tony Awards, two for Stroman herself. She then received Tonys for her choreography of the wordless, all-dance *Contact* (1999), which she also conceived, and for a remarkable Royal National Theatre revival of Rodgers and Hammerstein's *Oklahoma!*—all within a three-year period! What is remarkable about Stroman's choreography is its combination of humor, exuberance, inventiveness, and down-to-earth accessibility

across an enormously wide-ranging stylistic palette. The clever deployment of props is as close as Stroman comes to having a trademark: rustic mining implements in *Crazy for You* (1992), hurtling trays of dishes in the restaurant scene of *Contact*, eye-popping rope tricks in *Oklahoma!*, and a "Putting on the Ritz" chorus dressed in top hats, tails, and rugged combat boots in *Young Frankenstein* (2008). Yet Stroman resists such easy characterization: in *The Scottsboro Boys* (2010), about the 1931 arrest of nine African American teenagers for crimes they never committed and staged by the director-choreographer as a mock-minstrel show, Stroman displayed a profound sensitivity to cultural divisions in American culture of the early American century. While Stroman's subsequent Broadway productions—*Big Fish* (2012), *Bullets Over Broadway* (2014), and 2017's revue *Prince of Broadway*—each ran only for a few months, she remains a vital and influential presence.

STEPHEN SONDHEIM

While choreographers have exuded a powerful influence over musical theatre, no figure has had greater influence on the genre than the composer and lyricist Stephen Sondheim (born 1930), whose first important work was as lyricist for Leonard Bernstein's 1957 *West Side Story*. After one more assignment as a golden-age lyricist (for Jule Styne's *Gypsy*), Sondheim turned composer as well, winning high praise and success for both the lyrics and music to the songs in the highly original *A Funny Thing Happened on the Way to the Forum* (1962), drawn from the Roman comedies of Plautus.

In his work from 1970 onward, however, Sondheim departed from the standard formats of those early shows to develop a radically new style, marked by disturbing plots, an ironic and sometimes even cynical tone, skepticism about conventional morality, and highly sophisticated and intricate lyrics. Sondheim's first works in this period include *Company* (1970), a shrewd and incisive look at marriage and sex in contemporary Manhattan. While ironic and seemingly anti-romantic, however, Sondheim's tone remains amusing and surprisingly good-spirited. Somehow he has managed to leaven his gloomy message with buoyant music, penetrating observation, and fiendishly clever rhymes and rhythm breaks. *Company*'s song titles alone point to Sondheim's indelible combination of wistfulness and acidity: "Sorry-Grateful," "Marry Me a Little," "You Could Drive a Person Crazy."

Sondheim's subsequent musicals *Follies* (1971), set in Manhattan at an onstage reunion of able but aging musical theatre performers ("I'm Still Here" is the famous number from this show) and *A Little Night Music* (1973), adapted from an Ingmar Bergman film about summer dalliances on a country estate in Sweden, were widely heralded for their brilliantly acerbic but always entertaining portrayal of the eternal conflicts between social mores and romantic idealism (or, more bluntly, between laws and lust). Furthermore, particularly as all have been revived on Broadway twice since their premiere productions, they have established Sondheim's supremacy in the American musical form for the entire generation that followed.

Even after this initial burst of success, Sondheim continued to break new boundaries. His *Pacific Overtures* (1976) employs kabuki-inspired music and stage techniques to trace the history of relations between Japan and the United States since Commodore Perry's "opening" of Japan in 1853. His *Sweeney Todd* (1979) integrates Brechtian distancing techniques and elements from Italian grand opera, the English music hall, and Victorian melodrama in a wildly morbid story of a barber's revenge. *Sweeney*'s score is so powerful and its actions and images so compelling that the work has been staged by several European opera companies. Conversely, his *Sunday in the Park with George* (1984) is an elegant and minimal musical about the pointillist painter Georges Seurat; for this production, Sondheim invented an abstract style of music to echo Seurat's painting style. In 1986, Sondheim's *Into the Woods* offered a revision of the most traditional of forms, the fairy tale. In this retelling, however, familiar characters like Jack, Little Red Riding Hood, and Rapunzel suffer the same psychological crises and moral ambiguities as real people, long after their lives supposedly end "happily ever after." In fact, all of Sondheim's plays have received successful Broadway revivals in the twenty-first century. These days, Sondheim shows no sign of letting up or of compromising his ambition. Even in his late eighties, he is at work on a new musical, inspired by the films of the surrealist Mexican director Luis Buñuel.

Sondheim's most controversial works are *Assassins* (1991) and *Passion* (1994). The first is a musical review of presidential assassinations (and assassination attempts), which cascades through two centuries to portray the quirks, oddities, and motives of figures such as John Wilkes Booth, Lynette "Squeaky" Fromme, and John Hinckley Jr. *Passion*, a nineteenth-century gothic tragedy ("one long love song," Sondheim calls it) tells the strange story of Giorgio, a handsome Italian army officer who, though deeply in love with his beautiful mistress Clara, is relentlessly pursued by his superior's cousin Fosca, an ailing and obsessive woman. Giorgio yields to the intensity of Fosca's passionate fixation, much to Clara's despair. There being little for the Broadway audience to "root for" in this romantic tangle, *Passion* closed less than eight months after its Broadway premiere. Its innovations, however, are exhilarating, and the musical won the 1994 Tony Awards for Best Musical, Best Book of a Musical, and Best Original Score, while subsequent productions, including the nationally televised 2005 Lincoln Center concert version and a 2010 Donmar Warehouse London revival, have won great praise and new awards.

BLACK MUSICALS

More than a dozen major musicals by and about members of the African American community have found homes on the Broadway stage since the 1970s. As discussed earlier in this chapter, the history of race and the American musical is a complex one: white audiences enjoyed the copious entertainment produced by black artists even as rampant racism and segregation dominated American

For his 2005 Broadway revival of Stephen Sondheim's *Sweeney Todd*, the director John Doyle had his reduced cast of only ten actors play the orchestral instruments as well as perform the characters' roles. The innovation proved a great success, and the show was nominated for six Tony Awards, with Doyle winning one for Best Direction of a Musical.
©Paul Kolnik

society. As the wider American culture reckons with its own ugly past, however, black musicals deal more unflinchingly with the legacy of race relations—while also finding cause for celebration in distinctly black cultural figures and movements.

The last decades of the twentieth century featured Charlie Smalls's 1974 *The Wiz* (an adaptation of L. Frank Baum's novel *The Wonderful Wizard of Oz*); *Bubbling Brown Sugar* (1976) and *Eubie* (1978), both based on the music of ragtime composer-pianist Eubie Blake; *Ain't Misbehavin'* (1978) and *Sophisticated Ladies* (1981), which feature, respectively, the music of Fats Waller and Duke Ellington; *Jelly's Last Jam* (1992) about jazz pioneer Jelly Roll Morton; and *Bring in 'Da Noise, Bring in 'Da Funk* (1995), a furiously tap danced capsule history of racial injustice in America.

More recent black Broadway musicals like *Memphis*, *Fela!*, and *The Scottsboro Boys* celebrate—and often

Sahr Ngaujah plays the title role of Nigerian Afrobeat performer Fela Anikulapo Kuti in the 2009 Broadway musical *Fela!*, which depicts Fela's personal life as well as his musical genius. This production was directed and choreographed by Bill T. Jones, the coauthor of the book.
©Sara Krulwich/The New York Times/Redux

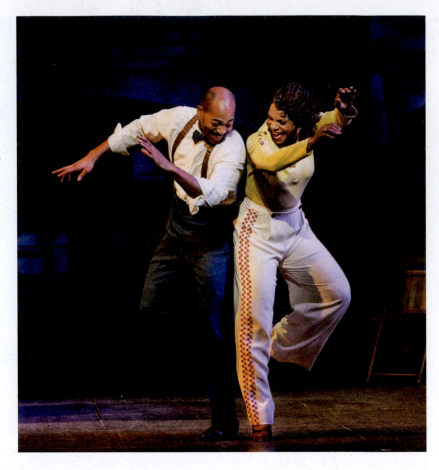

Black musicians and performers provide an integral and often-overlooked part of American musical history. The 2016 play *Shuffle Along, or the Making of the Musical Sensation of 1921 and All That Followed*, sought to unearth that history as it examined the behind-the-scenes process that led to the first bonafide Broadway hit created and performed by black artists. The play was directed and written by George Wolfe, with music from the original *Shuffle Along* by Eubie Blake and Noble Sissle. ©*Sara Krulwich/The New York Times/Redux*

criticize—the interaction between black music and white culture. *Memphis* (2009) deals with the transition from black rhythm and blues to white American rock & roll in Tennessee during the 1950s. *Fela!* (2009) showcases the legendary, and politically radical, Nigerian singer-musician Fela Anikulapo Kuti and the mesmerizing Afrobeat music he pioneered in his Lagos nightclub in the 1970s. And the Gershwins' *Porgy and Bess* (1935), set among the black inhabitants of Charleston's Catfish Row, was revised by Suzan-Lori Parks (see the chapter "The Playwright") and director Diane Paulus (with music adapted by Diedre Murray) to great acclaim on Broadway in 2012.

More recently, in 2016, *Shuffle Along, or the Making of the Musical Sensation of 1921 and All That Followed* dealt with—as its humorously wordy title indicates—the legacy of the early days of black entertainers on the musical stage, in particular the foundational 1921 work *Shuffle Along*, discussed earlier. This play glimpses behind the scenes to imagine the struggles and triumphs of the creative team behind the original work and featured the preeminent contemporary African American performers

Audra McDonald, Brian Stokes Mitchell, and Billy Porter. Like Parks's reimagining of *Porgy and Bess*, this version of *Shuffle Along* both celebrates and analyzes the American musical's troubled but vital relationship with race.

THE DISNEY MONOLITH

No one has better mastered the global theatrical musical than Disney, the quintessentially American company, which since the 1990s has infiltrated theatres worldwide with its productions of *The Lion King, Beauty and the Beast, Aida, Mary Poppins, The Little Mermaid, Tarzan, The Hunchback of Notre Dame, Newsies, Camp Rock, Freaky Friday, High School Musical* (and its sequel), *Aladdin*, and, in 2017—to great fanfare—*Frozen*. Disney musicals, mostly adaptations of very successful Disney animated and live-action films, have profited commercially from Disney's bottomless financial resources and worldwide name recognition. Disney has also been credited with great theatrical art, however, particularly in the designs of Bob Crowley for *Mary Poppins* and the amazingly innovative designs

Few plays were as hotly anticipated in the 2017–2018 Broadway season as *Frozen*, the adaptation of the 2013 Disney animated feature. Pictured here is Cassie Levy as Elsa, a queen whose magical ability to freeze anything she touches leads to her pursuit by suspicious townspeople, as well as wondrous special effects. ©*Sara Krulwich/ The New York Times/Redux*

and staging of *The Lion King* by longtime avant-garde director-designer Julie Taymor. The latter production (with music by Elton John) opened on Broadway in 1997 and, in April 2012, surpassed *The Phantom of the Opera* to become the highest-grossing Broadway play of all time. *The Lion King* has grossed over six billion dollars worldwide in box-office income and currently plays in major cities all over the world. Another popular Disney musical to hit America, *Frozen,* received above-average reviews in its preview in Denver—and yet, as is often the case with Disney productions, critical analysis is largely irrelevant in terms of box-office returns. *Frozen* is destined to become yet another smash hit; its source material, the animated film of the same name, is one of the highest-grossing movies in history. Clearly the musical theatre, thanks to Disney—and for better or worse—has become a global phenomenon in the twenty-first century.

ENGLAND AND FRANCE

American-born musicals dominated Broadway's musical theatre scene for the first six decades of the twentieth century. Then, beginning in 1970, European composers, lyricists, and directors came to the forefront. Leading the invasion of America's musical theatre capital was English composer Andrew Lloyd Webber, first with his rock opera *Jesus Christ Superstar* in 1970, followed in 1968 by his psychedelic biblical adaptation *Joseph and the Technicolor Dreamcoat,* and then by *Cats* (1981), a musical adaptation of famed poet T. S. Eliot's *Old Possum's Book of Practical Cats.* In 1988, Webber outdid the considerable success of these musicals with his legendary *Phantom of the Opera,* which has become the longest-running musical in Broadway history. All these works—including the successful *Evita* (1978)*, Starlight Express* (1984), and *Sunset*

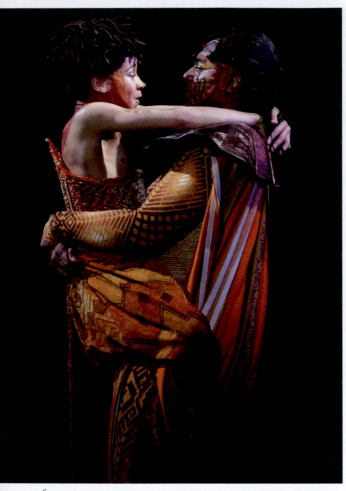

Alexander V. Bass plays Young Simba, here seen hugging his father Mufasa, played by Rufus Bonds Jr., as a 2004 production of *The Lion King* at the Orpheum Theatre in San Francisco. This musical juggernaut, created by Julie Taymor in 1997, had by the end of 2017 earned just over eight billion dollars worldwide. *©ZUMA Press, Inc./Alamy Stock Photo*

Following closely in Lloyd Webber's transatlantic steps were French composer Claude-Michel Schönberg and lyricist Alain Boublil. Their *Les Misérables* (1987, revived 2014) and *Miss Saigon* (1989, revived 2017) both became global megahits and rivaled Lloyd Webber's productions with their luxuriant scores and spectacular staging. The climax of *Miss Saigon* features a helicopter descending onto the roof of the American Embassy to rescue fleeing diplomats—a perfect example of their "more is more" philosophy. Not only were the composers and lyricists of these shows European, but the productions were mainly staged by top-tier British directors: Nicholas Hytner (*Miss Saigon*) and Trevor Nunn (*Cats*, *Les Misérables*, *Sunset Boulevard*, and *Starlight Express*).

MUSICALS OF THE TWENTY-FIRST CENTURY

The twenty-first century's musicals have clearly had their share of great commercial success. More than ever, it seems, audiences today crave the fantasy, romance, and comedy that musicals provide, flocking to recent hits like Steven Schwartz's *Wicked*, Harvey Fierstein's *Kinky Boots*, Alan Menken's *Aladdin*, Mel Brooks's *The Producers*, Steven Lutvak and Robert Freedman's *Gentleman's Guide to Love and Murder*, Andrew Lloyd Webber's *School of Rock,* and Trey Parker, Matt Stone, and Robert Lopez's *The Book of Mormon*.

However, the Broadway musicals of this century are also increasingly tackling serious subjects. Today's musicals have addressed topics as far-ranging as oppression in race relations (*Caroline, or Change*, 2004), sexual ignorance and its ramifications (*Spring Awakening*, 2006), the challenges of barrio life in New York City's Washington Heights (*In the Heights*, 2007), government corruption in Nigeria (*Fela!*, 2009), bipolar disorder and suicide (*Next to Normal*, 2009), judicial malfeasance (*The Scottsboro Boys*, 2010), conflicting sexual identities and depression within a single family (*Fun Home*, 2015), social anxiety disorder (*Dear Evan Hansen,* 2016), and—in one striking example—*Natasha, Pierre & the Great Comet of 1812,* a textually faithful (and musically playful) 2016 adaptation of a selection from Tolstoy's *War and Peace,* which deals with the sufferings of aristocrats during the Napoleonic Wars. This seriousness of theme has been joined, at times, with seriousness in approach; the critically adored and Tony Award–winning 2017 musical *The Band's Visit,* for instance, celebrates intimacy, quietness, and subtlety rather than loud and spectacular musical numbers.

Some recent musicals strike a balance between broad political and social protest and more intimate, personal

Boulevard (1994)—are known for their lush musical scores more than for their books or lyrics. Most are sung through (with no spoken dialogue), so they are easily accessible to global audiences who need little in the way of translation. The staging tends to be extravagant: *Starlight Express* featured a cast speeding on roller skates around an elevated track encircling the audience; in *Phantom* a chandelier seems to fall right in the midst of the audience, and the masked Phantom and his beloved cruise in a gondola on a fiery subterranean "lake" in the basement of the Paris Opera House. Lloyd Webber's more recent musical theatre creation has proven to be another hit: *School of Rock*, based on the comedic film of the same name, opened on Broadway in 2015 to great success.

Come From Away was a relatively unknown musical when it opened in New York in 2017, but it received seven Tony nominations that year and was still filling the house a year later. The play concerns an utterly unusual event: the landing of 7,000 airline passengers in Gander, Newfoundland, after the September 11 terrorist attacks caused thirty-eight airplanes to immediately switch courses and land in that tiny Canadian city. Here Jenn Collella (*left*), plays the pilot of one of the planes. ©*Sara Krulwich/The New York Times/Redux*

anguish. *Billy Elliott* (2008), written by Lee Hall with music by Elton John, tells the story of an English coal miner's son who wants to become a ballet dancer during the raucous turmoil of labor unrest and violent class antagonism in northern England in 1984. Termed a "protest musical," it became an enormous success on London's West End and won thirteen Tony Awards when it opened on Broadway in 2008. Tony Kushner's *Caroline, or Change* is more subdued, but still powerfully awash in bleak emotions. The 2016 musical *Come From Away* strikes an impeccable balance between the mournful and the sentimental. This musical, after all, is about the horrific terrorist attacks of September 11, 2001. Yet it looks to the side, rather than directly, at this event by examining the small Canadian town where a plane was forced to land after the Twin Towers fell. At once a celebration of human decency and a mournful demonstration of pathos, this play is a perfect emblem of the musical genre's capacity to move us and give us reason to celebrate.

In 2011, the audacious musical *The Book of Mormon* opened to rapturous reviews: a "raucously funny . . . nonstop fusillade of obscenities," the play "is earnestly about the power of faith," said Steven Suskin in the trade magazine *Variety*, and "some of the sweetest poison ever

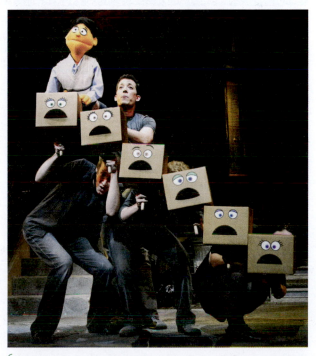

Avenue Q, an ironic and risqué musical of post-college life in New York City—with characters played by both humans and puppets—earned five Tony Awards in 2004. ©*Sara Krulwich/The New York Times/Redux*

Hamilton, the spectacular musical about the founding years of the United States, was created—music, lyrics, and book—by Lin-Manuel Miranda (*center*) who also starred in the title role; the show, which features a largely black or Latinx cast, immediately became the hit of the 2015–2016 Broadway season and has since grown into a global sensation. ©*Sara Krulwich/The New York Times/Redux*

poured," said Peter Marks in the *Washington Post*. The Tony Award voters, too, proved smitten by this outlandish comedy by *South Park* creators Trey Parker and Matt Stone, who teamed with Robert Lopez of *Avenue Q*. *Mormon* treats white, male, Mormon missionaries transported from Utah to Uganda; while the social, sexual, economic, religious, and cultural differences between these peoples are as extreme as could possibly be imagined, human linkage somehow seeps into every miscommunication, irritation, disappointment, and conflict that arises among the characters as the audience erupts, time and again, into joyous laughter and applause. The Broadway production still plays to sold-out houses nightly in New York.

No discussion of the contemporary American musical is complete, however, without mentioning *Hamilton*. Lin-Manuel Miranda's revelatory play has become more than another hit musical: it is a cultural monument, an astonishing larger-than-life work that has spawned the kind of worldwide adoration usually reserved for the absolute top tier of artistic objects. Yet the play itself cannot be overrated: it truly stands as a unique, genre-defying, moving, celebratory work. The musical charts the early days of America with exuberance and swagger; it celebrates democracy not only in its politics but in its array of musical influences and performers. Its songs include hip-hop showdowns, show-stopping Broadway musical torch songs, R&B duets, and more. Its characters are both instantly recognizable figures from history class *and* vital new archetypes of the American stage, and the casting celebrates diversity without losing the hard edges of different racial identities—all the while implicitly asking profound questions about labor, race, and cultural amnesia. *Hamilton* is a once-in-a-generation event, and its success gleefully signals that we seem to be heading for a truly new "golden age."

Chapter

10

Theatre Today

©Sara Krulwich/The New York Times/Redux

T HE THEATRE OF TODAY EXISTS in the world, not in the pages of this or any other book. It is being performed right now, in the multimillion-dollar theatres of the world's great cities as well as on simpler stages at schools, community theatres, and nightclubs. Theatre can be found in nontheatrical spaces such as city parks, streets, and even living rooms. Theatre is everywhere.

However, because it is everywhere, it is difficult to reach conclusions about today's theatre. We cannot evaluate the current theatre as we do the theatre of the past, with tidy labels and categories like "modernism" or "romanticism." It is also difficult to predict which plays today will stand the test of time; there is increasingly so much publicity surrounding new plays—rumors, interviews, think-pieces, reviews, and reflections—that actual artistic merit can become lost in the shuffle. No doubt many plays we are currently lavishing with attention will be forgotten in the future; likewise, work that flies under the radar or receives a critical shrug may turn out to be a masterpiece studied for generations. Ultimately, a permanent place in history books and on stages around the world is the achievement of very few. Among the playwrights once deemed equal to Shakespeare, after all, are such dimly remembered figures as John Fletcher, Joseph Addison, and Maxwell Anderson.

While we should avoid large pronouncements about all theatre today, we can still make observations about the many different trends on display on stages around the world. As a result, rather than talk about one kind of theatre today, we will identify in this chapter a variety of theatres that are now enjoying popularity: theatre of identity, spectacular theatre, performance art, dangerous theatre, theatre of community, physical theatre, solo performance, and intimate theatre. These categories are not exclusive: a play can be dangerous and intimate, identity-based and spectacular, physical and communal, and so on. We also do not want to limit these theatres only to new work. Many of the examples we discuss in this chapter are older plays—some very old—that receive new vitality in light of present-day concerns. Think of them instead as schools of thought, trends, and patterns.

All of these theatres speak, in some way, to our current day. This relationship is never quite direct; although many plays clearly address current events, many others do so subtly—or perhaps even unconsciously. After the tragic events of September 11, 2001, audiences in New York City flocked to a stage adaptation of *Metamorphoses*, a series of poems written thousands of years ago by the ancient Roman poet Ovid. When rehearsals began, the play's producers and artistic team could not have known about the terrorist attacks on the World Trade Center, yet the play's deeper themes of change, cosmic fate, and human resilience all resonated deeply with a public eager to find solace and reflection. Sixteen years later, at the 2017 Sibiu Theatre Festival, the renowned Romanian director Silviu Purcarete's adaptation of the same ancient poems received adulation and standing-room-only crowds. The ironic message here is clear: the only constant is change. And no medium reflects this idea better than the theatre, an ancient art form that disappears the moment the curtain falls; a timeless craft that produces timely works. It's no wonder we continue to find in the world's theatre a mirror of our own ever-changing condition.

What's Happening?

How does theatre reflect our condition today, in the beginning of the twenty-first century?

In order to find out the answer, we first need some history. The previous century was a violent and chaotic one: two world wars, assassinations of political and cultural leaders (Mahatma Gandhi, Martin Luther King Jr., John and Robert Kennedy, Anwar Sadat, Yitzhak Rabin, John Lennon), the Holocaust, the threat of nuclear annihilation and terrorist attack, the proliferation of dangerous drugs, outbreaks of lethal diseases, and the threatened destruction of Earth's vital resources. The arts responded to these social changes with a freedom often frightening in its extremity—nowhere more so than in the theatre, where by the 1970s Dionysian ecstasy had returned to the stage with a force almost equal to that of the ancient Greeks. As play-licensing laws fell in England and legal censorship became locally unenforceable in America, profanity, nudity, simulated sex, violence, and vicious verbal attacks on political institutions—all unknown on the legitimate stage since ancient times—became almost commonplace. Plays popular in America in the last third of the twentieth century featured accusations of a sitting president of murder (*MacBird*) and a recent pope of genocide (*The Deputy*), a soldier eating a dead baby while starving in a war-torn country (*Blasted*), teenage boys stoning a baby to death in its crib (*Saved*), and actors undressing and marching naked out into the street (*Paradise Now*). These were not always productions on the margins, either. Some of this Dionysian frenzy reached right into the theatre's mainstream when *Hair: The American Tribal Love-Rock Musical* (1968) ended its first act with its actors—who had already sung rapturously about "sodomy, fellatio, cunnilingus, pederasty"—brazenly stripping off all their clothes and facing the audience in a posture of mocking defiance.

Nor were theatre audiences themselves immune from such changes in theatrical convention. In the experimental theatre of the 1970s and 1980s, spectators almost routinely found themselves sat upon, fondled, assaulted, hurled about, handed lit joints of marijuana, and, in at least one case (in Finland), urinated on. These and other extreme behaviors had become part of the freedom claimed by a theatre that tried to make itself heard above the din of war, riots, and corruption. Or perhaps they wished to reflect the abject state of society in their treatment of spectators, as if to say: "You are not immune, even here, in the confines of this theatre building, from the horrors of the world." Or then again, perhaps its adherents, as many critics asked, were merely "acting out" to get attention. In any event, it was an era of violence and abandon that brought the age of modernism to a crisis, if not to a conclusion: the once-rebellious conventions of realism and antirealism seem tame compared to this newfound drive to create shocking, immersive theatre events.

Well before the century's end, however, this mood of violent protest was largely spent, and the theatre turned its focus from assaulting the audience to raising its social awareness. Profanity and nudity no longer seemed novel and, having lost their power to shock, became conventional tools for addressing serious issues. The American theatre, in particular, responded to the era's pervasive prejudices and privileges associated with gender, race,

No playwright in recent years has caused more controversy than England's Sarah Kane, whose postmodern, largely expressionistic works are filled with gruesome violence and carnality. Her first play, *Blasted*, presents shocking images of rape, racism, and cannibalism that caused a theatre scandal at its 1995 London premiere—which led to hundreds of productions of this and her four other plays throughout the theatre world. Kane was certainly England's most talked-about new playwright when, tragically, she took her own life in 1999, just weeks after her twenty-eighth birthday. In this production, directed by Thomas Ostermeier and seen at the Avignon Theatre Festival in 2005, Katharina Schüttler plays Cate, kneeling over her rapist Ian (played by Ulrich Mühe), who by this time has himself been raped, blinded, and battered to near-death by a soldier in the play's wartime environment. Scenery is by Jan Pappelbaum; costumes are by Almut Eppinger. ©Anne-Christine Poujoulat/AFP/Getty Images

class, and sexual orientation that were then coming under increasing fire as various movements—civil rights, feminism, gay rights—gained a more prominent cultural voice.

Internationally, the end of the twentieth century saw an explosion of new social and political groups and the rapid development of new technologies. A more global economy challenged local cultures with enhanced but often troubling prospects, while astonishing advances in telecommunications—social networks, text-messaging, smartphones—revolutionized the way the world's populations could connect. Today, we have the technology to create self-driving cars, remotely operated military drones, and—in the cinema and other media arts—near-perfect replicas of humans, objects, and landscapes. In the theatre, huge technological advances in sound and lighting design, spurred by globally touring rock concerts, create ear-splitting and eye-popping effects with the press of a button. Productions that had previously been seen only by the audiences seated in the theatres began to be broadcast live into theatres elsewhere in their countries, and soon after broadcast into theatres in various countries around the world.

And yet the world has not ceased its social and political chaos. The dominant stories of our recent historical progression are, on the one hand, the advancements in technology, medicine, and the arts and, on the other hand, an increase in global crises, such as the tumultuous and rancorous 2016 U.S. presidential election, massive influxes of refugees from battle-scarred countries, and the hovering threat of nuclear war, to name just a few.

This brings us to the present moment: a time of increased communication, broadening civil rights, and stunning technological innovation—but also of political instability and insecurity. The theatre has responded quickly to these new freedoms and opportunities. Once again, as in the days of Sophocles and Shakespeare, the stage has surfaced as an arena in which new thoughts, fashions, feelings, morals, opinions, and styles can be enacted. New methods and philosophies can be explored to help bring lucidity and structure to the confusions that beset us all—or to reflect those confusions back to us so that we can confront the character of our own time.

THEATRE AND IDENTITY

Who gets to be represented in the theatre? This seemingly simple question can lead us down some winding roads. The theatre has historically been a place to explore identity, and this relationship is quite complex. After all, the theatre is a place where an actor can "disappear" by taking on a role, yet it also gives that actor visibility—as well as a voice and an audience. A lot of theatre today endeavors—with varying levels of success—to represent different identities both in the characters who get to be represented and in the performers who get to represent them. As we learned in the chapter "The Director," the issue of casting is entwined with questions about history, selfhood, and empowerment— or, conversely, disenfranchisement. In this section, we will examine how theatre today grapples with questions of identity as they relate to gender and sexuality, race, and ability.

Paula Vogel has long been revered as a playwright and mentor, yet it wasn't until 2017 that her work opened on Broadway. The play, *Indecent*, follows the trials and travails of a theatre company producing the controversial play *God of Vengeance* in 1923. Vogel has long explored queer themes and identities in her work, and *Indecent* is no exception—the original cast of *God of Vengeance* was arrested on grounds of "obscenity" because the play featured a love scene between women. Pictured here are actors portraying the cast of *God of Vengeance* in a lighter moment. ©Sara Krulwich/The New York Times/Redux

Theatre, Gender, and Sexuality   Theatre today is richly engaged with questions of gender and sexuality. In many ways things are better than they have been in the past—recall that, for instance, in England women couldn't act onstage until the restoration of Charles II to the throne in 1660. But in other ways, there is much work to do. The Broadway season of 2016–2017 saw the first instance of two female playwrights, Lynn Nottage and Paula Vogel, having their plays in performance at the same time (*Sweat* and *Indecent*, respectively). This is something to celebrate, but it is also a timely reminder of how much work is yet to be done: plenty of plays by men are routinely produced concurrently. (And not too long ago, in the 2013–2014 season, there were *no* Broadway productions of plays by women.) While women comprise the majority of theatre audiences, they do not find equal representation onstage or in artistic management.

However, this sobering fact should not obscure the many achievements of women in theatre. Female directors, once a rarity, have now helm some of the most critically acclaimed and successful American plays: Julie Taymor, Anna Shapiro, Pam McKinnon, Rebecca Taichman, Jo Bonney, Susan Stroman, and Tina Landau are some of the most sought-after directors on and off Broadway. Since the 1980s, eight female playwrights (Vogel, Beth Henley, Marsha Norman, Wendy Wasserstein, Margaret Edson, Suzan-Lori Parks, Nottage, and Annie Baker) have received Pulitzer Prizes and six (Anna Deveare Smith, Naomi Wallace, Mary Zimmerman, Nottage, Sarah Ruhl, and Annie Baker) have been honored with MacArthur "Genius Grants." Meanwhile, women-centered theatre ensembles, such as the Women's Project in the United States and SheShePop in Germany, have gained prominence, and some have harnessed the power of theatre to combat pervasive sexism in cultures where women are systematically oppressed. In 2007, for example, The Wuturi Players, based in South Korea and directed by Aida Kari (born in the former Yugoslavia and now a resident of Austria), created an adaptation of Euripides' *The Trojan Women*, an ancient Greek tragedy about the women left in Troy as prisoners after the Greeks have sacked the city. The new adaptation, titled *Trojan Women: An Asian Story*, uses the plot of this classical work to explore the treatment of Korean "comfort women," or sex slaves, by invading Japanese forces. This is a fascinating example of an international women-led ensemble reworking a Western, male-authored play into a timely commentary on women's subjugation.

Drama has long engaged with other gender identities. LGBT+ people (lesbian, gay, bisexual, and transgender, with the plus sign standing in for other groups) have historically turned to the theatre as a reflection of their

Martin Sherman's 1979 *Bent* received a Tony nomination for its harrowing tale of the treatment of German homosexuals during the rise of Adolf Hitler, and it paved the way for the serious—even tragic—theatrical treatment of homophobia. In this 2006 English revival at the Trafalgar Studios in London, Max (Alan Cumming, *right*) and Rudy (Kevin Trainor, *left*) are gay men imprisoned by the Nazis. Max pretends to be Jewish under the misapprehension that he will be treated less harshly. Costumes are by Mark Bouman. ©*Geraint Lewis/Alamy Stock Photo*

Pictured here is Jefferson Mays as Charlotte von Mahlsdorf, a transgender woman who founded a "museum of everyday objects" in midcentury Germany, in Doug Wright's multiple-award-winning *I Am My Own Wife*. Charlotte is one of thirty-three roles Mays plays in the show. ©*Gary Friedman/Los Angeles Times/Getty Images*

Larry Kramer's 1985 off-Broadway production of *The Normal Heart* was instrumental in making the American public, and then the government, far more responsive to the AIDS crisis than it had been. Shown here, in the 2011 Broadway production, are Joe Mantello (*left*) as Ned Weeks, an AIDS activist, and John Benjamin Hickey (*right*) as Felix, Ned's love interest. Looming behind them are the names of the dead and dying. George C. Wolfe and Joel Grey codirected the production; Kramer, whose activism on this issue has never slowed, was out front after most performances, handing out blistering letters to exiting audience members "to get the word out, again." ©*Sara Krulwich/The New York Times/Redux*

lives—not only in the sense of portraying identities that have long been invisible, but also more abstractly because gender is increasingly thought of as a "performance" rather than a biological condition. Yet sexuality has remained buried in the closet during most of the theatre's history. As recently as 1958 the representation of gay life was illegal in England and widely (though not legally) suppressed in America. (Sexual acts between men were illegal in England as recently as 1967 and in the United States in 2003.) The love that "dared not speak its name" came to the stage only through authors' subtle references and audiences' inferences. Gay playwrights such as Oscar Wilde, Tennessee Williams, Gertrude Stein, Edward Albee, William Inge, and Mary P. Burrill were forced to speak at certain critical moments in their work only through innuendo and coded language.

Dramatic changes occurred in the late 1960s, when gay and lesbian life and gay and lesbian issues began to be treated as serious dramatic subjects, most notably by Mart Crowley in his groundbreaking American comedy *The Boys in the Band* (1968). Since then, issues of sexuality have become principal or secondary topics in hundreds of plays, including mainstream Broadway musicals (*Fun Home, La Cage aux Folles, March of the Falsettos, Kiss of the Spider Woman, The Wild Party, Avenue Q, Hedwig and the Angry Inch, Kinky Boots*), popular comedies (*Love! Valour! Compassion!, Jeffrey, The Little Dog Laughed, Buyer & Cellar, Significant Other*), and serious dramas (*Bent, M. Butterfly, Angels in America, Gross Indecency, Stop Kiss, The Laramie Project, Take Me Out, I Am My Own Wife, A Life*). Gay actors such as British star Ian McKellen have come out of the closet to advocate gay rights

worldwide. Gay plays have entered the global mainstream as well, as exemplified by the Shameless Theatre company, which opened a theatre in London's Victoria district in 2008 wholly dedicated to plays on gay themes, and the annual Gay Theatre Festival in Dublin, Ireland, which has presented plays from Poland, Germany, Zimbabwe, France, Spain, Australia, South Africa, Venezuela, Canada, America, England, and Ireland since its creation in 2004.

During the 1980s, in the wake of the devastation of the AIDS crisis, a growing genre of plays centered on the emotional and tragic impact of the disease in the gay community, most notably Larry Kramer's 1985 *The Normal Heart*, which also won the Tony Award for Best Revival in 2011. In 1992, Tony Kushner's *Angels in America* treated AIDS as central to what Kushner termed his "gay fantasia on national themes" and proved to be one of the country's most celebrated stage productions of the decade; it was revived on Broadway with an all-star cast in 2018. The recent success of the Broadway musical *Fun Home,* based on a graphic memoir by Alison Bechdel about a gay woman reflecting on her upbringing and complex relationship with her closeted father who committed suicide, affords us an opportunity to reflect on the rich history of lesbian theatre, as well. Lisa Kron, who wrote the book for *Fun Home,* was a groundbreaking lesbian theatre artist who performed regularly at the famous WOW Café Theatre in the early 1980s, alongside other queer female artists such as Holly Hughes, Fiona Shaw, and Deb Margolin.

As time goes on, people are openly identifying in ways that resist a simple binary of male-female or gay-straight, and the theatre has attended these shifts. *Hedwig and the*

When Lynn Nottage began writing *Sweat*, a work that focuses on down-on-their-luck working-class workers in rural Pennsylvania, she could not have anticipated just how timely the play would be in 2017. Yet *Sweat* is more than simply a ripped-from-the-headlines affair. It accomplishes one of the fundamental tasks of the theatre: to give a voice to the voiceless and visibility to the invisible. *Sweat* won the 2017 Pulitzer Prize for Drama and enjoyed an extended Broadway run. ©*Sara Krulwich/The New York Times/ Redux*

Angry Inch, an off-Broadway sensation in 1998 that premiered on Broadway in 2014, details the life of its titular character, a genderqueer performer who entertains the audience with rock ballads and empathetic reveals about her background. Artists like Cassils, who does not identify as man or woman, create solo acts that challenge our social preconceptions of gender. Becca Blackwell, a trans performer who similarly goes by "they" rather than "he" or "she," made waves in downtown New York in 2016's surreal musical-cabaret piece *A Ride on the Irish Cream* by Erin Markey in which they played a "Pontoon boat/ horse"—a clever and cartoonish representation of their own trans identity. Finally, the recent critical success *Inanimate* considers the love between a young woman and a fast-food sign—like *Irish Cream*, this play uses an absurd situation to reflect on the very real fluidity of desire and identification.

The rising visibility of people who identify as nontraditional sexualities is, of course, not simply an American issue but a global one. Non-Western venues such as the Delhi International Queer Theatre and Film Festival and the IndigNation festival in Singapore, along with non-Western authors like Amahl Khouri, from Lebanon, attest to the power of staging queer stories—even, perhaps especially, in political climates hostile to them.

Theatre and Race   The American theatre has a complex relationship to race. A brief examination of black, Latinx, Asian American, Middle Eastern, and Native American theatre will hopefully provide a better understanding of how minority populations both grapple with and feel liberated by working on stage. In this section we will focus on American identities in particular; later in the chapter we will examine more global contexts for theatre today.

A recent survey on diversity on Broadway and in American regional theatre found that African American actors were cast in 17 percent of all roles, Latinx actors in 3 percent, and Asian American actors in 9 percent; all other minorities combined comprised less than 1 percent. (Note that we have adopted the term "Latinx" as a gender-inclusive way of referring to people of Latin American descent.) For black theatre artists, that 17 percent figure is modest—there is still work to do—but significant, given the history of "whitewashing" of the American stage of years past. Midcentury black writers were hardly ever able to secure productions, and even the best black actors were often reduced to playing the roles of servants and "exotic" roles. However, in the decades following World War II, drama that focused on the lives of black Americans began to surge forward in the culture. Lorraine Hansberry's 1959 *A Raisin in the Sun*, a realistic study of black family life, marked the first appearance of a black playwright on Broadway, and its director, Lloyd Richards, became the first black director in the American theatrical mainstream. Soon, black theatre had become a truly revolutionary force with the startling work of Amiri Baraka, whose *Dutchman* and *The Toilet* appeared off-Broadway in

Samuel L. Jackson plays Dr. Martin Luther King Jr. and Angela Bassett plays a motel maid bringing him coffee in African American playwright Katori Hall's *The Mountaintop*, which takes place during the evening preceding the Nobel Prize winner's 1968 assassination at the Lorraine Motel in Memphis, Tennessee. The 2011 Broadway premiere was directed by Kenny Leon.
©*Sara Krulwich/The New York Times/Redux*

1964 and confronted American racism with astonishing ferocity. Baraka (then known as LeRoi Jones) refused to shrink from revolutionary violence, and his gut-wrenching urban plays provided a startling wake-up call not only to American society but also to the American stage. In 1967, actors Robert Hooks and Douglas Turner Ward created the Negro Ensemble Company, bringing forth dramatist Lonne Elder III's eloquent *Ceremonies in Dark Old Men* in 1969 and continuing to flourish to the present day. And in 1970 Charles Gordone became the first African American to win a Pulitzer Prize for Drama with *No Place to Be Somebody.*

The early 1980s brought to the fore the extraordinary August Wilson, whose ten-play dramatic cycle treats different aspects of African American life in each of the ten decades of the twentieth century. Wilson's plays received dozens of awards—including two Pulitzer Prizes—and have been regularly revived on Broadway and in regional theatres since his untimely death in 2005. In the current century, two black female dramatists have received Pulitzer Prizes—Suzan-Lori Parks for *Topdog/Underdog* in 2002 and Lynn Nottage for *Ruined* in 2009 and *Sweat* in 2017—while, in recent Broadway seasons, more black female playwrights, including Katori Hall (*The Mountaintop*), Lydia R. Diamond (*Stick Fly*), and Danai Gurira (*Eclipsed*), have had works presented. Playwrights like Robert O'Hara and Tarell Alvin McCraney, too, have brilliantly explored intersections of black and queer identity.

Latinx and Spanish-speaking theatre has also reached some notable heights onstage, although—as the aforementioned survey data show—progress can still be made to represent the rising Latinx population. Indeed, Latinx theatre is arguably at the roots of American theatre: the first play staged on this continent was *Los Moros y Los Cristianos* (*The Moors and the Christians*) at the San Juan Pueblo near Santa Fe in the sixteenth century. In 1954, in a foundational moment for Latinx theatre, the Puerto Rican director Roberto Rodriguez staged *La Carreta* (*The Oxcart*) at the Church of San Sebastian in New York. The success of this production inspired the powerful theatre impresario Joseph Papp to stage Spanish-language plays on bigger and more prominent stages, such as a revival of *La Carreta* in 1967 with Raúl Juliá and Míriam Colón—two bona fide Spanish-speaking stars. The success of this production in turn inspired Colón to found the Puerto Rican Traveling Theatre in 1967. Meanwhile, in 1965, the Mexican American Luis Valdez founded El Teatro Campesino, a company dedicated, in its early days, to inspire and entertain Latinx farmworkers in California. Valdez's Teatro electrified California audiences and won national acclaim, particularly for Valdez's groundbreaking *Zoot Suit* (1978) about riots in the Los Angeles *barrio* that pitted Mexican American migrants against the Los Angeles police and politicians in the early 1940s. In this work, Valdez employed Brechtian techniques to raise social, political, and economic questions, while retaining a

Denzel Washington plays Troy Maxson, a retired Negro League baseball star, and Viola Davis plays Rose, his wife, in a moment of reflective intimacy during August Wilson's most famous play, *Fences*. Kenny Leon directed this 2010 Broadway revival. ©*Sara Krulwich/The New York Times/Redux*

distinctly Latinx voice. The play went on to Broadway and was eventually adapted into a feature film. A recent revival of *Zoot Suit* in 2017 played to sold-out audiences, critical raves, and a rabid fanbase of repeat viewers who frequently dressed up in the flamboyant style of the Pachuco, the play's choral leader and cultural voice.

Today, the works of dozens of Latinx dramatists can be seen around the country. Cuban-born Nilo Cruz received the 2003 Pulitzer Prize for *Anna in the Tropics*, which portrayed Cuban migrant workers in a Florida cigar factory. His rapturous adaptation of Calderón's classic *Life Is a Dream* successfully premiered in California in 2007. Octavio Solis, born of Mexican immigrant parents in El Paso, Texas, was nominated for a 2009 Pulitzer for his intense *Lydia*. This realistic yet often mystical drama of a family not unlike Solis's own had earned extravagant praise in its initial productions in Denver and Los Angeles; his "dream play," *Se Llama Cristina*, enjoyed a "rolling world premiere" at the Kitchen Dog Theatre in Dallas, the Boston

Court Theatre in Los Angeles, and the Magic Theatre in San Francisco during the winter of 2014–2015. Puerto Rican–born José Rivera's *Marisol* (1992), a fantasy about a woman and her guardian angel in the tradition of magic realism, has been produced throughout the country; his *Sermon of the Senses* (2014) was the closing work of an epic fifty-play, fifty-four-actor, six-hour performance titled *The Mysteries* at New York's Flea Theater. Latinx theatre continues to flourish—if not on Broadway then certainly in other spaces, such as Chicago's Goodman Theatre, which started an annual festival dedicated to new Latinx work; Cleveland Public Theatre's formation of Teatro Publico de Cleveland; and—to save the most famous example for last—in the incredible success of Lin-Manuel Miranda, the composer, author, and star of the smash hit musical *Hamilton* and, before that, *In the Heights.*

Asian American theatre has claimed its share of the American theatrical scene as well—and also claimed, rightfully, its voice in debates about diversity onstage. In 2011, a Facebook post by an Asian theatre artist asked, "Where are all the Asian actors in mainstream New York theatre?" The ensuing debate in the comments grew into a formal survey—in fact, the same survey referenced earlier—and the robust and passionate discussion shows how vital questions of Asian and Asian American identities onstage continue to be. As recently as 2013, after all, white actors in a British production of *Mystery of Edwin Drood* used "brownface" to appear South Asian.

The watershed moment for Asian American theatre, in terms of sheer popularity, is undoubtedly the success of David Henry Hwang's *M. Butterfly*, which received both a Tony Award and a Pulitzer Prize during its 1988 Broadway premiere. Hwang's play boldly reinterprets the story of Giacomo Puccini's opera *Madama Butterfly*, with careful attention to its political and sexual prejudices, while incorporating both Western and Beijing opera (xiqu) techniques into a contemporary, highly postmodern play that explodes "Orientalist" stereotypes about Asians as viewed by Westerners. Hwang's career continues to flourish with his *Golden Child*, about the conflict between Chinese traditions (foot-binding in particular) and contemporary values, which was nominated for a best-play Tony Award, and his semiautobiographical 2008 play *Yellow Face*, which covers his own career as an Asian American playwright. Hwang's most recent plays, the comedy *Chinglish* and the Bruce Lee biography *Kung Fu*, had runs on Broadway in 2011 and off-Broadway in 2014, respectively. In 2016 Hwang cowrote the opera *Building the Dream*, which debuted at San Francisco Opera; and in 2017 a much-buzzed-about revival of *M. Butterfly,* starring Clive Owen and directed by Julie Taymor, opened on Broadway.

Austin Smith plays a black playwright who, before our eyes, applies white makeup to play white roles—both the heroic "George" (shown here) and the evil "M'Closky"—in Branden Jacobs-Jensen's *An Octoroon,* which was adapted from Dion Boucicault's *The Octoroon,* an 1859 melodrama rooted in American slavery, and performed in 2015 at Brooklyn's Theatre for a New Audience. Mary Wiseman plays the American heiress in love with Smith's "George." ©*Gerry Goodstein*

Gloria Garayua is Gracie in Octavio Solis's Christmas play, *La Posada Mágica* (*The Magic Journey*), which echoes the traditional Latin American procession honoring Joseph and Mary's search for lodging in which to bear the Christ child. This 2008 production, directed by playwright Solis himself, was presented for the fifteenth consecutive year at South Coast Repertory in Costa Mesa, California. ©*Henry DiRocco/South Coast Repertory Theatre*

Choctaw American actor Shyla Marlin plays Carlisle in Carolyn Dunn's *The Frybread Queen* in Native Voices's 2011 premiere production in Los Angeles. The playwright and cast members were all of Native American heritage. ©*Tony Dontscheff/Silvia Mautner Photography*

Hwang is only the most prominent of the many Asian Americans now solidly ensconced in the American repertoire, however. Philip Kan Gotanda's 1986 *Yankee Dawg You Die* provided a seminal moment in Asian American theatre history by addressing, with frank and hilarious honesty, the pervasive anti-Asian racism in American popular culture. Lonnie Carter, Diana Son, and Elizabeth Wong are among the others writing about relations between American and, respectively, Filipino, Korean, and Chinese cultures. And East West Players, formed in 1965 by actors frustrated with the opportunities afforded to Asians and Asian Americans, continues to foster new talent. Recently, the 2015 Broadway musical *Allegiance* addressed the experiences of the actor and social media personality George Takei—who also starred in the play—as a boy in a Japanese internment camp during World War II.

Native American theatre has also entered the American national theatre repertoire. The California-based Native Voices theatre company performs Native American plays regularly at its Autry Theatre home base in Griffith Park, Los Angeles, and tours plays and play readings to the La Jolla Playhouse in San Diego; the company's 2011 world premiere of Cherokee Carolyn Dunn's *The Frybread Queen*—with an all–Native American cast—was one of the highlights of the Southern California theatre season. Its most recent work, a 2015 presentation of *Off the Rails*, adapted from Shakespeare's *Measure for Measure* by Native Voices's artistic director Randy Reinholz, who is Choctaw, deals with Indian boarding schools in the American Wild West of the 1880s. Hanay Geiogamah, who founded a Native American theatre company in 1971, has been active in writing plays that deal specifically with Native experiences and are produced by Native American theatre artists. And the Thunder Theatre, operated by the Haskell Indian Nations University in Lawrence, Kansas, has also been devoted to producing Native American plays and training Native American theatre artists; its website lists more than one hundred Native American dramatists working around the country.

Theatre and Ability   Finally, people with disabilities are also represented by new plays, as well as by theatre companies that were created specifically for these voices and for expanding their outreach to include audience members with disabilities. In New York, Theatre Breaking Through Barriers (until 2008 known as Theatre by the Blind) employs blind actors, as well as actors with other disabilities, for all of its productions; in 2014 the theatre company traveled to Japan to perform in that country's National Sports Festival for People with Disabilities. The National Theatre of the Deaf in Connecticut and Deaf West in Los Angeles are two of several groups that create theatre by and for deaf and hard-of-hearing people, employing American Sign Language (ASL) as their primary verbal dramatic medium. The stories of deaf and hard-of-hearing people reached broad popular audiences with Mark Medoff's *Children of a Lesser God* (1980), which earned the deaf actor Phyllis Frelich the 1980 Tony Award for Best Actress, and Nina Raine's *Tribes*, about varying degrees of hearing ability within a family, which cast a deaf actor in the lead and won the 2012 Drama Desk Award for Outstanding Play. *Children of a Lesser God* was later revived on Broadway in 2018 and starred Joshua Jackson and the deaf actor Lauren Ridloff. In addition to plays that directly address the experience of people with disabilities, the theatre has reconsidered classic works that feature people with disabilities with new focus. For

Deaf West's production of the musical *Big River*, in which characters alternately speak, sing, and sign their roles, began on the company's tiny home stage. From there it moved to the much larger Mark Taper Forum and then to Broadway, winning critical acclaim for combining brilliant musical performances with the expressive potential of sign language. Tyrone Giordano (*left*) plays Huckleberry Finn, with Michael McElroy (*right*) as Jim, at the American Airlines Theatre in 2003. *©Sara Krulwich/The New York Times/Redux*

"We will lead you to young housewives with figures that will turn you on."

Anyone who has struggled to read a bad translation of a foreign language will find Asian American David Henry Hwang's *Chinglish* very funny indeed. The play, about an American businessman in China, is written in both Chinese and (fractured) English, helped (and often hindered, as above) by projected supertitles. Premiering at Chicago's Goodman Theatre, the play later enjoyed a three-month 2011–2012 Broadway run. Direction was by Leigh Silverman and scenic design by David Korins. *©Sara Krulwich/The New York Times/Redux*

📷 Photo Essay: Theatre in the Borderlands

1.

Not all—or even most—Latinx theatre activity in the United States is found in America's largest cities. The Borderlands Theatre was founded in Tucson, Arizona, in 1986 to provide theatrical entertainment for the local Mexican American population and create interchange among members of the Latinx and Anglo communities in the Arizona–Sonora "borderlands"—the area that at times links and at other times divides Mexico and the United States.

Borderlands has no permanent theatre and owns minimal equipment, but it recruits plays, performers, and directors from both countries with the aid of National Endowment of the Arts funding, along with a body of loyal community supporters. The pictured production, presented in English and Spanish versions on alternate nights, is Mexican playwright Javier Malpica's *Papá está en la Atlántida* (*Our Dad Is in Atlantis*), directed by Eva Tessler. It was a great success for the company in 2009, telling the heartbreaking story of two preteen Mexican brothers—played by adult actors Rafael E. Martinez and Bryant Ranier Enriquez—who, after their mother's death, try to walk through the Sonoran Desert to find their father, who has illegally crossed the border to Atlanta (which the younger brother thinks is the magical kingdom of Atlantis).

Similar bilingual theatre companies can be found in most cities along America's southern frontier—Teatro Promoteo in Miami, Latino Teatro in Los Angeles, the Latino Theatre Alliance in Austin, Texas—as well as in northern cities, including Teatro Pregones in New York City, the Gala Hispanic Theatre in Washington, and the all-female Teatro Luna in Chicago.

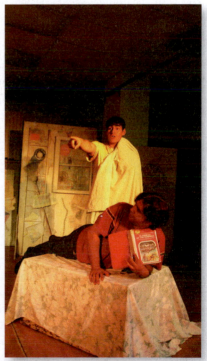

2.

instance, a 2017 Broadway production of Tennessee Williams's *The Glass Menagerie* cast in the role of Laura, whom the script describes as having a limp, an actor who uses a wheelchair, Madison Ferris. The opening moments of this production showed Laura dragging herself up the stairs to her dilapidated St. Louis apartment. The audience had to consider the difficulties of living in a world that does not accommodate the reality of your body.

Intersectional Theatre   The increasing visibility of the stories of people with disabilities onstage attests to the theatre's ability to accommodate new identities—oftentimes identities that have long existed but have existed in the margins. However, while this is to be celebrated, we should be hesitant to simply think of a constantly growing list of distinct theatres, one for each possible identity. The breakdown of different manifestations of the theatre of identity—women, LGBTQ+, black, Latinx, Asian American, and Native American—is convenient for learning of the histories of these groups, but it is also illusory. Theatre is above all not dedicated to one specific experience but rather a celebration of humanity; it is an intersectional space that provides a forum for identities to mingle, converse, and define themselves against and with each other. Such a designation does not diminish the vitality and singularity of different voices but instead strengthens them. There are traditions of theatre that exist in between the categories we have outlined here: plays can be queer and black, Latinx and feminist, or gay and Native American—or endless variations therein. Just like identity itself, theatre does not fall into neatly defined compartments but is an art form that embraces the whole continuum of life.

SPECTACULAR THEATRE

Aristotle considered spectacle the least important of his six components of theatre, but the recent decades have seen theatre emphasize spectacle more and more. However, the kind of spectacle in theatre today is different, in some ways, from the kind Aristotle disliked. Today, spectacle is less about simply adding visual elements as ornamentation to the other elements and more about creating an overwhelming and holistic experience that astounds the audience. This shift reflects the development of new technologies that have affected both visual and sound design. But sometimes spectacle is part of a new philosophy, as well: a deliberate attempt by artists to produce an overwhelming effect.

Some of the new theatre technology (see the chapter titled "Designers and Technicians") has been inspired by cinema, with its dazzling computer graphics, animations, and digitized motion capture, as well as from the contemporary circus. The special effects in films like *Wonder Woman* and the *Planet of the Apes* series have encouraged directors and designers to discover computerized technologies that in a matter of nanoseconds can create and remove landscapes, move lights and change their colors, and produce seemingly magical illusions. And the concert stage has created sound systems capable of reaching ear-blasting volume while still maintaining subtle characteristics. Today, the amplified voice can reach every seat in the house simultaneously with the clarity of someone speaking in the same room.

Such spectacular effects reach their apex in high-budget Broadway musicals, which feature onstage fireworks (*Aladdin*), high-flying actors (*Spider-Man: Turn Off the Dark*), falling chandeliers (*Phantom of the Opera*), and ascending helicopters (*Miss Saigon*). One of the clearer examples of a spectacle-laden, cinematic show is *King Kong,* which features a twenty-foot animatronic gorilla and opened on Broadway in 2018 after a tortuously long process of rewriting and reworking the script. However, today's typical Broadway theatregoer does not disdain these effects. Oftentimes, in fact, they are precisely why someone is attending the show.

There are international theatre events that feature spectacle as the main attraction as well. The Theatre Olympics is a global phenomenon, a festival of grand productions that was founded in 1993 by Theodoros Terzopoulos, Heiner Müller, Nuria Espert, Antunes Filho, Tony Harrison, Yuri Lyubimov, Suzuki Tadashi, and Robert Wilson. Wilson, in particular, stands as an international artist—his work is produced globally—who collaborates with multicultural artists to create jaw-dropping theatrical experiences. Wilson comes from a background in experimental theatre; spectacle is not only the purview of mass entertainment but also frequently an aspect of more avant-garde work as well. Along with the Theatre Olympics, Wilson has produced work for the actual Olympics—selections of his vast *the CIVIL warS: a tree is best measured when it is down* were featured in the opening ceremonies of the 1984 Summer Olympics in Los Angeles. The Olympics are frequently an opportunity to see theatrical spectacle on a grand scale; the Chinese director Zhang Yimou, for instance, created a sensation with his opening ceremonies for the 2008 Beijing Olympics, which featured Chinese opera, puppetry, and dancers covered in ink moving a giant scroll to create patterns and shapes.

There is also a more philosophical reason for the theatre's current turn to the spectacular. The French theorist Antonin Artaud argued fiercely in the 1930s that theatre should have "no more masterpieces" and that words

Puppet-theatre is an ancient form that has recently gained new popularity worldwide. The brilliant puppetry shown here is by the theatre artist Rezo Gabriadze, from a production at the Tovstonogov State Academic Bolshoi Drama Theatre in St. Petersburg, Russia. ©*Photoagency Interpress/ZUMA Press/Newscom*

in dramas should be valued more for their physical impact on the audience than for their meanings. Theatre, Artaud thought, should have the importance of dreams, and his proposed theatre was one of overwhelming sounds and visual images. While *Aladdin* might not exactly be what Artaud had in mind when he called for this theatrical revolution, other genres of theatre today have taken up his call.

PERFORMANCE ART

Performance art is a kind of theatre that is primarily conceptual and not "dramatic" in the traditional sense of having clear narrative, character development, or structure. Successful performance art can be meditative, arresting, shocking, political, and provocative—oftentimes all at once. The movement became prominent in the United

States in a famous presentation by noted performance artist Karen Finley in the late 1980s in which she smeared her naked body with chocolate to represent the exploitation and sexual abasement of women. This performance led to the National Endowment for the Arts (NEA) revoking the funding they had awarded her, and several other performance artists, in 1990. For her subsequent *Shut Up and Love Me*, Finley again smeared herself with chocolate, this time inviting audience members to lick it for a fee of twenty dollars to compensate for the loss of her NEA grant. By confronting viewers with their own lust and disgust—and their desire to be part of an outrageous news story—Finley created a vividly memorable unease.

Many other performance artists are active today. Among the best known is the American Laurie Anderson, a master of many voices, musical instruments, and original

One form of contemporary theatre that has gained popularity is verbatim drama, which, as the name suggests, bases its script on real-life interviews and transcripts. Here (*from left to right*), Paul James Corrigan, Paul Rattray, and Emun Elliott play members of Scotland's Black Watch in a verbatim drama by that name that deals with the horrors of the Iraq war. Created by the National Theatre of Scotland in 2006, it has been performed around the world, enjoying a sold-out, four-city American tour in 2011. ©*Geraint Lewis/Alamy Stock Photo*

ideas since the 1970s. Another is the Serbian Marina Abramović, whose 2010 performance titled "The Artist Is Present" at New York's Museum of Modern Art consisted of her sitting in complete silence all day every day for a month and a half—716 hours and 30 minutes in all—while museumgoers took a seat across from her one at a time to have a "silent conversation." All around her, performers reenacted many of her famous pieces, such as "Imponderabilia," in which the audience member passes between a nude man and woman in a door frame. Other recent

works of durational performance include "Pierre" by the French Abraham Poincheval, for which he lived inside a boulder for one week—nestled in a carved-out space in the shape of his body—in a museum in Paris.

Performance art has, as of late, attained a strange star power; actors such as James Franco and Tilda Swinton have—somewhat controversially—become enamored with the medium. Swinton, an electrifying British film star, recently created the work *Cloakroom,* in which she speaks with and licks the coats checked by audience members

Sometimes the dangerous theatre of yesterday can seem antiquated in the current age, but an electrifying 2014 production of *Hair* at the Hollywood Bowl, directed by Adam Shankman, proved that the 1968 musical still has legs—along with other parts of the human body—today. ©*Mathew Imaging/WireImage/Getty Images*

upon their arrival. This kind of art, like its forbears in the heady days of the 1960s and 1970s, is more of an "event" than a play, but it is, in its own way, highly theatrical.

DANGEROUS THEATRE

How can theatre be dangerous? The nudity and sensory assault of contemporary theatre no longer cause much protest, and audiences in the twenty-first century generally take these in stride. The first-act conclusion of the 2009 Broadway revival of *Hair*, rather than shocking its spectators, proved a rousing success. Most of its audiences considered its fully nude tableau far more thrilling than challenging.

Danger in today's theatre is more apt to come from depictions of violence. Of course, the theatre has long featured such acts. Ancient Greek tragedies often reach their climaxes in the aftermath of bloody acts: Oedipus Rex gouges out his eyes, Medea kills her children, and Clytemnestra murders her husband while he bathes.

Today our theatre has returned to depicting these primal acts of violence, filtered through our contemporary anxieties surrounding war, terror, and the aggressive oppression of women and minorities. At times the task of theatre seems to be to remind a complacent audience of the dangers facing many elsewhere in the world. The 2017 cabaret-theatre-dance piece *Unwanted,* by the Rwandan artist Dorothée Munyaneza, features spoken and sung real-life accounts of rape survivors from her native Rwanda, Chad, Syria, and other countries. Similarly, the 2015 play *Eclipsed,* by Danai Gurira, depicts the lives of women in Liberia forced into sexual slavery. The play premiered on Broadway in 2016 starring Lupita Nyong'o and received widespread critical appreciation.

Many recent plays have focused, in particular, on torture, such as a 2017 Broadway adaptation of *1984* that featured a torture sequence so harrowing that audience members reportedly fainted; David Wiener's 2011 *Extraordinary Chambers*, about the tortures and killings of Cambodia's Khmer Rouge regime; and the New Haven

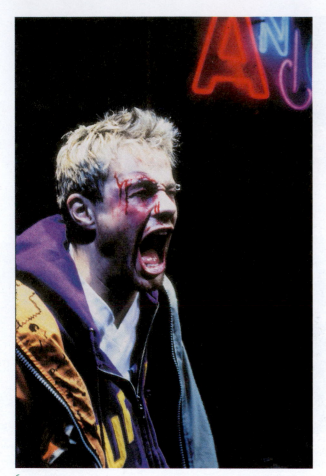

One of the most gripping contemporary plays about urban British violence is Mark Ravenhill's shockingly titled *Shopping and Fucking*. Andrew Clover is the besieged actor in the original London production at the Royal Court Theatre in 1996. ©*ArenaPal/Topham/The Image Works*

We might, then, think of a different kind of danger when discussing dangerous theatre: the political danger of voicing opinions in public. In 2017, an outdoor production of *Julius Caesar* produced by New York City's Public Theater was dangerous in both senses: it featured a title character whose costumes and physical appearance were clearly modeled after President Trump. Shakespeare's play contains a bloody depiction of Caesar's murder; in the Delacorte version, this scene led to outrage and protests. While audacious, however, the Public's *Caesar* offered a cautionary tale rather than an endorsement of violence: the conspirators who murder Caesar, after all, ended up dissolving Roman democracy and paving the way for the authoritarianism of the empire. The play was a critique of violence, not a celebration of it—a subtlety lost in the firestorm of media coverage. Other examples of politically dangerous theatre include higher stakes for participants: current theatre in Moscow, for instance, is a highly risky affair. With rampant government censorship and corruption, Russian theatre artists need to tread lightly. When they don't, we can surely call this kind of work dangerous. Teatr.doc, for instance, is a Russian theatre company whose play *BerlusPutin* viciously satirized Vladimir Putin, the president of Russia, and Silvio Berlusconi, the scandal-plagued former prime minister of Italy. The company was evicted from its theatre building in 2014 by the Russian government and forbidden to perform in Moscow's renowned Golden Mask Festival. Called "Russia's most daring theatre company" by the BBC, and actively antagonized by the Moscow government, Teatr.doc shows us another form of danger—the danger (and bravery) of speaking out.

Long Wharf's 2011 reading of Philippe Sands's book *Torture Team*. Even the language of theatre has become violent, perhaps starting in America with David Mamet's 1983 *Glengarry Glen Ross*—with lines like "Fuck marshalling the leads. What the fuck talk is that?" The trend caught on quickly. The titles of Mark Ravenhill's 1996 play *Shopping and Fucking* and Stephen Adly Guirgis's 2011 *The Motherfucker with the Hat* forced family newspapers to puzzle out how to list such works in their pages.

This kind of "dangerous" theatre, however, seems less startling today than it was in the first decade of this century. Perhaps the reason is the radically increased violence on television—not only in blood-soaked dramas like *Breaking Bad, Homeland, Game of Thrones,* and *The Walking Dead*, but also evening network broadcasts like *Criminal Minds, CSI,* and *Law & Order: SVU*—most of which invariably feature murder and willfully offensive language.

THEATRE OF COMMUNITY

Although most of the theatre discussed and pictured in this book was created by trained professional artists, we must never forget that theatre's origins are located in performances created not by theatre professionals but by social communities—religious and cultural—whose works were intended not for the entertainment of spectators but for the benefit, and often the rapture, of their own participants. The earliest forms of theatre were celebrations of their societies, and their performers were the primary celebrants. Such theatres continue today. They eventually may attract audiences, attain box-office income, and pay professional salaries, but they are foremost expressions, celebrations, and sometimes critiques of the cultures of their creators.

In the 1930s, several "workers' theatres" created theatre pieces by and for the American laborer. The most famous, Clifford Odets's *Waiting for Lefty*, was produced

Lynn Nottage's 2009 Pulitzer Prize–winning *Ruined* is dangerous both in terms of its political voice and depictions of the effects of violence. The play is set in a bar in the Ituri Rainforest of the Democratic Republic of Congo where women are forced into having sex with soldiers as a means of survival. Here, Coldola Rashad's Sophie, an 18-year-old Congolese girl, is approached by soldiers played by Kevin Mambo and William Jackson Harper. The play was directed by Kate Whoriskey, who co-researched it with Nottage in Uganda; it opened at the Goodman Theatre in Chicago in 2008 and at the Manhattan Theatre Club the following year. ©*Sara Krulwich/The New York Times/Redux*

in 1935 by the Group Theatre, which became one of the country's first prominent theatre ensembles dedicated to social causes. Other such theatre ensembles followed, many devoted not merely to creating theatre works by and for members of their community, but also to touring their productions to localities previously unserved by the theatre at all, including Luis Valdez's El Teatro Campesino (the "farmworkers' theatre," mentioned earlier) and the Free Southern Theatre founded in New Orleans by the playwright John O'Neal in 1965. The Los Angeles Poverty Department, a theatre company based in the Skid Row neighborhood of Los Angeles, dedicates itself to working with members of the community, such as the homeless and displaced, who lack a voice in mainstream theatre.

Applied drama refers to theatre that works with disenfranchised or traditionally marginalized communities to help explore and express their identities. One remarkable example of this work has been theatre in prisons. Across the country, inmates have participated in productions of Shakespeare or original works, oftentimes with stunning results. The renowned classical theatre director Arin Arbus regularly works at the Woodburne Correctional Facility to help the prisoners learn about Shakespeare's theatre and the theatrical process—and to learn about the human lessons Shakespeare's plays can teach us. One of modern drama's most famous productions was staged in a prison: in 1957, a production of *Waiting for Godot*—which had up until then puzzled critics and audiences alike—found a rapturous and understanding crowd at San Quentin State Prison. The Marin Shakespeare Company has kept up this practice to this day with its Shakespeare for Social Justice program, which works with inmates at San Quentin and California

Staged by the remarkably innovative director Rupert Goold, the often violent 2013 British musical *American Psycho* brilliantly satirizes the rock music, coke snorting, fervent consumerism, and rampaging capitalism of the American 1980s. A "ground-breaker," a "vivacious production," and a "serial-killer thriller," said its approving—and sometimes disapproving—critics following its London debut. ©*Elliott Franks/eyevine/Redux*

State Prison, Solano, as well as with veteran populations in the area. Shakespeare has the potential to be more vital in these productions than in traditional settings—to become a way for everyone, even those overlooked by most of society, to discover theatre's essential humanity.

A prominent presence in the community-based theatre movement in the United States is the Cornerstone Theater, founded in 1986 by Bill Rauch and Alison Carey and currently headed by Michael John Garcés. The Cornerstone's goal has been to engage with local cultural groups to create new theatrical works (often based on classic dramas) adapted to each group's interests, fears, and aspirations. These works are then performed—by the merged Cornerstone and community groups—within the community, usually on a free or pay-what-you-can basis. The response is usually electric: not only are these plays heralded as absorbing and entertaining, but they initiate new cultural discourse and even social change in almost every community where they have been engaged. Examples of Cornerstone's work are as varied as American culture

itself: for example *Tartoof*, adapted from Molière's *Tartuffe* and portraying a disintegrating farm family, with a cast and crew of fifty-five Kansans in Norcatur, Kansas (population 215); *Romeo & Juliet*, performed by a racially integrated cast in Port Gibson, Mississippi (population 2,371); and more recently, *Magic Fruit,* a riff on Mozart's opera *The Magic Flute* and the culmination of the ambitious six-year Hunger Cycle, which explores issues of global justice and hunger.

Rauch and Carey's vision was inspired by the influential Theatre of the Oppressed, a movement started in Brazil by Augusto Boal that focuses on using theatre as a tool for social good. Similar ideas can be found historically in the "Peasant's Theatre" of 1930s China and, more recently, in productions that use nonprofessional actors to tell stories of present-day crises. The 2017 Tunisian Canadian play *Al-Shaqaf* addresses the terrifying situation of refugees in the Middle East (the title is Yemeni for a small boat used to smuggle those escaping the country) and includes in its script interviews with actual refugees. The play toured

The three witches in Shakespeare's *Macbeth* are here performed by prisoners at San Quentin in 2015. The direction, costumes, and scenic elements were provided by the Marin Shakespeare Company in nearby San Rafael, California. *©Sean Mirkovich/Marin Shakespeare Company*

internationally and demonstrates how the communal act of staging stories can still be profound and radical.

PHYSICAL THEATRE

As theatre changes, the way we talk about theatre changes as well. These days, theatre listings often include events that previous generations would consider more dance, or simply physical movement. But *physical theatre* presents a valid new form that blurs the lines of what we consider drama to be. Physical theatre productions tend to consist almost entirely of expressive movement, dance, music, and lighting. Many companies enjoy enormous popularity in commercial as well as more experimental theatre communities.

The major crossover moment for this form occurred in 1991 when Luke Cresswell, a percussionist and composer, and Steve McNichols, an actor and writer, created *Stomp*, a story-less and purely percussive performance piece.

Blue Man Group, now running lavish and apparently permanent productions in six cities in the United States and Europe, began as an unknown three-man percussion ensemble performing in the streets and eventually in a tiny off-Broadway theatre. Extraordinary drumming, lighting, physical dexterity, and the now-famous iridescent blue makeup have characterized Blue Man Group performers since the beginning. *©Then Chih Wey Xinhua/eyevine/Redux*

Mixing dance and theatre, the work of Martha Clarke is difficult to categorize; whatever one calls it, though, her production *The Angel Reapers*, which premiered at the Signature Theatre, in New York, in 2016, was undoubtedly beautiful. The work—a collaboration with the playwright Alfred Uhry—celebrates the ecstatic spiritual practices of the Shakers, an American religious sect. ©*Sara Krulwich/The New York Times/Redux*

Stomp proved a great success in both London and New York and has run ever since in those cities and many others around the world. The production employs an assortment of garbage can lids, pipes, brooms, and other everyday objects for its drumming; its rhythms are furious, its choreography is explosive, and its intensity is relentless—and often comic.

Blue Man Group is a company that produces similarly plotless, percussive performance and also employs riotous clowning, interaction with the audience, and food fights; it is performed by three bald actors covered from the neck up in glossy blue goop. The group was created in New York City by former school pals Chris Wink, Matt Goldman, and Phil Stanton, who opened their first show, *Tubes*, at the tiny off-Broadway Astor Place Theatre in 1991. They (and their professional heirs) are now a near-permanent fixture in New York, Boston, Chicago, Berlin, Orlando, and Las Vegas. In 2017, Blue Man Group was purchased by Cirque du Soleil, another global physical

theatre sensation that plans on expanding the Blue Men even farther and wider.

One form of physical theatre, *dance-drama*, uses a mixture of speech and dramatic choreography to create a dance-centered theatre event—or, depending on how you look at it, a very theatrical form of dance. Dance-theatre was popularized in Germany by the late Pina Bausch, whose Tanztheatre Wuppertal company created playful and harrowing dances that flirted with a plot without ever resolving into a clear sense of story. In America, dance-theatre gained prominence through the work of Martha Clarke, a veteran of the Pilobolus dance troupe. Clarke first received wide acclaim for her dance-theatre pieces in the late 1980s, particularly *The Garden of Earthly Delights*, based on the famous painting by Hieronymus Bosch. She refashioned and revived this production to wide acclaim in 2008–2009. Her major works in the current century include *Vienna: Lusthaus*, which evokes the artistic and sexual ferment of Vienna at the time of painter-designer

The Synetic Theatre in Arlington, Virginia's 2014 production of *Hamlet . . . the rest is silence* is, like all of its productions, wordless. Directed by the company leader, Paata Tsikurishvili, it is a combination of music, mime, and movement, the latter created by choreographer Irina Kavsdze, who is also featured in this production as Ophelia, shown here surrounded by the ensemble. *©Koko Lanham*

Gustav Klimt; *Kaos,* a dance-theatre piece based on stories by Italian playwright Luigi Pirandello that conveys tales of tragic madness, sexual passion, and despair among the inhabitants of a dusty Sicilian village; and most recently *Angel Reapers,* in 2016, which saw Clarke collaborate with the renowned playwright Alfred Uhry to create a work inspired by the Shakers, an eighteenth-century ecstatic religious sect.

The dance-theatre of the present has also been enhanced by innovative choreographers who work in pure dance. A prize example of this is Susan Stroman, who has choreographed for the New York City Ballet as well as choreographed and directed Broadway's *The Producers, The Scottsboro Boys, Bullets Over Broadway,* and the revue *Prince of Broadway.* The versatile Stroman scored an immense success with her all-but-wordless *Contact* in 2000, which surprisingly won the Tony Award for Best Play while Stroman took the Tony for Best Director. (For more on Susan Stroman, see the photo essay in the chapter titled "The Director.")

One of the newest movement-based companies is the Synetic Theatre in the Washington, D.C., suburb of Arlington, Virginia. Founded in 2001 by a Georgian expatriate couple, Paata and Irina Tsikurishvili, the Synetic group (the word combines "synthesis" and "kinetic") performs completely wordless works, yet their favorite playwright is one of the world's wordiest dramatists: William Shakespeare. The plays' missing words are not replaced merely with music and ballet but with intense passion, persuasive actions, visible props and symbols, and a surprising level of comedy and fantasy. Since there are no words spoken, character intentions are physically exhibited. For example, in their 2014 *Hamlet . . . the rest is silence,* when the prince Hamlet would normally tell his mother Gertrude to "look upon this picture and on this," Hamlet (played by Paata) grabs Gertrude (played by Irina) and forces her to look at actors dressed and posing as King Hamlet and King Claudius, who are seen glaring at each other from opposite sides of the stage, making

The Argentine movement art company De La Guarda was founded in 1993 by a group of theatre students who, unable to find acting jobs upon graduation, created their own highly original form of expression in interactive aerial ballet. Company performers mostly fly over and into their standing, swaying audience—which is simultaneously assaulted by rain, smoke, and wind and blasted by pummeling music and sound. The company's most recent production, *Fuertzabruta* (*Brute Force*)—seen here in its run at the 2007 Edinburgh International Festival in Scotland—has elements of circus, rave, rock concert, striptease, and fraternity party and has been performed around the world. ©*Geraint Lewis/ Alamy Stock Photo*

their brotherly hatred all the more frightful. The production's intense choreography, created by Irina, and its original musical score take care of most of the rest. Synetic's wordless action creates a continuously building arc of Shakespearean tragedy that regularly receives standing ovations from the audience. In 2014, the Tsikurishvili cofounders, already the winners of many awards, were honored as "Washingtonians of the Year" by *Washingtonian* magazine. Synetic's 2017 production of *Peter Pan* quickly became another hit for the company, this time for adults and children alike.

SOLO PERFORMANCE

Although Anton Chekhov wrote a short play for a single actor in 1886 (*On the Harmfulness of Tobacco*, in which the solo character is a lecturer addressing his audience),

only in recent times have authors seriously entertained the possibilities of full-length plays employing just one performer. Sometimes these are little more than star vehicles or extended monologues, often based on historical characters, such as Hal Holbrook's long-running portrayal of America's great writer in *Mark Twain Tonight*, James Whitmore's rendition of America's feisty thirty-third president in *Give 'Em Hell, Harry!*, and Julie Harris's tours as Emily Dickinson in *The Belle of Amherst*. More fully dramatized works followed in the 1990s, however, when Jay Presson Allen wrote two intriguing and generally successful Broadway plays for solo actors, most notably *Tru*, about novelist and socialite Truman Capote in his last, despairing days. Other noteworthy solo performances include Lily Tomlin's portrayal of all seventeen characters in Jane Wagner's amusing and affecting *Search for Signs of Intelligent Life in the Universe;* Billie Allen embodying a

The celebrated solo performer John Leguizamo here presents his fifth one-man show, *Ghetto Klown*, free of charge to all comers in New York's Central Park in 2014. In this show he reflects on—and performs—everything from his Latinx upbringing in Queens to his twenty-year career interactions with Al Pacino, Sean Penn, and his late acting teacher, Lee Strasberg. "The beautiful thing I've learned about being an artist," he says, is seeing "beauty in the darkest parts of human nature." *©Jack Vartoogian/ Archive Photos/Getty Images*

Without a doubt, the most virtuosic display of endurance in New York theatre in 2017 was Taylor Mac's daylong exploration of American music, *A 24-Decade History of Popular Music*. Mac, an accomplished and gender-fluid performer, dedicated each hour to a decade of American history, from the Civil War to the present day. Audiences were enraptured, euphoric, and exhausted. *©Sara Krulwich/The New York Times/Redux*

character who in turn takes on numerous "selves" such as the Duchess of Hapsburg and Jesus in Adrienne Kennedy's *Funnyhouse of a Negro;* Patrick Stewart's one-man presentation of Charles Dickens's *A Christmas Carol,* in which the celebrated Shakespearean actor (and *Star Trek* star) played all the roles; and Jefferson Mays playing forty roles, both men and women (and winning the 2004 Tony Award for it) in Doug Wright's *I Am My Own Wife.*

In the United States, more socially engaged solo performances have redefined the genre. Jeff Weiss's epic narratives of his life on the Lower East Side, collectively titled *. . . And That's How the Rent Gets Paid,* probably began this trend at the Performing Garage in New York's SoHo neighborhood during the 1970s and 1980s. In the next decade, Eric Bogosian's series of intense and penetrating performances, savage and comic by turns, featured an indelible cast of American low-life characters, such as pimps and prostitutes, addicts and agents, executives and rock stars, and panhandlers and jocks (*Drinking in America; Sex, Drugs,* and *Rock & Roll; Wake Up and Smell the Coffee*). Anna Deveare Smith's *Fires in the Mirror, Twilight: Los Angeles 1992, Lay Me Down Easy,* and most recently *Notes from the Field* are all solo performances, in multiple voices, that portray verbatim testimonies from people embroiled in major crises: the 1991 three-day riot in Crown Heights, Brooklyn, sparked by the death of an African American child and culminating in the violent death of a Hasidic Jew; the 1992 Los Angeles riots following the acquittal of white police officers charged with the beating of the black motorist, Rodney King; the current crisis in health care; and the state of American public education.

Many solo performances are autobiographical; Colombian-born John Leguizamo's performances of *Freak* and *Sexaholix,* both set in Leguizamo's childhood borough of Queens, New York, are hugely comic and often deeply poignant autobiographical journeys of his childhood and adolescence; his 2011 Broadway hit *Ghetto Klown* describes his later battles trying to combine a stage and film career with fame, family, and friendships. In 2017 Leguizamo again found himself headed to Broadway with his comical and politically fierce lecture *Latin History for Morons.* In 2016 Taylor Mac wowed audiences with *A 24-Decade History of Popular Music,* which, as its title suggests, leads the audience through the last 240 years of music—with each hour dedicated to a different decade.

That adds up to 24 hours: an entire day of one person leading us through centuries of artistic expression. Internationally, the Fujairah Festival, in Iran, is dedicated entirely to "monodrama"—the festival's term for solo performance—and offers works that mingle Western theatre forms with Arab traditions, such as the *sirah,* a kind of storytelling that centers on biographical narrative. And in one subversive example of solo performance, the Austrian author Thomas Bernhard's *Minetti* deals with an actor who cannot take on the role of King Lear: the play is a study of one man's failure even though, as audience members, we are watching the virtuosity of one man's performance. A recent Russian production of *Minetti* received rapturous reviews at the 2017 Sibiu Theatre Festival in Romania.

INTIMATE THEATRE

One trend in global theatre has been toward intimacy: rather than shock, prod, or assault the audience, more productions are inviting them into the world of the play—sometimes quite literally. Theatre today is increasingly focused on blurring boundaries between spectator and performer, stage and seating.

Many plays today are *site-specific:* they are realized fully in particular environments outside the traditional facilities with curtains and theatre seats. Site-specific plays have occurred in apartments, restaurants, and even—in one 2017 adaptation of *Macbeth*—a shipping crate. The 2011 Romanian production of *The Cioran Temptation*, written and directed by Gavriil Pinte, was staged in a streetcar traveling from the city of Sibiu, Romania, to Rasinari, where the actual Emil Cioran (a twentieth-century Romanian philosopher) was born: as the play progressed, the character of Cioran escorted the audience to and from his hometown, sharing his reactions to his town, his country, and his life. Here, the actual site of the performance is where actions described in the play are considered to take place. Similarly, the South African theatre artist Brett

Director Stephen Burdman calls the New York Classical Theatre, which he founded in 1999, a form of "panoramic theatre" because it stages plays outdoors in wide-open public venues with the audience standing, seated on the ground, or settled in folding chairs. Here Connie Castanzo (*left*) and Kristan Calagro (*right*) perform a scene from *The Rivals,* a classic comedy written by Richard Brinsley Sheridan in 1775 and staged by Burdman in New York's Central Park in 2017. ©*Miranda Arden/New York Classical Theatre*

Gavriil Pinte's *The Cioran Temptation*, seen at the 2011 Sibiu International Theatre Festival, is literally staged in and around a streetcar that travels during the performance to and from the same Romanian cities that its title character, the Romanian philosopher Emil Cioran, visited often as a young man. *Sibiu International Theatre Festival ©Mihaela Marin/Radu Stanca National Theatre Sibiu*

Sleep No More, presented in New York in 2011 by England's Punchdrunk company, is a radical reconstruction of Shakespeare's *Macbeth*. The production requires audience members to don identical masks, then invites them to follow—and occasionally interact with—individual actors as they move from floor to floor and room to room in a bizarrely decorated five-story "hotel." The fascinating action—impossible to follow in its entirety—climaxes in a scene where the spectators are herded together to see Macbeth and Lady Macbeth wash the murderous blood from their bodies in a basement bathtub. *©Sara Krulwich/The New York Times/ Redux*

Bailey recently created a disturbing theatrical environment in a colonial mansion in Chile; as audience members wandered through the house, actors played slaves and servants at work; spectators saw history come alive in the place where it first occurred. In fact, the very role of "spectator" was challenged, as visitors became woven into the history itself. A 2016 production of Shakespeare's *Merchant of Venice* occurred outside, in the original Jewish ghetto in Venice—precisely where the play takes place. (The production was fortuitously timed with the 500th anniversary of the ghetto's formation and the 400th anniversary of Shakespeare's death.) Like Bailey's work, the characters seem to be ghosts from the landscape, returned to remind us of the past.

Another kind of intimate theatre, known as *immersive theatre,* does not necessarily take place in a "real" location but does fully invite its audience to be a part of the show. One of the biggest recent immersive hits in New York has been *Sleep No More*, an imaginative work inspired by *Macbeth*. Staged by England's Punchdrunk company in three

Participatory theatre doesn't get more participatory than this: an actor is given a never-before-seen script and proceeds to read it for the first time in front of a live audience. Such is the case with *White Rabbit Red Rabbit* by the Iranian playwright Nassim Soleimanpour, which became a sensation in New York in 2016. Different well-known actors would take on the lead role on different nights. Pictured here is Darren Criss; other notable performers include Brian Dennehy, F. Murray Abraham, Nathan Lane, Cynthia Nixon, and Stana Katic. *©Bruce Glikas/FilmMagic/Getty Images*

Immersive theatre reaches a literal apex in *Here Lies Love* at the New York Public Theater in 2014, where the actors (Jose Llana and Ruthie Ann Miles) playing the late president and first lady of the Philippines, Ferdinand and Imelda Marcos, stand above, talk to, and eventually dance with the audience. *©Sara Krulwich/The New York Times/Redux*

Juma Sharkah plays a fourteen-year-old girl disguised as a boy in Diana Nneka Atuona's immersive play *Liberian Girl* in its 2015 Royal Court Theatre production in London. The audience chose either to stand around her on a red-earth "killing field," replete with rifle-bearing revolutionaries, or sit apart from the cast in an upper tier of seats. ©*Elliott Franks/eyevine/Redux*

interconnected, long-abandoned Manhattan warehouses, the audience is invited to wander wherever they wish among some 100 rooms in the six floors of the building, which has been converted to resemble a 1930s hotel out of a classic film noir. Audience members wear masks and wander wherever they want—to follow an actor, sit in the chairs, lie on the beds, type on the typewriters, and open the cabinets and study their contents. Without producing a straightforward version of Shakespeare's play, *Sleep No More* remains true to its source material's core themes. As *Macbeth* is a

tragedy with ghosts and witches, *Sleep No More* is both brooding and blood-soaked, with ominous music, occult images, and simulated violent sex. The power of the production is that you are not just observing it, you are *in* it.

In 2017, immersive theatre came to Broadway: the play *Natasha, Pierre & the Great Comet of 1812* originated in a tent in downtown Manhattan, where audience members sat at a Russian nightclub and enjoyed caviar and pierogis as they watched the play. When it transferred to Broadway, the play kept its immersion intact: audience members were seated onstage, mere inches from the performers (who had to sing and dance around the spectators). Other actors and musicians danced through the audience, and lucky playgoers received presents from the cast.

This sense of co-participation between actor and audience has led to the rise of the immersive genre in today's dramatic repertoire. One recent international success takes this immersion to its extreme. In the 2016 *White Rabbit Red Rabbit,* a different notable actor who has never read the play receives the script at each performance and immediately walks onto the stage and reads it aloud to the audience. The text, by the Iranian Nassim Soleimanpour, addresses the very absence of its author, who is forbidden to leave his native land. The performer is, in a sense, another audience member, surprised by each word in the script. This play has toured throughout the world and become a sensation. It seems that intimacy—with the setting, the dramatic world, and even the performers—has become a new form of provocation, perhaps to compensate for our increasingly plugged-in lives.

Finding Theatre in the United States

The American theatre is one of the world's most active, and while its capital is the small island of Manhattan, in America's most populated city, it also takes place in every state in the nation. Theatre is flourishing in regional theatres, festivals, summer and dinner theatres, and amateur theatres in communities and colleges. Wherever you are, theatre is happening right now.

THEATRE IN NEW YORK

New York is the site of more performances, openings, revivals, tours, and dramatic criticism than any half dozen other American cities put together. The city's hundred-plus playhouses are a prime tourist attraction and a major pillar of the local economy.

Moreover, in the minds of most theatre artists—actors, directors, playwrights, and designers—New York is the town where the standards are the highest, the challenges the greatest, and the rewards the most magnificent. The professional New York theatre comes in three different and quite distinct categories: Broadway, off-Broadway, and off-off-Broadway.

Broadway   When people talk about Broadway, they refer to a concept rather than a street. Broadway is simply the historic and commercial apex of the American theatre.

Known as the "Great White Way" (which refers to its bright lights), Broadway provides the destination for tourists from around the world. Forty-one theatres make up today's official Broadway Theatre District, most within a dozen blocks north of Times Square. The great growth of twentieth-century American drama took place right here: the Broadway district is where Eugene O'Neill, Arthur Miller, Tennessee Williams, William Inge, and Edward Albee premiered their masterpieces; where George M. Cohan, Ethel Merman, and Liza Minelli sang and danced; and where Marlon Brando, Barbra Streisand, Sean Penn, Meryl Streep, Robert Redford, and thousands of others acted their way into America's hearts and, often, into Hollywood's films. Broadway flourishes now as never before; the 2016–2017 season recorded Broadway's highest gross income ($1.45 billion, $80 million more than the previous season) and second-highest attendance (13.27 million people) in history. Most excitingly, its glamour is readily accessible: the TKTS Booths (at Times Square, South Street Seaport, Downtown Brooklyn, and Lincoln Center) and several websites sell up-to-half-price tickets for many shows to make the Broadway experience affordable for almost everyone. And Broadway touring companies extend the "Broadway experience" to audiences almost as numerous as those attending the same shows in "the Big Apple."

The Broadway stakes are higher than anywhere else in theatre, and as a result, its energy is electric. However, the Great White Way is no longer the place where new plays routinely originate, as it was in 1947 when it hosted the debuts of Tennessee Williams's *A Streetcar Named Desire* and Arthur Miller's *All My Sons.* Today, Broadway is primarily the staging ground for extravagantly produced musicals, both new (*Hamilton, Aladdin, Dear Evan Hansen, Waitress*) and revived (*Hello, Dolly!, Cats, Cabaret, Sunday in the Park with George*). Second, Broadway is the showcase for the best—or at least most commercially promising—new plays from America's off-Broadway (*Natasha, Pierre & the Great Comet of 1812; Indecent; The Band's Visit*); for new plays from abroad (from England, *Farinelli and the King* and *Harry Potter and the Cursed Child*); and for new works that premiered earlier at America's top-ranking nonprofit theatres—including the Pulitzer Prize winners *Sweat* by Lynn Nottage, which had premiered at the Oregon Shakespeare Festival; *August: Osage County* by Tracy Letts, which had premiered at Chicago's Steppenwolf Theatre; and *Clybourne Park* by Bruce Norris, which had its premiere a few blocks away at off-Broadway's Playwrights Horizons. Finally, Broadway is the site of many major revivals from the international dramatic repertory, including recent star-heavy productions

The Bushwick Star, in Brooklyn, New York, has lately been a hotbed for exciting and experimental off-off-Broadway theatre. Pictured here is a 2018 production, *The Brobot Johnson Experience,* a solo performance that blends science fiction and West African mythology. ©*Richard Termine/The New York Times/Redux*

of modern and contemporary classics, such as *Angels in America* by Tony Kushner, revived in 2018 and starring Nathan Lane; *M. Butterfly* by David Henry Hwang, revived in 2017 and starring Clive Owen; and Noel Coward's *Present Laughter,* also revived in 2017 and featuring a Tony Award–winning performance by Kevin Kline.

The main reason a new play rarely premieres directly on Broadway today is because the costs are usually far too high to risk on an untested product. Despite high ticket prices, which in 2017 ascended to as much as $998 for musicals and $373 for nonmusicals, the majority of Broadway productions charge far less and, even so, fail to recoup their expenses. Increasingly, therefore, Broadway producers look for new plays whose worth has been proven in less-expensive off-Broadway venues, in the subsidized European (chiefly English) theatre, or on a not-for-profit American regional stage. Only a star-studded

revival or a new musical with Tony Award potential is otherwise likely to be bankable and offer sufficient opportunity for commercial success. Nonetheless, Broadway remains the primary showcase for some of the most fully realized theatrical entertainment—and often inspiration—that America has to offer.

Off-Broadway and Off-Off-Broadway   Not all of New York theatre is performed in official Broadway theatres. At least 200 New York theatres are not in the Broadway category. Many of them are fully professional, and most of the others are semiprofessional (that is, they engage professional actors and other artists who, by mutual agreement, are not paid minimum union salaries). The importance of Broadway, however, is so strong that these theatres are named for their relation to Broadway: some are "off-Broadway" theatres, and others are "off-off-Broadway."

Off-Broadway is a term that came into theatrical parlance during the 1950s and now includes forty to sixty theatres found throughout New York neighborhoods. Originally the designation referred to the theatre building's distance from Broadway, but now it refers to the seating capacity: off-Broadway theatres seat between 100 and 499 people. Some of the best stage productions in America—including eventual Tony and Pulitzer Prize winners—have come from these companies in recent years.

Off-off-Broadway, a designation dating from the 1960s, denotes semiprofessional or amateur theatres located in the New York metropolitan area that seat fewer audience members than off-Broadway theatre. Off-off broadway theatres are often the site of experimental and boundary-pushing works, and often take place in church basements, YMCAs, coffeehouses, fringe festivals, and converted studios or garages. The actors' union oversees off-off-Broadway productions under its "Showcase Code," which allows union actors to perform for next to nothing to allow them to enjoy the public exposure and press reviews that could lead to the off-Broadway and eventually Broadway roles to which they aspire.

Many artists, however, find the artistic excitement of off-off-Broadway productions more appealing than the money and glamour of Broadway or even Hollywood. The annual Obie Awards, given by the *Village Voice*, recognize outstanding work in both off- and off-off-Broadway theatres and are often more accurate indicators of national theatre trends than are the more glamorous Tony Awards.

Non-Broadway New York theatre generates passionate and vigorous theatrical creativity. Leaner and less costly than their Broadway competitors, off- and off-off-Broadway productions attract audiences of their own, many of whom would never think of going to Times Square to see a play. And with their lower ticket prices (particularly for off-off-Broadway) and subscription seasons (particularly for off-Broadway), many companies have lured successive generations of audiences to new and exciting works before they reach the Broadway masses.

REGIONAL AMERICAN THEATRE

Very little professional theatre was produced on a regular basis outside of New York City until 1950, when the Arena Stage was founded in Washington, D.C. Over the next fifteen years other "regional" theatres opened, including Houston's Alley Theatre, San Francisco's Actors' Workshop, and Minneapolis's Guthrie Theater. Now there are nearly five hundred such professional theatres, operating in almost every state.

These theatres, though professional to varying degrees, are nearly all not-for-profit (or nonprofit)—meaning they are in business not to make money but to create art. Not-for-profit theatres receive box-office revenue, of course, but they supplement that income with government and foundation grants and from private donations that, if the theatre has been legally registered as a nonprofit corporation, provide tax deductions to the donors. Some of these theatres, such as the Public Theater, the Manhattan Theatre Club, and Playwrights Horizons, operate as off-Broadway theatres in the New York metro area. The vast majority, however, are scattered throughout the country and produce more than two thousand productions each year, providing Americans in hundreds of cities and towns an opportunity to see professional theatre, often at its very best. An annual Tony Award for regional theatre cites the most distinguished of these groups, and forty-two such theatres have been so honored, some in large cities such as Washington, D.C.; Chicago; Los Angeles; Denver; Minneapolis; Seattle; Boston/Cambridge; and Dallas, as well as some in smaller towns, including Williamstown, Massachusetts; Waterford, Connecticut; and Costa Mesa, California.

Nonprofit theatres vary enormously in character. Some concentrate on world classics, some on new American plays, some on the work of specific cultures, some on the European avant-garde, and many on theatrical experiments. Some operate in ninety-nine-seat spaces with extremely modest five-figure budgets and others on multiple stages with funds to match.

The regional theatre is where the vast majority of America's best-known plays have first been shaped and exposed since the 1970s. As a result, what was known as a regional theatre "movement" during the 1960s and 1970s has now become, quite simply, America's national theatre. More and more, the American national press is attuned to major theatre happenings in the nonprofit sector. And more and more, the Broadway audiences, while admiring the latest hit, are aware they are seeing that hit's second, third, or fourth production after debuting in a regional theatre. National theatre prizes such as the Pulitzer, once awarded only for Broadway productions, are now increasingly claimed by plays that premiered in off-Broadway theatres (*Rabbit Hole, Ruined, Clybourne Park, Hamilton,* and *The Flick*) and by regional companies (*August: Osage County, Water by the Spoonful,* and *Disgraced.*) World-renowned actors such as Al Pacino, John Mahoney, Dianne Wiest, Mary Louise Parker, Maggie Gyllenhaal, and Matthew Broderick, once seen live only on Broadway stages and on tour, now also appear in many of the country's nonprofit theatres. These days, the vast majority of

Regional theatre produces much of America's greatest drama. Tracy Letts's *August: Osage County,* a large-scale (thirteen actors, three-plus hours) realistic comedy about a wildly dysfunctional Oklahoma family, was created by Chicago's Steppenwolf Theatre Company, long famed for its ensemble acting. Following its Chicago premiere, the show went on to Broadway, where it was awarded the 2008 Pulitzer Prize for Drama, along with Tony, New York Critics Circle, and Drama Desk Awards. Steppenwolf's artistic director Anna D. Shapiro ingeniously staged the quarrelings and couplings—of the many characters shown here in the now-famous dinner scene in the second act—so audience members felt they knew each one of the characters personally. Deanna Dunagan (*center, with pearl necklace*) plays the central role of Violet, the drug-addicted family matriarch, for which she received the Best Actress Tony Award. Steppenwolf's designers included Todd Rosenthal (scenery), Ana Kuzmanic (costumes), and Ann G. Wrightson (lighting). ©*Sara Krulwich/The New York Times/Redux*

Americans can see first-class professional theatre created in or near their hometowns, and professional theatre artists can live in any major city in the country—not only in New York. Regional theatres are also proving to be a site of artistic innovation offstage. For example, Minneapolis's award-winning Guthrie Theater announced a new initiative in 2016 to create a small theatre space with inexpensive tickets (nine dollars) and featuring new, innovative work.

SHAKESPEARE FESTIVALS

During Broadway's mid-twentieth-century heyday, various theatres opened up as *summer stock* companies. This network of theatres, mainly located in resort areas throughout the Northeast, provided summer entertainment for tourists and assorted local communities. Summer stock companies produced recent and not-so-recent Broadway shows, mainly comedies, with a mix of professional theatre artists from New York and young theatrical hopefuls from around the country. They provided America's vacation theatre and professional training ground.

Summer stock is not as vibrant today, but in its place has risen another phenomenon that, like summer stock, has found massive popularity in the United States. This is the vast array of Shakespeare festivals, begun during the Great Depression and now flourishing in almost every state. The Oregon Shakespeare Festival, in rural Ashland,

Many American regional theatres fill their houses with families in December with productions of a Christmas play—nearly always an adaptation of Charles Dickens's novel *A Christmas Carol.* This production, with South Coast Repertory veteran Hal Landon front and center as Scrooge, is from the final scene of South Coast's twenty-ninth annual production of the play in 2008, adapted by Jerry Patch. *©Henry DiRocco/South Coast Repertory Theatre*

was the first in America. Founded by local drama teacher Angus Bowmer, whose three-night amateur production of *The Merchant of Venice* in 1935 was preceded by an afternoon boxing match "to draw the crowds," the Oregon festival now produces no fewer than eleven plays each year and attracts 350,000 spectators during a ten-month season in a town of less than 20,000 people. There are now more than 200 North American Shakespeare festivals, many of them largely or partially professional, with two of them (Oregon's and Utah's) winning regional Tony Awards. Characteristic of each is a core of two to four Shakespearean productions, normally performed outdoors, together with more contemporary plays often performed on adjacent indoor stages—an arrangement not unlike that of Shakespeare's King's Men, which by the end of the playwright's career performed plays of many authors at both the outdoor Globe and the indoor Blackfriars. In addition to providing exciting classical and modern theatre to audiences around North America, these Shakespeare festivals provide a bridge for aspiring performers and designers to segue from college training to professional employment.

SUMMER AND DINNER THEATRES

There remain some notable professional summer theatres without the word "Shakespeare" in their names. The Williamstown Theatre Festival in Massachusetts is one of the most notable, as it employs many of New York's better-known actors, designers, and directors eager to leave the stifling city in July and August to spend a month or two in this beautiful Berkshire village, where they stage Chekhov, Brecht, Ibsen, Williams, and newer plays in elegantly mounted productions. The Berkshire Theatre Festival in Stockbridge, Massachusetts, is also a highly accomplished professional summer theatre, located in a culturally rich

One of the most acclaimed American theatrical institutions is the Oregon Shakespeare Festival, which celebrates the timeless appeal of classical works while also engaging with our contemporary cultures—as it did in 2018, when it featured a production of the beloved musical *Oklahoma!* with same-sex couples in leading roles. Pictured here is its lovely Renaissance-style outdoor space, the Allen Elizabethan Theatre. *©T. Charles Erickson*

area just two hours north of New York City, where, in the afternoons, visitors can also drop in at Tanglewood to see the Boston Symphony Orchestra rehearsing.

Dinner theatres were introduced to suburban America in the 1970s, offering a "night-on-the-town" package of dinner and a play in the same facility. Their novelty has worn relatively thin, however, and only a few of them remain, generally offering light comedies, mystery melodramas, and pared-down productions of golden-age Broadway musicals.

AMATEUR THEATRE: ACADEMIC AND COMMUNITY

There is an active amateur theatre in the United States, some of it operating in conjunction with educational programs. More than a thousand U.S. colleges and universities have theatre or drama departments that offer degrees in these fields, and another thousand collegiate institutions put on plays, or give classes in drama, without having a full curriculum of studies. Several thousand high schools, summer camps, and private schools also teach drama and mount plays. Much of this dramatic activity is directed toward general education. The educational staging of plays has been pursued at least since the Renaissance as a way to explore dramatic literature, human behavior, and cultural history—as well as to teach skills such as public speaking, self-presentation, and foreign languages. Practical instruction in drama has the virtue of making the world's greatest literature physical and emotional; it gets drama not only into the mind but into the muscles. Learning about history becomes embodied, rather than just thought about. Some of the world's great theatre has emerged from just such academic activity. Four or five "University Wits," Cambridge-educated authors who wrote works influenced by their classical learning, dominated Elizabethan playwriting before Shakespeare arrived on the scene, and Shakespeare's company competed with publicly presented school plays that had become popular

Snow falls on a barren landscape in this 2011 University of California, Irvine, production of Samuel Beckett's *Waiting for Godot*. The portrayed actors (*from left,* Ben Jacoby as Vladimir and Chris Klopatek as Estragon) and the designers (Robin Darling, scenery; Gwyn Conoway Bennison, costumes; Karen Lawrence, lighting; Patricia Cardona, sound) were all graduate drama students. ©*Paul Kennedy*

in London during his career. Several plays that changed theatre history—such as Alfred Jarry's *Ubu Roi* and Tom Stoppard's *Rosencrantz and Guildenstern Are Dead*—were first conceived as extracurricular college projects.

The founding of the Yale Drama Department (now the Yale School of Drama) in 1923 signaled an expanded commitment on the part of American higher education to assume not merely the role of theatre educator and producer but also that of theatre trainer. Today, the majority of American professional theatre artists receive their training in American college and university departments devoted, in whole or in part, to that purpose. As a result, academic and professional theatres have grown closer together, and many artists work as both theatre professionals and theatre professors. For this reason, performances at many university theatres may reach sophisticated levels of excellence and, on occasion, equal or surpass professional productions of the same dramatic material.

Community theatres are amateur groups that put on plays for their own enjoyment and for the entertainment or edification of their community. There are occasions when these theatres, too, reach levels of excellence. But polished perfection is not the goal. Rather, as the name suggests, community theatre aims to entertain and bring together a local town, neighborhood, or district. One should always remember that many of the greatest companies in the theatre's history, including Konstantin Stanislavski's Moscow Art Theatre and André Antoine's Parisian Théâtre Libre, began, essentially, as amateur community theatres. The word *amateur*, after all, means "lover," which suggests that the artist who creates theatre out of love rather than commercial expedience aims for the highest levels of art. Community theatre has, then, a noble calling: it is the theatre a community makes out of and for itself, and it can tell us a lot about who we are and what we want.

The Stage Coach Players of DeKalb, Illinois, offer an excellent example of a locally beloved community theatre. *©Kim Karpeles/Alamy Stock Photo*

The Global Theatre

While this book is published in the United States (it also appears in Mandarin Chinese in China), its readers who find theatre attractive should be aware of seeing theatre beyond their borders, for few spectator experiences are as challenging and fascinating as seeing plays from a culture—and a country—other than your own. Theatre from other countries—and continents—presents a variety of styles, techniques, and ideas that will make your eyes pop and your mind explode. The global theatre transcends local ideologies; it can make antagonists into partners and turn strangers into friends. As theatre once served to unite the ten tribes of ancient Attica, so it may serve in the coming era to unite a world too often fractured by prejudice and ignorance. Nothing could be more vital in today's world than sharing popular "entertainment" and being reminded of the original meaning of entertain: "to bring together" (from the French *entre* [between] and *tenir* [to hold], thus "to hold together" or "to bring together").

A trip to an international drama festival, in the United States or abroad, is a superb way to sample the theatres of several countries within a short period of time. But nothing can quite match a theatre tour abroad, where an adventurous theatregoer can see the theatrical creativity of another culture in its own setting and with its own intended audience. Seeing kabuki in Tokyo, with the audience shouting *kakegoe* (cries of approval) at climactic moments, or attending an Igbo *mmonwu* (masquerade) under the Nigerian sun, with the audience sitting and standing around the performers, cheering them on and swaying to the beat of their drums, is an experience that cannot be equaled.

Admittedly, few Americans are able or willing to devote the time and resources to travel to Asia or Africa solely for theatregoing, and those who do will find the theatrical attractions on those continents far apart and hard to get to. But there are increasingly international theatre festivals throughout the non-Western world—in Singapore, Uganda, and Egypt, to name only a few. Seeing theatre troupes from all over the world descend into a

A global team was behind the Royal Shakespeare Company's 2015 production of *Othello*, which featured black actors in both of the lead roles: the Ghanaian-born Hugh Quarshie as Othello and British-Tanzanian Lucian Msamati, as Iago. The play is set in today's times (there's a Venetian gondola, a rapping contest, and a tortuous waterboarding scene), and created by an international team: Indian Iqbal Khan directed and Irish Ciaran Bagnall designed the setting and lighting. ©*Nigel Norrington/Camera Press/Redux*

vibrant city in a foreign country and witnessing them present their own work, each with distinct traditions and artistic vision, is a truly vital and unique experience.

THEATRE IN ENGLISH-SPEAKING COUNTRIES

Europe also presents a navigable destination for the theatre-curious. Literally millions of Americans each year find their way to England for this very reason. Americans often account for up to one-third of the theatre audiences in London, where they might see, in addition to revered classics and extravagant musicals, new and provocative works by such celebrated current English dramatists as Tom Stoppard, Mark Ravenhill, Alan Ayckbourn, Charlotte Jones, Martin Crimp, Martin McDonagh, Howard Brenton, David Hare, and Caryl Churchill. Highlighting London's theatre scene are the government-subsidized National Theatre (NT), which houses three stages in a modern complex on the South Bank of the River Thames; the nearby Globe Theatre, a replica of Shakespeare's

original outdoor playhouse that produces Shakespearean-era drama during the summer months; and the West End theatre district on and around Shaftesbury Avenue and Covent Garden, which is comparable to New York's Broadway in its mix of musicals, new dramas, and classical revivals. There is also a London "Fringe" of smaller theatres, roughly comparable to off-Broadway, which includes the adventurous companies Almeida, Cheek by Jowl, Complicite, Donmar Warehouse, and the Royal Court. And in Shakespeare's hometown of Stratford-upon-Avon, little more than an hour's train ride from London, you can see productions by the Royal Shakespeare Company, which produces their namesake's work (and much more) in three theatres in that town, as well as seasonally in London and on tours throughout the United Kingdom. Theatre ticket prices in England are less than in the United States, and an official half-price TKTS Booth, comparable to the ones in New York City, may be found in London's Leicester Square.

World travelers can explore other English-speaking dramatic centers as well. Ireland has provided a vast

The timeless tale of Peter Pan, the boy who wouldn't grow up, has been adapted for the theatre for centuries. Here, a 2016 National Theatre production of *Peter Pan* in London shows off its special effects as Paul Hilton, as the titular character, and Madeleine Worrall, as Wendy, fly through the air, to the enchantment of the audience. ©*Robbie Jack/ Corbis/Getty Images*

One can always count on the London theatre to present, in addition to new plays and avant-garde productions of older ones, "conventional" but still intensely stimulating productions of classic plays, both comedies and tragedies. Here the English National Theatre presents Oliver Goldsmith's eighteenth-century classic *She Stoops to Conquer* with Sophie Thompson (*left*) as the hilariously scandalized Miss Oldcastle; this production, which was probably not very different from its premiere in Goldsmith's time, was so popular it was telecast live (by National Theatre Live) after its 2012 London opening. *©Robbie Jack/Corbis Entertainment/Getty Images*

"Panto" is a traditional English Christmastime entertainment for both adults and children. (The word is short for "pantomime" but bears little relation to the American art of that name.) Here (*from left to right*), Roger Allam plays Abbanazar, Ian McKellen plays Widow Twankey, Neil McDermott plays Aladdin, and Frances Barber plays Dimsum in a 2004–2005 production of *Aladdin* staged at London's Old Vic. The outrageous costuming is by Mark Bouman. *©Nigel Norrington/Camera Press/Redux*

South African playwright Athol Fugard cowrote *The Island* with actors John Kani and Winston Ntshona, who played the two roles of convicts sentenced to hard labor in South Africa's brutal Robben Island prison. The play premiered in 1973 in Cape Town and in London and Broadway showings the following year, which attracted international attention to the play and, in New York, earned Tony Awards for the two actors. Here Kani and Ntshona repeat their roles in a 2000 revival at the Royal National Theatre. ©*Nigel Norrington/Camera Press/Redux*

Tourist literature portrays the island of Ireland as a peaceful and beautiful land, but unfortunately it has suffered fiercely contentious rule for most of its political history. Martin McDonagh, English-born but of Irish parents, writes about the island's notorious "troubles," as they are famously called there, in his 2002 *The Lieutenant of Inishmore*, a dark (and many say tasteless) comedy of violence, torture, and killings (of both humans and animals), which both shocked and fascinated London audiences. Paul Lloyd (*hanging upside down*) and Peter McDonald are shown here in one of the play's grimmer scenes. ©*Theodore Wood/Camera Press/Redux*

repertoire to the stage since the seventeenth century. Indeed, most of the great "English" dramatists of the eighteenth and nineteenth centuries—George Farquhar, Oliver Goldsmith, Richard Sheridan, Oscar Wilde, and George Bernard Shaw—were actually Irish by birth. In the twentieth century, a distinctly Irish tradition of drama became immensely popular in the hands of William Butler Yeats, Sean O'Casey, and Brendan Behan. But possibly no period of Irish drama is as rich as the current one, which includes major established playwrights such as Brian Friel (*Philadelphia, Here I Come; Translations; Dancing at Lughnasa*) and newer ones such as Sebastian Barry (*The Steward of Christendom, Whistling Psyche*), Conor McPherson (*The Weir, The Seafarer, The Night Alive*), and English–Irish Martin McDonagh (*The Beauty Queen of Leenane, The Cripple of Inishmaan, The Pillowman, A Behanding in Spokane*). Most of these plays make their way to the United States, but seeing them in their natural surroundings, as at the Abbey or Gate Theatres of Dublin and the Druid Theatre of Galway, is a special treat.

In Canada, theatre flourishes in every province. The city of Toronto alone boasts 200 professional theatre companies and is, after London and New York, the largest professional theatre metropolis in the English-speaking world. But Canada is a bilingual country, and its major playwrights cover a broad international spectrum; its dramatists today include the veterans Michel Tremblay (a French Canadian writing in French) and Daniel David Moses (a First Nations, or Indigenous, playwright of Delaware descent), and relative newcomers such as Wajdi Mouawad (born in Lebanon, educated in Quebec, and

Set in a South African graveyard, Athol Fugard's *The Train Driver* tells of the anguished Roelf Visagie (*right*), a white train engineer whose locomotive has unintentionally run over and killed a woman and her baby. Seeking to uncover what might be her gravesite, Roelf meets up with the cemetery's local black caretaker, Simon Hanabe (*left*), and the two have a ninety-minute discourse that quickly leads to the horrors and hatreds of South African racism, political apartheid, and desperate human poverty—particularly in areas such as Hanabe's. New York's 2012 Signature Theatre production was directed by the playwright; Ritchie Coster played Roelf Leon, and Addison Brown played Simon. The grimy setting was designed by Christopher H. Barreca. ©*Sara Krulwich/The New York Times/Redux*

writing in French). Canada is also known for its globally renowned playwright/director Robert Lepage, its two major theatre festivals (one for Shakespeare in Stratford, the other for George Bernard Shaw in Niagara-on-the-Lake), a strong network of repertory companies and avant-garde groups, and its spectacular and world-famous Cirque du Soleil performance troupe. With a virtual flood of new playwrights, directors, and theatre critics working in multiple languages, Canadian theatre, in addition to its growing popularity at home, is developing a wide recognition abroad.

Australia also has a fine theatrical tradition and a lively contemporary scene. Veteran playwrights David Williamson (his *Sorting Out Rachel,* a contemporary comedy of manners, opened at Sydney's Ensemble Theatre in 2018)

and Louis Nowra (*The Emperor of Sydney* in 2007) have long flooded that country's stages with provocative plays. They are now supplemented by a host of younger writers who flourish in both standard repertory and offbeat, alternative theatres in Melbourne, Sydney, and Brisbane—as well as at Australia's biennial Adelaide Arts Festival.

South Africa has also given the world one of its most prominent living playwrights, Athol Fugard, author of *Sizwe Banzi Is Dead, The Island, Master Harold . . . and the Boys, A Lesson from Aloes, Valley Song, My Children! My Africa*!, and *Playland*, most of which premiered at the Market Theatre of Johannesburg. Both Fugard and the Market Theatre have won their reputations not only for the outstanding quality of their work but also for their courageous and effective confrontation of that country's

This opening moment of Thomas Ostermeier's radical 2015 production of Shakespeare's *Richard III* does not take place with Richard giving his famous soliloquy to the audience; rather it is an explosion (literally) of thousands of gold and silver shavings, falling not only over an elegant black-tie celebration of English royals, but also over the thousand-seat audience of the Avignon Opera House—one of the three main stages of the world-famous Avignon Theatre Festival. The play was performed in German (it had opened at the Berlin Schaubühne) with French subtitles, but Lars Eidinger, playing the title role, broke into English colloquialisms—and even ad libs to the audience—from time to time, entertaining his crowd while exasperating his supposed colleagues. *©Boris Horvat/AFP/Getty Images*

apartheid, or institutional segregation, which lasted until 1991. In the post-apartheid era, Fugard has written new plays, often autobiographical, dealing with his continuing struggles to reconcile contemporary South Africa with both its roots and its future; these include the notable *Valley Song* (1996) and its sequel, *Coming Home* (2009). Now living in California, his play *The Painted Rocks at Revolver Creek* earned critical raves when it opened in 2015.

THEATRE IN NON-ENGLISH-SPEAKING COUNTRIES

Outside of these English-speaking countries, France and Germany, which spawned the theatre of the absurd and the theatre of alienation, respectively, are immensely rewarding theatre destinations. Each country provides an outstanding mix of traditional and original theatre. French and German theatre, like that of most European countries, enjoys strong government support, which keeps ticket prices at a fraction of what they are in the United States and England.

France has five fully supported national theatres. Four of them are in Paris—including the historic Comédie-Française, founded in 1680 out of the remains of Molière's company shortly after his death; the Odèon, now a "Theatre of Europe," presenting home-based plays as well as productions from around the continent; and the Théâtre du Chaillot, which focuses on new plays and dance pieces.

In Germany, where major dramatic activity is spread more broadly throughout the country, federal and city governments support more than 150 theatres and about 60 theatre festivals in just about every large city on the

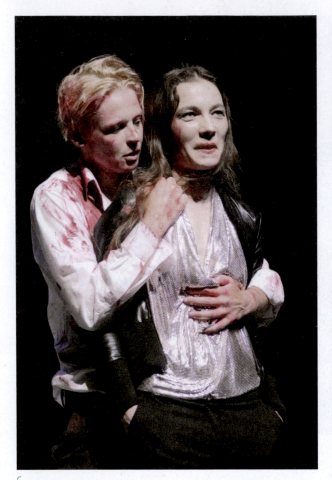

Different global cultures can often converge in a single production. In Karin Henkel's radically adapted 2011 version of Shakespeare's *Macbeth* in Germany at the Munich Kammerspiele (Chamber Theatre), the bloody Macbeth is played by the female actor Jana Schulz (*left*), with Katja Bükle (*right*) playing his Lady—as well as one of the witches. The production emphasizes Lady Macbeth's famous "unsex me here" line, making gender as well as political points as it goes, all with mixed languages that include German, Flemish, Swiss-German, and English. Despite the startling text and plot changes, the production was still titled *Macbeth von William Shakespeare*, making clear that German (and Eastern European) theatregoers no longer expect productions of classic plays to always stick to their original texts. ©*Silke Rößner*

The acclaimed Austrian playwright Felix Mitterer wrote the irreverent musical comedy *The Weavers (Die Weberischen)* about the life of Mozart, pictured here in a 2008 production. ©*Stephan Trierenberg/AP Images*

map. The modern German theatre, whose brash, experimental style of most productions takes off from the influence of Bertolt Brecht, is considered revolutionary in its breaking of theatrical stage conventions. German directors Peter Stein, Matthais Langhoff, Claus Peymann, Thomas Ostermeier, Karin Henkel, and Frank Castorf have pioneered theatrical innovations that have influenced theatres around the world. In addition to the Berliner Ensemble, currently headed by Peymann, Berlin boasts Castorf's radical Volksbühne theatre and each

May mounts an annual Theatretreffen (Theatre Meeting), bringing what a jury of critics selects as the ten best German-language theatre productions (out of the 400 they evaluate) from Germany, Austria, and Switzerland. Theatretreffen productions are chosen almost entirely for their innovative direction and design, as well as for their contribution to the future of theatre in the German-speaking world. Attending such events puts the audience in contact with the most adventurous theatre in Western Europe.

Other Western European countries—particularly Spain, Italy, Sweden, Denmark, Finland, Switzerland, Belgium, and the Netherlands—also have extremely active theatre communities and their own legendary actors and directors. And they too are wonderful places to engage in the theatre of the present and see a glimpse of the theatre of the future.

The most exciting theatre in Europe today, however, according to many observers, is in Eastern Europe. Because the theatres of Eastern European countries faced strict government censorship from 1945 until the early 1990s, their playwrights weren't allowed to talk directly about current events. Therefore, directors, rather than writers, took the lead in creating a form of dangerous theatre to express subversive ideas. The directors mounted classical plays to avoid any scrutiny. What Communist Party official, after all, would dare complain about a director who wanted to stage a 2,000-year-old Greek tragedy? But these directors made these ancient plays newly relevant. As a result, Eastern European directors created a theatre of ancient plays produced with hidden, often subversive, meanings clear to intelligent audiences but lost on the government. Indeed, the Eastern European theatre played a major role in the sweeping away of Communist rule in the Soviet bloc, particularly in Czechoslovakia, where in 1989 the "Velvet Revolution" led by Václav Havel, a prominent dissident Czech playwright, brought about the overthrow of the Communist government and the election of Havel as president.

Within Eastern Europe, the country of Romania deserves special recognition, because, with a population smaller than that of Texas, it has produced an extraordinary collection of world-famous directors. Andrei Serban, Mihai Maniutiu, Gábor Tompa, and Silviu Purcarete have international reputations for innovative brilliance and creativity. "In the field of directing, it is not Romania but America that needs to catch up," said Senior Editor Randy Gener in a 2007 cover story on Romanian theatre for *American Theatre*, the country's most distinguished publication in that field.

Each of those Romanian directors has reinvented the theatre itself by questioning the way it works, the way we think about it, and the way it projects ideas and images to its audiences. Each has worked frequently in Europe, Asia, and the United States. Serban directs regularly at the American Repertory Theater in Cambridge, Massachusetts, and teaches at Columbia University in New York.

Current Latin American theatre is usually experimental and often intensely political. Here, in the Teatro Ubu (San José, Costa Rica) premiere of Argentinian-Quebecois Luis Thenon's *Los Conquistadores*, Maria Bonilla (director-actor at Costa Rica's National Theatre) kneels in anguish at the plight of her son, whom she discovers listed among citizens who mysteriously "disappeared" but were generally known to have been tortured and killed by official goon squads. *Photo by Ana Muñoz*

Purcarete's internationally renowned work includes a magnificent *Faust*, which received once-in-a-lifetime reviews when on tour at the Edinburgh Theatre Festival. Tompa and Maniutiu not only head the Hungarian-language and Romanian-language national theatres of Cluj, Romania, where both of those languages are spoken, but they both also now teach and direct at University of California campuses at, respectively, San Diego and Irvine. All four also continue to direct in their home country, where they face increasing competition from a new generation of Romanian disciples who are actively building on their discoveries.

The live theatre is now a global art, with plays, actors, and theatre companies increasingly touring around the world. This centuries-old kabuki dance masterpiece, *Kaidan Chibusa no Enoki* (or *The Ghost Tale of the Wet Nurse* Tree), was updated and in part modernized by Japan's Heisei Nakamura-za company—which has also toured to Berlin, Boston, Washington, and Sibiu, Romania; the production opened the 2014 Lincoln Center Festival at New York's Rose Theatre. Shown here is the company's master, Nakamura Kankuro, displaying the classic cross-eyed *mie*—a frozen moment in kabuki which provokes wild cheers from the Japanese audience. Yet the company employs contemporary tropes as well, at times running down the aisles making English language asides to their American audiences, and tapping messages onto their smartphones. As with most foreign-language stage productions that tour the world, projected subtitles or supertitles are provided for local audiences. *©Sara Krulwich/The New York Times/Redux*

Romanian theatre is intellectually bold, stylistically innovative, physically demanding of its performers, and emotionally demanding of its audiences. There is no doubt that Gener's estimate of Romania's importance to the theatre's future is accurate; the entire Spring 2009 issue of Yale University's Theatre journal was also devoted to Romanian theatre today, and the international festivals Romania now hosts annually in Bucharest, Cluj, Craiova, and Sibiu are attended by theatre practitioners, students, and fans from all over the world. (The 2017 Sibiu Festival has, not coincidentally, provided this chapter with several examples of cutting-edge theatre.)

And for those readers—the vast majority, of course—who aren't making foreign theatre tours this year, the Internet provides a wonderful way to catch a glimpse of and a feeling for the works described in these pages. A quick Internet search—beginning with the theatre companies or the directors named here—quickly leads to photos and, in many cases, videos of their latest work, as well as archival photos of many of the productions mentioned.

Theatre Innovators Today

There are many artists currently redefining theatre today, four exemplary cases of which are identified in this section. Ivo van Hove, Jesusa Rodríguez, Rimini Protokoll, and Ong Keng Sen may not be the most well-known theatre artists, but they are innovators who are pushing the limits of what the medium can do. They both exemplify different types of theatre identified earlier in this chapter (dangerous, communal, intimate, and so on) and combine different facets of theatre today. As a result they are, in their own way, utterly unique and inspiring.

IVO VAN HOVE

Depending on whom you ask, the Flemish director Ivo van Hove is considered either a minimalist or a maximalist, a theatrical innovator or a blasphemer, a classicist or a renegade. Since the 1990s, van Hove has risen to prominence by directing an eclectic selection of dramatic works, including Shakespeare, adaptations of films (by Michelangelo Antonioni, John Cassavetes, and Ingmar Bergman), and—most famously—plays that are firmly entrenched in the American canon. As an outsider to American culture, van Hove's interpretations of American drama contain no cultural "baggage" that we might associate with them. Instead, they attempt to get to the soul of the text—the elemental idea that propels the drama. His staging tends to reflect this desire for primal simplicity: for example, his celebrated production of Arthur Miller's *A View from the Bridge* had no set, barefoot actors, and only two small props; his take on Tennessee Williams's *A Streetcar Named Desire* was dominated by a giant clawfoot bathtub and little else; and his staging of Tony Kushner's epic *Angels in America* made use only of an IV tube and a record player on the floor.

Most of all, though, van Hove's productions strip away naturalism, a style he actively dislikes. By removing any pretense to reality, his plays paradoxically reach a distinctly theatrical kind of truth, one unburdened by convention and instead focused on the fundamental instrument of the actor's body. His performers are renowned for their physical bravery—notoriously, van Hove does not choreograph any violence and instead has his actors improvise their conflicts—and their intense, almost dreamlike ferocity, which has led to some indelible images: an overturned can of tomato soup spilling onto the title character of Ibsen's *Hedda Gabler*; the angel from Tony Kushner's *Angels in America* viciously and repeatedly throwing the AIDS-stricken Walter Prior onto the floor; and Katherina, from Shakespeare's *The Taming of the Shrew*, urinating on a kitchen table. Also memorable are the unexpected musical choices he makes, often scoring his works with more contemporary pop songs—like Joni Mitchell in *Hedda* or Randy Newman in Eugene O'Neill's *Long Day's Journey into Night*. These bold gestures replace any attempts at restrained, psychological nuance—van Hove believes that all subtext should be expressed, not hidden.

With his signature blend of simplicity and surprising imagery, Ivo van Hove's 2016 production of *Lazarus* paid homage to the great rock & roll shapeshifter David Bowie. Pictured here are Sophie Anne Caruso (*left*) and Michael C. Hall (*right*). *©Robbie Jack/Corbis/Getty Images*

This attitude recalls distinctly European traditions—expressionism, Bertolt Brecht's epic theatre, Antonin Artaud's theatre of cruelty—yet van Hove marries them, time and again, to American works that are typically portrayed more realistically. As a result of this clash of sensibilities, he was met with both adulation and shock when his work first traveled to the United States in 1997, with a production of O'Neill's sprawling, unfinished *More Stately Mansions*. This first trip started a long relationship with New York Theatre Workshop, where he brought his first American critical success with *Hedda Gabler*—and where he began cultivating regular American performers, such as Elizabeth Marvell, and inspiring a younger generation of American directors, including Sam Gold. After years of fame as a singular downtown figure, van Hove found more commercial success with the Broadway transfer of his *A View from the Bridge* from the National Theatre in London, and shortly thereafter another Broadway success—and another Miller play—with a celebrated production of *The Crucible* starring Saoirse Ronan, Ben Whishaw, and Sophie Okonedo. Lately the floodgates seem to be open for van Hove's work, which continues to engage and surprise audiences; in 2017 he brought to New York's Brooklyn Academy of Music (BAM) a four-hour adaptation of Ayn Rand's controversial novel *The Fountainhead*—proof that, while his work is gaining international popularity, he certainly hasn't compromised his ability to provoke.

JESUSA RODRÍGUEZ

Jesusa Rodríguez has portrayed many figures that loom large in the history of her native Mexico: Frida Kahlo, former president Carlos Salinas de Gortari, the renowned seventeenth-century author Sor Juana Inés de la Cruz, and—perhaps most strikingly—the Aztec goddess Coatlicue, depicted in mythology as having two serpentine heads and a necklace made of human hearts, who gave birth to the moon and stars.

These performances are not reverent, however. In fact, they are just the opposite: Rodríguez is renowned for her expressive, in-your-face style, deft wordplay, kinetic energy, and raunchy sense of humor. She does not portray history as if it belongs in a museum, but as if it were alive right now—living, breathing, and, most of the time, with a score to settle. When embodying Coatlicue, for instance, Rodríguez chose to play her like a nagging mother, chastising spectators with cries of "madre solo hay una y esa ¡¡ingratos!!" ("There is only one mother, ingrates!!"). She also complains that no one put up 50,000 posters to announce her arrival—a remark that has specific resonance with Rodríguez's Mexican audience, as when she initially performed as Coatlicue, the pope had just visited the predominantly Catholic country. Her question is both cheeky and serious—why isn't anyone remembering the older past of this country, in all its feminine and (to use Rodríguez's word) "freaky" glory?

Beneath its humorous appearance, Rodríguez's work has a deadly serious objective: to take aim against systems of power. It is no wonder, then, that she cites two of her idols as Jonathan Swift, the English satirist who penned the devastating essay "A Modest Proposal," and Lucas Cranach, the Renaissance engraver whose grotesque images depicted royalty and religion in absurd, cutting caricature. Recently, Rodríguez, who often blurs the line between activism and art, collaborated with the American performance studies scholar Diana Taylor to create *Sin Maíz No Hay Vida* ("Without Corn, There Is No Life"), a raucous protest against Monsanto, the multinational agricultural corporation. Monsanto had recently struck a controversial deal with the Mexican government to plant crops of genetically modified vegetables. Rodríguez and Taylor enlisted passersby and other activists to parade through the streets, decked in body paint, pigs' heads, and flamboyant costumes; the march ended at a volleyball game between "People of the Corn" and "Monsanto," with spectators invited to pick a side. (Most chose "People of the Corn.")

Rodríguez's work spans many different forms: solo performance, street protest, opera, and even academic lecture. One recent theatrical lecture, created in collaboration with Rodríguez's creative and life partner Liliana Felipe, featured Rodríguez taking the role of a real-life nineteenth-century scientist who published an examination of an intersex person and concluded that the person was "nobody" as a result of having no discernible genitalia. As always, Rodríguez played the part with gusto, brimming with humor just at the edge of—and at times beyond—good taste. And as always, underneath the farcical humor was a deadly serious topic: the historic mistreatment of women by the male-dominated medical industry. Rodríguez is equally at home in a public park as she is in a more traditional theatre space, such as Teatro Capilla, which Rodríguez and Felipe run together in Mexico City, or in downtown New York, where she won an Obie Award for her collaboration with the American experimental group Mabou Mines in 1999. Wherever she performs, Rodríguez has shown a capacity to provoke, as well as a chameleon-like ability to take on larger-than-life roles (in addition to Cruz, Coatlicue, and Kahlo, she has also played the devil and Charles Darwin). It is hardly surprising to hear that the *New York Times* once declared that, when performing, Rodríguez "may be the most powerful woman in Mexico."

In the sprawling, collaborative 2013 work *Sin Maíz No Hay Vida* ("Without Corn, There Is No Life"), Jesusa Rodríguez organized and performed with the Hemispheric Institute of Performance and Politics, a celebratory parade through the streets of Mexico City to protest the involvement of the agricultural corporation Monsanto in Mexican farming. The performance was both deadly serious in its satirical target and lighthearted in its freeform use of parody—a mixture familiar to Rodríguez, whose work often mixes outrage with the outrageous. ©*Marlène Ramírez-Cancio*

RIMINI PROTOKOLL

It seems fitting to include Rimini Protokoll—a three-person team of theatre artists made up of Helgard Haug, Stefan Kaegi, and Daniel Wetzel—on a list of theatre innovators that otherwise contains individuals. This is a group, after all, that has dedicated itself to questioning what it means to be a community at all—and how a lone person can relate to, or make up a part of, the larger whole.

The Germany-based group is perhaps best known for its work *100%,* an endlessly adaptable performance concept that has toured through the United States and Europe. The idea is fiendishly simple: the company recruits 100 local people in exact proportion to the gender, age, and racial makeup of the city where it is staged. For instance, in San Diego, thirty of the performers are Latinx, to reflect the roughly 30 percent of that city's population. The production reflects the city back to itself and gives each performer—and by extension each identity—a voice. During one section, half of the stage is labeled "Agree" and the other "Do Not Agree"; different statements are read on the loudspeaker ("I support the death penalty," for instance) and performers go to the side of the stage that corresponds to their view.

One hundred residents of Berlin occupy the stage in Rimini Protokoll's *100% Berlin,* pictured here in 2008. These nonactors proceed to answer questions—and physically divide themselves based on their answer—to give a sense of the cultural makeup of the city. The *100%* series has proved one of Rimini Protokoll's most enduring works, traveling all over the world to reflect and analyze different local communities. ©*Lieberenz/ ullstein bild/Getty Images*

If this feels radically different from the other types of theatre discussed in this book, that's because it is—Rimini Protokoll is often hailed as the vanguard of a new form of documentary theatre, one that goes beyond the genre's previous conventions. At times, the company breaks free from the theatre altogether and instead trains its eye on discovering theatricality in everyday life. In its work *Hauptversammlung* ("General Meeting"), the group does not stage a work so much as ask its audience members to view a piece of corporate life as the theatre. Rimini Protokoll invited a large audience to attend a general meeting of the shareholders of Daimler, a vast German automotive company. This meeting is open to the public, though typically audiences are shareholders or other interested parties. Rimini Protokoll asked people to attend as if they were theatre spectators, thus emphasizing how the event is a kind of theatre. Attendees—both those invited by the Rimini Protokoll and those who were going to be there anyway—were given booklets that contained essays and art about general meetings, along with a phone number that, when called, played the sounds of a theatre audience (applause, booing, catcalls) out of their cell phones. There were breakout talks about the event during the meeting and follow-up discussions with participants. The group ingeniously provided the scaffolding of the theatre to something that strikes us, on most days, as resolutely undramatic: company bureaucracy.

There is perhaps no topic less thrilling than institutional decorum, yet Rimini Protokoll has addressed it time and again with innovative results. Its piece *50 Kilometres of Files* gives audience members headphones and leads them through the streets of Berlin while piping in actual taped conversations from the archives of the Stasi, or former East German secret police. The recordings sync up with the locale of the walk—so, for instance, a phone call alerting the police to a protest on Alexanderplatz plays as the participants walk through that very neighborhood. The past comes vividly to life, overlaying itself onto the present, and again, a seemingly banal walk down the street reveals itself to be theatrically dynamic.

Rimini Protokoll may challenge our understanding of the theatre, but the group is increasingly welcomed by more traditional theatre establishments. In the 2017–2018 season it claimed a slot in the Denver Center for the Performing Arts—a company that had recently premiered the mega-blockbuster musical *Frozen*—and created a performance wherein fifty audience members left the theatre wearing headphones and received instructions to perform, at times in unison with each other, as they toured the city. Without compromising its vision, this company has found a way to spread its challenging, illuminating methods of revealing the world around us in a new light.

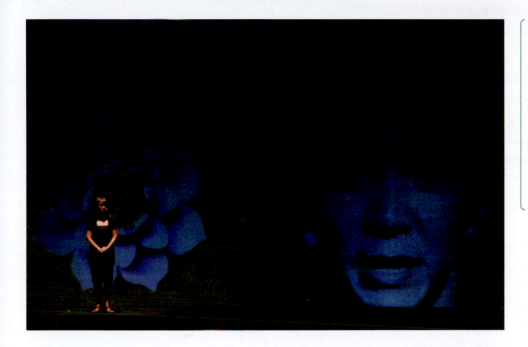

Ong Keng Sen's 2009 production of *Diaspora* incorporated media, live performance, and orchestral accompaniment to tell stories of migration across a variety of contexts, including Vietnamese Americans, Indonesian Chinese, and the Orang Laut, a group of "sea nomads" who live around Singapore. ©*Robbie Jack/ Corbis/Getty Images*

ONG KENG SEN

Ong Keng Sen's 2002 adaptation of *Hamlet,* titled *Search: Hamlet,* took place at Kronborg, a Danish castle that served as the basis of Elsinore in Shakespeare's play. Ong's production featured four different languages, several different paths for the audience to follow, a broad array of performance styles—including Japanese noh, Chinese xiqu opera, and martial arts—and precisely zero people playing Hamlet. As the title suggests, Ong is more interested in the search for Hamlet than he is in actually finding the famously melancholy Dane. Instead, audience members wander the castle, immersing themselves in various scenes and media events inspired by the play.

Hamlet was another in a series of Shakespeare adaptations for Ong. He has previously adapted *King Lear* (as simply *LEAR*) and *Othello* (as *Desdemona*). Ong, who was born in Singapore to Chinese immigrant parents, tends to resist having his productions labeled as "Asian Shakespeare." Rather than be pigeonholed—and rather than accept a generalized understanding of Asian theatre as a monolithic tradition—Ong instead embraces a wide swath of cultures and traditions, including an increasingly popular new trend in theatre of "Global Shakespeare." The title may sound like the simple act of staging Shakespeare's work in different international contexts, but the reality is more complex and rewarding: Global Shakespeare stages the interactions of different cultures in the meeting-ground of Shakespeare's work. In other words, it poses vital questions about culture, identity, and communication, and it does so with a spectacular mingling of styles from all over the world.

Ong's work extends beyond Shakespeare, however, and beyond just directing—he has also been an active cultivator of theatre from around the world. After serving as artistic director of the award-winning company TheatreWorks in Singapore from 2013 to 2017, he was appointed the director of the Singapore Arts Festival, which has brought in internationally renowned work from artists such as the American director Robert Wilson, the Iranian director Amir Reza Koohestani, and Singapore's own critically acclaimed theatre company Wild Rice. Ong has also premiered his own recent work at the festival. Among those works is the timely play *The Incredible Adventures of Border Crossers* (2015), which featured actual refugees among its acting ensemble, as well as a 2017 production of Euripides' ancient tragedy *The Trojan Women,* in collaboration with the National Theatre of Korea. The festival, under Ong's leadership, has become a hub of theatrical innovation and has received critical and commercial success. Ong has received many accolades, including a Cultural Medallion from the Singaporean government and a Fulbright scholarship. In his artistic and administrative work, he acutely demonstrates a key concept for theatre today: its ability to be global without sacrificing the specificity of any individual culture or voice—its ability, in short, to be truly democratic.

Conclusions about Theatre Today?

Can we draw any definite conclusions about theatre today?

In a word, no. We cannot because what is current is never concluded. Today's theatre is current because it is in process, but it is "current" in another sense, as well: it is like a river that is continually running, newly replenished with fresh rainwater and snowmelt. What is hot today may be cold tomorrow, but the theatre of today is *our* theatre and it is *your* theatre: there to apprehend, to enjoy, to appreciate, and to respond to. It is not just a series of plays or an array of styles, but a communication between individuals and peoples that raises levels of human discourse and artistic appreciation. It responds to individual impulses of creativity and collective demands for human contact and understanding. It synthesizes the impulses of artists and audiences, and it fosters a focused interaction that incorporates our human experience, aspirations, and values. Like a river, theatre began long before the advent of recorded history and "keeps on rolling."

Theatre is also always new. As Heraclitus said 2,500 years ago, "We cannot step twice in the same river; for when I step in the river for a second time, neither I nor the river are the same."

Chapter

11

The Audience

©Sara Krulwich/The New York Times/Redux

IT IS 10:30 P.M. THE lights fade a final time, the curtain falls, the spectators applaud, and the play is over. The actors go back to their dressing rooms, take off their makeup, and depart. The audience disperses into the night.

But the theatrical experience is not over. In many ways, it is just beginning.

A play does not begin and end its life on a stage. It begins in the mind of its creator, and it ends in the memories of its audiences. The stage is just one stop among many. After the performance is over, the play's impact remains: it is something to think about, talk about, fantasize about, become inspired by, get frustrated with, and live with for hours, days, and even years to come.

Some plays we remember all our lives: plays whose characters are as sharp in our memories as people we have long known, whose settings are as deeply experienced as our childhood locales, and whose themes resonate with many of our own deeply held beliefs. Like the

fictional characters onstage, we have experienced indecision, romantic yearnings, thwarted ambitions, uproarious hilarity, and deep sorrow. And the questions plays ask resonate with those of the "real" world: Shall we be as determined as Oedipus? as passionate as Romeo? as deceptive as Shin Te? We talk about these matters with our fellow theatregoers—our friends who accompanied us, and perhaps other audience members, former strangers with whom we have shared this experience—once the curtain has fallen.

We also talk about the acting, costumes, scenery, and sound effects. Were we convinced? impressed? moved? transported? changed? Did the production hold our attention throughout? Did our involvement with the action increase during the play, or did we feel a letdown after the intermission? Did we accept the actors as the characters they were playing, or were we uncomfortably aware they were simply "acting" their parts rather than embodying their roles?

We do not even need to be in a theatre to engage deeply with a play. The printed text can also prompt important questions. That play the teacher or director asked you to read yesterday: Did it "get to" you? Could you follow the story? Were you interested in the characters? Did it stimulate you intellectually? Did it move you to tears or laughter? Did it make you want to take action politically? Why? Why not? Could you visualize its actions, its settings, its impact on a theatre audience? Could you imagine casting it with actors you have seen on stage or screen? Were there aspects of the play you thought could be changed for the better?

When you address any of those sorts of questions about a performance or a play text, you are engaging in dramatic analysis. To be an audience member—whether in the theatre or as a reader—is to be an analyzer of work. Some people do this for a living. People who do so publicly, explaining to readers or listeners their reactions to a play or a play performance, are creators of *dramatic criticism* and are called *drama critics*. But all that is required of criticism is that you have experienced art. By being an audience member, and by thinking about the theatrical art you have witnessed, you have become a critic.

Dramatic analysis is the informed, articulate, and communicative response of critics or reviewers to what they have seen in the theatre. It can appear as a production review in a newspaper, blog, periodical, or on the radio; as a feature newspaper or magazine article about individual theatre artists or companies; as an essay in a scholarly book about dramatic literature, history, or theory; or simply as a class discussion or chat at a social gathering after the show. Sharing your post-performance responses to a theatre experience can provide, in fact, some of the most illuminating discussions life can offer.

Critical Perspectives

What makes a play particularly successful? What gives a theatrical production significance and impact, and what makes it unforgettable? What should we be looking for when we read a play or see a dramatic production?

Of course, we have complete freedom in making up our minds. As audience members, we have the privilege of thinking what we wish and responding as we will. But five perspectives can be particularly useful in helping us focus our response to any individual theatrical event: the play's social significance, human (or personal) significance, artistic quality, theatrical expression, and capacity to entertain.

SOCIAL SIGNIFICANCE

Theatre, as we have seen throughout this book, is always tied to its surrounding society. Sometimes this relationship is very direct, as when a theatre has been directly created or sponsored by governments and ruling elites. The Greek theatre of the fifth century B.C.E. was a creation of the state, early Indian drama was a thoroughly public medium that was sustained by civic engagement, and the theatre of the Royal era was a direct extension of monarchical power. Even in modern times, government often serves as a funder or benefactor of the theatre.

However, the intellectual ties between a theatre and its society extend well beyond politics. Thematically, the theatre has at one time or another served as an arena for the discussion of every social issue imaginable. In modern times, the theatre has approached issues such as alcoholism, gay rights, overseas labor, venereal disease, prostitution, public education, racial prejudice, health care reform, capital punishment, thought control, prison reform, political assassination, civil equality, political corruption, police brutality, and war crimes. The best of these productions have presented the issues in all of their complexity and have proffered ideas not as dogma but as food for thought. Great theatre has never sought to purvey pure propaganda, after all. It asks profound questions rather than gives pat answers.

Playwrights are not necessarily brighter than the audience or even better informed, but they may be better attuned. Playwriting is, in a way, the art of listening. And it can be valuable to pay attention. Playwrights and their collaborators may be able to focus public debate, stimulate dialogue, and turn public attention and compassion toward social injustices. Theatre artists are traditionally nonconformists; artists' points of view are generally out of the social mainstream, and their perspectives are of necessity somewhat unusual. Therefore, the theatre is in a strong position to force and focus public confrontation with social issues, and at its best it succeeds in putting members of the audience in touch with their own thoughts and feelings about those issues.

HUMAN SIGNIFICANCE

While cultural and political themes help give the theatre its power, more personal qualities characterize a great play, as well. The theatre is a highly individual art, in part because it stems from the unique perspectives of its artists. The greatest plays, in fact, transcend social and political issues to confront the hopes, concerns, and conflicts faced by all humankind: personal identity, courage, compassion, deception, kindness, love, and the inescapable problems of growing up and growing old, of wasting away and dying, and of loss. These are some of the basic themes of the finest plays and of our own consciousness, as well. The best plays link up with our deepest musings and help us put our oftentimes random or suppressed ideas into some sort of order or philosophy. The theatre is a medium in which we invariably see reflections of ourselves, and in the theatre's best achievements, those reflections lead to certain discoveries and evaluations concerning our own personalities.

ARTISTIC QUALITY

A play may be politically powerful and personally distinctive, but it still might not represent a well-wrought piece of theatre. As critics, we judge a play as we do any piece of art—in comparison to similar works and in the execution of its different elements. This is the oldest form of evaluation, practiced by the ancient Greek philosopher Aristotle, one of the very first—and best—theatre critics (see the chapter titled "What Is a Play?")

We can form such opinions quickly. The theatre is such a distinctive art form that even with the briefest exposure we can develop a sense of what we like to see. We quickly come to know—or think we know—honesty onstage, for without being experts we feel we can recognize false notes in acting, in playwriting, and even in design.

Beyond that, we can ask a number of questions of ourselves. Does the play excite our emotions? Does it stimulate the intellect? Does it surprise us? Does it thrill us? Does it seem complete and unified? Are the characters credible? Are the actors convincing? enchanting? electrifying? Does the play seem alive or dead? Does it seem in any way original? Is it logically sound? Is the action purposeful, or is it gratuitous? Are we transported, or are our

Few plays are as probing, fascinating, and thought-provoking as Shakespeare's *Hamlet,* and the play is produced with regularity throughout the theatregoing world. But how do directors and designers make it fresh and exciting to see again and again? How do they make it a work of contemporary art? This 2009 production by the Kolyada Theatre of Yekaterinberg, Russia, portrayed the Danish prince at the beginning of the play as a fragile and spoiled child who bites his nails but later assumes the role of an avenger and eventually a national hero. The production, directed by Nikolai Kolyada, who considers himself a "great provocateur," surprised and generally thrilled French audiences in its 2011 showing at the Odéon Theatre in Paris with its imaginative imagery and novel ideas. Kolyada also designed the scenery; the costumes were by Elena Getsevich, lighting was by Denis Novoselov, and the grinning child-Hamlet was played by Oleg Yagodine. ©Laurencine Lot

minds wandering? Finally, does the play fit our idea of what a play should be—or, even better, does it force us to rewrite our standards altogether?

Judgments of this sort are subjective. What seems original to one member of the audience may be clichéd to another; what seems an obvious gimmick to a veteran theatregoer can seem brilliantly innovative to a less jaded patron. None of this should intimidate us. An audience does not bring absolute standards into the theatre—and certainly any standards it brings are not shared absolutely. The theatrical response is collective, a combination of many individual reactions.

Each of us has our own distinct sensibility and response. We appreciate certain colors, sights, sounds, words, actions, behaviors, and people that please us. We appreciate constructions that seem to us balanced, harmonic, expressive, and assured. We appreciate designs, ideas, and performances that exceed our expectations, that reveal patterns and viewpoints we didn't know existed. We take great pleasure in sensing underlying structure: a symphony of ideas, a sturdy architecture of integrated style and action. We begin to develop our own sensibility and taste, as distinct as the voice of the play itself. By reading this book, you have been introduced to a vocabulary that helps you articulate and defend your own sensibility with greater acuity.

THEATRICAL EXPRESSION

As we've already discussed, plays are not simply things that happen in the theatre; they *are* theatre—which is to say that each play or play production redefines the theatre itself and makes us reconsider, at least to a certain extent, the value and possibilities of the medium. In some cases the playwright makes this reconsideration mandatory by dealing with theatrical matters in the play itself. Some plays are set in theatres where plays are going on (Luigi Pirandello's *Six Characters in Search of an Author*) or where people are learning to act (Annie Baker's *Circle Mirror Transformation*); other plays are about dramatic characters (Tom Stoppard's *Rosencrantz and Guildenstern Are Dead*); and still other plays contain dramatic works within themselves (Robert O'Hara's *Barbecue*) or the rehearsals of such plays (Shakespeare's *A Midsummer Night's Dream*, Jean Anouilh's *The Rehearsal*).

As discussed in the chapter "The Modern Theatre," the term *metatheatre* describes those plays that specifically refer back to themselves in this manner, but in fact all plays and play productions can be analyzed and evaluated on the way they use the theatrical format to their best advantage and the way they make us rethink the nature of theatrical

Spotlight

Performance Studies

"All the world's a stage, and all the men and women merely players," said Shakespeare. Not surprisingly, one of the growing areas in theatre education is the area of Performance Studies—or how we "perform" in nontheatrical spaces such as everyday life, sports, and consumerism, or even how we "act out" our own identities.

Rather than examine staged theatre, the discipline of Performance Studies encompasses all human action as its object of study. As a result, everything we do—make war, play sports, take museum tours, engage in political activism—is seen as a kind of performance. Even everyday events, such as buying groceries, become part of an exhibition. We perform with dialogue ("I'll be paying with my credit card") and follow blocking (when the customer ahead is finished, we move up one place in the line), and we depend on proper costumes and properties to complete our actions. Perhaps most radically, we perform without meaning to—we perform our identity in the infinite small gestures and habits that constitute our "role" of our selves. At times this performance is even dictated by others: we act as different selves in different contexts. By becoming aware of our constant dependence on the theatre, we are encouraged to study performance as a way of understanding the entire world.

Performance Studies is open-ended and draws influences from many different disciplines, but its two most prominent forefathers are anthropology and linguistics. From anthropology, it draws an interest in ritual and ancient practices from all parts of the world. From linguistics, it focuses on the construction of meaning through language. Other important influences are avant-garde art, sociology, and cognitive psychology. What unifies this diverse set of inspirations is the rejection of solely text-based knowledge. Instead, Performance Studies embraces the medium of our bodies in time and space. Rather than pore over the written word, Performance Studies looks at the moving actor.

As it has risen in popularity, more universities and colleges have begun offering classes and degrees in Performance Studies, and several academic journals specialize in its practice. By giving us a theatrical vocabulary to describe our lives, this exciting discipline places us all onstage, and encourages us to think critically about the entrances, exits, and scenes that we make every day.

production. All plays stand within the spectrum of a history of theatre and a history of theatrical convention. And all plays and productions can be studied, often with illuminating results, from the perspective of how they adopt or reject prevailing theatrical conventions, how they fit into or deviate from prevailing dramatic genres, how they echo

Entertainment rarely comes more exquisite than *An American in Paris*, a 2014 musical based on the classic 1951 American film. Directed by Christopher Wheeldon, the play proved a ravishing hit for aficionados of theatre and dance in equal measure; as this image demonstrates, Wheeldon's keen eye for stage composition, honed in his experience as a choreographer, created indelible images. ©*Bettina Strenske/Alamy Stock Photo*

various elements of past plays or productions—and what theatrical effects, good and bad, such historical resonances may have. Sometimes a play's reflection of the theatre allows us to recognize the "theatre" of everyday life: the roles that we play, the ways that we present ourselves, and the spectacles that fill us with awe in our own world.

ENTERTAINMENT VALUE

Finally, we look upon all theatre as entertainment. Great theatre is never less than pleasing. Even tragedy delights. People go to see *Hamlet* not to wallow in despair but, rather, to celebrate its theatrical form and experience the liberating emotions that become released in the play's murderous finale. Hamlet himself knows the thrill of staged tragedy:

HAMLET: What players are they?

ROSENCRANTZ: Even those you were wont to take such delight in, the tragedians . . .

What is this entertainment value that all plays possess? Most obviously, the word "entertainment" suggests "amusement," and so we think immediately of the hilarity of comedy and farce. Most of the literature regarding theatrical entertainment concentrates on the pratfalls and gags that have been part of the comic theatre throughout its history.

But entertainment goes far beyond humor. Another definition for "entertainment" is "that which holds the attention." This definition casts more light on our question. Entertainment includes the enchantment of romance; the dazzle of brilliant debate, witty epigram, and biting repartee; the appeal of the different and the grotesque; the beauty and grandeur of spectacle; and the nuance and crescendo of a musical or rhythmic line.

Entertainment encompasses suspense and adventure, sexuality and desire, and the splendor of sheer talent. Finally, of course, it includes any form of drama that profoundly stirs our feelings and heightens our awareness of the human condition. It is no wonder that Hamlet delights in the performance of tragedians—and that we delight in *Hamlet*. The mixture of ideas, language, poetry, feelings, and actions that constitute great tragedy confers one of life's sublime entertainment experiences. The best kind of theatre gets us to feel something, and even if—*especially* if—that feeling is one of sadness or loss, we still revel in the thrill of our emotions.

The theatre is a storehouse of pleasures, not only for the emotional, intellectual, spiritual, and aesthetic stimulation it provides, but also for its intrinsic social excitement. Theatre is a favored public meeting place for people who care about each other. Being an audience member implies more than a location; it implies companionship in the theatrical experience. The theatre is a place to commune in an especially satisfying way with strangers. When we are gripped by a staging of romantic passion or stunned by a brilliantly articulated argument or moved by a touching denouement, the excitement is enhanced by the fact that we are not alone in these feelings, that possibly every member of the audience has been stirred to the same response—or perhaps they feel differently; disagreement, after all, is a form of communication and communion as well. Theatre, in its essence, serves to rescue humankind from an intellectual and emotional aloneness, and therein lies its most profound "entertainment" value.

Critical Focus

These five perspectives on the theatre experience—its social and human significance, artistic quality, theatrical expression, and entertainment value—can be taken up by all audience members regardless of their experience or credentials. These are the five angles from which we view and judge plays, and place ourselves in a storied history. The judgment of plays and performances, which has been done formally since ancient Greek times, continues today through the well-publicized Tony and Obie Awards, Pulitzer Prizes, and Critics Circle citations. It is one of the fundamental aspects of theatrical participation. And it is open to professionals and amateurs alike.

PROFESSIONAL CRITICISM

Professional criticism takes the basic form of production reviews, as well as scholarly books and articles written, for the most part, by people who specialize in this activity, often as an entire career.

Newspaper reviews of play productions remain common throughout the theatre world, and the box-office success of most theatres depends on favorable journalistic coverage. In the commercial Broadway theatre, a positive write-up—particularly from the extremely influential *New York Times*—is almost essential to guarantee a successful run, and sternly unfavorable reviews may mean the play will close within a month or two. Today's newspaper theatre coverage has, in the past decade, been joined by an explosion of theatre websites and social media reviews. If you type "*Hamlet* review" into a search engine, you will probably come up with hundreds of reviews—from newspapers, blogs, online publications, Facebook posts, and even tweets—of productions of *Hamlet* around the world. If you add the name of a city or theatre where such a production was staged, you will find the full complement of critical response the work has so far engendered. To find professional criticism, select those reviews from esteemed publications (although Facebook posts are important too, as we'll discuss in the section on the amateur critic).

In New York (and most theatre capitals around the world), newspaper reviews generally appear the morning after the opening performance, which usually takes place in late afternoon rather than evening to meet the paper's press deadline. Customarily, after that performance, actors and producers and their fans gather at Sardi's restaurant in Broadway's Theatre District, where they pretend to eat dinner while awaiting the advance word of what will appear in the following morning's *Times*, published just blocks away. As they wait for the print copy, some are checking their phones to see if the review has been posted on the newspaper's website. The televised and printed reviews are examples of "instant criticism," and the reporters or journalists who tackle such assignments must be very skilled at articulating their impressions immediately.

Ultimately, the journalist's or blogger's review must be limited to a brief reaction rather than a detailed or exhaustive study. It provides a firsthand, audience-oriented response to the production, often vigorously and wittily expressed, and may serve as a useful consumer guide for the local theatregoing public. Writing skill rather than dramatic expertise is often the newspaper critic's principal job qualification, and at many smaller papers, staff reporters with little dramatic background are assigned to the theatre desk. But many fine theatre critics throughout the years—the *New Yorker*'s Hilton Als, for instance—have written highly intelligent dramatic criticism that remains pertinent long after its consumer-oriented function has run its course.

More scholarly critics, writing without the deadlines or strict space restrictions of journalists, are able to analyze plays and productions within detailed, comprehensive, and rigorously researched critical contexts. They are therefore able to understand and evaluate, in a more complex way, the achievements of playwrights and theatre artists within any or all of the five perspectives we have

No plays from the twentieth century have been more subject to critical examination by theatre scholars and play reviewers than those by Samuel Beckett, whose *Waiting for Godot* and *Endgame* revolutionized the theatre with their strange characters and plot complexities that generated examinations by theatre scholars and critics around the world. Here, Juliet Stevenson plays Winnie, permanently buried in sand (for no known reason), and David Beames plays her husband Willie, who hardly says a word, in Beckett's comic but ironic *Happy Days*, directed by Natalie Abrahami at the Young Vic Theatre in London 2015. *©Geraint Lewis/Alamy Stock Photo*

discussed. Scholarly critics aim to uncover hidden aspects of a play's structure, analyze its deep relationships to social or philosophical issues, probe its various meanings and dramatic possibilities, define its place in cultural history, amplify its resonance with earlier works of art, and theorize about larger issues of art and human understanding. Such criticism is itself a literary art, and the great examples of dramatic criticism have included brilliantly styled essays that have outlasted the theatrical works that were their presumed subjects: Aristotle, Samuel Johnson, Goethe, Shaw, and Nietzsche are among the drama critics who, simply through their analyses of drama, have helped shape our vision of life itself.

Scholarly critics, ordinarily distinguished by their broad intellectual background and exhaustive research, write with a comprehensive knowledge of the specific subject—a knowledge that includes the work of all important previous scholars who have studied the same materials. The professional scholar is not content to repeat the opinions or discoveries of others but seeks to make fresh insights from the body of literature (play texts and productions, production records, previous scholarship) that constitutes the field of study.

Scholarly critics tend to work within accepted frameworks of engagement, or "methodologies," which develop and change rapidly in contemporary academic life. Traditional methodologies include historical and biographical approaches, thematic and rhetorical analyses, studies of character and plot, examinations of staging and theatrical styles, and detailed explications of meaning. More advanced methodologies include systems and theories developed since the 1970s; these analyses tend to bypass traditional questions of history, biography, and character to focus instead on the internal relationships of various dramatic ingredients. Such methodologies, which draw heavily from the fields of philosophy, linguistics, anthropology, and literary theory, are intellectually demanding and difficult to master; they provide, however, stunning insights to those properly initiated.

AMATEUR CRITICISM

Anyone who watches a play can be a critic. For students, writing dramatic criticism for a school paper is a wonderful way to affect—and become a part of—the theatre. Writing a play review, in fact, is a common class assignment, and a relatively easy way to get published and read within your local community. Similarly, writing a review on a blog is an easy way to share your thoughts and impressions with a large audience; more and more, impassioned theatre writers in the blogosphere have become respected and prominent critical voices.

More and more, people on social media express their opinions through Facebook, Twitter, or other apps that

The venerable New York restaurant Sardi's has, since its 1927 opening, installed over a thousand caricatures of theatrical celebrities on its walls to fascinate the hordes of actors, directors, producers, and theatregoers who dine at this famous American eatery in the midst of forty-one professional Broadway theatres. ©*Elizabeth D. Herman/The New York Times/Redux*

allow people to elaborate on their personal takes to friends, family, and the wider public. At times social media responses have produced profound and controversial effects in the theatre world more widely, as when a campaign on Twitter criticized the racial implications of casting Mandy Patinkin, a white actor, in the lead role of the musical *Natasha, Pierre & the Great Comet of 1812*. Patinkin's run would have cut short the work of the previous actor, Okieriete Onaodowan, who is Nigerian American. However, the campaign convinced Patinkin, who announced—via Twitter—that he would not take over the role after all. We now live in a time of increased communication and interconnectedness, and the theatre is no longer immune—nor should it be—from this phenomenon.

We Are the Critics

As audience members, we are also critics—and that carries with it responsibility. To be an audience is ultimately an ethical act. In fact, it is an ethical *art,* a form of

expression just as vital as the object of its study. As audiences, we are a party to the theatrical experience, not passive receptacles for its contrived effects. The theatre is a forum of communication, and communication demands mutual and active participation.

To be an observant critic, we need only go to the theatre with an open mind and sharply tuned senses. Unfettered thinking should be a part of every theatrical experience, and provocative discussion should be its aftermath.

To be an informed critic, we need sufficient background to provide a context for opinion and evaluation. A play may be moving, but is it as moving as *The Three Sisters*? as provocative as *Dutchman*? as witty as *The Way of the World*? as communal as a ta'ziyeh ritual? as confounding as *Waiting for Godot*? An actor's voice may be thrillingly resonant, but how does it compare with the voice of Benedict Cumberbatch in *Hamlet*? Is that line of music enunciated as sinuously as Daveed Diggs sings in *Hamilton*? If our opinions are to have weight and distinction, they may do so only against a background of knowledge and

One recent surprise U.S. hit was the 2015 Broadway musical *Fun Home,* a tragicomedy adapted from a memoir by American graphic novelist Alison Bechdel. The Alison character was played by three actors: Sydney Lucas (*not pictured*), representing Alison as a child; Emily Skeggs (*right*), representing college-age Alison; and Beth Malone (*left*), representing her throughout the play both as present-day Alison and narrator. ©*Sara Krulwich/The New York Times/Redux*

experience. And so, the more we see, the more we learn—and the more we think.

To be a sensitive critic, we must be receptive to artistic experience and to life itself. The most sensitive criticism comes from a compassionate approach to humankind and expression. When we attune ourselves to the world around us, it provokes a more compassionate and personalized response to dramatic works. Sensitive criticism admits to life's messiness: it begins from the view that life is difficult and problematic and that relationships are demanding. Perceptive critics are open to learning new things, not smug—humane, not self-absorbed. They are eternally

eager for personal discovery and the opportunity to share it. They recognize that we are all groping in the dark, hoping to encounter helping hands along the way in the adventure of life, which is the hope of theatre artists too.

To be a demanding audience member is to hold the theatre to the highest standards of which it is capable. As we have seen so often in this text, the theatre wants to be liked. It has tried from its very beginning to assimilate what is likable in the other arts. Like a hungry scavenger, it absorbs the latest music and dance forms; the most trendy arguments, vocabularies, philosophies, and technologies; and the most fashionable artistic sensibilities. In

Theatre audiences can provide a sort of spectacle themselves, as with this enchanted crowd that is being covered in fake snow during the finale of 2007's *How the Grinch Stole Christmas*. ©Sara Krulwich/ The New York Times/Redux

the process, though, it often panders to tastelessness and propagates the meanest and most shallow values of its time. And here the drama critic in each of us can play a crucial role. Cogent, fair-minded, penetrating criticism keeps the theatre mindful of its own artistic ideals—the ideals that transcend the fashions of the moment—and its essential responsibility to communicate. Criticism can prevent the theatre from either selling out completely to the current whim or bolting the other way into hopeless indulgence.

To be an articulate critic is to express our thoughts with precision, clarity, and grace. An utterance of "I loved it" or "I hated it"—or, perhaps most deadly of all, "I didn't get it"—is not criticism but rather a crude expression of a general opinion, or an admission of not having an opinion at all. Articulation means the careful building of clear ideas through a presentation of evidence, logical argument, the use of helpful analogy and example, and a style of expression neither dry and pedantic nor wildly freewheeling. Good criticism should be a pleasure to write and read; it should make us want to go deeper into the mysteries of the theatre and not suffocate us with the prejudices or egotistical displays of the critic.

In sum, the presence of a critical focus in the audience—observant, informed, sensitive, demanding, and articulate—keeps the theatre honest. It inspires the theatre to reach its highest goals. It ascribes importance to the theatrical act. It telegraphs the expectations of the audience to producer, playwright, director, and actor alike, saying, "We are out here, we are watching, we are listening, we are hoping, we care: we want your best—and then we want you to be better yet." The theatre needs such demands from its audience. The theatre and its audience need to be worthy co-participants in a collective experience that enlarges life as well as art.

If we are to be critics of the theatre, then, we must be knowledgeable, fair, and open-minded; receptive to stimulation and excitement; and open to wisdom and love. We must also admit that we have human needs.

In exchange, the theatre must enable us to see ourselves in the characters of the drama and in the performers of the theatre. We must see our situations in the situations of plays and our hopes and possibilities in the behavior staged before us. We must be drawn to understand the theatre from the inside and to participate, in our own way, in a play's performance.

In this way, we become critics, audience members, and participants in one. The theatre is then no longer simply a remote subject encountered in a book, in a class, or in the entertainment columns of the world press; the theatre is part of us.

It is *our* theatre.

Design Elements: *Spotlight Icon: ©McGraw-Hill Education; Theatrical Masks: ©Ingram Publishing/Alamy Stock Photo; Camera: ©Tatiana Popova/Shutterstock*

Glossary

Within the definitions, terms that are defined in this glossary appear in *italic*.

absurdism The notion that the world is meaningless, derived from the essay "The Myth of Sisyphus" by Albert Camus, which suggests that human beings have an unquenchable desire to understand that the world is unknowable. The resulting conflict puts individuals in an "absurd" position, like Sisyphus, who, according to Greek myth, was condemned for eternity to push a rock up a mountain, only to have it always roll back down before it reached the top. The philosophical term gave the name to a principal postwar dramatic *genre: theatre of the absurd.*

act (*verb*) To perform in a play. (*noun*) A division within a play. Acts in modern plays are separated by an *intermission.* Full-length modern plays are customarily divided into two acts, sometimes three. Roman, Elizabethan, and *neoclassical* plays were usually printed in five acts, but the actual stage productions were not necessarily divided by intermissions, only stage clearings.

ad-lib A line improvised by an actor during a performance, usually because the actor has forgotten the line or because something unscripted has occurred onstage. Sometimes an author directs actors to ad-lib, as in crowd scenes during which individual words cannot be distinguished by the audience.

aesthetic distance The theoretical separation between the created artifice of a play and the "real life" the play appears to represent.

agon "Action," in Greek; the root word for "agony." Agon refers to the major struggles and interactions of Greek *tragedy.*

amphitheatre In Rome, a large elliptical outdoor theatre, originally used for gladiatorial contests. Today the term is often used to designate a large outdoor theatre of any type.

anagnorisis "Recognition," in Greek. Aristotle claimed that every fine *tragedy* has a recognition scene in which the *protagonist* discovers either some unknown fact or some moral character flaw. Scholars disagree as to which of these precise meanings Aristotle had in mind. See also *hamartia.*

angle wing A flat wing to which is hinged a second flat wing at an angle—usually between 90 and 115 degrees. Used extensively in seventeenth-century scenery, where it was painted to represent, among other things, diagonal walls on either side of the stage or exterior corners of buildings. See also *flat; wings.*

antagonist In Greek *tragedy,* the "opposer of the action"; the opponent of the *protagonist.*

antirealism A broad term that encapsulates many individual movements, such as symbolism, absurdism, and postmodernism. Antirealist movements rebelled against the conventions of realism by emphasizing highly stylized and non-naturalistic stage conventions.

Apollonian That which is beautiful, wise, and serene, in the theories of Friedrich Nietzsche, who believed *drama* sprang from the junction of Apollonian and *Dionysian* impulses in Greek culture.

applied drama The use of theatre and theatrical exercises to help a specific community, such as those who are imprisoned or those who are differently abled, gain means of self-expression and explore aspects of their identity.

apron The part of the stage located in front of the *proscenium;* the forward-most portion of the stage. The apron was used extensively in the English *Restoration* period, from whence the term comes. Today, it is usually called the *forestage.*

aragoto The flamboyant and exaggerated masculine style of acting employed in certain *kabuki* roles.

arena stage A stage surrounded by the audience; also known as *theatre-in-the-round.* Based on a Latin term meaning "sand," the arena originally referred to the dirt circle in the midst of an *amphitheatre.*

aside A short line in a play delivered directly to the audience; by dramatic convention; the other characters onstage are presumed not to hear it. Popular in the works of William Shakespeare and dramatists of the *Restoration* period, the aside has made a comeback and is used to good effect, in conjunction with the longer *direct address,* by contemporary American playwrights such as Margaret Edson and Braden Jacob-Jenkins.

audition The process whereby an actor seeks a role by presenting to a director or casting director a prepared reading or by reading from the text of the play being presented.

avant-garde Artists who abandon conventional models and create works that are in the forefront of new movements and styles.

backstage The offstage area hidden from the audience that is used for *scenery* storage, for actors preparing to make entrances, and for stage technicians running the show. "Backstage plays," such as *The Torchbearers* and *Noises Off,* "turn the set around" and exploit the furious activity that takes place backstage during a play production.

biomechanics An experimental acting system, characterized by expressive physicalization and bold gesticulation, developed by the Russian director Vsevolod Meyerhold in the 1920s.

black-box theatre A rectangular room with no fixed seating or stage area; this theatre design allows for a variety of configurations in staging plays.

blackface The practice, once very common, of white actors using makeup to darken their faces and embody racist caricatures of African Americans.

black musical See *black theatre.*

black theatre In America, theatre that is generally by, with, and about African Americans.

blocking The specific staging of a play's movements, ordinarily by the director. Often this is worked out ("blocked out") on paper by the director beforehand.

book In a *musical*, the *dialogue* text, apart from the music and song lyrics.

border A piece of flat *scenery*, often black velour but sometimes a *flat*, which is placed horizontally above the set, usually to *mask* the lighting instruments. Borders are often used with side *wings*, in a scenery system known as "wing and border."

box set A stage set consisting of hard scenic pieces representing the walls and sometimes the ceiling of a room, with one wall left out for the audience to peer into. This set design was developed in the nineteenth century and remains in use today primarily in *realistic* plays.

Broadway The major commercial theatre district in New York, roughly bordered by Broadway, Eighth Avenue, 42nd Street, and 52nd Street.

bunraku A Japanese puppet-theatre, founded in the sixteenth century and still performed today.

burlesque Literally, a *parody* or mockery, from an Italian amusement form. Today the term implies broad, coarse humor in *farce*, particularly in parodies and *vaudeville*-type presentations.

business The minute physical behavior of the actor—fiddling with a tie, sipping a drink, drumming the fingers, lighting a cigarette, and so forth. Sometimes this is controlled to a high degree by the actor or the director for precise dramatic effect; at other times the business is *improvised* to convey *verisimilitude*.

call An oral command, normally whispered over an intercom by the stage manager to the appropriate operator, to execute a specific lighting, sound, or scene-shift cue as, for example, "Sound cue number 121—go!" See also *cue sheet; tech run-through.*

call book or **calling book** See *prompt book.*

caricature A character portrayed very broadly and in a stereotypical fashion, ordinarily objectionable in *realistic* dramas. See also *character.*

catharsis In Aristotle's *Poetics,* the "purging" or "cleansing" of the terror and pity that the audience feels during the *climax* of a *tragedy.*

character A "person" in a play, as performed by an actor. Hamlet, Oedipus, Juliet, and Willy Loman are characters. Characters may or may not be based on real people.

chiton The full-length gown worn by Greek tragic actors.

choral ode See *ode.*

chorus (1) In classic Greek plays, an ensemble of characters representing the general public of the play, such as the women of Argos or the elders of Thebes. Originally, the chorus numbered fifty; Aeschylus is said to have reduced it to twelve and Sophocles to have increased it to fifteen. More recent playwrights, including Shakespeare and Jean Anouilh, have occasionally employed a single actor (or a small group of actors) as "Chorus," to provide narration between *scenes.* (2) In *musicals,* an ensemble of characters who sing or dance together (in contrast to soloists, who mostly sing or dance independently).

chou In *xiqu,* clown characters and the actors who play them.

classic drama Technically, plays from classical Greece or Rome. Now used frequently (if incorrectly) to refer to Elizabethan, Jacobean, and French *neoclassical* masterpieces. See also *modern classic.*

climax The point of highest tension, when the conflicts of the play are at their fullest expression.

colorblind casting The controversial belief that race should play no factor in casting decisions, so that an actor of any background can play a part regardless of the character's ethnicity.

comedy Popularly, a funny play; classically, a play that ends happily; metaphorically, a play with some humor that celebrates the eternal ironies of human existence ("divine comedy").

comic relief In a *tragedy,* a short comic scene that releases some of the built-up tension of the play—giving the audience momentary "relief" before the tension mounts higher. The porter scene in Shakespeare's *Macbeth* is an often-cited example; after the murder of Duncan, a porter jocularly addresses the audience as to the effect of drinking on sexual behavior. In the best tragedies, comic relief also provides an ironic counterpoint to the tragic action.

commedia dell'arte A form of largely improvised, masked street theatre that began in northern Italy in the late sixteenth century and still can be seen today. The principal characters—Arlecchino, Pantalone, Colombina, Dottore, and Scapino among them—appear over and over in thousands of commedia stories.

company A group of theatre artists gathered together to create a play production or a series of such productions. See also *troupe.*

convention A theatrical custom that the audience accepts without thinking, such as "when the curtain comes down, the play is over." Each period and culture develops its own dramatic conventions, which playwrights may either accept or violate.

cue The last word of one speech that then becomes the "signal" for the following speech. Actors are frequently admonished to speak "on cue" or to "pick up their cues," both of which mean to begin speaking precisely at the moment the other actor finishes.

cue sheet A numbered list of lighting, sound, or scene-shift changes coordinated with precise moments marked in the stage manager's *prompt book.*

curtain call The last staged element, in which the actors, after the play ends and the audience has begun to applaud, come forward to graciously accept the applause by bowing.

cycle plays In medieval England, a series of *mystery plays* that, performed in sequence, relate the story of the Judeo-Christian Bible, from the Creation of the Universe to the Crucifixion to Doomsday. The York Cycle includes forty-eight such plays.

cyclorama In a *proscenium theatre,* a large piece of curved *scenery* that wraps around the rear of the stage and is illuminated to resemble the sky or to serve as an abstract neutral background. It is usually made of fabric stretched between curved pipes but is sometimes a permanent structure made of concrete and plaster.

dada A provocative and playful European art movement that followed World War I and is characterized by seemingly random, unstructured, and "anti-aesthetic" creativity. It was briefly but deeply influential in poetry, painting, and theatre.

dan In *xiqu,* the female roles and the actors who play them.

dance-drama As its name suggests, this kind of performance mixes the genres of dance and theatre by adding narrative and dramatic elements to physically expressive movement.

denouement The final *scene* or scenes in a play devoted to tying up the loose ends after the *climax* (although the word originally meant "the untying").

deus ex machina In Greek *tragedy,* the resolution of the *plot* by the device of a god ("deus") flying onstage by means of a crane ("machina") and solving all the characters' problems. Today, this term encompasses any contrived play ending, such as the sudden arrival of a long-lost husband or father. This theatrical element was considered clumsy by Aristotle and nearly all succeeding critics; it is occasionally used ironically in the modern theatre, as by Bertolt Brecht in *The Threepenny Opera*.

devised theatre A process for making a play that relies on the improvisations, research, and exercises of an entire company, rather than on a pre-written script.

dialogue The speeches—delivered to one another—of the *characters* in a play. Contrast with *monologue*.

diction One of the six important components of *drama*, according to Aristotle, who meant by the term the intelligence and appropriateness of the play's speeches. Today, the term refers primarily to the actor's need for articulate speech and clear pronunciation.

didactic drama Drama dedicated to teaching lessons or provoking intellectual debate beyond the confines of the play; a dramatic form espoused by Bertolt Brecht. See also *distancing effect*.

dimmer The electrical device that regulates the amount of light emitted from lighting instruments.

dim out To fade the lights gradually to blackness.

Dionysia The weeklong Athenian springtime festival in honor of *Dionysus*; after 534 B.C.E., it was the major play-producing festival of the ancient Greek year. Also called "Great Dionysia" and "City Dionysia."

Dionysian Characterized by passionate revelry, uninhibited pleasure-seeking; the opposite of *Apollonian*, according to Friedrich Nietzsche, who considered *drama* a merger of these two primary impulses in Greek culture.

Dionysus The Greek god of *drama* as well as the god of drinking and fertility. Dionysus was known as Bacchus in Rome.

direct address A character's speech delivered directly to the audience, common in Greek *Old Comedy* (see *parabasis*), in Shakespeare's work (see *soliloquy*), in *epic theatre,* and in some otherwise *realistic* modern plays (such as Tennessee Williams's *The Glass Menagerie*).

discovery A *character* who appears onstage without making an entrance, as when a curtain opens. Ferdinand and Miranda are "discovered" playing chess in Shakespeare's *The Tempest* when Prospero pulls away the curtain that was hiding them from view.

distancing effect A technique, developed by German playwright Bertolt Brecht, by which actors deliberately present rather than represent their characters and "illustrate" the characters without trying to embody the roles fully, as *naturalistic* acting technique demands. This effect may be accomplished by "stepping out of character"—as to sing a song or to address the audience directly—and by developing a highly objective and *didactic* mode of expression. The actors are distanced from the role in order to make the audience more directly aware of current political issues. This technique is highly influential, particularly in Europe.

dithyramb A Greek religious rite in which a *chorus* of fifty men, dressed in goatskins, chanted and danced; the precursor, according to Aristotle, of Greek *tragedy*.

divertissement A French term, now accepted in English, for a frothy entertainment, intended to "divert" the audience from more serious matters.

documentary drama Drama that presents historical facts in a nonfictionalized, or slightly fictionalized, manner.

doggerel Coarse, unsophisticated poetry, usually with short lines and overly obvious rhymes, often used comically by Shakespeare to indicate simplistic verse written or performed by characters in his plays, such as Orlando's amateurish love poems to

Rosalind in *As You Like It* or the play of "Pyramus and Thisbe" presented by inexperienced performers in the last act of *A Midsummer Night's Dream*.

domestic tragedy A *tragedy* about ordinary people at home.

double (*verb*) To play more than one role. An actor who plays two or more roles is said to "double" in the second and following roles. Ordinarily the actor will seek, through a costume change, to disguise the fact of the doubling; occasionally, however, a production with a *theatricalist* staging may make it clear that the actor doubles in many roles. (*noun*) To Antonin Artaud, the life that drama reflects, as discussed in his book *The Theatre and Its Double*. See also *theatre of cruelty.*

downstage The part of the stage closest to the audience. The term dates back to the eighteenth century, when the stage was *raked* so that the front part was literally lower than the back (or *upstage*) portion.

drama The art of the theatre; plays, playmaking, and the whole body of literature of and for the stage.

dramatic Plays, scenes, and events that are high in conflict and believability and that would command attention if staged in the theatre.

dramatic criticism A general term that refers to writings on drama, ranging from journalistic play reviews to scholarly analyses of dramatic *genres,* periods, *styles,* and theories.

dramatic irony The device of letting the audience know something the characters don't, as in Shakespeare's *Macbeth,* when King Duncan remarks on his inability to judge a person's character—while warmly greeting the man (Macbeth) who we already know plans to assassinate him.

dramaturg (also spelled "dramaturge") A specialist in play construction and the body of dramatic literature, dramaturgs are frequently engaged by professional and academic theatres to assist in choosing and analyzing plays, to develop production concepts, to research topics pertinent to historic period or play production *style,* and to write program essays. The dramaturg has been a mainstay of the German theatre since the eighteenth century and is becoming increasingly popular in the English-speaking world.

dramaturgy The art of play construction; sometimes used to refer to play structure itself.

drapery Fabric—often black—mainly used as neutral *scenery* to *mask* (hide) actors when they leave the lit (active) area of the stage. Also refers to a front curtain (a "main drape"), which is often red.

dress rehearsal A *rehearsal* in full costume; usually also with full *scenery, properties,* lighting, sound, and technical effects. Such rehearsals are ordinarily the last ones prior to the first performance before an audience.

drop A flat piece of *scenery* hung from the *fly gallery,* which can "drop" into place by a flying system.

emotion memory A technique in which actors stimulate emotion by remembering the feelings they experienced during a previous, real-life event. Employed since ancient times, it was developed and named by Konstantin Stanislavski (who, however, subsequently disowned it) and was promoted in America by Lee Strasberg. Also called "affective memory."

empathy Audience members' identification with dramatic characters and their consequent shared feelings with the plights and fortunes of those characters. Empathy is one of the principal effects of good drama.

ensemble Literally, the group of actors (and sometimes directors and designers) who put a play together; metaphorically, the rapport and shared sense of purpose that bind such a group into a unified artistic entity.

environmental theatre Plays produced not on a conventional stage but in an area where the actors and the audience are intermixed in the same "environment" and there is no precise line distinguishing stage space from audience space.

epic theatre As popularized by Bertolt Brecht, a *style* of theatre in which the play presents a series of semi-isolated episodes intermixed with songs and other forms of *direct address,* all leading to a general moral conclusion or set of integrated moral questions. Brecht's *Mother Courage* is a celebrated example. See also *distancing effect.*

epilogue In Greek *tragedy,* a short concluding *scene* of certain plays, generally involving a substantial shift of tone or a *deus ex machina.* Today, the epilogue is a concluding scene set substantially beyond the time frame of the rest of the play, in which characters, now somewhat older, reflect on the preceding events.

episode In Greek *tragedy,* a *scene* between characters and between choral *odes.* The word literally means "between odes."

existential drama A play based on the notions of existentialism, particularly as developed by playwright/philosopher Jean-Paul Sartre. Existentialism, basically, preaches Sartre's principal tenet in *No Exit* that "you are your acts, and nothing else" and that people must be held fully accountable for their own behavior.

exodos In Greek *tragedy,* the departure *ode* of the *chorus* at the end of the play.

exposition In play construction, the conveyance, through *dialogue,* of story events that occurred before the play begins.

expressionism An artistic *style* that greatly exaggerates perceived reality in order to express inner truths directly. Popular mainly in Germany between the world wars, expressionism in the theatre is notable for its gutsy dialogue, piercing sounds, bright lighting and coloring, bold scenery, and shocking, vivid imagery.

farce Highly comic, lighthearted, gleefully contrived drama, usually involving *stock situations* (such as mistaken identity or discovered lovers' trysts), punctuated with broad physical stunts and pratfalls.

flat A wooden frame covered by fabric or by a hard surface and then painted, often to resemble a wall or portion of a wall. The flat is a traditional staple of stage *scenery,* particularly in the realistic theatre, because it is exceptionally lightweight, can be combined with other flats in various ways, and can be repainted and reused many times over several years.

fly To raise a piece of *scenery* (or an actor) out of sight by a system of ropes or wires. This theatre practice dates back at least to ancient Greek times. See also *deus ex machina.*

fly gallery The operating area for flying scenery, where fly ropes are tied off (on a pinrail) or where ropes in a counterweight system are clamped in a fixed position.

follow-spot A swivel-mounted spotlight that can be pointed in any direction by an operator.

footlights In a *proscenium theatre,* a row of lights across the front of the stage, used to light the actors' faces from below and to add light and color to the setting. Footlights were used universally in previous centuries but are employed only on special occasions today.

forced perspective A principle of design that simulates depth in a narrow space, so that a backdrop creates a sense of distance even though its images are in two dimensions.

forestage See *apron.*

found object In scene or costume design (and art in general), an item that is found (rather than created) and is incorporated into the finished design.

full house Audience seating filled to capacity. See also *house.*

gel (*noun*) Short for "gelatin," a sheet of colored plastic placed over a light source to color the beam emitted from a lighting instrument. (*verb*) To insert gels into the instruments.

genre A French noun meaning "kind"; a term used in dramatic theory to signify a distinctive class or category of play—*tragedy, comedy, farce,* and so on.

geza The *stage right,* semienclosed musicians' box in *kabuki* theatre. This term also refers to the music that is played in this box.

gidayu The traditional style of chanting in *kabuki* and *bunraku* theatre.

gobo A perforated sheet of metal that, when placed in front of the lens of a sharply focused lighting instrument, projects designs on the floor or wall the light falls on.

greenroom A room near the stage where actors may sit comfortably before and after the show or during scenes in which they do not appear. This room is traditionally painted green; the custom arose in England, where the color was thought to be soothing.

ground plan A schematic drawing of the stage setting, as seen from above, indicating the location of stage-scenery pieces and furniture on (and sometimes above) the floor. A vital working document for directors in *rehearsal,* as well as for technicians in the installation of *scenery.*

hamartia In Aristotle's *Poetics,* the "tragic flaw" of the *protagonist.* Scholars differ as to whether Aristotle was referring primarily to a character's ignorance of certain facts or to a character's moral defect.

hanamichi In the *kabuki* theatre, a long narrow runway leading from the stage to a door at the back of the auditorium that is used for raised and highly theatrical entrances and exits through the audience. For some plays, a second hanamichi may be added.

Hellenistic theatre Ancient Greek theatre during the fourth and third centuries B.C.E. The surviving stone theatres of Athens and Epidaurus date from the Hellenistic period, which began well after the great fifth-century tragedies and comedies were written. The Hellenistic period did produce an important form of comedy *(New Comedy),* however, and Alexandrian scholars during this period collected, edited, and preserved the masterpieces of the golden age.

high comedy A comedy of verbal wit and visual elegance, primarily peopled with upper-class characters. The *Restoration* comedies of William Congreve (1670–1729) and the Victorian comedies of Oscar Wilde (1854–1900) are often cited as examples.

hikimaku The traditional striped curtain of the *kabuki* theatre.

himation The gownlike basic costume of the Greek tragic actor.

house The audience portion of the theatre building.

hubris In Greek, "an excess of pride"; the most common *character* defect (one interpretation of the Greek *hamartia*) of the *protagonist* in Greek *tragedy.* "Pride goeth before a fall" is a biblical expression of this foundation of tragedy.

immersive theatre Theatre that fully invites its audience to be part of the dramatic action.

improvisation *Dialogue* or stage *business* invented by the actor, often during the performance itself. Some plays are wholly improvised, even to the extent that the audience may suggest situations that the actors must then create. More often, improvisation is used to "fill in the gaps" between more traditionally memorized and rehearsed scenes.

inciting action In play construction, the single action that initiates the major conflict of the play.

ingenue The young, pretty, and innocent female role in certain plays; also used to denote an actor capable of playing such roles.

interlude A *scene* or staged event in a play not specifically tied to the *plot;* in medieval England, a short moral play, usually comic, that could be presented at a court banquet amid other activities.

intermission A pause in the action, marked by a fall of the curtain or a fade-out of the stage lights, during which the audience may leave their seats for a short time, usually ten or fifteen minutes. Intermissions divide the play into separate *acts*. In England, known as "the interval."

jing In *xiqu*, the "painted-face" roles, often of gods, nobles, or villains.

jingju "Capital theatre" in Chinese; the Beijing (Peking) opera is the most famous form of *xiqu*.

kabuki One of the national theatre styles of Japan. Dating from the seventeenth century, kabuki features magnificent flowing costumes; highly stylized *scenery,* acting, and makeup; and elaborately styled choreography.

kakegoe Traditional shouts that *kabuki* enthusiasts in the audience cry out to their favorite actors during the play.

kathakali Literally, "story play"; a traditional dance-drama of India.

kōken Black-garbed and veiled actors' assistants who perform various functions onstage and offstage in *kabuki* theatre.

kunqu (sometimes **kunju**) The oldest form of Chinese *xiqu* still performed, dating from the sixteenth century.

kyōgen A comic, often farcical, counterpoint to Japanese *noh* drama, to which it is, surprisingly, historically related.

lazzo A physical joke, refined into traditional *business* and regularly inserted into performances of *commedia dell'arte.* "Eating the fly" is a famous lazzo.

LED The recently developed light-emitting diode is a light source that, because of its extremely long life, is beginning to replace incandescent sources in a variety of stage lighting instruments.

Lenaea The winter dramatic festival of ancient Athens. Because there were fewer foreigners in town in the winter, comedies that might embarrass the Athenians were often performed at this festival rather than at the springtime *Dionysia*.

light plot The layout—on paper—showing the positions where stage lights are to be hung and how they are wired (connected) into the numbered electrical circuits of the theatre facility.

liturgical drama *Dramatic* material that was written into the official Catholic Church liturgy and staged as part of regular church services in the medieval period, mainly in the tenth through twelfth centuries. See also *mystery play*.

low comedy Comic actions based on broad physical humor, scatology, crude punning, and the argumentative behavior of ignorant and lower-class *characters*. Despite the pejorative connotation of its name, low comedy can be inspired, as in the "mechanicals" scenes in Shakespeare's *A Midsummer Night's Dream*. Good plays, such as this one, can mix low comedy with *high comedy* in a highly sophisticated pattern.

mask (*noun*) A covering of the face, used conventionally by actors in many periods, including Greek, Roman, and *commedia dell'arte*. The mask was also used in other sorts of plays for certain occasions, such as the masked balls in Shakespeare's *Romeo and Juliet* and *Much Ado About Nothing*. The mask is a symbol of the theatre, particularly the two classic masks of Comedy and Tragedy. (*verb*) To hide backstage storage or activity by placing in front of it neutrally colored *flats* or drapery (which then become "masking pieces").

masque A minor dramatic form combining dance, music, a short allegorical *text,* and elegant *scenery* and costuming; often presented at court, as in the royal masques written by Ben Jonson, with scenery designed by Inigo Jones, during the Stuart era (early seventeenth century).

master electrician (ME) The person in charge of coordinating the hanging, focusing, and "gelling" (putting color media in) lighting instruments prior to and during technical rehearsals and maintaining the lighting technology during the run of a show.

melodrama Originally a term for *musical* theatre, by the nineteenth century this became the designation of a suspenseful, plot-oriented *drama* featuring all-good heroes, all-bad villains, simplistic *dialogue,* soaring moral conclusions, and bravura acting.

metaphor A literary term designating a figure of speech that implies a comparison or identity of one thing with something else. It permits concise communication of a complex idea by use of associative imagery, as with Shakespeare's "morn in russet mantle clad."

metatheatre Literally, "beyond theatre"; plays or theatrical acts that are self-consciously theatrical, that refer back to the art of the theatre and call attention to their own theatrical nature. Developed by many authors, including Shakespeare (in plays-within-plays in *Hamlet* and *A Midsummer Night's Dream*) and particularly the twentieth-century Italian playwright Luigi Pirandello (*Six Characters in Search of an Author, Tonight We Improvise*), thus leading to the term "Pirandellian" (meaning "metatheatrical"). See also *theatricalist* and *play-within-the-play*.

mie A "moment" in *kabuki* theatre in which the actor (usually in an *aragoto* role) suddenly "freezes" in a tense and symbolic pose.

mime A stylized art of acting without words. Probably derived from the *commedia dell'arte,* mime was revived in France during the mid-twentieth century and is now popular again in the theatre and in street performances in Europe and the United States. Mime performers traditionally employ whiteface makeup to stylize and exaggerate their features and expressions.

mise-en-scène The composition of a scene of theatre through the arrangement of bodies and objects onstage; literally, "seen in the scene."

modern A difficult term to pin down because it literally refers to work of "the present"—which, however, is always changing. The term popularly means "up-to-date," but arts scholars employ it mainly in reference to works created between approximately 1890 and 1945, which were called modern in their own time (e.g., "Modern art") and now—in contrast to *postmodern* works—can be roughly categorized into identified various artistic *styles* (e.g., realism, naturalism, expressionism, absurdism, epic theatre) of those years.

modern classic A term used to designate a play of the *modern* era that has nonetheless passed the test of time and seems as if it will last into the century or centuries beyond, such as the major works of Anton Chekhov, George Bernard Shaw, and Samuel Beckett. Contrast with *classic drama.*

monologue A long unbroken speech in a play, often delivered directly to the audience (in which case it is more accurately called a *soliloquy*).

morality play An allegorical medieval play in which the characters represent abstractions (Good Deeds, Death, and so on) and the overall impact of the play is moral instruction. The most famous in English is the anonymous *Everyman* (fifteenth century).

motivation That which can be construed to have determined a person's (or a *character's*) behavior. Since Konstantin Stanislavski, actors have been encouraged to study the possible motivations of their characters' actions. See also *objective.*

music theatre A dramatic *genre* that employs, normally in addition to spoken dialogue (but see *sung-through*), a musical score with a dozen or more songs and dances. Also called "musical theatre."

musical (*noun*) A single work of *music theatre*—such as *Oklahoma!* or *The Producers.*

musical comedy A *musical* intended mainly as light comic entertainment, emphasizing comedy and youthful romance as well as singing.

musical drama A subgenre of the *musical* that incorporates serious themes in its texts and musical treatments

mystery play The most common term referring to medieval plays developed from liturgical drama that treated biblical stories and themes. (They were also known as "pageant plays" in England, as "passion plays" when dealing with the Crucifixion of Jesus, and as "Corpus Christi plays" when performed in conjunction with that particular festival.) Unlike *liturgical dramas,* which were in Latin, mystery plays were written in the vernacular (English, French, German, Italian, Spanish, and Russian versions exist) and were staged outside the church.

naturalism A version of *realism* advancing the notion that the natural and social environment, more than individual willpower, controls human behavior. Its proponents, active in the late nineteenth and early twentieth centuries, sought to dispense with all theatrical convention in the search for *verisimilitude*—or, as the naturalists would say, a *slice of life.*

neoclassicism Literally, "new classicism." A renewed interest in the literary and artistic theories of ancient Greece and Rome and an attempt to reformulate them for the current day. A dominant force in seventeenth-century France, neoclassicism promoted restrained passion, balance, artistic consistency, and formalism in all art forms; it reached its dramatic pinnacle in the tragedies of Jean Racine.

New Comedy Greek comic dramas—almost all of which are now lost—of the late fourth to the second centuries B.C.E. Considerably more realistic than the *Old Comedy* of Aristophanes, New Comedy employed *stock characters* and domestic scenes; it strongly influenced Roman author Plautus and, through him, Renaissance comedy.

noh The classical dance-drama of Japan. Performed on a bare wooden stage of fixed construction and dimensions and accompanied by traditional music, noh is the aristocratic forebear of the more popular *kabuki* and has remained generally unchanged since its fourteenth-century beginnings.

objective The basic "goal" of a *character.* Also called "intention," "goal," or "victory." Since Konstantin Stanislavski, actors have been urged to discover their characters' objectives and, by way of "living the life of the character," to pursue their characters' objective during the course of the play.

ode In Greek *tragedy,* a song chanted or sung by the *chorus* and often accompanied by dance. Also called "choral ode."

off-Broadway The New York professional theatre located outside the *Broadway* district; principally in Greenwich Village and around the Upper East and West Sides. Developed in the 1950s, when it was considered *avant-garde,* the off-Broadway theatre is now more of a scaled-down version of the Broadway theatre, featuring *musicals* and commercial *revivals* as much as (or more than) original works.

off-off-Broadway A term designating certain theatre activity in New York City, usually nonprofessional (although with professional artists involved) and usually experimental and *avant-garde.* Off-off-Broadway developed in the 1970s as a supplement to the commercialism of both Broadway and, increasingly, off-Broadway.

Old Comedy Ancient Greek comedy of the fifth century B.C.E., mainly known to us through the bawdy, satirical, and even slapstick comedies of Aristophanes.

onnagata "Women-type" roles in *kabuki,* which, like all the roles, are played by men.

"open the house" A direction to admit the audience. See also *house.*

orchestra (1) In the ancient Greek or Roman theatre, the circular (in Rome, semicircular) ground-level acting area in front of the stagehouse, or *skene.* It was used primarily by the *chorus.* (2) In modern U.S. theatre buildings, the ground-level section of the audience, which usually slopes upward at the rear. Distinct from the mezzanine and balconies and ordinarily containing the more expensive seats. In England, known as "the stalls."

parabasis The "coming-forward" of a *character* in Greek *Old Comedy* who then gives a *direct address* to the audience in the middle of the play. In Aristophanes's plays, the parabasis is often given in the author's name and may have been spoken by Aristophanes himself. The parabasis was often unrelated to the *plot* and dealt with the author's immediate political or social concerns.

parados (1) The *ode* sung by the *chorus* entering the orchestra in a *Greek tragedy.* (2) The space between the stagehouse *(skene)* and audience seating area *(theatron)* through which the chorus entered the orchestra.

parody Dramatic material that makes fun of a dramatic *genre* or mode or of specific literary works; a form of theatre that is often highly entertaining but rarely has lasting value.

passion play A medieval play about Jesus and his trial and crucifixion, still performed in many towns and villages around the world during Easter week.

pathos "Passion," in Greek; also "suffering." The word refers to the depths of feeling evoked by *tragedy;* it is at the root of our words "sympathy" and "empathy," which also describe the effect of drama on audience emotions. See also *empathy.*

performance Any form of scrutinized human action. As opposed to theatre, which takes place in a more formal setting, "performance" encompasses such activities as sports, religious rituals, and political speeches. The discipline that studies performance is known as performance studies.

peripeteia The change of course in the *protagonist's* fortunes that, according to Aristotle, is part of the *climax* of a *tragedy.*

physical theatre With an emphasis on the actors' bodies, rather than the spoken word, this form of theatre often uses only movement, dance, music, and lighting.

platform A tablelike construction of any height, built to be stood upon, that creates raised flooring for a designated portion of the stage.

play-within-the-play A play "presented" by characters who are already in a play, like "The Murder of Gonzago," which is presented by the "Players" in *Hamlet*. Many plays are in part about actors and plays and contain such plays-within-plays; these include Anton Chekhov's *The Seagull*, Jean Anouilh's *The Rehearsal*, and Shakespeare's *A Midsummer Night's Dream* and *The Taming of the Shrew*.

plot The events of the play, expressed as a series of linked dramatic actions; in common terms, the story of the play. Plot is the most important component of a play, according to Aristotle.

postmodern A wide-ranging term describing certain post–World War II artistic works characterized by nonlinearity, self-referentiality if not self-parody, and multiple/simultaneous sensory impressions.

practical A *property* that works onstage the way it does in life. For example, a "practical" stove, in a stage setting, is one on which the characters can actually cook. A "nonpractical" stove, by contrast, is something that only looks like a stove (and may in fact be a stove without insides).

preview A performance prior to a production's formal opening, primarily intended to allow the director and cast to make final changes in response to audience reactions. There may be one preview or many; the musical *Spider-Man* had 183 of them before its opening night.

problem play A realistic play that deals, often narrowly, with a specific social problem. George Bernard Shaw's *Mrs. Warren's Profession*, for example, is virtually a dramatic tract on prostitution. The term was most popular around the beginning of the twentieth century.

producer (1) In America, the person responsible for assembling the ingredients of a play production: financing, staff, theatre, publicity, and management. Not ordinarily involved in the day-to-day artistic direction of the production, the American producer nonetheless controls the artistic process through her or his authority over personnel selection and budgeting. (2) Until recently in the English theatre, the theatre artist whom Americans refer to as the director.

production stage manager (PSM) The overseer of a production's scheduling, staffing, and budgeting of every element of the production, including the acting rehearsals and the building, loading in, and operation of all the design and technical elements.

prologue In Greek *tragedy*, a speech or brief *scene* preceding the entrance of the *chorus* and the main action of the play, usually spoken by a god or gods. Subsequently, the term has referred to a speech or brief scene that introduces the play, as by an actor in certain Elizabethan plays (often called the chorus) and in the *Restoration*. The prologue is rarely used in the modern theatre.

prompt book The annotated script maintained by the production stage manager during rehearsal identifying the cues—chiefly lighting, sound, and scene changes—to be implemented during the production. When performances begin, this book is often renamed the *call book* or the *calling book*.

properties Or "props"; the furniture and handheld objects (hand props) used in play productions. These are often real items (chairs, telephones, books, etc.) that can be purchased, rented, borrowed, or brought up from theatre storage; they may also, particularly in period or stylized plays, be designed and built in a property shop.

proscenium The arch separating the audience area from the main stage area. The term derives from the Roman playhouse, in which the proscenium (literally, *pro skene*, or "in front of the stage") was the facing wall of the stage. Modern *thrust* and *arena stages* have no proscenium.

proscenium theatre A rectangular-roomed theatre with a *proscenium arch* separating the audience on one end from the stage at the other. The proscenium theatre was first popular in the late seventeenth century and reached its apogee in the late nineteenth and early twentieth centuries. Still the basic theatre architecture of America's Broadway and of major European theatre companies.

protagonist In Greek *tragedy*, the "carrier of the action"; in any drama, the principal *character*, often opposed by an *antagonist*.

raked stage A sloped stage, angled so that the rear (*upstage*) area is higher than the forward (*downstage*) area. A raked stage was standard theatre architecture in the seventeenth century and is often used today in scene design but rarely in a theatre's permanent architecture.

realism The general principle that the stage should portray, in a reasonable facsimile, ordinary people in ordinary circumstances and that actors should behave, as much as possible, as real people do in life. Although the roots of realism go back to Euripides, it developed as a deliberate contrast to the florid *romanticism* that swept the European theatre in the mid-nineteenth century. See also *naturalism,* which is an extreme version of realism.

recognition See *anagnorisis.*

rehearsal The gathering of actors and director to put a play into production; the period in which the director stages the play and the actors develop and repeat their *dialogue* and actions; etymologically, a "reharrowing," or repeated digging into. In French, the comparable term is *répétition.*

repertory The plays a theatre company produces. A company's current repertory consists of those plays available for production at any time.

Restoration In England, the period following the restoration of the monarchy in 1660. In the theatre, the period is particularly noted for witty and salacious comedies, through to William Congreve's brilliant *The Way of the World* in 1700.

revival The remounting of a play production after its initial closing.

rising action In play construction, the escalating conflict; events and actions that follow the *inciting action.*

ritual A traditional cultural practice, usually religious, involving precise movements, music, spoken text, or gestures, that serves to communicate with deities. Ritual is often incorporated into plays, either as *conventions* of the theatre or as specific dramatized actions.

romanticism A nineteenth-century European movement away from *neoclassical* formalism and restraint and toward outsized passions, exotic and grotesque stories, florid writing, and all-encompassing worldviews. Supplanted late in the century by *realism,* romanticism survives today primarily in grand opera and nineteenth-century-based *musicals.*

rotating repertory The scheduling of a series of plays in nightly rotation. This is customary in most European theatres and in many American Shakespeare festivals; it is otherwise rare in America. See also *repertory.*

samisen The three-stringed banjolike instrument used in *kabuki* and *bunraku.*

satire A play or other literary work that ridicules social follies, beliefs, religions, or human vices, almost always in a lighthearted vein. Satire is not usually a lasting theatre form, as summed up by dramatist George S. Kaufman's classic definition: "Satire is what closes on Saturday night."

satyr A mythological Greek creature, half man and half goat, who attended *Dionysus* and represented male sexuality and drunken revelry; goatskin-clad followers of Dionysus who served as the *chorus* of the *satyr play*.

satyr play The fourth play in a Greek *tetralogy*. Satyr plays were short bawdy *farces* that parodied the events of the *trilogies* that preceded them.

scansion The study of verse for patterns of accented and unaccented syllables; also known as "metrics."

scene (1) The period of stage time representing a single location during a continuous period of time, now usually marked by a stage clearing and a noticeable change in the lighting; the subdivision of an *act*. (2) The locale where the events of the play are presumed to take place, as represented by *scenery* (as in "the scene is the Parson's living room"). (3) Of scenery, as "scenic design."

scenery Physical constructions that provide the specific acting environment for a play and that often indicate, by representation, the locale where a *scene* is set; the physical *setting* for a scene or play.

scenography Scenic design, particularly as it fits into the moving pattern of a play or series of plays. Scenography is four-dimensional, comprising the three physical dimensions plus time.

scrim A theatrical fabric woven so finely that when lit from the front it appears opaque and when lit from behind it becomes transparent. A scrim is often used for surprise effects or to create a mysterious mood.

script The written version of a play.

selective realism A style of stage design that combines realistic and expressive elements.

semiotics The study of signs, as they may be perceived in literary works, including plays. Semiotics is a contemporary tool of *dramaturgical* analysis that offers the possibility of identifying all the ingredients of *drama* (staging as well as language) and determining the conjunctions between them.

set piece A single piece of *scenery* that represents a fixed object, such as a tree or a bathtub.

setting or **set** The fictional location where the play's action is presumed to take place (e.g., "a forest").

sheng In *xiqu*, the male roles and the actors who play them.

shite The principal *character* (the "doer") in *noh*.

site-specific theatre Plays that become fully realized in environments outside traditional theatre facilities.

skene The Greek stagehouse (and root word of *scene*). The skene evolved from a small changing room behind the *orchestra* to a larger structure with a raised stage and a back wall during the Greek period.

slapstick Literally, a prop bat made up of two hinged sticks that slap sharply together when the bat is used to hit someone; a staple gag of the *commedia dell'arte*. More generally, slapstick is any sort of very broad physical stage humor.

slice of life Pure *naturalism*: stage action that realistically represents an ordinary and arbitrary "slice" of the daily activity of the people portrayed.

soliloquy A *monologue* delivered by a single actor with no one else onstage, sometimes played as the *character* "thinking aloud" and sometimes as a seeming *dialogue* with the (silent) audience.

sound effects A term referring to single sounds, normally played from offstage and often prerecorded, that represent specific (and usually realistic) sounds, such as a telephone ringing, a car braking, or a cannon firing. Today, such effects are mostly incorporated into a play's overall sound design.

spotlight A mounted lighting unit, operated remotely or manually, that is capable of illuminating certain characters (or props or set pieces) more than others to direct the audience's attention toward those visual elements.

stage business See *business*.

stage directions Scene descriptions, *blocking* instructions, and general directorial comments written, usually by the playwright, in the *script*.

stage left Left, from the actor's point of view.

stage machinery A variety of mechanical devices, including hoists, cranes, rolling carts, and turntables, used to move or change actors or *scenery*. Many, though now electric, date from ancient Greek times.

stage right Right, from the actor's point of view.

stasimon A choral *ode* between scenes (*episodes*) in a Greek *tragedy*.

stock characters *Characters* recognizable mainly for their conformity to a standard ("stock") dramatic stereotype: the wily servant, the braggart soldier, the innocent virgin, and so on. Most date from at least Roman times.

stock situation One of a number of basic *plot* situations—the lover hiding in the closet, twins mistaken for each other, and so on—that, like *stock characters*, have been used in the theatre since Plautus and before.

storyboard A series of rough preliminary drawings that, when looked at in sequence, visually illustrate an imagined order of stage moments—the sequencing of the *scenery* and the flow of the action—in a play being prepared for production.

style The specific manner in which a play is shaped, as determined by its *genre*, its historical period, the sort of impact the director wishes to convey to the audience, and the skill of the artists involved. The term generally refers to these aspects inasmuch as they differ from *naturalism*, although it could be said that naturalism is a style.

stylize To deliberately shape a play (or a setting, a costume, etc.) in a specifically non-naturalistic manner.

subplot A secondary *plot*, usually related to the main plot by play's end. The Gloucester plot in *King Lear* and the Laertes plot in *Hamlet* are examples.

subtext According to Konstantin Stanislavksi, the deeper and usually unexpressed "real" meanings of a *character*'s spoken lines. Of particular importance in the acting of realistic plays, such as those of Anton Chekhov, where the action is often as much between the lines as in them.

summer stock Theatre companies, located mostly in vacation areas of the American Northeast, that produce a season of plays (often one per week) during the summer months. Particularly popular in the three decades following World War II, when they mainly offered light, Broadway-styled comedies and provided pleasant entertainment for vacationers, salaries for unemployed New York actors, and break-in opportunities for student apprentices. The surviving companies, such as the Williamstown Theatre Festival in Massachusetts, have since become much more artistically ambitious.

sung-through A *musical* that has no spoken *dialogue*.

surrealism An art movement of the early twentieth century, in which the artist sought to go beyond *realism* into superrealism.

symbolism The first major antirealistic movement in the arts and in the theatre. Symbolism, which emphasizes the symbolic nature of theatrical presentation and the abstract possibilities of drama, flourished as a significant movement from the late nineteenth century to the early twentieth century, when it broke into various submovements: *expressionism, surrealism,* theatricalism, and many others.

tableau A "frozen moment" onstage, with the actors immobile, usually employed at the end of a *scene,* as the curtain falls or the lights dim.

technical director (TD) The person in charge of the building and operation of scenery and stage machinery.

technical rehearsal A stop-and-start *rehearsal,* in which a play's technical elements—mainly scene shifts, lighting, and sound cues—are precisely timed and integrated with the acting. See also *cue sheet.*

tech run-through A nonstop *rehearsal* of the play with all technical elements called by the stage manager and executed. See also *call; cue sheet.*

tetralogy Four plays performed together in sequence. In ancient Greek theatre, this was the basic pattern for the tragic playwrights, who presented a *trilogy* of tragedies, followed by a *satyr play.*

text A play *script.* This term is sometimes used to indicate the spoken words of the play only, as apart from the stage directions and other material in the script.

theatre and drama These words are often used interchangeably, yet they also have distinct meanings. "Theatre" is the broader term and can denote all of the elements of theatrical production (plays, scenery, staging, acting). "Drama" mainly focuses on plays performed in a theatrical environment. This difference in meaning reflects the words' separate etymologies: theatre is that which "is seen," and drama is that which "is done." So "theatre" can mean a building, but "drama" cannot. And "dramatic" suggests actions, in both plays and life, that are compelling; but "theatrical," when referring to real-life behavior, implies overly showy or sensationalistic.

theatre and theater *Theatre* is the French and British spelling; *theater* the German. Both spellings are common in the United States.

theatre-in-the-round See *arena stage.*

theatre of alienation See *distancing effect; epic theatre.*

theatre of cruelty A notion of theatre developed by the French theorist Antonin Artaud (1896–1948). Artaud's goal was to employ language more for its sound than for its meaning and to create a shocking stream of sensations rather than a coherent *plot* and cast of *characters.* Although Artaud's practical achievement was slight, his theories have proven extraordinarily influential.

theatre of the absurd A theatrical style, named by Martin Esslin in his 1961 book of that title, that has been applied to the post–World War II plays of Samuel Beckett, Eugène Ionesco, Jean Genet, and others, mostly Europeans. Esslin employed the term, derived from an essay by Albert Camus (see *absurd*), to describe plays with unrealistic and illogical plots, repetitious and disconnected language, and unclear themes, reflecting a world in which humans "absurdly" seek meaning but never find it.

theatricalist A contemporary style that boldly exploits the theatre itself and calls attention to the theatrical contexts of the play being performed. This term is often used to describe plays about the theatre that employ a *play-within-the-play.* See also *metatheatre.*

theatricality A quality of particularly vivid and attention-grabbing showmanship, either onstage or in daily life.

theatron The original Greek theatre; from the Greek for "seeing place."

thespian Actor; after Thespis, the first Greek actor.

thrust stage A stage that projects into the seating area and is surrounded by the audience on three sides.

timing The overall effect of the individual paces that the director and actors have determined.

tragedy From the Greek for "goat song," originally meaning a serious play. Tragedy was later refined by Greek playwrights (Thespis, sixth century B.C.E., being the first) and subsequently the philosopher Aristotle (384–322 B.C.E.) into the most celebrated of dramatic *genres:* a play that treats, at the most uncompromising level, human suffering. The reason for the name is unclear; a goat may have been the prize, or the *chorus* may have worn goatskins.

tragic flaw See *hamartia.*

tragicomedy A play that begins as a *tragedy* but includes comic elements and ends happily. Tragicomedy was a popular *genre* in the eighteenth century but is rarely employed, at least under that name, in the modern theatre.

traveler A curtain that, instead of flying out (see *fly*), moves horizontally and is usually opened by dividing from the center outward.

trilogy Three plays performed in sequence; the basic pattern of ancient Greek tragedies, of which one—Aeschylus's *The Oresteia (Agamemnon, The Libation Bearers,* and *The Eumenides)*—is still extant.

trope A written text, usually in dialogue form, incorporated into the Christian worship service. In the tenth century, tropes became the first *liturgical dramas.*

troupe A group of actors who perform together, often on tour. See also *company.*

unities The unity of place, unity of time, unity of action, and unity of tone were the four "unities" that *neoclassical* critics of the seventeenth century claimed to derive from Aristotle; plays said to "observe the unities" were required to take place in one locale, to have a duration of no more than one day (in an extreme interpretation, in no more time than the duration of the play itself), and to concern themselves with no more than a single action. Aristotle made no such demands on playwrights, however, and very few authors have ever succeeded in satisfying these restrictive conventions.

unit set A set that, by the moving on or off of a few simple pieces and perhaps with a change of lights, can represent all the scenes from a play. The unit set is a fluid and economical staging device, particularly useful for Shakespeare productions.

unity The conceptual quality that gives a play a sense of visionary wholeness.

upstage *(noun)* In a *proscenium theatre,* the part of the stage farthest from the audience; the rear of the stage, so called because it was in fact raised ("up") in the days of the *raked stage.* *(verb)* To stand upstage of another actor. Upstaging is often considered rude, inasmuch as it forces the *downstage* actors to face upstage (and away from the audience) in order to look at the actor to whom they are supposed to be speaking. Figuratively, the term may be used to describe any sort of acting behavior that calls unwarranted attention to the "upstaging" actor and away from the "upstaged" one.

vaudeville A stage variety show, with singing, dancing, comedy skits, and animal acts; highly popular in America from the late 1880s to the 1930s, when it lost out to movies, radio, and subsequently television.

verisimilitude Lifelikeness; the appearance of actual reality (as in a stage *setting*).

wagoto In *kabuki,* "soft-style" acting performed by certain male romantic characters.

waki The secondary *character* in *noh.*

well-made play *Pièce bien faite* in French; in the nineteenth century, a superbly plotted play, particularly by such gifted French playwrights as Eugène Scribe (1791–1861) and Victorien Sardou (1831–1908); today, generally used pejoratively, as to describe a play that has a workable *plot* but shallow characterization and trivial ideas.

West End The commercial theatre district of London, England.

wings In a *proscenium theatre,* vertical pieces of *scenery* to the left and right of the stage, usually parallel with the *footlights.*

working drawings Designer's drawings that show how a prop or a piece of *scenery* looks, and indicate how it should be constructed. See also *properties.*

xiqu Chinese for "tuneful theatre"; the general term for all varieties of traditional Chinese theatre, often called "Chinese opera."

zadacha Russian for "task" (though commonly translated as "objective"); according to Konstantin Stanislavski, a character's (fictional) tasks (or goals), which the actor must pursue during the play.

Selected Bibliography

Historical Surveys of Theatre and Drama

Banham, Martin, ed. *The Cambridge Guide to Theatre.* 9th ed. Cambridge: Cambridge University Press, 1995.

Boardman, Gerald, and Thomas S. Hischak. *The Oxford Companion to American Theatre.* New York: Oxford University Press, 2004.

Brockett, Oscar G., and Franklin J. Hildy. *History of the Theatre.* Boston: Allyn & Bacon, 2003.

Deeney, John F., and Maggie B. Gale, eds. *The Routledge Drama Anthology and Sourcebook: From Modernism to Contemporary Performance.* New York: Routledge, 2010.

Gerould, Daniel. *Theatre/Theory/Theatre: The Major Critical Texts from Aristotle and Zeami to Soyinka and Havel.* New York: Applause Books, 2003.

Hill, Errol. *The Theatre of Black Americans.* New York: Applause Books, 1987.

Kanellos, Nicolás, ed. *A History of Hispanic Theatre in the United States: Origins to 1940.* Austin: University of Texas Press, 1990.

Kennedy, Dennis. *The Oxford Encyclopedia of Theatre and Performance.* Oxford: Oxford University Press, 2003.

Knapp, Raymond, Mitchell Morris, and Stacy Wolf, eds. *The Oxford Handbook of the American Musical.* Oxford: Oxford University Press, 2012.

Lee, Esther Kim. *A History of Asian American Theatre.* Cambridge: Cambridge University Press, 2006.

Liu, Siyuan, ed. *Routledge Handbook of Asian Theatre.* New York: Routledge, 2016.

Nagler, Alois M. *A Source Book in Theatrical History.* New York: Dover, 1959.

Pavis, Patrice. *Dictionary of the Theatre: Terms, Concepts, and Analysis.* Toronto: University of Toronto Press, 1999.

Sanders, Leslie C. *The Development of Black Theatre in America.* Baton Rouge: Louisiana State University Press, 1988.

General Studies of Theatre and Drama

Armstrong, Anne Elizabeth, and Kathleen Juhl, eds. *Radical Acts: Theatre and Feminist Pedagogies of Change.* San Francisco: Aunt Jute Books, 2007.

Bentley, Eric. *The Life of the Drama.* New York: Applause Books, 1991.

Chinoy, Helen, and Linda Jenkins, eds. *Women in American Theatre.* 3rd ed. New York: Theatre Communications Group, 2006.

Elswit, Kate. *Theatre & Dance.* New York: Palgrave Macmillan, 2017.

Esslin, Martin. *An Anatomy of Drama.* New York: Hill & Wang, 1977.

Granville-Barker, Harley. *On Dramatic Method.* New York: Hill & Wang, 1956.

Hayman, Ronald. *How to Read a Play.* 2nd ed. New York: Grove Press, 1999.

Mamet, David. *Three Uses of the Knife: On the Nature and Purpose of Drama.* New York: Columbia University Press, 1998.

Proehl, Geoffrey S., with D. D. Kugler, Mark Lamos, and Michael Lupu. *Toward a Dramaturgical Sensibility.* Madison, NJ: Fairleigh-Dickinson Press, 2008.

Puchner, Martin. *The Drama of Ideas: Platonic Provocations in Theatre and Philosophy.* New York: Oxford University Press, 2014.

Schechner, Richard. *Environmental Theatre.* 2nd ed. New York: Applause Books, 1994.

———. *Performance Studies.* 2nd ed. New York: Routledge, 2006.

Styan, J. L. *The Elements of Drama.* New York: Cambridge University Press, 1960.

———. *Drama, Stage, and Audience.* New York: Cambridge University Press, 1975.

Worthen, W. B. *Drama: Between Poetry and Performance.* Hoboken, NJ: Wiley, 2010.

Specialized Studies

Asian Theatre

Akihiko, Senda. *The Voyage of Contemporary Japanese Theatre.* Honolulu: University of Hawai'i Press, 1997.

Brandon, James R., ed. *Nō and Kyōgen in the Contemporary World.* Honolulu: University of Hawai'i Press, 1997.

Chelkowski, Peter J. *Ta'ziyeh, Ritual, and Drama in Iran.* New York: New York University Press, 1979.

Ernst, Earle. *The Kabuki Theatre.* New York: Grove Press, 1956.

Goldman, Andrea. *Opera and the City: The Politics of Culture in Beijing, 1770–1900.* Palo Alto, CA: Stanford University Press, 2012.

Huang, Alexander C. Y. *Chinese Shakespeares: Two Centuries of Cultural Exchange.* New York: Columbia University Press, 2009.

Immoos, Thomas. *Japanese Theatre.* Translated by Hugh Young, photographs by Fred Mayer. London: Studio Vista, 1977.

Keene, Donald. *Nō and Bunraku.* New York: Columbia University Press, 1970.

Kominz, Laurence R. *The Stars Who Created Kabuki.* Tokyo: Kodansha International, 1997.

Ma, Qiang. *The Pictorial Album of Costumes in Chinese Traditional Opera.* Shanxi, China: Shanxi Education Press, 1992.

Mackerras, Colin. *The Performing Arts in Contemporary China.* 2nd ed. London: Routledge, 2005.

Miettinen, Jukka O. *Classical Dance and Theatre in South-East Asia.* Oxford: Oxford University Press, 1992.

Richmond, Farley P., Darius L. Swann, and Phillip B. Zarilli, eds. *Indian Theatre: Traditions of Performance.* Honolulu: University of Hawai'i Press, 1990.

Rogers, Amanda. *Performing Asian Transnationalisms: Theatre, Identity, and the Geographies of Performance.* New York: Routledge, 2014.

Scott, A. C. *The Classical Theatre of China.* London: Simson Shand, 1957.

———. *The Theatre in Asia.* London: Weidenfeld and Nicholson, 1972.

Seizer, Susan. *Stigmas of the Tamil Stage: An Ethnography of Special Drama Artists in South India.* Durham, NC: Duke University Press, 2005.

Toita, Yasuji, and Chiaki Yoshida. *Kabuki.* Translated by Don Kenny. Osaka, Japan: Hoikusha Publishing, 1992.

Wang-ngai, Siu, with Peter Lovrick. *Chinese Opera.* Vancouver: University of British Columbia Press, 1997.

Wichmann, Elizabeth. *Listening to Theatre: The Aural Dimension of Beijing Opera.* Honolulu: University of Hawai'i Press, 1991.

Premodern Theatre (Ancient, Medieval, Renaissance, and Royal)

Beacham, Richard C. *The Roman Theatre and Its Audience.* Cambridge, MA: Harvard University Press, 1996.

Bosher, Kathryn, ed. *Theatre Outside Athens: Drama in Greek Sicily and South Italy.* Cambridge: Cambridge University Press, 2012.

Bradby, David, and Andrew Calder. *The Cambridge Companion to Moliere.* Cambridge: Cambridge University Press, 2006.

Chambers, E. K. *The Medieval Stage.* 2 vols. Oxford: Clarendon Press, 1903.

Dillon, Elizabeth Maddock. *New World Drama: The Performative Commons in the Atlantic World, 1649–1849.* Durham, NC: Duke University Press, 2014.

Enders, Jody. *The Medieval Theatre of Cruelty: Rhetoric, Memory, Violence.* Ithaca, NY: Cornell University Press, 2002.

Garber, Marjorie. *Shakespeare after All.* New York: Random House, 2005.

Hart, Mary Louise. *The Art of Ancient Greek Theatre.* Los Angeles: Getty Publications, 2010.

Henke, Robert. *Performance and Literature in the Commedia dell'Arte.* Cambridge: Cambridge University Press, 2010.

Mackay, Ellen. *Persecution, Plague, and Fire: Fugitive Histories of the Stage in Early Modern England.* Chicago: University of Chicago Press, 2011.

Nussbaum, Felicity. *Rival Queens: Actresses, Performance, and the Eighteenth-Century British Theatre.* Philadelphia: University of Pennsylvania Press, 2010.

Symes, Carol. *A Common Stage: Theatre and Public Life in Medieval Arras.* Ithaca, NY: Cornell University Press, 2007.

Modern and Postmodern Theatre

Artaud, Antonin. *The Theatre and Its Double.* Translated by Mary C. Richards. New York: Grove Press, 1958.

Bentley, Eric. *The Playwright as Thinker.* 4th ed. Minneapolis: University of Minnesota Press, 2010.

Bigsby, C. W. E. *A Critical Introduction to Twentieth-Century American Drama.* 3 vols. Cambridge: Cambridge University Press, 1985.

Bradby, David. *Modern French Drama 1940–1980.* Cambridge: Cambridge University Press, 1984.

Brecht, Bertolt. *Brecht on Theatre.* Translated by John Willett. New York: Hill & Wang, 1965.

Brook, Peter. *The Empty Space.* New York: Atheneum, 1968.

Brotchie, Alastair. *Alfred Jarry: A Pataphysical Life.* Cambridge, MA: The MIT Press, 2011.

Craig, Edward Gordon. *On the Art of the Theatre.* 2nd ed. Boston: Small, Maynard, 1924.

de Jongh, Nicholas. *Not in Front of the Audience: Homosexuality on Stage.* London: Routledge, 1992.

Esslin, Martin. *The Theatre of the Absurd.* Rev. ed. New York: Vintage, 2004.

Grotowski, Jerzy. *Towards a Poor Theatre.* Eugenio Barba, ed. Rev. ed. New York: Routledge, 2002.

Harding, James Martin. *The Ghosts of the Avant-Garde: Exorcising Experimental Theatre and Performance.* Ann Arbor: University of Michigan Press, 2013.

Hercher, Jutta, and Peter Urban, eds. *Chekhov on Theatre.* London: Nick Hern Books, 2012.

Innes, Christopher. *Modern German Drama: A Study in Form.* New York: Cambridge University Press, 1979.

Knowles, Ric, Joanne Tomkins, and W. B. Worthen, eds. *Modern Drama: Defining the Field.* Toronto: University of Toronto Press, 2003.

Marranca, Bonnie, and Gautam Dasgupta, eds. *Interculturalism and Performance.* New York: PAJ Publications, 1991.

Miller, Hillary. *Drop Dead: Performance in Crisis, 1970s New York.* Evanston, IL: Northwestern University Press, 2017.

Murphy, Brenda. *American Realism and American Drama, 1880–1940.* Cambridge: Cambridge University Press, 2008.

Puchner, Martin. *Stage Fright: Modernism, Anti-Theatricality, and Drama.* Baltimore, MD: Johns Hopkins University Press, 2011.

Roose-Evans, James. *Experimental Theatre: From Stanislavski to Peter Brook.* 4th ed. New York: Routledge, 1996.

Salamon, Julie. *Wendy and the Lost Boys: The Uncommon Life of Wendy Wasserstein.* New York: Penguin Press, 2011.

Savran, David. *Breaking the Rules: The Wooster Group.* New York: Theatre Communications Group, 1993.

Shaw, George Bernard. *The Quintessence of Ibsenism.* London: Constable, 1913.

Vanden Heuvel, Michael. *Performing Drama/Dramatizing Performance.* Ann Arbor: University of Michigan Press, 1991.

Wekwerth, Manfred. *Daring to Play: A Brecht Companion.* New York: Routledge, 2011.

Williams, Mance. *Black Theatre in the 1960s and 1970s.* Westport, CT: Greenwood Press, 1985.

Musical Theatre

Bloom, Ken. *American Song.* 2nd ed. New York: Schirmer, 1996.

Bordman, Gerald. *American Musical Theatre.* 2nd ed. New York: Oxford, 1992.

Bradley, Ian, ed. *The Complete Annotated Gilbert and Sullivan.* New York: Oxford University Press, 1996.

Buch, David. *Magic Flutes and Enchanted Forests: The Supernatural in Eighteenth-Century Musical Theatre.* Chicago: University of Chicago Press, 2008.

Everett, William A., and Paul R. Laird. *The Cambridge Companion to the Musical.* Cambridge: Cambridge University Press, 2002.

Ganzl, Kurt. *The Encyclopedia of Musical Theatre.* Oxford: Blackwell, 1994.

Hammerstein, Oscar. *Lyrics.* New York: Simon & Schuster, 1949.

Hischack, Thomas S. *Boy Loses Girl: Broadway's Librettists.* Lanham, MD: Scarecrow Press, 2002.

Hollis, Alpert. *125 Years of Musical Theatre.* New York: Arcade Publications, 1991.

Jones, John Bush. *Our Musicals, Ourselves: A Social History of the American Musical Theatre.* Waltham, MA: Brandeis University Press, 2003.

Knapp, Raymond. *The American Musical and the Formation of Personal Identity.* Princeton, NJ: Princeton University Press, 2005.

———. *The American Musical and the Performance of Personal Identity.* Princeton, NJ: Princeton University Press, 2006.

Magee, Jeffrey. *Irving Berlin's American Musical Theatre.* New York: Oxford University Press, 2012.

Most, Andrea. *Making Americans: Jews and the Broadway Musical.* Cambridge, MA: Harvard University Press, 2004.

Naden, Corinne. *The Golden Age of the American Musical Theatre: 1943–1965.* New York: Scarecrow Press, 2011.

Peterson, Bernard L. *A Century of Musicals in Black and White.* Westport, CT: Greenwood Press, 1993.

Wolf, Stacy. *A Problem Like Maria: Gender and Sexuality in the American Musical.* Ann Arbor: University of Michigan Press, 2002.

Theatre Today

Erven, Eugene van. *Community Theatre: Global Perspectives.* New York: Routledge, 2001.

Farcas, Stephanie Barton. *Disability and Theatre: A Practical Manual for Inclusion.* New York: Taylor and Francis, 2017.

Giguere, Amanda. *The Plays of Yasmina Reza on the English and American Stage.* Jefferson, NC: McFarland, 2010.

Harvie, Jen, and Andy Lavender, eds. *Making Contemporary Theatre: International Rehearsal Processes.* Manchester, UK: Manchester University Press, 2010.

Hoffman, Warren. *The Great White Way: Race and the Broadway Musical.* New Brunswick, NJ: Rutgers University Press, 2014.

Johnson, E. Patrick, and Ramón H. Rivera-Servera, eds. *Blacktino Queer Performance.* Durham, NC: Duke University Press, 2016.

Kuftinec, Sonja. *Staging America: Cornerstone and Community-Based Theatre.* Carbondale: Southern Illinois University Press, 2003.

Larson, Jennifer. *Understanding Suzan Lori-Parks.* Columbia: South Carolina University Press, 2012.

Majumdar, Ramendu, and Mofidul Hoque, eds. *The World of Theatre: 2008 Edition.* Dhaka, Bangladesh: Bangladesh Centre of ITI, 2008.

Pearson, Mike. *Site-Specific Performance.* New York: Palgrave Macmillan, 2010.

Román, David. *Performance in America: Contemporary U.S. Culture and the Performing Arts.* Durham, NC: Duke University Press, 2005.

Acting and Directing

Acker, Barbara, and Marion Hampton, eds. *The Vocal Vision.* New York: Applause, 1997.

Benedetti, Jean. *Stanislavski: An Introduction, Revised and Updated.* 2nd ed. New York: Routledge, 2004.

Berry, Cecily. *Voice and the Actor.* London: Harrap, 1973.

Bogart, Ann. *And Then, You Act: Making Art in an Unpredictable World.* New York: Routledge, 2007.

Boleslavski, Richard. *Acting: The First Six Lessons.* New York: Theatre Arts Books, 1933.

Carnicke, Sharon Marie. *Stanislavsky in Focus.* Amsterdam: Harwood Press, 1998.

Chaikin, Joseph. *The Presence of the Actor.* 2nd ed. New York: Theatre Communications Group, 1993.

Cohen, Robert. *Acting One/Acting Two.* New York: McGraw-Hill Education, 2007.

———. *Acting Professionally* (with James Calleri). London: Palgrave Macmillan, 2009.

———. *Acting Power: The 21st Century Edition.* London: Routledge, 2013.

Cohen, Robert, and John Harrop. *Creative Play Direction.* 2nd ed. Englewood Cliffs, NJ: Prentice-Hall, 1984.

Cole, Toby, and Helen K. Chinoy, eds. *Directors on Directing.* Rev. ed. Indianapolis: Bobbs-Merrill, 1963.

———. *Actors on Acting.* Rev. ed. New York: Crown, 1995.

Diderot, Denis. "The Paradox of Acting." In William Archer, *Masks or Faces?* New York: Hill & Wang, 1957.

Donnellan, Declan. *The Actor and the Target.* 2nd ed. London: Nick Hern Books, 2005.

Giannachi, Gabriella, and Nick Kaye. *Performing Presence: Between the Live and the Simulated.* Manchester, UK: Manchester University Press, 2011.

Gordon, Robert. *The Purpose of Playing: Modern Acting Theories in Perspective.* Ann Arbor: University of Michigan Press, 2006.

Hagen, Uta. *Respect for Acting.* 2nd ed. Hoboken, NJ: Wiley, 2008.

Herrera, Brian Eugenio. "The Best Actor for the Role, or the Mythos of Casting in American Popular Performance." *The Journal of American Drama and Theatre* 27.2 (Spring 2015).

Hethmon, Robert. *Strasberg at the Actors Studio.* New York: Viking, 1965.

Krasner, David. *Method Acting Reconsidered: Theory, Practice, Future.* New York: St. Martin's Press, 2000.

Lewis, Robert. *Advice to the Players.* New York: Theatre Communications Group, 1980.

Linklater, Kristin. *Freeing the Natural Voice: Imagery and Art in the Practice of Voice and Language.* Rev. ed. New York: Drama Publishers, 2006.

Mitchell, Katie. *A Director's Craft: A Handbook for the Theatre.* New York: Routledge, 2008.

Oddey, Allison. *Devising Theatre: A Practical and Theoretical Handbook.* New York: Routledge, 1994.

Roach, Joseph R. *The Player's Passion: Studies in the Science of Acting.* Newark: University of Delaware Press, 1985.

Shevtsova, Maria, and Christopher Innes. *Directors/Directing: Conversations on Theatre.* Cambridge: Cambridge University Press, 2009.

Spolin, Viola. *Improvisation for the Theatre.* 3rd ed. Evanston, IL: Northwestern University Press, 1999.

Stanislavsky, Konstantin. *An Actor Prepares.* Translated by Elizabeth Reynolds Hapgood. New York: Theatre Arts Books, 1936.

_____. *An Actor's Work.* Translated by Jean Benedetti. London: Routledge, 2008.

Design

Aronson, Arnold. *American Set Design.* New York: Theatre Communications Group, 1985.

Bicat, Tina. *Costume and Design for Devised and Physical Theatre.* Marlborough, UK: Crowood Press, 2012.

Collins, Jane, and Andrew Nisbet. *Theatre and Performance Design: A Reader in Scenography.* New York: Routledge, 2010.

Corson, Richard. *Stage Make-up.* 8th ed. Englewood Cliffs, NJ: Prentice-Hall, 1989.

Crabtree, Susan, and Peter Beudart. *Scenic Art for the Theatre.* 3rd ed. Waltham, MA: Focal Press, 2011.

Essig, Linda. *Lighting and the Design Idea.* Belmont, CA: Thomson/Wadsworth, 2005.

Essin, Christin. *Stage Designers in Early Twentieth Century America: Artists, Activists, Cultural Critics.* New York: Palgrave Macmillan, 2012.

Goodwin, John, ed. *British Theatre Design: The Modern Age.* London: Weidenfeld & Nicholson, 1989.

Izenour, George C. *Roofed Theatres of Classical Antiquity.* New Haven, CT: Yale University Press, 1996.

_____. *Theatre Design.* 2nd ed. New Haven, CT: Yale University Press, 1996.

Jones, Robert Edmund. *The Dramatic Imagination.* New York: Meredith, 1941.

Mielziner, Jo. *Designing for the Theatre.* New York: Atheneum, 1965.

Motley. *Designing and Making Stage Costumes.* Rev. ed. New York: Routledge, 1992.

Oddey, Alison, and Christine White, eds. *The Potentials of Spaces: The Theory and Practice of Scenography and Performance.* Bristol, UK, and Portland, OR: Intellect Books, 2006.

Payne, Darwin Reid. *Scenographic Imagination.* Carbondale: Southern Illinois University Press, 1993.

_____. *Computer Scenographics.* Carbondale: Southern Illinois University Press, 1994.

Pecktal, Lynn. *Costume Design.* New York: Back Stage Books, 1993.

Reid, Francis. *Designing for the Theatre.* New York: Routledge, 1996.

_____. *The Stage Lighting Handbook.* 5th ed. New York: Routledge, 1996.

Smith, Ronn. *American Set Design 2.* New York: Theatre Communications Group, 1991.

Sofer, Andrew. *The Stage Life of Props.* Ann Arbor: University of Michigan Press, 2003.

Svoboda, Joseph. *The Secret of Theatrical Space.* New York: Applause Theatre Books, 1993.

Walne, Graham, ed. *Effects for the Theatre.* New York: Drama Book Publishers, 1995.

Index

Page numbers in italics indicate a photograph.

A

Abbey Theatre (Ireland), 287
Abbott, George, 166
Abdinezhad, Anita, 176, *176*
Abraham, F. Murray, 274
Abrahami, Natalie, 305
Abramović, Marina, "The Artist Is Present," 262
absurdist theatre
   playwrights, notable, 226–227
   Waiting for Godot (Beckett) example of, *227*, 227–228, 233
Abydos Passion Play, 185
academic critics/criticism, 304–305
academic model (in actor training), 50
academic theatre, 281–282, *282*
acoustics, 9
act, 5
ACTER (Actors from the London Stage), 53
acting, 11, 36. *See also* performance
   exercises, 44–45
   film stars onstage, 18, 53
   Islamic cultures on, 45
   paradox of, 5, 41–42, 45
   Plato on public order threat of, 42
acting approaches
   American Method, 41
   external method, 37–39
   internal method, 37–38, 39–40
   "the Method," 39–40, 41
   Stanislavski method, 39–41, 45–46
   Suzuki method, 38, 41
   Viewpoints method, 38
actor(s). *See also* casting
   actors coaching other, 168, *168*
   audience assessment by, 50
   auditioning process for, 49, 152
   backstage energy for, 36
   blocking for, 49, 158–159, 161
   with Broadway beginnings, 276
   character immersion for, 41–42, 45–46, 49–50, 54
   Confucius decree of death for, 42
   directors coaching, 161, 163, 171, *171*
   directors relationship with, 142, *142*, 143, *143*, 161, 163, 165

income for, 36–37
   kabuki lineage of, 204
   labor union, 152, 278
   musical instruments played by, 120, 241, *241*
   paradoxes of, 5, 41–42, 45
   playwrights collaboration with, 57
   PSM role in management of, 130, 131
   spontaneity challenges for, 50, 54
   onstage acting, 18, 53
   theatre conventions common for, 30
   theatrical separation of, 6–7, 8, 272
   vocal abilities, Greek theatre emphasis on, 38
   women, first appearance of, 196
An Actor Prepares (Stanislavski), 40
actor routine
   auditioning in, 49
   performances in, 50, 54
   rehearsals in, 49–50, 168, *168*, 173–174, *173–174*, 176, *176*
actor training
   academic and apprentice models compared for, 50
   on artistic discipline, 48–49
   Asian theatre traditions of, 50, 197
   of body (actor's instrument), 46–48
   on character creation, 45–46
   dance in, 47, *47*
   mask work in, 48
   on voice and vocal abilities, 46–47, 52, *52*, 53
actor-coaching
   between actors, 168, *168*
   by directors, 161, 163, 171, *171*
Actors' Equity Association, 152
Actors from the London Stage (ACTER), 53
Actors' Gang (Los Angeles), 190, *190*
Actors Studio, 41
The Adding Machine (Rice), 220, 222, *222*
Addison, Joseph, 247
Adler, Richard
   Damn Yankees, 237
   The Pajama Game, 237
Aeschylus, 135, 186
   Agamemnon, 98
   Oresteia, 2, 22
   roles of, multiple theatre, 11, 233
   The Suppliants, 187

African theatre. *See also* South African theatre
   makeup for traditional, 118, *118*
   masks in tribal, *184*, 184–185, *185*
   mmonwu masquerades in, 13, 283
   theatre origins in, 13, 180, 181, *181*, *184*, 184–185, *185*
Agamemnon (Aeschylus), 98
Aidem, Betsy, 19, *19*
AIDS crisis, 252, *252*, 293
Ain't Misbehavin' (musical), 241
Airline Highway (D'Amour), 96, *96*
Akhtar, Ayad
   American Dervish (novel), 76
   Disgraced, 75–76, *76*
   Junk, 76
   The War Within (film), 76
Akitaya, Kazunori, *20*, 23, *23*
Aladdin (Menken), 244, 286, *286*
Albee, Edward, 252
   dialogue skill of, 64
   Three Tall Women, 64, *64*
   Who's Afraid of Virginia Woolf?, 53, 155
Alda, Alan, 60, *60*
Aldredge, Theoni, 109, 239
The Aliens (Baker), 71–72
Alita, Adrian, 177, *177*
All My Sons (Miller), 86, 276
All That Jazz (film), 239
All the Way (Schenkkan), *6*, 19, *19*, 153
Allam, Roger, 160, *160*, 286, *286*
Allegiance (musical), 257
allegory, contemporary, 218, 228–229
Allen, Jay Presson, *Tru*, 270
Allen Elizabethan Theatre (Oregon), 281, *281*
Almeida Theatre (London), 92, 222, 285
amateur theatre, *281*, 281–282, *282*, 283
Ambrose, Lauren, 212, *212*
Ambruster, Heidi, 76, *76*
The America Play (Parks), 61, 74
American Airlines Theatre, 258, *258*
American Buffalo (Mamet), 90
American Dervish (Akhtar), 76
An American in Paris (musical), 303, *303*
American Method acting approach, 41
American Psycho (musical), 266
American Repertory Theater, 19, 75, 144, 291